Lecture Notes in Computer Science   8985

Commenced Publication in 1973
Founding and Former Series Editors:
Gerhard Goos, Juris Hartmanis, and Jan van Leeuwen

More information about this series at http://www.springer.com/series/7410

Christos G. Panayiotou · Georgios Ellinas
Elias Kyriakides · Marios M. Polycarpou (Eds.)

Critical Information Infrastructures Security

9th International Conference, CRITIS 2014
Limassol, Cyprus, October 13–15, 2014
Revised Selected Papers

 Springer

Editors
Christos G. Panayiotou
University of Cyprus
Nicosia
Cyprus

Georgios Ellinas
University of Cyprus
Nicosia
Cyprus

Elias Kyriakides
University of Cyprus
Nicosia
Cyprus

Marios M. Polycarpou
University of Cyprus
Nicosia
Cyprus

ISSN 0302-9743   ISSN 1611-3349   (electronic)
Lecture Notes in Computer Science
ISBN 978-3-319-31663-5   ISBN 978-3-319-31664-2   (eBook)
DOI 10.1007/978-3-319-31664-2

Library of Congress Control Number: 2016934196

LNCS Sublibrary: SL4 – Security and Cryptology

Printed on acid-free paper

This Springer imprint is published by Springer Nature
The registered company is Springer International Publishing AG Switzerland

Preface

This volume contains revised selected papers from the proceedings of the 9th International Conference on Critical Information Infrastructures Security (CRITIS 2014), which was held in Limassol, Cyprus during October 13–15, 2014. The workshop was organized by the KIOS Research Center for Intelligent Systems and Networks and the Department of Electrical and Computer Engineering of the University of Cyprus and was held in a beautiful five-star hotel in the historic Amathus area of Limassol. The conference participants had the opportunity to enjoy an excellent technical program, as well as the rich cultural heritage of Cyprus, whose nine-thousand-year cultural legacy has been at the crossroads of world history. Currently, Cyprus is a full member of the European Union and combines European culture with ancient enchantment.

CRITIS 2014 continued a well-established tradition of successful annual conferences. CRITIS aims at bringing together researchers and professionals from academia, industry, and governmental organizations working in the field of security of critical infrastructure systems. Critical infrastructure systems are made up of unreliable components that may fail at any point in time. Despite component failures, it is expected that the infrastructure as a whole will continue to function. For this reason, this year's program was enhanced with topics from the fault diagnosis and fault tolerant control areas.

The full technical program of the three-day conference included four plenary lectures by accomplished researchers in the field, 37 technical papers organized in two parallel sessions, a panel discussion, a case study session, as well as two special sessions. The four plenary talks were the following:

- "System of Systems Simulation in a Cooperative Multinational Environment," José R. Martí, University of British Columbia, Vancouver, Canada
- "Methodologies for the Identification of Critical Information Infrastructure Assets and Services," Rossella Mattioli, ENISA, Greece
- "Risk Prediction for Increasing Critical Infrastructure Protection: A Key Issue for Enhancing City Resilience," Vittorio Rosato, Head of the ENEA Laboratory of Technological and Computing Infrastructures, Italy
- "Water Distribution Systems Security Enhancement through Monitoring," Avi Ostfeld, Technion Institute of Technology, Israel

The Technical Program Committee (TPC) received 74 high-quality submissions, which were thoroughly reviewed by the expert members of the TPC. Out of these papers, 42 with mature work or promising work-in-progress were retained for oral presentations during the conference. The technical papers were organized in sessions that included topics on cyber-physical systems and sensor networks, security of water systems, power and energy system security, security and recovery policies, cyber security, and security tools and protocols. Furthermore, six of the accepted papers were presented in the CIPRNet Young CRITIS Award (CYCA) Session. This award recognizes outstanding research by young experts in critical infrastructure security and protection and was sponsored by the FP7 Network of Excellence CIPRNet. Mature work papers were selected to be presented as full papers in this volume, while work-in-progress papers as short papers.

The panel discussion *"Current Status and Future Challenges in Critical Infrastructure Protection (CIP) in Cyprus"* was organized by G. Boustras (European University, Cyprus), and included panelists from the Cyprus police, civil defense, water development board, and ADITESS, an SME software company. Furthermore, COncORDE (Development of Coordination Mechanisms During Kinds of Emergencies), an FP7 research project, held the case study session *"COncORDE Emergency Response Stakeholders Case Studies,"* which was moderated by T. Kotis, Cambridge University Hospitals, and included presentations by the project coordinator as well as representatives of the Cyprus Department of Crisis Management of the Ministry of Foreign Affairs, the Cyprus Fire Brigade, the Cyprus Ministry of Health, the Cyprus Civil Defense, and the Cyprus Joint Rescue Coordination Center. The Technical Program concluded with two invited sessions: the *CRIS2014 Special Session* and the *COncORDE—Coordination Mechanisms and Decision Support in Emergency Environments Special Session*. These two sessions focused on specific aspects of the security of power systems and the health-care emergency response management.

It is our pleasure to express our gratitude to everybody that contributed to the success of CRITIS 2014. In particular, we would like to thank the Vice-Chairs and the members of the Program Committee who did a tremendous job under strict time limitations during the reviewing process. We also thank the members of the Executive Committee for the great effort and their assistance in the organization of the workshop. We are also grateful to ADITESS—Advanced Integrated Technology Solutions and Services, IOActive—Comprehensive Computer Security Services, the European Research Council (ERC), the CIPRNet Network of Excellence, the University of Cyprus, and the Cyprus Tourism Organization for their financial support. We thank the conference secretariat, Top Kinisis, and especially Marianna Charalambous, for their excellent and timely support in the organization of the workshop. We are grateful to the administrative personnel and several researchers from the KIOS Research Center who assisted in various ways in the organization of CRITIS 2014, and especially Despina Petrou for managing the workshop organization. We would also like to thank the publisher, Springer, for their cooperation in publishing the selected papers from the proceedings in the prestigious series of *Lecture Notes in Computer Science*. Finally, we thank all the authors who contributed to this volume for sharing their new ideas and results with the community. We hope that these ideas will generate further new ideas and innovations for securing our critical infrastructures for the benefit of society and the environment.

February 2016

Christos G. Panayiotou
Georgios Ellinas
Elias Kyriakides
Marios M. Polycarpou

Organization

Executive Committee

General Chairs

Marios Polycarpou   University of Cyprus, Nicosia, Cyprus
Elias Kyriakides   University of Cyprus, Nicosia, Cyprus

Program Chair

Christos Panayiotou   University of Cyprus, Nicosia, Cyprus

Program Co-chairs

Vicenç Puig   Universitat Politècnica de Catalunya, Barcelona, Spain
Erich Rome   Fraunhofer Institute for Intelligent Analysis
                          and Information Systems, Germany
Stephen Wolthusen   Gjøvik University College, Norway and Royal Holloway,
                          University of London, UK

Publicity Chairs

Cristina Alcaraz   University of Malaga, Spain
Demetrios Eliades   University of Cyprus, Nicosia, Cyprus

Publications Chair

Georgios Ellinas   University of Cyprus, Nicosia, Cyprus

Steering Committee

Chairs

Bernhard M. Hämmerli   University of Applied Sciences Lucerne, GUC Gjøvik
                          and Acris GmbH
Javier Lopez   University of Malaga, Spain

Members

Robin Bloomfield   City University London, UK
Sandro Bologna   AIIC, Italy
Sokratis Katsikas   University of the Aegean, Greece
Eric Luiijf   TNO, The Netherlands
Reinhard Posch   Technical University Graz, Austria
Saifur Rahman   Advanced Research Institute, Virginia Tech, USA
Roberto Setola   Università Campus Bio-Medico, Italy

Nils Kalstad Svendsen	Gjøvik University College, Norway
Erich Rome	Fraunhofer IAIS, Germany
Stephen Wolthusen	Gjøvik University College, Norway and Royal Holloway, University of London, UK

Program Committee

Cristina Alcaraz	University of Malaga, Spain
Sandro Bologna	AIIC, Italy
George Boustras	European University, Cyprus
Stefan Brem	Swiss Federal Office for Civil Protection, Switzerland
Arslan Broemme	GI Biometrics Special Interest Group (BIOSIG), Germany
Emiliano Casalicchio	Univarsità di Roma Tor Vergata, Italy
Gabriella Cembrano	CetAqua, Spain
Jorge Cuellar	Siemens, AG, CT T, Germany
Gregorio D'Agostino	ENEA, Italy
Geert Deconinck	K.U. Leuven, Belgium
Eric Duviella	Université de Lille Nord de France, France
Demetrios Eliades	University of Cyprus, Cyprus
Georgios Ellinas	University of Cyprus, Cyprus
Dimitris Gritzalis	Athens University of Economics and Business, Greece
Stefanos Gritzalis	University of the Aegean, Greece
Bernhard Haemmerli	Acris, Switzerland
Pieter Hartel	University of Twente, The Netherlands
Constantinos Heracleous	University of Cyprus, Cyprus
Sokratis Katsikas	University of Piraeus, Greece
Stefan Katzenbeisser	TU Darmstadt, Germany
Marieke Klaver	TNO, The Netherlands
Panayiotis Kolios	University of Cyprus, Cyprus
Panayiotis Kotzanikolaou	University of Piraeus, Greece
Christoph Krauß	Fraunhofer AISEC, Germany
Elias Kyriakides	University of Cyprus, Cyprus
Javier Lopez	University of Malaga, Spain
Eric Luiijf	TNO, The Netherlands
Konstantinos Manousakis	University of Cyprus, Cyprus
Fabio Martinelli	IIT-CNR, Italy
Michalis Michaelides	Cyprus University of Technology, Cyprus
Igor Nai Fovino	Joint Research Centre, Italy
Eiji Okamoto	University of Tsukuba, Japan
Stefan Pickl	Bundeswehr University Munich, Germany
Vasso Reppa	Supelec, France
Andre Samberg	Sec-Control, Finland
Roberto Setola	Università Campus Bio-Medico, Italy
Angelos Stavrou	George Mason University, USA

Marianthi Theoharidou	Athens University of Economics and Business, Greece
Stelios Timotheou	University of Cyprus, Cyprus
Anthony Tzes	University of Patras, Greece
Christos Xenakis	University of Piraeus, Greece
Zinon Zinonos	University of Cyprus, Cyprus

Contents

Power and Energy System Security

Security and Recovery Policies

Cyber Security

Security Tools and Protocols

Cyber-Physical Systems and Sensor Networks

Fault Detection and Isolation in Critical Infrastructure Systems

Vicenç Puig$^{(\boxtimes)}$, Teresa Escobet, Ramon Sarrate, and Joseba Quevedo

Advanced Control Systems (SAC), Universitat Politcnica de Catalunya (UPC),
Campus de Terrassa, Rambla Sant Nebridi, 10, 08222 Terrassa, Barcelona, Spain
{vicenc.puig,teresa.escobet,ramon.sarrate,joseba.quevedo}@upc.edu

Abstract. Critical infrastructure systems (CIS) are complex large-scale systems which in turn require highly sophisticated supervisory control systems to ensure that high performance can be achieved and maintained under adverse conditions. The global CIS Real-Time Control (RTC) need of operating in adverse conditions involves, with a high probability, sensor and actuator malfunctions (faults). This problem calls for the use of an on-line Fault Detection and Isolation (FDI) system able to detect such faults. This paper proposes a FDI mechanism that extends the classical Boolean fault signature matrix concept taking into account several fault signal properties to isolate faults in CIS. To exemplify the proposed FDI scheme in CIS, the Barcelona drinking water network is used as a case study.

1 Introduction

Critical infrastructure systems (CIS), such as water, gas or electrical networks, are complex large-scale systems which in turn require highly sophisticated supervisory control systems. CIS are geographically distributed and decentralized with a hierarchical structure. Each subsystem is composed of a large number of elements with time-varying behavior, exhibiting numerous operating modes and subject to changes due to external conditions (e.g., weather) and operational constraints. But, in order to take profit of these expensive infrastructures, it is also necessary to have a highly sophisticated real-time control (RTC) scheme which ensures that high performance can be achieved and maintained under adverse conditions (Schütze et al., 2004; Ocampo et al., 2008). The advantage of RTC applied to CIS has been demonstrated by an important number of researchers during the last decades. Comprehensive reviews that include a discussion of some existing implementations are given by Schilling et al. (1996), Schütze et al. (2004) and Ocampo et al. (2013), and cited references therein, while practical issues are discussed by Schütze et al. (2002), among other. The RTC scheme in CIS might be local or global. When local control is applied, regulation devices use only measurements taken at their specific locations. While this control structure is applicable in many simple cases, in large systems with a strongly interconnected and complex infrastructure of sensors and actuators, it may not be the most efficient alternative. Conversely, a global control strategy

© Springer International Publishing Switzerland 2016
C.G. Panayiotou et al. (Eds.): CRITIS 2014, LNCS 8985, pp. 3–12, 2016.
DOI: 10.1007/978-3-319-31664-2_1

is suitable for large scale systems with slow and coupled multivariable dynamic response such as water networks, which computes control actions taking into account real-time measurements all through the network, is likely the best way to use the infrastructure capacity and all the available sensor information.

The global RTC need of operating in adverse conditions involves, with a high probability, sensor and actuator malfunctions (faults) since due to the large scale nature of the systems, an important number of components are involved. This problem calls for the use of an on-line fault detection and isolation (FDI) system able to detect locally such faults, and correct them (if possible) by activating fault tolerant control (FTC) mechanisms. FTC techniques prevent the global RTC system from stopping every time a fault occurs by using techniques such as virtual sensors/actuators or retuning of the controller.

The FDI process aims at carefully identifying which fault (including hardware or software faults, and malicious attacks) can be hypothesized to be the cause of some monitored events. In general, when addressing the FDI problem, two approaches can be found in the literature: hardware redundancy based on the use of redundancies (adding extra sensors and actuators), and software (or analytical) redundancy based on the use of software/intelligent sensors (or model) combining information provided by sensor measurements or using other actuators to compensate a faulty actuator. In CIS, hardware redundancy is preferred. However, for large-scale systems, the use of hardware redundancy is very expensive and increases the number of maintenance and calibration operations. This is the reason why, in CIS applications, systems that allow combining both hardware and analytical redundancy (Carrozza, 2008) must be developed.

This paper proposes a FDI mechanism that extends the classical Boolean fault signature matrix (FSM) concept taking into account several fault signal properties to isolate faults in CIS. To exemplify the proposed FDI scheme in CIS, the Barcelona drinking water network is used as a case study.

2 Proposed Methodology

2.1 Foundations

The proposed FDI procedure is based on checking the consistency between the observed and the normal system behavior using a set of analytical redundancy relations, which relate the values for measured variables according to a normal operation (fault-free) model of the monitored system. When some inconsistency is detected, the fault isolation mechanism is activated in order to identify the possible fault.

The design of a model-based FDI system is based on utilizing the CIS mathematical model (that is obtained from the constitutive elements and their basic relationships) to build a set of consistency tests that only involve observed variables, known as Analytical Redundancy Relations (ARRs). A convenient description of the mathematical model of a CIS regarding FDI is by means of the following discrete-time model:

$$x_{k+1} = g(x_k, u_k, \theta_k) + w_k$$
$$0 = f(x_k, u_k, \theta_k) + \eta_k \qquad (1)$$
$$y_k = h(x_k, u_k, \theta_k) + \nu_k$$

where: $x \in \mathbb{R}^{n_x}$ is the vector of system states, $u \in \mathbb{R}^{n_u}$ is the vector of control actions and $y \in \mathbb{R}^{n_y}$ is the vector of system outputs; $\theta_k \in \mathbb{R}^{n_\theta}$ is a vector of uncertain parameters; $w_k \in \mathbb{R}^{n_w}$ and $\eta_k \in \mathbb{R}^{n_\eta}$ are unmodelled dynamics and disturbances and; $\nu_k \in \mathbb{R}^{n_\nu}$ are measurement noises; $g : \mathbb{R}^{n_x} \to \mathbb{R}^{n_x}$ and $h : \mathbb{R}^{n_x} \to \mathbb{R}^{n_y}$ are the state-space and measurement nonlinear functions, respectively; and f is the nonlinear static relation function.

To obtain ARRs for state space representation such as (1), it is necessary to manipulate the model to eliminate unobserved variables (i.e., the state x).

As it has been defined in Cordier et al. (2004), an ARR is a constraint derived from the system model which contains only observed variables, and which can therefore be evaluated from any observation obtained from measurements provided by the installed sensors. The evaluation of an ARR is denoted as r and is called the residual of the ARR. In ideal conditions (no uncertainty and no noise), $r = 0$ in a non-faulty situation, while $r \neq 0$ otherwise. Thus, residual r is the basis for fault detection.

Given the model defined in (1) with observed variables y_k and u_k, consistency tests can be derived from an ARR by generating a computational residual in the following way:

$$r_i = \Psi_i(y_k, u_k) = 0 \qquad (2)$$

where Ψ_i is called the residual ARR expression. The set of ARR can be represented as

$$\mathcal{R} = \{r_i = \Psi_i(y_k, u_k) = 0, i = 1, \ldots, n_r\} \qquad (3)$$

where n_r is the number of obtained ARRs.

In CIS, these ARRs can be efficiently derived applying structural analysis techniques. The analysis of the model structure has been widely used in the area of model-based diagnosis (Blanke et al., 2006). A structural model of a system is an abstraction of the analytical model where only the relation between variables and equations is taken into account, neglecting the mathematical expression of this relation. The diagnosis analysis based on structural models is performed by means of graph-based methods which have no numerical problems and are more efficient, in general, than analytical methods. In (Sarrate et al., 2014), a structural model of a water distribution network is obtained for FDI system design. See (Rosich et al., 2012) and (Travé-Massuyés et al., 2006) for a comprehensive description of ARR design methodologies based on structural analysis.

2.2 Fault Detection

In the literature, there are different approaches to solve this problem. For example, statistical decision methods (Basseville and Nikiforov, 2003) can be used when unknown dynamics and measurement noise are stochastically modeled. In many practical situations, this assumption is not realistic, being more natural to assume that disturbances/model errors and measurement noise are bounded and their effect is propagated to the residuals using, for example, interval methods (Puig et al., 2008). Taking into account bounded uncertainties, the residual of the ARR (2) is monitored by evaluating an interval:

$$[r_i] = \{r_i | r_i = \Psi_i(y_k, u_k, \delta_k), \delta_k \in D\} \tag{4}$$

where D is the interval box $D = \{\delta \in \mathbb{R}^{n_\delta} | \underline{\delta} \leq \delta \leq \overline{\delta}\}$, that includes all the bounded uncertainties. Fault detection is formulated as ARR consistency checking using a set-membership approach (Tornil-Sin et al., 2012).

Given a system described by (3) and a sequence of measured inputs u_k and outputs y_k of the real system at time k, an ARR is consistent with those measurements and the known bounds of uncertain parameters and noise if there exists a set of sequences $\delta_k \in D$ which satisfies the ARR.

Given a sequence of observed inputs u_k and outputs y_k of the real system, a fault is said to be detected at time k if there does not exist a set of sequences $\delta_k \in D$ to which the set of ARRs is consistent.

Based on interval reasoning, a fault is detected when $0 \notin [r_i]$ where $[r_i]$ is defined in (5). The information provided by the consistency checking is stored as fault signal $\phi_i(k)$:

$$\phi_i(k) = \begin{cases} 0 \text{ if } 0 \in [r_i] \\ 1 \text{ if } 0 \notin [r_i] \end{cases} \tag{5}$$

From computation point of view (6) are generated as $r(k) = y(k) - \hat{y}(k, \delta)$, where $\hat{y}(k, \delta)$ is the estimated value of the output obtained from (1), using for example parity equations or observers.

2.3   Fault Isolation

While a single residual is sufficient to detect faults, a set (or a vector) of residuals is required for fault isolation (Gertler, 1998). Once the jth residual has been generated, it is evaluated in order to detect normal or abnormal behaviors. In general, a fault f affects a subset of ARRs, $R_f \subseteq \mathcal{R}$.

In model based FDI, the fault effects on the residual can be expressed in terms of the residual fault sensitivity that leads to the residual internal form (Gertler, 1998). For example, in the case of residual r_1 is affected by faults f_1 and f_2, the internal form can be expressed as follows

$$r_1(k) = S_{f_1}(q^{-1})f_1(k) + S_{f_2}(q^{-1})f_2(k) \tag{6}$$

where, $S_{f_1}(q^{-1})$ and $S_{f_2}(q^{-1})$ are the residual fault sensitivity transfer functions that characterize the fault effect on the residual and q^{-1} is the delay operator of discrete time models.

The fault isolation module proposed in this paper is a generalization to a CIS of the one used in Puig et al. (2005) (see Fig. 1). The first component is a memory that stores information on the fault signal occurrence history and

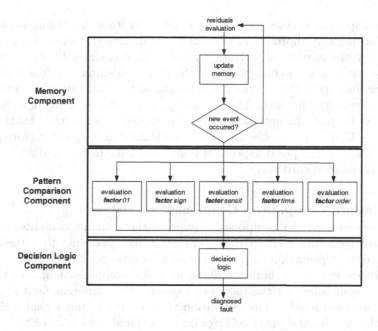

Fig. 1. Fault detection and isolation logic scheme.

it is cyclically updated by the fault detection module. The pattern comparison component compares the memory contents with the stored fault patterns. The classical Boolean fault signature matrix concept (Gertler, 1998) is generalized by extending the binary interface to take into account more fault signal properties. The last component represents the decision logic part of the method whose aim is to propose the most probable fault candidate.

2.3.1 Memory Component

The memory component consists of a table in which events in the residual history are stored. When $\phi_i = 1$, the occurrence time, identified by k_0, is stored in the first column; the maximum nominal residual $r_{i,max}$ is stored in the second column and computes as follow:

$$r_{i,max} = \max_{k \in [k_0, k_0+T_w]} (|r_i^0(k)|) \tag{7}$$

where r_i^0 is computed according to (6) considering the center of the uncertainty interval δ_0; and, the *sign* of the residual is stored in the last column. If the fault detection component detects a new fault signal, the memory is updated by filling out all those fields. The problem of different time instant appearances of the fault signal $\phi_i(k)$ is solved by disabling the isolation decision until a prefixed waiting time T_w has elapsed from the first fault signal appearance. This T_w is calculated from the larger transient time response from a non-faulty situation to any faulty situation. After this time has elapsed, a diagnosis is proposed and the memory component is reset in order to be ready to start the diagnosis of a new fault. Following the approach of Combastel et al. (2003), inside this diagnosis time window, the maximum activation value of the memory-table $r_{i,max}$ at time k_0 and for one residual i changes only if the current nominal residual is superior to the previous ones. Due to the max-operator activation values can only rise. Using this strategy the effect of noise and non-persistence fault indicators are filtered because just the activation peaks are stored. The memory table makes the residual history accessible for later computation by explicitly storing that data. In this way, temporal aspects of fault isolation can be handled in a very easy and straightforward way.

2.3.2   Pattern Comparison Component

The pattern comparison component compares the memory contents with the stored fault patterns. Fault patterns are organized according to a theoretical **FSM**. This interpretation assumes that the occurrence of f_j is observable in r_i, hypothesis known as fault exoneration or no compensation, and that f_j is the only fault affecting the monitored system. Five different fault signature matrices are considered in the evaluation task: Boolean fault signal activation (**FSM**01), fault signal signs (**FSM** sign), fault residual sensitivity (**FSM** sensit), and, finally, fault signal occurrence order (**FSM** order) and time after the first residual is activated (**FSM** time). Theses matrices can be obtained from the analysis of residual fault sensitivity (8). Details on the general rules to obtain those matrices from (8) can be found in Meseguer et al. (2010).

2.3.3   Decision Logic Component

The decision logic algorithm starts when the first residual is activated (that is, $\phi_i = 1$) and lasts T_w time instants or till all fault hypotheses except one are rejected because they do not fulfill the observed residual activation order/time or because an unexpected activation signal has been observed according to those fault hypotheses. Rejection is based on using the results of **factor**01$_j$, **factor**sign$_j$ and **factor**order$_j$. If any of these factors is "zero" for a given fault hypothesis, it will be rejected. Every factor, with a range of [0,1], represents some kind of a filter, suggesting a set of possible fault hypotheses. At the end of the time window T_w, for each non-rejected fault hypothesis, a fault isolation indicator is calculated using **factor**sensit$_j$ and **factor**time$_j$ factors. Thus, the biggest fault isolation indicator will determine the diagnosed fault. The fault isolation indicator associated to the fault hypothesis f_j is determined as it follows:

$$d_j = \max(|\boldsymbol{factor}\, sensit_j|, \boldsymbol{factor}\, time_j) \qquad (8)$$

So, the final diagnosis result can be expressed as a set of fault candidates with their associated fault isolation indicator.

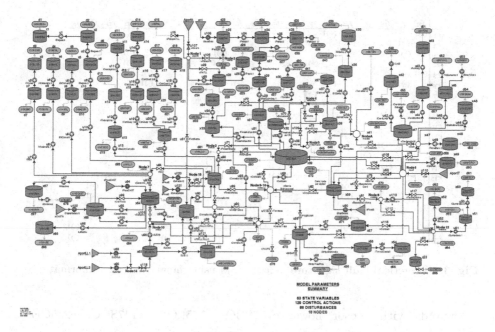

Fig. 2. Barcelona water transport network description.

3   Application to the Barcelona Water Transport Network

3.1   Description of Network

The Barcelona water network supplies water to approximately 3 million consumers, distributed in 23 municipalities in a $424 \, km^2$ area. Water can be taken from both surface and underground sources. The most important ones in terms of capacity and use are Ter, which is a surface source, and Llobregat, where water can be taken from one surface source and one underground source. Water is supplied from these sources to 218 demand sectors through around $4645 \, Km$ of pipes. The complete transport network has been modeled using: 63 storage tanks, 3 surface sources and 7 underground sources, 79 pumps, 50 valves, 18 nodes and 88 demands. The network is controlled through a SCADA system (Fig. 2) with sampling periods of 1 hour. For the predictive control scheme a prediction horizon of $24 \, h$ is chosen. This record is updated at each time interval.

3.2   FDI in the Barcelona Water Network

The case study used to illustrate the FDI methodology proposed in this paper is based on part of this network. It includes two subsystems, known as Orioles and Cervello. This part of the network includes the following elements:

- Tanks: d150SBO, d175LOR, d147SCC, d205CES, d263CES
- Actuators with sensor flows: iStBoi, iOrioles, iStaClmCervello, iCesalpina1

	f_{P1}	f_{P2}	f_{P3}	f_{P4}	f_{P5}	f_{F1}	f_{F2}	f_{F3}	f_{F4}	f_{F5}	f_{L1}	f_{L2}	f_{L3}	f_{L4}	f_{L5}	f_{d1}	f_{d2}	f_{d3}	f_{d4}	f_{d5}
r_1	(-)1					(+)1														
r_2		(-)1					(+)1													
r_3		(+)1										(+)1					(-)1			
r_4							(+)1					(+)1					(-)1			
r_5	(+)1	(-)1									(+)1					(-)1				
r_6		(-)1					(+)1				(+)1					(-)1				
r_7	(+)1							(-)1			(+)1					(-)1				
r_8							(+)1	(-)1			(+)1					(-)1				
r_9			(-1)1					(+)1												
r_{10}				(-)1				(+)1												
r_{11}				(-)1				(+)1												
r_{12}			(+)1	(-)1									(+)1					(-)1		
r_{13}				(-)1				(+)1					(+)1					(-)1		
r_{14}			(+)1						(-)1				(+)1					(-)1		
r_{15}								(+)1	(-)1				(+)1					(-)1		
r_{16}				(+)1	(-)1									(+)1					(-)1	
r_{17}					(-)1				(+)1					(+)1					(-)1	
r_{18}				(+)1						(-)1				(+)1					(-)1	
r_{19}									(+)1	(-)1				(+)1					(-)1	
r_{20}					(+)1									(+)1					(-)1	
r_{21}										(+)1				(+)1					(-)1	

Fig. 3. Theoretical fault signature matrix FSM using binary and sign information.

- Demands with sensor flows: c157SBO, c175LOR, c147SCC, c205CES, c263CES
- Sensor levels: d150SBO, xd175LOR, xd147SCC, xd205CES, xd263CES

This case study can be modeled by the system described by (1), with a 5-dimensional state space vector where each x_i is the ith tank level, $q_{in,i}$ and $q_{out,i}$ are the input and output tank flows, and d_i is the demand. The set of known variables is $O = \{u_i, y_j\}$ for $i = 1, \ldots, 5$ and $j = 1, \ldots, 15$, where u_i are the actuator command variables and y_j concerns all measured variables, including the sensors described above.

Applying the algorithm proposed by (Travé-Massuyés et al., 2006), 21 ARRs have been obtained. From these ARRs, the same number of residuals can be generated. Considering faults in the actuators, f_{Pi}, flow transducers, f_{Fi}, level transducers, f_{Li}, and demand transducers f_{di}, for $i = 1, \ldots, 5$, the fault signature matrix shown in Fig. 3 is obtained. This fault signature matrix includes binary and sign information.

If just binary information is considered, all faults are detectable, but only f_{Pi} and f_{Fi} are isolable. For instance, faults $\{f_{Li}, f_{di}\}$ can not be isolated because both can not observed independently. But if *sign* information is taken into account, both can be distinguished. Moreover, notice that the information provided by both sensors, $\{f_{Li}, f_{di}\}$ is essential for computing residuals because there is not enough redundancy, Thus, they can be considered as critical sensors. A fault in one of these sensors modifies the ARR sets, resulting to an undetectable fault. The fault detection and isolation procedure described in Sect. 2 has been applied in a simulation case. Figure 4 shows the first 8 ARR residuals and fault signal evolution when a drift in sensor iOrioles flow, f_{F2}, is introduced at hour 362. Notice that residuals r_2, r_4, r_7 and r_8 are non-consistent, indicating as potential fault $\{f_{P2}, f_{F1}, f_{F2}, f_{L1}, f_{L2}, f_{d1}, f_{d2}\}$.

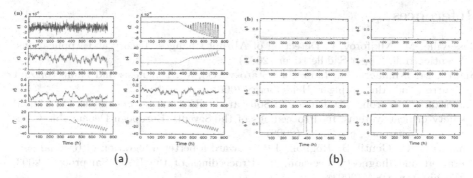

(a)   (b)

Fig. 4. (a) Residuals and (b) fault signal evolution with a drift fault in sensor iOrioles flow.

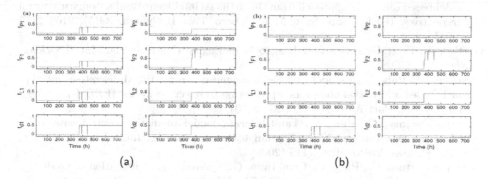

(a)   (b)

Fig. 5. Fault signal analysis based on (a) *factor*01 and (b) *factor*sign.

The time evolution of *factor*01 and *factor*sign are plotted at every time instant in Fig. 5. It can be seen that both factors indicate as a maximum fault hypothesis f_{P2}, with $d_{P2} = 1$ (10). There are also others activated factors but with a smaller indication magnitude. In this example, the time needed for detection and isolation is of two sampling times.

4   Conclusions

CIS are complex large-scale systems which in turn require highly sophisticated supervisory-control systems to ensure that high performance can be achieved and maintained under adverse conditions. The global RTC need of operating in adverse conditions involve, with a high probability, sensor and actuator malfunctions (faults). This problem calls for the use of an on-line FDI system able to detect such faults and correct them (if possible) by activating fault tolerant mechanisms. The proposed FDI mechanism extends the classical Boolean fault signature matrix concept taking into account several fault signal properties to isolate the faults in CIS. To exemplify the FDI methodologies in CIS, the Barcelona drinking water network is used as the case study.

References

Basseville, M., Nikiforov, I.: Detection of Abrupt Changes: Theory and Applications. Prentice Hall, Upper Saddle River (2003)

Blanke, M., Kinnaert, M., Lunze, J., Staroswiecki, M.: Diagnosis and Fault-Tolerant Control, 2nd edn. Springer, Heidelberg (2006)

Carrozza, G., Cotroneo, D. Russo, S.: Software faults diagnosis in complex OTS based safety critical systems. In: Proceedings of the Seventh European Dependable Computing Conference, pp. 25–34 (2008)

Combastel, C., Gentil, S., Rognon, J.P.: Toward a better integration of residual generation and diagnostic decision. In: Proceedings of the IFAC Safeprocess 2003, Washington, USA (2003)

Cordier, M.-O., Dague, P., Levy, F., Montmain, J., Staroswiecki, M., Travé-Massuyés, L.: Conflicts versus analytical redundancy relations: a comparative analysis of the model based diagnosis approach from the artificial intelligence and automatic control perspectives. IEEE Trans. Syst. Man Cybern. Part B Cybern. 34(5), 2163–2177 (2004)

Gertler, J.: Fault Detection and Diagnosis in Engineering Systems. Marcel Dekker, New York (1998)

Meseguer, J., Puig, V., Escobet, T.: Fault diagnosis using a timed discrete-event approach based on interval observers: application to sewer networks. IEEE Trans. Syst. Man Cybern. Part A 40(5), 900–916 (2010)

Ocampo-Martnez, C., Puig, V.: Fault-tolerant model predictive control within the hybrid systems framework: application to sewer networks. Int. J. Adapt. Control Signal Process. 23(8), 1099–1115 (2008)

Ocampo-Martnez, C., Puig, V., Cembrano, G., Quevedo, J.: Application of predictive control strategies to the management of complex networks in the urban water cycle. IEEE Control Syst. Mag. 33(1), 15–41 (2013)

Puig, V., Quevedo, J., Escobet, T., Pulido, B.: A new fault diagnosis algorithm that improves the integration of fault detection and isolation. In: Proceedings of ECC-CDC 2005, Sevilla, Spain (2005)

Puig, V., Quevedo, J., Escobet, T., De las Heras, S.: Passive robust fault detection of dynamic processes using interval models. IEEE Trans. Control Syst. Technol. 16(5), 1083–1089 (2008)

Rosich, A., Frisk, E., Åslund, J., Sarrate, R., Nejjari, F.: Fault diagnosis based on causal computations. IEEE Trans. Syst. Man Cybern. Part A 42(2), 371–381 (2012)

Sarrate, R., Blesa, J., Nejjari, F.: Water Supply. doi:10.2166/ws.2014.037.

Schilling, W., Anderson, B., Nyberg, U., Aspegren, H., Rauch, W., Harremoës, P.: Real-time control of wasterwater systems. J. Hydraul. Resour. 34(6), 785–797 (1996)

Schütze, M., Butler, D., Beck, B.: Modelling, Simulation and Control of Urban Wastewater Systems. Springer, Heidelberg (2002)

Schütze, M., Campisanob, A., Colas, H., Schilling, W., Vanrolleghem, P.: Real time control of urban wastewater systems: where do we stand today? J. Hydrol. 299, 335–348 (2004)

Tornil-Sin, S., Ocampo-Martinez, C., Puig, V., Escobet, T.: Robust fault diagnosis of nonlinear systems using interval constraint satisfaction and analytical redundancy relations. IEEE Trans. Syst. Man Cybern. Syst. Part B 44(1), 18–29 (2014)

Travé-Massuyés, L., Escobet, T., Olive, X.: Diagnosability analysis based on component supported analytical redundancy relations. IEEE Trans. Syst. Man Cybern. Syst. Part A 36(6), 1146–1160 (2006)

Critical Infrastructure in the Future City
Developing Secure and Resilient Cyber–Physical Systems

Hugh Boyes[⊠], Roy Isbell, and Tim Watson

Cyber Security Centre, WMG, University of Warwick, Coventry, UK
{hb,ri,tw}@warwick.ac.uk

Abstract. Cities face serious challenges that affect competitiveness, sustainability and their occupants' safety & security. In response, investment is made in city infrastructure projects. Given the complexity of the systems architecture, and interactions between physical and cyber domains, this paper shows how a multi-disciplinary approach can be adopted to address the challenges. It introduces an analysis methodology for use by multi-disciplinary teams to allow the dependencies and interactions of cyber–physical systems in physical–cyber environments to be explored. The analysis methodology offers a systematic way to study the cyber–physical systems and identify safety, security or resilience issues that need to be addressed in the systems design or operation.

Keywords: Smart cities · Cyber–physical systems · Cyber security · Resilience · Trustworthy software · Critical infrastructure · Physical–cyber environment · Future city

1 Introduction

Projections indicate that 60 % of the world's population will be urbanised by 2030 [1]. This compares to less than 40 % of the global population living in cities in 1990 and with fewer than 10 % of urban dwellers living in cities with populations <500,000 people [2]. The WHO anticipates that population growth in cities over the next 30 years will occur in developing countries [2]. This indicates that by the middle of the 21st century, the urban population of developing countries will more than double. This growth will result in the expansion of existing cities and development of new ones. Areas where these cities develop are often on coastal plains, putting them at greater risk from severe weather events and changes in sea levels [3].

The increasing size of urban populations creates significant challenges for future cities, dubbed as 'smart cities', where complex interactions between Cyber–Physical Systems (CPS) will aim to improve the quality of life and to proactively manage demand for scarce or costly resources. Creating future cities will present significant technical and economic challenges for both developed and developing nations.

Use of technology is not without risks, particularly with regard to the resilience and cyber security of critical city infrastructure. Future cities will

© Springer International Publishing Switzerland 2016
C.G. Panayiotou et al. (Eds.): CRITIS 2014, LNCS 8985, pp. 13–23, 2016.
DOI: 10.1007/978-3-319-31664-2_2

evolve into sophisticated platforms, comprising systems-of-systems-of-systems or physical–cyber environments. There will also be a greater degree of system autonomy where humans will be relegated to the role of supervisor or maintainer, giving birth to a new breed of 'Cyber Janitor'.

Future cities will challenge existing safety and security engineering models e.g. the United States electricity blackout in 2003 [4] showed that in interdependent networks a very small failure in one network might lead to catastrophic consequences [5]. New and complex cascading failure modes will arise out of unforeseen or emergent system characteristics as they are developed in an incremental and ad hoc fashion, especially where more sophisticated technologies are added to an already ageing physical infrastructure.

This paper examines some challenges to be addressed if we are to understand and manage the potential future impacts. It starts by examining the nature of CPS and the evolution of the city as a platform. To understand the requirements this paper considers a city from three perspectives: the context of its data and systems, understanding resilience of systems and services, and an approach to deriving its cyber security needs. These perspectives form the basis of an analysis methodology under development by the authors.

2   Cyber–Physical Systems and the City as a Platform

There are a number of definitions of CPS [6–9]. Common features effectively describe control systems, networked and/or distributed, incorporating a degree of intelligence (adaptive or predictive), and work in real time to influence outcomes in the real world. These definitions point to the diverse nature of CPS found in transportation, utilities, buildings, infrastructure, manufacturing, and health care.

Although CPS have similarities with traditional data processing systems, e.g. their networked or distributed nature and a degree of automation, the real-time nature of their interactions with the physical world is a significant difference. Interactions are sensors detecting and measuring physical parameters with actuators to control physical processes. Feedback loops allow data about the environment and the physical processes to be collected and computed. Actuation may be automatic or by an alert to a human operator.

Critical infrastructure systems are CPS, whose failure would have economic or social impact. Society expects systems will operate in a safe, secure and consistent manner [10]. In response to environmental, demographic and societal pressures, cities may no longer conduct business as usual. Traditional city models are no longer appropriate, as transport and utility infrastructures becomes unsustainable and requires significant investment [11].

Some cities have embraced the concept of the 'city as a platform', a hyperconnected urban environment that harnesses the network effects, openness, and agility of the real-time web [12]. The focus has been on access to data, leading to development of smartphone apps and portals allowing citizens to 'connect' with city services and institutions [13,14]. To address cyber security requirements we

need to understand the proliferation of functions in this hyper-connected world
[15]. Where functions in individual CPS interact, they will create new functions that will proliferate over time. To protect these complex systems we need
to understand their network of functions, relationships and interdependencies.
A study of critical infrastructure interdependencies [16] led to the identification
of six dimensions, which can be used to examine CPS and supporting infrastructures:

- Type of interdependency, e.g. cyber, physical, logical or geographic;
- Environment, e.g. business, economic, public policy, legal, regulatory, security,
  technical, health/safety, or social/political;
- Coupling and response behaviour, e.g. adaptive, inflexible, loose/tight or lin-
  ear/complex;
- Infrastructure characteristics, e.g. spatial, operational, organisational or tem-
  poral;
- Type of failure, e.g. common cause, escalating or cascading;
- State of operation, e.g. normal, stressed/disrupted, restoration or repair.

The study is a useful starting point in understanding interdependencies between
city systems and infrastructure, however, the sophistication of solutions today is
greater than those contemplated in 2001. The increased integration and automation of city systems requires a broader understanding of the 'city as a platform'
if solutions are to deliver resilience and cyber security.

3 Future Cities Analysis Framework

We propose an analysis framework, which examines the critical city infrastructure and services from three perspectives: context, resilience, and cyber security.
The analysis framework (Fig. 1), builds on our work regarding the cyber security
of buildings [17], adapted to focus at a city level on critical infrastructure and
related services.

3.1 Identifying Critical City Infrastructure

Whilst there are a number of definitions for critical national infrastructure [18–
20], from a city perspective the concept of critical infrastructure is not well
defined. The UK's definition of critical national infrastructure (CNI) is: "those
facilities, systems, sites and networks necessary for the functioning of the country and the delivery of the essential services upon which daily life in the UK
depends" [19]; where criticality is determined based on a Criticality Scale [21],
which assesses impact of events or scenarios on a national scale. From a city perspective, we propose that criticality addresses elements necessary for the delivery
of essential services to the populace who are resident and/or work in the city and
that impact is focused at city rather than national level. The critical infrastructure must encompass both the city's normal operating state, and its ability to

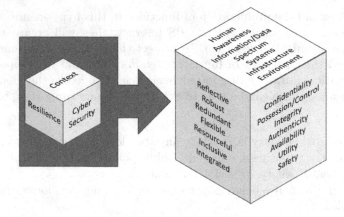

Fig. 1. Analysis Framework for secure and resilient Future Cities

effectively respond to natural or other disasters [22]. Our definition of a city's critical infrastructure translates the principles underlying criticality at a national level to apply them at a city level based on four factors:

- the impact on delivery of essential societal functions and services, e.g. to provide water, food and shelter, and to maintain law and order;
- the economic impact on the well-being and viability of the city, e.g. the ability to operate as a business and financial centre and provide employment;
- the impact on life, health and well-being of city occupants, e.g. to provide medical and social services to protect and care for citizens;
- the ability to respond to major incidents or disasters, e.g. to provide emergency services including sites to manage emergency operations and to provide housing in the event of a disaster.

The result of applying these factors to a typical city's infrastructure is illustrated in Table 1, which also identifies whether an element would normally be regarded as part of the critical national infrastructure.

The extension of generally accepted critical infrastructure to include education and leisure facilities recognises the critical role they can play in emergencies. For example, in Hurricane Katrina the New Orleans Superbowl was used as an emergency relief centre. Large open spaces, such as parks or sports fields can also be used as locations for temporary accommodation or to provide alternative sites for managing disaster operations in the event of a natural disaster [22].

3.2   Understanding the Context

The resilience and cyber security requirements of a future city require a holistic view of the relevant systems, services and their interdependencies. This is important where a network of independently operated systems including systems operating external to the city provides the essential functionality. A smart

Table 1. Proposed components of critical city infrastructure

Critical city infrastructure	Critical national infrastructure
Communications	Yes
Education (Schools, Colleges, Universities)	No
Emergency services	Yes
Energy (Electricity, Gas, Oil/Petroleum products)	Yes
Financial services	Yes
Food	Yes
Government (City administration)	Yes
Health	Yes
Leisure (Parks, Sport facilities)	No
Transport (Road, Rail, Air, Waterborne)	Yes
Water	Yes

environment must be able to both detect the current state or context in the environment and determine what actions to take based on this context information [23].

To establish the resilience and cyber security requirements for a future city's CPS, the seven dimensions of cyber [24,25] need to be analysed and the context under which they are operating understood. The dimensions are: human, awareness/understanding, information/data, spectrum, systems, infrastructure, and the environment. For example, understanding the spectrum and channels used for communications and sharing both data and control signals will help to understand the impact of interference, jamming, electro-magnetic pulses and solar weather events on the city's infrastructure.

3.3   Resilience of a City's Cyber–Physical Systems

The Rockefeller Foundation and Arup developed a City Resilience Framework [26]. The Framework defines a resilient system as having seven qualities: reflective, robust, redundant, flexible, resourceful, inclusive, integrated. These indicators are important as they provide a holistic view of resilience as it applies to a city. For example, a resilient city has effective city leadership, good infrastructure, social cohesion, collective identity and relative prosperity. This is illustrated in the contrast between the recovery of Port au Prince, Haiti following an earthquake in 2010 and New York's response to Hurricane Sandy in 2012 [26].

3.4   Defining Cyber Security for Cyber–Physical Systems

The future city will be a complex environment comprising a variety of technologies, existing and emerging. The cyber security approach adopted may vary

Table 2. Application of cyber security elements

Element	Relevance to cyber–physical systems
Confidentiality	Protection of personal and other sensitive data
Possession/Control	Prevent unauthorised manipulation or control of systems
Integrity	Prevention of unauthorised changes to or deletion of data, and maintenance of system configuration
Authenticity	Prevention of fraud or tampering with data
Availability	City infrastructure able to operate without disruption or impairment
Utility	Maintaining data and systems in a useful state throughout their lifecycle
Safety	Prevention of harm to individuals, assets and the environment

considerably, depending on factors such as asset and systems complexity, ownership and use. The supply chain supporting design, construction, operation and occupation of individual assets or systems also affect the future city. Applying current information security practice to deliver cyber security of the city as a platform is extremely complex if not impossible. The fragmented ownership of individual components within the platform, diverse interfaces and constant change will all limit the effectiveness of traditional control measures. Cyber security of CPS is complicated by the real-time nature of the systems and the potential safety critical elements of their functionality. Applying the traditional CIA triad [27], used by the information security community, does not adequately address the safety and control aspects of CPS. An alternative approach that combines engineering good practice with information security may be achieved by adapting the Parkerian Hexad [28] with the addition of safety as a seventh element [25]. This results in cyber security being considered using the following elements: confidentiality, possession and/or control, integrity, authenticity, availability, utility, safety. Table 2 illustrates how these elements relate to the design and operation of the city's CPS.

4   Applying the Framework to City Infrastructure

With the increasing sophistication and integration of city systems and the need to protect their growing populations, there is a need for city planners to consider risk, resilience and cyber security in a holistic manner. The two examples below illustrate how critical CPS and poor planning may disable generators and transport systems. The example from Hurricane Sandy of cross-sector dependencies was the impact of the storm on energy supplies. A post storm study [29] exposed risks that were not understood by dependent critical sectors and government officials, due in part to their limited understanding of sector operations and distribution. The study highlights that:

- without power, even well stocked gasoline service stations were unable to pump fuel to customers;
- emergency managers struggled to determine which gasoline stations had both fuel and power;
- refineries and supply terminals that lost power also had major water damage to primary switch gear and other critical electrical components that delayed restoration long after power was restored;
- many critical dependent sites limited to 24 hours of fuel storage required repeated daily refuelling runs for generators;
- the regulation on fuel storage creates disincentives to store greater supplies.

The analysis framework, which is summarised in Fig. 2, is a structured approach to analysing city infrastructure and systems. Due to the interdependencies between city systems and services, it should be applied on a citywide basis rather than focused on single systems or services. Whilst the framework is intended to work at an overall systems level, by addressing the interactions and dependencies of the 'city as a platform', it may also be used within systems to understand complex sub-system relationships and behaviour. The framework has been tested on the CCTV and associated area management systems in a major UK city [30].

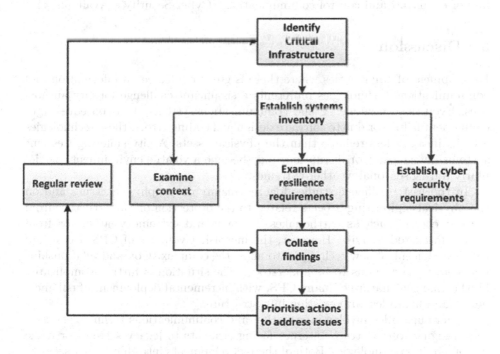

Fig. 2. Applying the analysis framework to a city

The approach used to test the framework was to identify the set of affected systems, which included a number of control rooms. The context and role of the control rooms was examined, including the relationships between the areas of coverage. The resilience requirements were investigated, taking into account the need to manage major annual events and public safety incidents. Finally the cyber security requirements and current systems issues were investigated. In collating the results a number of deficiencies were identified, including a significant loss of capability following a system upgrade. The discovery of this loss and the rapid advances in the technology employed in 'smart' cities confirmed the need for regular reviews, to monitor changes in systems and infrastructure, identify new dependencies and emergent functionality arising from systems integration or interconnectivity.

The framework draws together information that may not be apparent to an infrastructure owner or operator, e.g. one recently discovered correlation between the three perspectives occurred in a power distribution network. The operator is increasing the use of the mobile telephony network to manage the field maintenance workforce. The mobile telephone network is not robust when there are power supply interruptions. In the event of a major supply outage, e.g. following a severe weather incident, due to the operator's reliance on the mobile telephone network (Context – Spectrum), the field workforce will not have access to a robust communications platform (Resilience – Robust), leading to a potential loss of command and control communications (Cyber Security – Availability).

5   Discussion

Development of smart cities where there is greater reliance on information and communications technologies represents a significant challenge for city authorities. Even as standalone IT and communication systems, as a consequence of component failure or due to software design and coding errors, these technologies are significantly less reliable than the physical assets. A city suffering frequent systems outages and/or disruptions may become a volatile environment, particularly during seasonal weather extremes.

In the past, resilience studies focused mainly on geophysical issues and on the physical engineering aspects related to the protection of infrastructure from natural events, such as earthquakes, tsunami and extreme weather, or from terrorism-related activity. However, the increasing volumes of CPS necessitate the development of new techniques to allow the complexity of, and relationships between, these systems to be understood. The situation is further complicated by the emergent nature of many CPS, with incremental deployment of enhancements and upgrades onto existing infrastructure.

Where upgrades involve information and communications technologies, system designers often attach Internet facing elements to legacy systems or make use of wireless technologies. Both of these developments introduce cyber security and resilience vulnerabilities.

The systems architecture of a future city is likely to be constantly evolving, with new components added and existing elements progressively upgraded or replaced. At any instant, the future city is therefore likely to be a complex hybrid of established, proven systems, with known constraints and defects, and newer systems whose behaviour and performance are still being established. It is likely that technical standards will also evolve over time, so systems will be built to differing risk profiles, availability and security standards.

This analysis framework provides a structured, systematic way of examining CPS, to identify any safety, security or resilience issues that need to be addressed in the design or operation of the systems. The three perspectives combine information about environmental, societal, process and technical dependencies and risks. This approach is not intended to replace the technical risk assessment techniques used in systems engineering, such as Failure Mode and Effects Analysis (FMEA), Hazard and Operability studies (HAZOP), Fault Tree Analysis (FTA) or Cause and Effect Analysis. Instead it provides an approach, which may be used at city level to explore vulnerabilities in the design and use of complex integrated CPS.

6   Conclusions

The expectation of future cities is that information and communications technologies, autonomy and CPS will be harnessed to deliver a safe, secure and sustainable environment for their rapidly growing populations. This dependence on technology is not without significant risk as the complex CPS that are already being developed will increasingly interact with each other. When the systems start to behave as a platform, the city becomes exposed to cascading failure modes, where apparently unrelated events may cause significant disruption or even loss of life.

The analysis framework described in this paper is intended to provide an approach for analysing the city level risks and vulnerabilities to inform both system planning and design. It should also enable the city authorities and infrastructure owner to make informed decisions about where systems need to be reinforced or reengineered to improve resilience and reduce cyber security risks.

Without a clear framework such as the one proposed here, it will be difficult to analyse the complex interactions and relationships between cyber–physical systems in a future city. The approach to systems thinking outlined in this paper enables multi-disciplinary teams to adopt a common approach to sharing information about the operation, dependencies and potential vulnerabilities of their systems or infrastructure. Using this consolidated view should enable security and resilience issues to be identified and addressed.

A comprehensive analysis methodology is under development by the authors, which builds on the framework outlined in this paper. Further work is also underway regarding the definition of cyber security of CPS. The work in both of these areas will be published in due course.

References

1. Doytsher, Y., et al.: Rapid urbanization and mega cities: the need for spatial information management. Research study by FIG Commission 3. FIG Publication No 48 (2010)
2. World Health Organisation: Global Health Observatory (GHO) - Urban population growth. http://www.who.int/gho/urban_health/situation_trends/urban_population_growth/en/. Accessed 17 April (2014)
3. Campbell-Lendrum, D., Corvalan, C.: Climate change and developing-country cities: implications for environmental health and equity. J Urban Health **84**(Suppl 1), 109–117 (2007). doi:10.1007/s11524-007-9170-x
4. Biello, D.: Is the US grid better prepared to prevent a repeat of the: blackout? Scientific American (2003). doi:10.1038/nature.2013.13559. http://www.nature.com/news/is-the-us-grid-better-prepared-to-prevent-a-repeat-of-the-2003-blackout-1.13559. Accessed 17 April 2014
5. Bashan, A., Berezin, Y., Buldyrev, S.V., Havlin, S.: The extreme vulnerability of interdependent spatially embedded networks. Nature Phys. **9**, 667–672 (2013). http://www.nature.com/news/us-electrical-grid-on-the-edge-of-failure-1.13598. Accessed 17 April 2014
6. CHESS: CHESS - Center for Hybrid and Embedded Software Systems (2013). http://chess.eecs.berkeley.edu/. Accessed 17 April 2014
7. Baheti, R., Gill, H.: Cyber-physical systems. In: Samad, T., Annaswamy, A.M. (eds.) The Impact of Control Technology, pp. 161–166. IEEE Control Systems Society, New York (2011). http://ieeecss.org/main/IoCT-report. Accessed 17th April 2014
8. Poovendran, R.: Cyber-physical systems: close encounters between two parallel worlds. Proc. IEEE **98**(8), 1363–1366 (2010)
9. Shafi, Q.: Cyber physical systems security: a brief survey. In: 12th International Conference on Computational Science and its Applications (ICCSA), 2012, pp. 146–150. IEEE (2012)
10. Boyes, H.A.: Trustworthy cyber-physical systems - a review. In: 8th IET International System Safety Conference incorporating the Cyber Security Conference 2013, pp. 1–8, 16–17 October 2013. doi:10.1049/cp.2013.1707
11. Institution of Civil Engineers: The state of the nation - Infrastructure 2010. London: Institution of Civil Engineers (2010). http://www.ice.org.uk/Information-resources/Document-Library/State-of-the-Nation-Infrastructure- 2010. Accessed 17 April 2014
12. Davis, P.M.: How to Rebuild the City as a Platform (2012). http://www.shareable.net/blog/rebuilding-cities-as-platforms. Accessed 17 April 2014
13. Coleman, E.: The City as a Platform - Stripping out complexity and Making Things Happen (2014). http://www.emercoleman.com/2/post/2014/02/the-city-as-a-platform-stripping-out-complexity-and-making-things-happen.html. Accessed 23 April 2014
14. The Bartlett Centre for Advanced Spatial Analysis: CityDashboard: London (2014). http://citydashboard.org/london/. Accessed 23 April 2014
15. World Economic Forums: Perspectives on a Hyperconnected World (2013)
16. Rinaldi, S.M., Peerenboom, J.P., Kelly, T.K.: Identifying, understanding, and analyzing critical infrastructure interdependencies. Control Syst. IEEE **21**(6), 11–25 (2001). doi:10.1109/37.969131. December 2001

17. Boyes, H.A.: Cyber Security in the Built Environment. Institution for Engineering and Technology, London (2014)
18. Moteff, J., Parfomak, P.: Critical Infrastructure and Key Assets: Definition and Identification. Congressional Research Service Library of Congress, Washington DC (2004)
19. Centre for Protection of National Infrastructure: The national infrastructure (2014). http://www.cpni.gov.uk/about/cni/. Accessed 17 April 2014
20. Federal Office of Civil Protection and Disaster Assistance: Critical Infrastructure Sectors and Subsectors. http://www.kritis.bund.de/SubSites/Kritis/EN/introduction/sectors/sectors_node.html. Accessed 23 April 2014
21. Cabinet Office: Strategic Framework and Policy Statement on Improving the Resilience of Critical Infrastructure to Disruption from Natural Hazards (2010). https://www.gov.uk/government/uploads/system/uploads/attachment_data/file/62504/strategic-framework.pdf. Accessed 23 April 2014
22. O'Rourke, T.D.: Critical Infrastructure, Interdependencies and Resilience. Bridge 37(1), 25–29 (2007). http://www.nae.edu/File.aspx?id=7405. Accessed 23 April 2014
23. Dey, A.K., Abowd, G.D., Salber, D.: A context-based infrastructure for smart environments. In: Nixon, P., Lacey, G., Dobson, S. (eds.) Managing Interactions in Smart Environments, pp. 114–128. Springer, London (2000)
24. Isbell, R., Boyes, H., Watson, T.: Deconstructing Cyber: The Seven Dimensions of Cyberspace. In preparation
25. Boyes, H.A.: Cyber security attributes for critical infrastructure systems. Cyber Security Review. Summer 2014, pp. 47–51 (2014). ISSN 2055-6950
26. Arup: City Resilience Framework. Arup, London (2014)
27. Bishop, M.: Introduction to Computer Security. Addison-Wesley Longman, Amsterdam (2004)
28. Parker, D.B.: Toward a new framework for information security. In: Bosworth, S., Kabay, M. (eds.) Computer Security Handbook, Chapter 5, 4th edn. Wiley, New York (2002)
29. National Infrastructure Advisory Council: Resilience through National, Regional, and Sector Partnerships: Draft Report and Recommendations (2013). http://www.dhs.gov/sites/default/files/publications/niac-rrwg-report-final-review-draft-for-qbm.pdf. Accessed 19 April 2014
30. Boyes, H.A., Isbell, R., Watson, T.: The resilient city and the role of cyber-physical systems. In: Infrastructure Risk and Resilience: Managing Complexity and Uncertainty in Developing Cities. London: The Institution of Engineering and Technology (2014). ISBN 978-1-84919-920-9

Exploitation of HART Wired Signal Distinct Native Attribute (WS-DNA) Features to Verify Field Device Identity and Infer Operating State

Juan Lopez Jr.$^{(\boxtimes)}$, Michael A. Temple, and Barry E. Mullins

Department of Electrical and Computer Engineering,
US Air Force Institute of Technology, Dayton, OH, USA
{juan.lopez,michael.temple,barry.mullins}@afit.edu

Abstract. Infusion of Information Technology (IT) into Industrial Control System (ICS) applications has increased Critical Infrastructure Protection (CIP) challenges. A layered security strategy is addressed that exploits Physical (PHY) features to verify field device identity and infer normal-anomalous operating state using Distinct Native Attribute (DNA) features. The goal is inferential confirmation that Human Machine Interface (HMI) indicated conditions match the system's true physical state. Feasibility is shown using Wired Signal DNA (WS-DNA) from Highway Addressable Remote Transducer (HART) enabled field devices. Results are based on experiments using an instrumented Process Control System (PCS) with smart field devices communicating via wired HART. Results are presented for two field devices operating at two different set-points and suggest that the WS-DNA technical approach is promising for inferring device physical state.

Keywords: CIP · ICS · HART · DNA · Anomaly detection · Process control

1 Introduction

CIP has become increasingly difficult as ICS architectures have migrated from simple point-to-point networks [8,9] to IT-based architectures interconnecting ICS and business enterprise networks. Although increasing both efficiency and reducing cost [10–13], this migration comes at the expense of increased vulnerability [14–20,22,24] and higher potential for catastrophic events that are inherent in IT systems [21]. The migration cost is high from a security perspective, and ICS Internet connectivity presents what some consider an "unresolved security issue" that must be addressed [23].

Some security solutions work well in traditional IT systems but are less effective for CIP intrusion and anomaly detection [23,25,26,29,31]. Most ICS intrusion

---

The rights of this work are transferred to the extent transferable according to title 17 U.S.C. 105.

© Springer International Publishing Switzerland 2016
C.G. Panayiotou et al. (Eds.): CRITIS 2014, LNCS 8985, pp. 24–30, 2016.
DOI: 10.1007/978-3-319-31664-2_3

detection schemes do not detect bit-level protocol vulnerability attacks given they do not understand "application level" protocols [32]. Some single packet detection capability for Supervisory Control And Data Acquisition (SCADA) traffic do exist [28–30,32,33], but these methods are unreliable for detecting sequential "allowed" commands that can progressively drive a SCADA system to become unstable (Stuxnet-like events). ICS/SCADA protection strategies that exploit device level PHY state information can complement upstream bit-level protection approaches. The envisioned multi-layer security strategy integrates both levels with a goal of countering Stuxnet-like attacks, e.g., detect cases where the HMI indicates coolant is flowing normally while in reality the control valve being monitored is physically closed, no coolant flowing, and physical damage is imminent. Current bit-level detection strategies have proven to be ineffective against these types of attacks. Sensing PHY state information from downstream field devices provides potential for confirming that desired physical device changes (open, close, etc.) have occurred and that HMI reporting is reliable.

This work supports a PHY-based Security (PhySEC) approach for verifying that the indicated HMI status is consistent with field device operating state. A WS-DNA fingerprinting process is formalized using signals from a wired HART field device in a closed-loop PCS–more than 35 million Hart devices have been deployed [27]. As used to achieve human-like discrimination of device hardware [18] and operations [1], the Radio Frequency DNA (RF-DNA) fingerprinting methodology was adopted for recent HART device level field bus work [2] which motivated WS-DNA formalization for SCADA PhySEC application. The HART WS-DNA fingerprints are used here to discriminate selected device-state combinations using a Multiple Discriminant Analysis, Maximum Likelihood (MDA/ML) process. The initial approach is promising for device hardware and state discrimination, so the investigation continues.

2   Discrimination Methodology

Exploitable DNA features have been extracted from both intentional and unintentional waveform responses that generally differ with device type [3,5,17,21]. Wireless techniques were adopted here for WS-DNA demonstration with a goal of identifying discriminating PHY features in FSK signals of a $4 - 20$ mA control loop. Of interest is unintentional electromechanically induced signal variation that is expected to possess unique characteristics dictated by component manufacturing process, component tolerances, device aging, environmental conditions, etc. [4]. The WS-DNA fingerprinting methodology here is consistent with work in [6,7] and includes: (1) Burst Detection, (2) Down-Conversion and Baseband Filtering, (3) Analysis Signal Generation, (4) Fingerprint Generation, and (5) Class Discrimination.

Wired HART signal collections were made on a Lab-volt 3531 PCS running an automated fluid level control process [2] using a collection receiver (Agilent Oscilloscope) and a desktop workstation for post-collection processing. The HART field devices were Endress+Hauser PMD75 differential pressure

Table 1. Hardware Device (D) and State (S) Notation.

Description	Notation
Low Pressure DPT-SP10	D1:S1
Low Pressure DPT-SP50	D1:S2
High Pressure DPT-SP10	D2:S1
High Pressure DPT-SP15	D2:S2

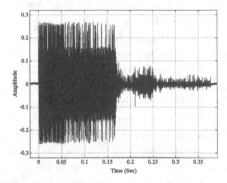

Fig. 1. Mean of 456 experimentally-collected HART FSK bursts.

transmitters. High-level $(0 - 400$ psi$)$ and low-level $(0 - 10$ psi$)$ pressure trans-mitters were used to measure column fluid level at two set points (SP): including (1) SP-10 for 2.0 inches of fluid, and (2) SP-50 for 20.0 inches of fluid. HART FSK signals were collected directly from pressure transmitter maintenance ports. A 2×2 experimental design was conducted using each of the two field devices sensing the two fluid levels. The various factor level combinations followed the Device:State (D:S) notation in Table 1. The assessments used WS-DNA finger-prints from a total of $N_B = 456$ independent HART bursts for all four D:S cases considered.

Figure 1 shows a representative mean response for 456 experimentally col-lected bursts; the response was similar for all four D:S cases. Of note is the constructive response of the *Preamble* during $0 < t < 0.055$ s and the Device ID Region (*DevIDRgn*) during $0.055 < t < 0.165$ s; note that the *DevIDRgn* designation is used here for presentation and does not represent a formal HART protocol designation.

As in prior DNA-based fingerprinting work, the invariant cross-burst responses such as the *Preamble* and *SigIDRgn* responses in Fig. 1 are generally most favorable for discrimination. Thus, the *SigIDRgn* region was first consid-ered for WS-DNA extraction and MDA/ML classification. This choice was sup-ported by Fig. 2 which shows *SigIDRgn* responses relative to a D1:S1 reference, i.e., the D1:S1 response was subtracted from responses for the other D:S cases to highlight differences. These responses reflect (1) discriminating *Device* (D) information in the $0.080 < t < 0.120$ s interval and (2) discrimination *State* (S)

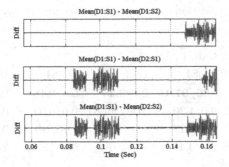

Fig. 2. Difference between *SigIDRgn* responses using D1:S1 as the reference. The $0.080 < t < 0.120$ s region reflects *device* similarity and the $t > 0.140$ s region reflects *state* similarity.

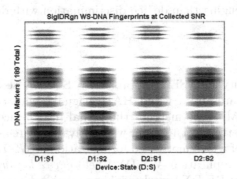

Fig. 3. Average DNA fingerprint features at $SNR_C \approx 22.0$ dB based on 200 independent *SigIDRgn* fingerprints for each D:S cased considered.

information in the $t > 0.140$ s interval. Similar behavior and conclusions were drawn using D2:S1 as the reference.

2.1 Discrimination Results

Initial assessments considered 456 FSK bursts for all four D:S cases using WS-DNA features extracted from *SigIDRgn* responses. The entire *SigIDRgn* response was used with statistical features of variance, skewness, and kurtosis calculated across $N_R + 1 = 20 + 1 = 21$ sub-regions of the *SigIDRgn* instantaneous amplitude, phase and frequency responses. Thus, the resultant fingerprints included a total of $21 \times 3 \times 3 = 189$ WS-DNA features (DNA markers). The characteristic fingerprint differences for the D:S cases considered are illustrated in Fig. 3 which shows clear visual discrimination. The discriminability was confirmed using the MDA/ML classifier using the *SigIDRgn* WS-DNA fingerprints to discriminate both device and state. The discriminability is quantitatively reflected in Table 2 MDA/ML confusion matrix results which are presented for both $CollectedSNR_C \approx 22.0$ dB and degraded $AnalysisSNR_A \approx 2.0$ dB conditions. Diagonal entries reflect 100 % and 92.7 % correct classification (discrimination) for the two SNRs

Table 2. MDA/ML classification confusion matrix results. Presented for SNR$_C$ ≈ 22.0 dB / SNR$_A$ ≈ 2.0 dB.

		Called (%)			
		D1:S1	D1:S2	D2:S1	D2:S2
Input	D1:S1	**100/97.19**	0.0/2.45	0.0/0.18	0.0/0.18
	D1:S2	0.0/4.30	**100/95.61**	0.0/0.09	0.0/0.0
	D2:S1	0.0/0.27	0.0/0.0	**100/90.61**	0.0/9.12
	D2:S2	0.0/0.44	0.0/0.0	0.0/11.93	**100/87.63**

and suggest the process is relatively robust for varying channel conditions. Off-diagonal elements for SNR_A ≈ 2.0 dB indicate that state discrimination is generally more challenging than device discrimination with decreasing SNR.

3   Conclusions

A PHY-based Security (PhySEC) approach to SCADA security is addressed using WS-DNA features from wired HART signals, with a goal of verifying that the observed HMI state matches the actual field device physical state to counter Stuxnet-like attacks. The paper was motivated by related HART fieldbus work [2], the results of which motivated formalization of WS-DNA fingerprinting for SCADA PhySEC application. WS-DNA field *device hardware discrimination* is consistent with prior RF-DNA works yielding reliable device discrimination. Of greater importance to near-term SCADA security improvement is the introduction of an *inferential device state estimation* process using the same WS-DNA features. While results here are indeed limited (two devices operating in each of two states), they are sufficiently promising to warrant additional research. Thus, additional equipment has been procured and experimentation is underway to extend the findings and further develop the envisioned SCADA PhySEC approach.

References

1. Cobb, W.E., et al.: Physical layer identification of embedded devices using RF-DNA fingerprinting. In: Military Communications Conference, pp. 2168–2173 (2010)
2. Lopez Jr., J., Temple, M.A.: Inferring field device identity and operating state using physical features of highway addressable remote transducer (HART) signals. In: 9th International Conference on Critical Information Infrastructures Security, Limassol, October 2014
3. Reising, D.R. et al.: Gabor-based RF-DNA fingerprinting for classifying 802.16e WiMAX mobile subscribers. In: International Conference on Computing, Networking and Communications, January 2012

4. Suski II, W.M., et al.: Using spectral fingerprints to improve wireless network security. In: IEEE Global Communications Conference, New Orleans (2008)
5. Williams, M.D., et al.: Augmenting bit-level network security using physical layer RF-DNA fingerprinting. In: IEEE Global Communications Conference, December 2010
6. Cobb, W., et al.: Intrinsic physical layer authentication of ICs. IEEE Trans. Inf. Forensics Secur. **2**(4), 793–808 (2011)
7. Stone, S., Temple, M.: RF-based anomaly detection for programmable logic controllers in the critical infrastructure. Int. J. Crit. Infrastruct. Prot. **5**(2), 66–73 (2012)
8. Igure, V., Laughter, S., Williams, R.: Security issues in SCADA networks. Comput. Secur. **25**, 498–506 (2006)
9. Rameback, C.: Process automation systems history and future. In: IEEE Conference on Emerging Technologies and Factory Automation (ETFA 2003), Lisbon (2003)
10. Stouffer, K., et al.: Guide to Industrial Control System (ICS) Security (Special Publication 800–82). Nat'l Inst of Stands and Tech, Gaithersburg (2013)
11. Parthasarathy, S., Kundur, D.: Bloom filter intrusion detection for smart grid SCADA. In: 25th IEEE Canadian Conference on Electrical and Computer Engineering, Montreal (2012)
12. Langner, R.: Robust Control System Networks: How to Achieve Reliable Control After Stuxnet. Momemtum Press, New York (2012)
13. Lewis, T.: Critical Infrastructure Protection in Homeland Security: Defending a Networked Nation. Wiley, Hoboken (2006)
14. Baker, S., Waterman, S., Ivanov, G.: In the Crossfire: Critical Infrastructure in the Age of Cyber War. McAfee Inc., Santa Clara (2010)
15. Powner, D., Rhodes, K.A.: Critical Infrastructure Protection: Multiple Efforts to Secure Control Systems Are Under Way, but Challenges Remain [GAO-07-1036]. Government Accounting Office, Washington, DC (2007)
16. Baker, S., et al.: In the Dark: Crucial Industries Confront Cyberattacks. McAfee, Santa Clara (2011)
17. Government Accountability Office, Cybersecurity national strategy, roles, and responsibilities need to be better defined and more effectively implemented (GAO-13-187). Government Printing Office, Washington, DC (2013)
18. Government Accountability Office, Critical infrastructure protection: Challenges in addressing cybersecurity (GAO-05-827T). GAO, Washington, DC (2005)
19. Chertoff, M.: National infrastructure protection plan: Partnering to enhance protection and resiliency (2009). www.dhs.gov/files/programs/editorial_0827.shtm
20. Northcote-Green, J., Wilson, R.: Control and Automation of Electrical Power Distribution Systems. Taylor and Francis, Boca Raton (2007)
21. Markey, E., Waxman, H.: Electric Grid Vulnerability: Industry Responses Reveal Security Gaps. US House of Representatives, Washington, DC (2013)
22. Leverett, E., Stajano, F., Crowcroft, J.: Quantitatively Assessing and Visualising Industrial System Attack Surfaces. University of Cambridge, Cambridge (2011)
23. Phillippe, J., Axelrod, J.: Industrial control system security,: Protecting your operational technology network from cyber attacks. Ernst and Young LLP (2012)
24. Government Accountability Office, Defense Critical Infrastructure: Actions needed to improve the identification and management of electrical power risks and vulnerabilities to DOD critical assets (GAO-10-147). Government Printing Office, Washington, DC (2009)

25. Abshier, J., Weiss, J.: Securing your control system, 22 November 2004. www.controlglobal.com/articles/2004/238.html?page=1
26. Liu, A.: Critical U.S. infrastructure at risk of cyber attack, experts warn, 22 March 2011. www.foxnews.com/scitech/201103/22/major-industries-vulnerable-cyber-attack/
27. Control Global, The Once & Future Protocol: HART is the Most Widely Used Communication Protocol in the Process Industries and the Best Choice for the Future, 11 September 2012. www.controlglobal.com/articles/2012/hart-future-protocol/?show=all
28. Akella, R., et al.: Analysis of information flow security in cyber physical systems. Int. J. Crit. Infrastruct. **3**(3–4), 157–173 (2010)
29. Campbell, R., Rrushi, J.: Detecting cyber attacks on nuclear power plants. In: IFIP Advances in Information and Communication Technology (AICT), vol. 290, pp. 1–54 (2011)
30. Solomakhin, R., Tsang, P., Smith, S.: High security with low latency in legacy SCADA systems. In: Moore, T., Shenoi, S. (eds.) Critical Infrastructure Protection IV, pp. 63–79. Springer, Heidelberg (2010)
31. Verba, J., Milvich, M.: Idaho national laboratory supervisory control and data acquisition intrusion detection system (IDS). In: IEEE Conference on Technologies for Homeland Security, pp. 469–473 (2008)
32. Parthasarathy, S., Kundur, D.: Bloom filter based intrusion detection for smart grid SCADA. In: IEEE Canadian Conference on Electrical and Computer Engineering, pp. 1–6 (2012)
33. Yang, Y., et al.: Rule-based intrusion detection system for SCADA networks. In: 2nd IET Renewable Power Generation Conference, pp. 1–4 (2013)

Processing and Communications Rate Requirements in Sensor Networks for Physical Thread Assessment

Ioannis Kyriakides[1](✉), Stelios Neophytou[1], Anastasis Kounoudes[2],
Konstantinos Michail[2], Yiannis Argyrou[2], and Thomas Wieland[3]

[1] Department of Electrical Engineering, University of Nicosia, Nicosia, Cyprus
{kyriakides.i,neophytou.s}@unic.ac.cy
[2] SignalGeneriX Ltd, Limassol, Cyprus
{tasos,k.michail,yiannis}@signalgenerix.com
[3] Fraunhofer Application Center Wireless Sensor Systems, Coburg, Germany
thomas.wieland@iis.fraunhofer.de

Abstract. Sensor networks for the assessment of physical threats in critical infrastructure have the potential to provide continuous and reliable information on illegal activity over wide areas. In order to reach that potential, it is essential for the sensor network to operate efficiently by conducting processing and communication operations on a very limited power budget. In this work, it is shown that when sequentially assessing physical threats using a sensor network, the required processing and communication load is directly related to estimation uncertainty. It is, furthermore, shown that the processing and communications rate required for sequential estimation using a sensor network is much less than the rate required for processing and transmitting all data available at the nodes. This result can be used to reduce hardware cost and power requirements of the sensor network.

Keywords: Bayesian target tracking · Critical infrastructure security

1 Introduction

This work addresses the issue of reducing the processing rate on-board of sensor nodes and the communication rate between sensor nodes and the fusion center. This reduction is made possible based on two factors. One is the existence of information on the target state provided by the sequential estimation process. This information can be used to restrict the amount of processing performed on the raw data and the size of the resulting measurement statistics to be communicated. The second is the availability of reconfigurable sensors with

This work was co-funded by the European Regional Development Fund and the Republic of Cyprus through the Research Promotion Foundation (Project $TEXNOΛOΓIA/MHXAN/0311(BIE)/03$).

© Springer International Publishing Switzerland 2016
C.G. Panayiotou et al. (Eds.): CRITIS 2014, LNCS 8985, pp. 31–36, 2016.
DOI: 10.1007/978-3-319-31664-2_4

on-board processing capabilities that are able to process measurements based on the instructions of the fusion center and communicate the result to the fusion center. In background work for signal processing for detection and estimation, raw measurements are processed using a number of matched filtering operations resulting to an equal number of measurement statistics. In [1] the concept of tessellated resolution cells was used which resulted to exhaustively covering the entire measurement statistics space. Using a particle filtering method, however, it was shown that measurement statistics can be taken at irregular intervals of the measurement space, instead of having to lie on a grid [2].

In this work, it is shown that the size of the set of measurement statistics that is useful for sequential estimation is less than the total number of measurement statistics from all possible matched filtering operations on the raw data. This means that the amount of processing on the raw data and the size of the resulting processed data on each sensor node can both be reduced without compromising estimation accuracy. This result can then be applied in the case where processing capabilities are available on-board of configurable sensor nodes of a sensor network [3–6]. The processing that each of the sensor nodes needs to perform on the data is determined by the fusion center based on data from all sensors. It is noted that in this work, the size of data to exchange between the fusion center and node is not considered in terms of communication noise, but rather in terms of sensing noise and the uncertainty in estimating the target state. The determination of the size of the measurement statistics useful for detection and estimation described in this work can be then combined with work on modelling the channel between sensors and the fusion center and the use of coding schemes.

The reduction in processing and communication costs in a sensor network is also demonstrated with simulations using real thermal imaging data. Thermal imagery is used in this work as an example of a sensing modality that imposes large bandwidth and computational demands on the tracking system. These requirements are mainly due to the collection of a large amount of data from the image sensor that needs to be transmitted to the tracker and the subsequent need for the tracker to process that data on-line. In the simulation results, it is shown that the number of processing operations and the number of the resulting measurements statistics that need to be communicated to the fusion center at each time step of the multiple tracking scenario by a particle filtering based tracker depends on the available information on the target state. Therefore, the total volume of measurement statistics that need to be collected and communicated is much less than the volume of measurement statistics that would be generated by processing all pixels and communicating the result, which would correspond to the case where no information exists on the target.

In Sect. 2, the evolution of the target state to be estimated and the measurement model are described. In Sect. 3, the state prediction process is explained that leads to a representation of the uncertainty in the state to be estimated prior to the arrival of new measurements. In Sect. 4, a multitarget tracking example is provided to demonstrate the theoretical results on the processing and communication rates required for sequential estimation.

2 State Evolution and Measurement Model

2.1 State Evolution Model

The unknown state to be estimated at each time step k describes the unknown position and velocity of a single target given by $\mathbf{x}_k = [\chi_k \, \dot{\chi}_k \, \psi_k \, \dot{\psi}_k]^T$ where χ_k and ψ_k denote the position and $\dot{\chi}_k$ and $\dot{\psi}_k$ denote the velocity of the target in the Cartesian coordinates. Then the evolution of the state is described by a constant velocity model as:

$$\mathbf{x}_k = \mathbf{F}\mathbf{x}_{k-1} + \mathbf{V}\eta_k, \tag{1}$$

where $\mathbf{F} = [1 \, \delta t \, 0 \, 0; 0 \, 1 \, 0 \, 0; 0 \, 0 \, 1 \, \delta t; 0 \, 0 \, 0 \, 1]$ and δt is the time difference between state transitions. The matrix $\mathbf{V}$ is a diagonal process noise covariance matrix and the column vector η_k represents a zero-mean, unit variance Gaussian process that models errors in velocity. The kinematic distribution $p(\mathbf{x}_k|\mathbf{x}_{k-1})$ is a Gaussian. In a multi-target scenario the state vector $\mathbf{x}_k$ would be extended by concatenating the Cartesian positions and velocities of the multiple targets [8].

2.2 Measurement Model

Next the relationship between state space and measurement space is described. The state vector described above maps onto a template in the measurement space expressed as an M-dimensional vector

$$\mathbf{s}_l = f_{\mathbf{s},k}(\mathbf{x}_k) \tag{2}$$

via $f_{\mathbf{s},k}(\cdot)$ that represents the mapping from the state space to the measurement space. $\mathbf{s}_l$ in (2) is indexed by $l \in \mathcal{L}$ in set $\mathcal{L}$ with cardinality $\bar{L} = |\bar{\mathcal{L}}|$. Specifically in this work, the above formulation corresponds to mapping targets from the Cartesian coordinates to pixels on the image plane for a certain pan-tilt position of a thermal imager. Then each template $\mathbf{s}_l$ represents a block of pixels shifted at a certain pixel coordinate location and a specific pan-tilt position of the imager.

2.3 Measurement Processing

At every time step k measurements $\mathbf{r}_k$ are matched filtered with templates, indexed by $l \in \tilde{\mathcal{L}}$, as

$$y_{l,k} = \mathbf{s}_l^* \mathbf{r}_k \tag{3}$$

and the likelihood ratio is given by

$$\Lambda(\mathbf{y}_k|\mathbf{x}_k) = \frac{p(\mathbf{y}_k|\mathbf{x}_k)}{p(\mathbf{y}_k|0)} \tag{4}$$

where $p(\mathbf{y}_k|\mathbf{x}_k)$ and $p(\mathbf{y}_k|0)$ is the likelihood if a target is present and not present respectively. $\mathbf{y}_k = \{y_{l,k}\}_{l=1}^{\tilde{L}}$ represents a vector of all the matched filter statistics needed at the fusion center. A set of unique templates in $\tilde{\mathcal{L}}$ is then requested by the fusion center and delivered by each sensor node.

Table 1. Particle filtering tracking with reduced processing and communications

Having available state $\{\mathbf{x}_{k-1}^n\}_{n=1}^N$ with weights $\{w_{k-1}^n\}_{n=1}^N$ from time $k-1$, perform
Prediction:
- For each particle $n = 1, \ldots, N$ and each sensor node
  - Sample $\mathbf{x}_k^n = f_{\mathbf{x},k}(\mathbf{x}_{k-1}^n, \eta_k^n)$, or $\mathbf{x}_k^n \sim p(\mathbf{x}_k^n | \mathbf{x}_{k-1}^n)$
  - Obtain $p_k^n(l) = \sum\limits_{n:\mathbf{x}_k^n \to l} p(\mathbf{x}_k^n | \mathbf{x}_{k-1}^n) w_{k-1}^n$
- Create set $\mathcal{L}_k$ with unique templates $l : p_k^n(l) > \epsilon \ \forall n$
- Register correspondence between unique templates with particles $n : \mathbf{x}_k^n \to l$
- Communicate set $\mathcal{L}_k$ from fusion center to sensor node
Measurement update at each sensor node:
- For each unique template $l \in \mathcal{L}_k$
  - Form templates $\mathbf{s}_l$
  - Obtain measurements $\mathbf{r}_k$
  - Calculate $y_{l,k} = \mathbf{s}_{l,k}^* \mathbf{r}_k$
  - Communicate measurement statistics $y_{l,k}, l \in \mathcal{L}_k$ to fusion center
Measurement update at fusion center:
- Calculate weights $w_{l,k} = w_{l,k-1} \Lambda(y_{l,k} | \mathbf{x}_{l,k}), l \in \mathcal{L}_k$
- Use correspondence $n : \mathbf{x}_k^n \to l$ to assign weights to each particle $\{w_k^n\}_{n=1}^N$ from $\{w_{l,k}\}, l \in \mathcal{L}_k$
Estimation:
- Estimate $\hat{\mathbf{x}}_k = \sum_{n=1}^N w_k^n \mathbf{x}_k^n$

3 State Prediction and Representation of the Uncertainty

The posterior distribution of the unknown state, using measurements up to time step $k-1$, is provided by the Chapman–Kolmogorov equation [7] as

$$p(\mathbf{x}_k | \mathbf{y}_{k-1}) = \int_{\mathbf{x}_{k-1}} p(\mathbf{x}_k | \mathbf{x}_{k-1}) p(\mathbf{x}_{k-1} | \mathbf{y}_{k-1}) d\mathbf{x}_{k-1}. \tag{5}$$

In order to express this information in the measurement space the state $\mathbf{x}_k$ is mapped onto templates with indices $l \in \tilde{\mathcal{L}}$ using (2). Therefore, the probability distribution associated with an index l appearing in the measurements at time k can be expressed in terms of the posterior $p(\mathbf{x}_k | \mathbf{y}_{k-1})$ as

$$p_k(l) = \int_{\mathbf{x}_k : \mathbf{x}_k \to l} p(\mathbf{x}_k | \mathbf{y}_{k-1}) d\mathbf{x}_k \tag{6}$$

for $l \in \mathcal{L}_k$. The integral above is taken over all target states $\mathbf{x}_k$ such that $\mathbf{x}_k$ maps onto template index l in set $\mathcal{L}_k$ according to (2).

The set of templates $\mathcal{L}_k$, consists of templates with non-zero probability $p_k(l)$ of appearing in the measurements given by (6). Therefore, the dictionary is a set $\mathcal{L}_k$ with cardinality $L_k = |\mathcal{L}_k|$ with templates $l \in \mathcal{L}_k$ for $p_k(l) > \epsilon$ where ϵ represents a probability threshold. Moreover, this set is a subset of the total set of templates in $\tilde{\mathcal{L}}$ that may appear in the entire sequential estimation scenario which

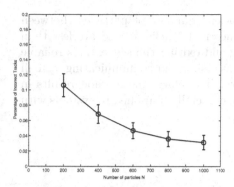

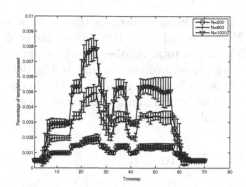

Fig. 1. Percentage of false tracks versus the number of particles.

Fig. 2. Matched filtering operations per time step and different number of particles.

was defined in Sect. 2.2 (i.e. $\mathcal{L}_k \subseteq \tilde{\mathcal{L}}$, with cardinality $L_k = |\mathcal{L}_k| \leq \tilde{L} = |\tilde{\mathcal{L}}|$). A sampling importance resampling (SIR) particle filtering [7,9] version of the estimation and sensor node configuration process is outlined in Table 1 which can be used in non-linear, non-Gaussian scenarios.

4 Numerical Assessment

In order to demonstrate the reduction in measurement processing and the communication of measurement statistics to the fusion center, a multiple target tracking scenario involving cars was used with measurements from a FLIR F-Series thermal imager. From the thermal imager a 576×704 pixel grayscale image is extracted at each time step of the scenario. The tracking scenario is comprised of 70 time steps, where 5 targets in total enter and exit the scene. The number of particles varies as $N = 200, 400, 600, 800, 1000$. A track is confirmed if the sum of weights following a track exceeds .95 for 4 consecutive time steps. Also, a confirmed track is removed if the sum of weights of the particles that follow the track drop below .95 for two consecutive time steps.

In Fig. 1 the percentage of incorrect tracks averaged over 350 Monte Carlo runs are provided for different numbers of particles. An incorrect track was counted if the root mean squared error of an estimated target trajectory was above 3 m from the nearest true target trajectory for more than 6 time steps. The percentage of matched filtering operations, which equal the percentage of measurement statistics that need to be communicated to the fusion center at each time step of the scenario, are provided in Fig. 2. The percentage was given with respect to the total marched filter statistics that would need to be processed and communicated exhaustively over the image per time step and per template. This is taken to be equal to the image size. Plot lines for numbers of particles $N = 400$ and $N = 800$, which were omitted in order to improve clarity in the figure, lie between the plot lines corresponding to numbers of particles $N = 200, 600$ and $N = 600, 1000$ respectively and follow a similar trend as the plot lines shown.

The results demonstrate that with a sufficient number of particles (between $N = 800$ and $N = 1000$) the number of incorrect tracks formed are less than 5 % of the total number of targets entering and exiting the scene. This reliable tracking performance is achieved by only processing and communicating a small fraction of data compared to the image size. Therefore, the method results in large savings in power and communications, especially if applied to systems with multiple sensor nodes.

5   Conclusion

In this work the processing and communications rate required for the assessment of physical threats by a sensor network is determined. It is shown that the processing and communications rate can be reduced below the rate required to process all raw data from sensors and communicate the total number of measurement statistics that result from that processing. The reduction is possible due to the information on the target state obtained when sequentially assessing physical threats. The reduction in processing and communications rate is demonstrated using simulation results from tracking multiple targets using real thermal image data.

References

1. Rago, C., Willett, P., Bar-Shalom, Y.: Detection-tracking performance with combined waveforms. IEEE Trans. Aerosp. Electron. Syst. **34**(6), 612–624 (1998)
2. Kyriakides, I., Konstantinidis, I., Morrell, D., Benedetto, J.J., Papandreou-Suppappola, A.: Target tracking using particle filtering and CAZAC sequences. In: Waveform Diversity and Design, pp. 367–371 (2007)
3. Muise, R., Mahalanobis, A.: Recent results of integrated sensing and processing using a programmable hyperspectral imaging sensor. In: Proceedings of SPIE, Optical Pattern Recognition XVII, vol. 6245, April 2006
4. Priebe, C.E., Marchette, D.J., Healy, D.M.: Integrated sensing and processing decision trees. IEEE Trans. Pattern Anal. Mach. Intell. **26**(6), 699–708 (2004)
5. Waagen, D., Schmitt, H.A., Shah, N.: Activities in integrated sensing and processing. In: Proceedings of the Intelligent Sensors, Sensor Networks and Information Processing Conference, pp. 295–300, December 2004
6. Sira, S.P., Papandreou-Suppappola, A., Morrell, D.: Time-varying waveform selection and configuration for agile sensors in tracking applications. In: Proceedings of IEEE ICASSP, Philadelphia, April 2005
7. Arulampalam, M.S., Maskell, S., Gordon, N., Clapp, T.: A tutorial on particle filters for online nonlinear/non-Gaussian Bayesian tracking. IEEE Trans. Sig. Process. **50**(2), 174–188 (2002)
8. Kyriakides, I., Morrell, D., Papandreou-Suppappola, A.: Sequential Monte Carlo methods for tracking multiple targets with deterministic and stochastic constraints. IEEE Trans. Sig. Process. **56**(3), 937–948 (2008)
9. Kyriakides, I.: A configurable compressive acquisition matrix for radar tracking using particle filtering. In: European Radar Conference (2012)

A Comprehensive Approach for Security Assessment in Transport

Simona Cavallini[1]([✉]), Francesca D'Onofrio[1], Pedro Ferreira[2],
Anabela Simoes[2], and Nicanor Garcia[3]

[1] Fondazione FORMIT, Rome, Italy
s.cavallini@formit.org
[2] Centro de Investigação em Gestão, Lisbon, Portugal
[3] Autoridad Portuaria de Gijón, Gijón, Spain

Abstract. Transport is one of the most important economic sectors in Europe with its infrastructure being essential for the functioning of the entire society. Directive 2008/114/EC outlines the approach Member States are required to follow to identify, designate, and protect European Critical Infrastructures also in the transport sector. The paper illustrates a benchmarking methodology which could be used to assess security in terms of awareness, preparedness and maturity in operators belonging to transport sub-sectors. The final goal is to provide a relevant informative base, taking into consideration sub-sector differences useful to enhance awareness in security in the transport sector.

Keywords: Transport security · Security awareness · Security preparedness · Security maturity · Critical infrastructure · Benchmarking methodology

1 Introduction

This paper proposes a conceptual benchmarking methodology which aims to assess security awareness, preparedness and maturity levels of transport operators[1] belonging to the five sub-sectors listed in the Council Directive 2008/114/EC on the *identification and designation of European Critical Infrastructures and the assessment of the need to improve their protection* [3,4][2]. Transport is one of the most important economic sectors in Europe, with its infrastructure being essential for the well functioning of the entire society [1].

---

[1] Transport operators are intended as the organizations performing functions for the production and delivery of transport services (e.g. carriers, infrastructure managers, terminal/port/airport managers).

[2] This benchmarking methodology is part of the research activities carried out by AMLETO project (*Assessing security awareness and increasing maturity level of transport operators to strengthen Critical Infrastructure Protection*) co-funded by the EC DG Home Affairs under the *"Prevention, preparedness and consequence management of terrorism and other security-related risks"* Programme.

© Springer International Publishing Switzerland 2016
C.G. Panayiotou et al. (Eds.): CRITIS 2014, LNCS 8985, pp. 37–42, 2016.
DOI: 10.1007/978-3-319-31664-2_5

Operators of transport infrastructures are faced with multiple challenges that can range from normal traffic to accidents as well as major disruptions due to natural disasters or acts of intentional man-made attacks. For this reason, transport operators must be aware of the risks they are exposed to and be prepared for potential threats [6]. This translates into the operator's responsibility to hold adequate information and knowledge to protect itself and to employ concrete resources and capabilities to ensure its security [2]. In addition, operators of transport sub-sectors behave differently in the security field: the lack of security measures in land transport and inland waterways is balanced by the comprehensive security measures already in place in the aviation and maritime sub-sector[3]. Accordingly, security awareness, preparedness and maturity vary across transport sub-sectors and countries. The aim of the benchmarking methodology presented in this paper is to propose an horizontal approach able to highlight the distinguishing elements of each transport sub-sector in the security domain and to enhance Critical Infrastructure protection thanks to the definition of tailored protection strategies [5].

2   Concepts of Security Awareness, Preparedness and Maturity

The concepts of security awareness, preparedness and maturity are proposed as founding aspects *(fa)* for the assessment of security performance in transport. *Awareness* for a transport operator can be broadly defined as the state resulting from the acquisition of a meaningful knowledge on security (in terms of vulnerabilities, threats, as well as protection measures and response mechanisms) through information gathering. The notion of *preparedness* focuses on assessing conditions necessary to deploy efficient response in case of failures of the transport operator in order to guarantee prompt recovery to normal operations. In this context, *Maturity* is intended as achievement of pre-established states of development: this does not necessarily mean that higher levels of security are progressively attained but rather that security measures are improved in terms of effectiveness and efficiency in view of existing vulnerabilities and threats.

Maturity levels should lead to the recognition that both awareness and preparedness measures are robust and well embedded into every function of the operator and that the resources mobilised are in fact an investment and an added value to the operator.

---

[3] Regulation (EC) No 300/2008 of the European Parliament and of the Council of 11 March 2008 on *common rules in the field of civil aviation security* and repealing Regulation (EC) No 2320/2002 (OJ L 97 11.3.2008); Regulation (EU) No 185/2010 of 4 March 2010 *laying down detailed measures for the implementation of the common basic standards on aviation security* (OJ L 55, 4.3.2010); Regulation (EC) No 725/2004 of the European Parliament and of the Council of 31 March 2004 on *enhancing ship and port facility security,* (OJ L 129/6, 29.4.2004).

3   A Comprehensive Methodology to Assess Security

The proposed methodology on a comprehensive approach which intends to assess security levels in the five transport sub-sectors streamlining, as a final output, their distinguishing features. The benchmarking methodology is based on:

- three *founding aspects (fa)*: awareness *(F1)*, preparedness *(F2)*, maturity *(F3)*,
- *four cornerstones (c)*: security oriented knowledge *(cA)*, management of asset security *(cB)*, resources for security *(cC)* and security capabilities *(cD)*.

To be able to assess security levels the comprehension of the logical flow of the three *fa* is crucial. Each operator needs to be aware of security issues, of external security-related information sources (including existing legislation and standards) to be able to plan a tailored security strategy for responding to security risks and guaranteeing service continuity. Together, appropriate levels of awareness and preparedness allow the operator to achieve a satisfactory level of security maturity.

The four *cornerstones* are main security-related aspects.

Security oriented knowledge (cA) includes factors referring to the degree of information on security issues present in the operator (awareness) as well as elements providing details on how such information is used to plan the operator's security policy (preparedness). In few words, an operator can plan its security only if it is aware of the security issue in general (awareness) and if it is able to translate information into action (preparedness). *Management of Asset security (cB)* refers to the knowledge of critical assets/functions/operations, their vulnerabilities and possible uncertainty sources which could involve them (awareness) and it also relates to the effective protection measures in use to avoid or reduce security failures affecting key assets of the transport system (preparedness). *Resources for Security (cC)* are about the importance given to security-related investments and to specific HR within the operator (awareness) and about their concrete allocation and implementation within the operator (preparedness). *Security capabilities (cD)*, relate to the importance given to security training and the development of internal skills to make sure that the staff has appropriate abilities to protect critical assets/functions/operations from security threats (awareness). From a preparedness perspective, *cD* refers to the effective existence and implementation of capabilities to protect critical assets/function/operations within the considered operator (preparedness).

Theoretically levels of awareness, preparedness and maturity of the operator in each cornerstone contribute to the overall concept of Awareness *(F1)*, Preparedness *(F2)* and Maturity *(F3)* (1).

$$Fn = fncA + fncB + fncC + fncD \quad n = 1, 2, 3. \tag{1}$$

3.1   Combining Founding Aspects and Cornerstones

Within the proposed methodology, the practical assessment of transport operators' *F1* and *F2* levels is made through an on-line survey proposed to EU28 transport operators (and in particular to managers dealing with security issues) with
a set of questions which combine each founding aspect with each cornerstone.
The elaboration of results coming from both the awareness and the preparedness
sections produces the degree of maturity *(F3)*.

For instance, looking at *cD* (security capabilities), questions relating to the
collection of data on awareness *(F1)* aim at understanding how knowledgeable
are operators regarding the importance of developing and implementing internal
capabilities and skills to face security issues, while from a preparedness *(F2)*
point of view, they investigate to what extent such security capabilities are
concrete in place within operators.

The survey proposes several questions related to awareness and preparedness. Looking at awareness, questions are related to the importance of training
for threat identification and security monitoring and to the identification of the
relevant professional target profiles to whom training *should* be dedicated (i.e. all
the staff, security-related staff, top management levels). Concerning preparedness, questions focus on procedures used to detect and report security incidents
and to the professional target profiles which are periodically involved in security
training session (i.e. all the staff, security-related staff, top management levels).

3.2   Assessing Security Awareness, Preparedness and Maturity
of Operators

A weighted score is assigned to each answer selected by the respondent for the
operator. Each combination of *fa* and *c* (e.g. *f1cD*) is given by the sum of the
answer scores weighted by the number of questions included in the section dedicated to the specific *fa* and *c* combination.

As result, Awareness value derived from the answers to the questionnaire
F1q contains the total awareness level of the operator, based on the degree of
awareness reached in each one of the four cornerstones and the Preparedness,
F2q, the total preparedness level of the operator referring to the same four
cornerstones.

$$Fnq = \frac{fncA + fncB + fncC + fncD}{4} \quad n = 1, 2 \qquad (2)$$

As previously mentioned, maturity *(F3q)* is given by the weighted sum of
F1q and *F2q*.

To be able to benchmark resulting values of the operators, awareness, preparedness and maturity levels range from 0 (minimum level) to 1 (maximum
level). Apart form the absolute value of the own indexes, each operator has the
opportunity, through the developed benchmarking methodology, to assess security levels (in *F1, F2, F3*) of the other operators belonging to the same sub-sector
or to the same country that answered to the questionnaire.

The on-line tool used to propose the benchmarking exercise to EU28 transport operators shows graphs reporting indexes measuring awareness, preparedness and maturity according to answers given by participants. *F1*, *F2* and *F3* indexes range from 0 to 1 and offer an overall view of the level of security (Fig. 1).

In the specific case below reported, the indexes show that the operator at issue has a higher level of preparedness (*F2*) than the population of operator respondents and than the other operators belonging to its same sub-sector, but its level of *F2* is lower when compared at country level.

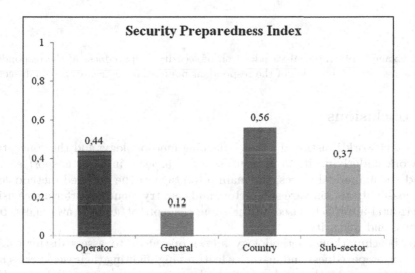

Fig. 1. Example of graphical visualization of security preparedness index (respectively, of the respondent operator, of the respondent population, by country, by sub-sector)

The benchmarking tool also allows respondents to visualise a set of radar graphs (Fig. 2) which represent results of each of the four cornerstones for the respondent operator, for the population of operator respondents, by country for the respondent operator, by sub-sector for the respondent operator. As a result, operators are able to gain an immediate perception of which cornerstones *(c)* should be enhanced. For instance, isolating the radar graph reporting subsectoral level in Fig. 2, the operator at issue is more prepared than others (average value) in *Security oriented knowledge (cA)* and in *Security Resources (cC)*, but less prepared than other operators in the *Management of Asset Security (cB)* and in *Security capabilities (cD)*. Furthermore, the operator at issue scored its highest rate in *f2cA* combination.

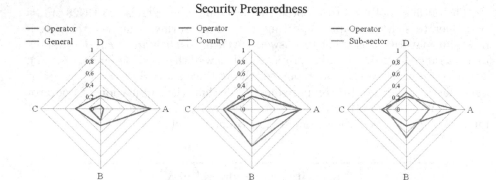

Fig. 2. Example of graphical visualization of security preparedness of the respondent operator respect to the value of the respondent population, by country, by sub-sector

4   Conclusions

The present work illustrated a benchmarking methodology, and the conceptual framework underlying it, to measure security aspects in the transport sector. Beyond the numerical scores, the main advantage of the outlined methodology is the possibility to compare sub-sectors and country security performance using an horizontal approach based on the same concepts of security awareness, preparedness and maturity.

The benchmarking methodology allows operators to assess distinguishing awareness, preparedness and maturity features highlighting their weaknesses and strengths respect to their sub-sectors and country competitors. Policy makers may benefit from the benchmarking tool having indications on security gaps and needs useful to set up appropriate policies aimed to enhance security in transport sector.

References

1. EC, commission staff working document on enhancing supply chain security. SWD, 251 final, 27 February 2006
2. EC, commission staff working document on transport security. SWD, 143 final, 31 May 2012
3. EC, commission staff working document on a new approach to the European programme for critical infrastructure protection. Making European Critical Infrastructure more Secure, SWD, 318 final, 28 August 2013
4. EC, Council Directive (EC) 114/2008 on the identification and designation of European critical infrastructures and the assessment of the need to improve their protection (2008)
5. Palmatier, T.E.: Building secure critical infrastructures. Int. J. Crit. Infrastruct. Prot. **6**, 8586 (2013)
6. Peltier, T.R.: Implementing an information security awareness program, security management practices, pp. 37–49, May/June 2005

Security of Water Systems

Decentralised Hierarchical Multi-rate Control of Large-Scale Drinking Water Networks

Ajay Kumar Sampathirao, Pantelis Sopasakis$^{(\boxtimes)}$, and Alberto Bemporad

IMT Institute for Advanced Studies, Lucca, Italy
{ajay.sampathirao,pantelis.sopasakis,alberto.bemporad}@imtlucca.com

Abstract. We propose a decentralised hierarchical multi-rate control scheme for the control of large-scale systems with state and input constraints. The large-scale system is partitioned into sub-systems each one of which is locally controlled by a stabilising linear controller which does not account for the prescribed constraints. A higher-layer controller commands reference signals at a lower uniform sampling frequency so as to enforce linear constraints on the process variables. Worst-case subsystem interactions are modeled and accounted for in a robust manner. By optimally constraining the magnitude and rate of variation of the reference signals to each lower-layer controller we prove that closed-loop stability is preserved and the fulfillment of the prescribed constraints is guaranteed. We apply the proposed methodology to Johansson's quadraple-tank system and we compare it to a centralised control approach.

1 Introduction

1.1 Motivation and Background

Large-scale systems (such as drinking water networks and power distribution networks) call for control strategies based on the spatial and temporal decomposition of the overall dynamics so as to leverage the high computational cost of a centralised control approach [1,2]. In large scale systems hierarchical control is often the basis for a decentralised control scheme [3] and various decentralised and hierarchical control schemes have been proposed in the literature for which Scattolini [4] provides a thorough review. An overview of the current architectural trends in decentralised control for large-scale interconnected systems is provided by Bakule [5].

Drinking Water Networks (DWNs) are large-scale systems whose operation is liable to set of operating, safety and quality-of-service constraints. The optimal management of DWNs is a complex task with outstanding socio-economic and environmental implications and has received considerable attention by the scientific community [6,7]. One key reason for the use of decentralised control

This work was supported by the European Research Projects HYCON2 (FP7, Network of Excellence grant agreement no 257462) and EFFINET (FP7, "Efficient Integrated Real-time monitoring and Control of Drinking Water Networks," grant agreement no. 318556).

© Springer International Publishing Switzerland 2016
C.G. Panayiotou et al. (Eds.): CRITIS 2014, LNCS 8985, pp. 45–56, 2016.
DOI: 10.1007/978-3-319-31664-2_6

schemes is the need to isolate certain parts of the network for maintenance purposes without the need to re-model the overall system.

Recently, Sampathirao *et al.* [8] proposed a control framework for large-scale DWNs where pumping actions are computed by minimising a cost index. Such approaches are in the spirit of economic model predictive control (MPC) [9], and, despite the fact that are proven to lead to improved closed-loop behaviour, may fail to guarantee the satisfaction of state constraints in closed loop. The proposed methodology allows the operator to command reference signals to the sub-systems of the network according to some cost-optimisation strategy in such a way so as to satisfy the constraints during controlled operation.

The use of reference governors has been recommended by various authors so as to mitigate the computational burden of a centralised approach by separating the constraint satisfaction problem from the stabilisation problem [10]. Recently, Kalabić and Kolmanovsky [11] proposed a methodology for the design of reference governors for constrained large-scale linear systems. Two-layer hierarchical control systems are considered in the majority of relevant publications (see [13] and references therein).

Multirate control schemes are quite popular as they increase the flexibility in the quest for the desired properties (stability, optimality, constraints satisfaction) [12–14]. A multi-rate control approach is adopted in this paper with a quantification of the effect that the ratio of the two sampling rates has on the control of the system. We will show that the adoption of different reference rates in the upper and the lower control layers offers great flexibility and enables us to strike a balance between responsiveness to set-point changes and optimality.

In this paper we propose a hierarchical multi-rate decentralised control scheme for the control of large-scale systems whose states and inputs are subject to linear constraints. The hierarchical scheme comprises two control layers: At the lower one, a linear controller stabilises the open-loop process without considering the constraints. A higher-layer controller commands reference signals at a lower uniform sampling frequency so as to enforce linear constraints on the process variables. We propose a methodology for large-scale dynamically coupled linear systems which are partitioned into interconnected subsystems with state and input constraints. Worst-case interactions between subsystems are modeled and accounted for in a robust manner. By optimally constraining the magnitude and rate of variation of the reference signals to each lower-layer controller, quantitative criteria are provided for selecting the ratio between the sampling rates of the upper and lower layers of control at each location, in a way that closed-loop stability is preserved and the fulfillment of the prescribed constraints is guaranteed. This paper builds on previous work by Barcelli *et al.* [15,16] and on the ideas presented in [17].

2   Multirate Decentralised Hierarchical Control

2.1   Notation

Let $\mathbb{R}, \mathbb{R}^n, \mathbb{R}^{n \times m}, \mathbb{N}, \mathbb{N}_{[k_1,k_2]}$ denote the sets of real numbers, the n-dimensional vectors, the n-by-m real matrices, the set of natural numbers, and the natural numbers in the interval $[k_1, k_2]$. The infinity-norm of $x \in \mathbb{R}^n$ is defined as $\|x\|_\infty \triangleq \max_{i \in \mathbb{N}_{[1,n]}} |x_i|$.

Let $A \in \mathbb{R}^{n \times m}$, $\mathcal{I} \subseteq \mathbb{N}_{[1,n]}$ and $\mathcal{J} \subseteq \mathbb{N}_{[1,m]}$; we denote by $A_{\mathcal{I}\mathcal{J}} \in \mathbb{R}^{|\mathcal{I}| \times |\mathcal{J}|}$ the submatrix of A formed by the rows and columns of A whose indices are in $\mathcal{I}$ and $\mathcal{J}$ respectively and $|\mathcal{I}|$ stands for the cardinality of the set $\mathcal{I}$. For a vector $x \in \mathbb{R}^n$, $x_\mathcal{I}$ denotes the vector of $\mathbb{R}^{|\mathcal{I}|}$ formed by the elements of x whose indices are in $\mathcal{I}$. We denote by $(A)_i$ the i-th row of A, while $(x)_i$ denotes the i-th element of x. Finally, we denote by 1_n the n-vector having all entries equal to 1.

2.2 Problem Formulation

The proposed setting comprises two control layers: the lower-layer controller (LLC) and the upper-layer controller (ULC) which operate at different sampling frequencies. The lower control layer comprises m independent controllers whose role is the stabilisation of the open-loop dynamics of the controlled system without taking into account the prescribed state and input constraints. The lower layer controllers operate at a higher sampling frequency, namely $1/T_L$, and receive reference signals from corresponding upper layer controllers which operate at lower sampling frequencies $1/T_H^{\langle i \rangle}$, $i \in \mathbb{N}_{[1,m]}$. We define $N^{\langle i \rangle} \triangleq T_H^{\langle i \rangle}/T_L$ to be the ratio between sampling frequencies of ULC and LLC which are positive integers refereed to as *reference rates*. To simplify the notation, the state variable of the system (involving all sub-systems) at the LLC sampling instants is denoted by x_k for $k \in \mathbb{N}$ (referring to all sub-systems) and the state at the ULC sampling instants is denote by $x^\nu \triangleq x_{\nu N}$ for $\nu \in \mathbb{N}$.

Let x_k, u_k, y_k respectively be the state, the input and the output of the lower layer process in discrete time and the dynamics of the system be given by:

$$x_{k+1} = \bar{A}x_k + \bar{B}u_k, \tag{1a}$$

$$y_k = \bar{C}x_k + \bar{D}u_k, \tag{1b}$$

where $x_k \in \mathbb{R}^{n_x}$, $y_k \in \mathbb{R}^{n_r}$, $u_k \in \mathbb{R}^{n_u}$ and $\bar{A}$, $\bar{B}$, $\bar{C}$ and $\bar{D}$ are given matrices of proper dimensions. The feedback law defining the LLC is:

$$u_k = Fx_k + Er_k, \tag{2}$$

where $r_k \in \mathbb{R}^{n_r}$ stands as a reference signal to be decided by the Upper Layer Controller (ULC). The reference-to-output gain $\Theta \in \mathbb{R}^{n_r \times n_r}$ of (1) under feedback control law (2), is:

$$\Theta \triangleq ((\bar{C} + \bar{D}F)(I - \bar{A} - \bar{B}F)^{-1}\bar{B} + \bar{D})E. \tag{3}$$

The closed-loop system (1) can be rewritten as

$$x_{k+1} = Ax_k + Br_k, \tag{4a}$$

$$y_k = Cx_k + Dr_k, \tag{4b}$$

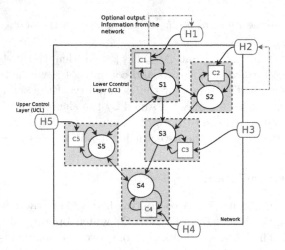

Fig. 1. Two-layer (LLC and ULC) decentralised hierarchical control scheme over a network of interconnected, dynamically coupled components. Upper-layer controllers command reference signals to the lower-layer ones which are updated at a lower frequency.

where $A \triangleq \bar{A} + \bar{B}F$, $B \triangleq \bar{B}E$, $C \triangleq \bar{C} + \bar{D}F$ and $D \triangleq \bar{D}E$. Additionally, matrix E must be chosen so that (A, B) is a stabilisable pair (Fig. 1).

The sparsity pattern of $\bar{A}$ in (1) can be exploited so as to decompose (1) into m subsystems which are as decoupled as possible; the components of the state vector are rearranged so that $\bar{A}$ in the new coordinates is as close as possible to a block-diagonal form [18]. Let $\mathcal{I}_x^{\langle i \rangle}$, $\mathcal{I}_u^{\langle i \rangle}$ and $\mathcal{I}_r^{\langle i \rangle}$ ($i \in \mathbb{N}_{[1,m]}$) denote the sets of state, input and output indices that participate in the i-th subsystem and let $n_x^{\langle i \rangle}$, $n_u^{\langle i \rangle}$ and $n_r^{\langle i \rangle}$ be their cardinalities respectively. These sets are not assumed to be necessarily disjoint as some states and input may belong to multiple subsystems.

Assumption 1. The pair $(\bar{A}, \bar{B})$ is stabilisable and F is an asymptotically stabilising gain for $(\bar{A}, \bar{B})$ and E possess the structure $F_{s,j} = 0, \forall s \in \mathcal{I}_u^{\langle i \rangle}$, and $j \notin \mathcal{I}_x^{\langle i \rangle}, \forall i \in \mathbb{N}_{[1,m]}$, and $E_{s,j} = 0, \forall s \in \mathcal{I}_u^{\langle i \rangle}$, and $j \notin \mathcal{I}_r^{\langle i \rangle}, \forall i \in \mathbb{N}_{[1,m]}$.

Under Assumption 1 the LLC can be decomposed into a set of local controllers whereby the i-th controller produces the control action $u^{\langle i \rangle} \in \mathbb{R}^{n_u^{\langle i \rangle}}$ using state measurements only from the i-th subsystem according to:

$$u_k^{\langle i \rangle} = F^{\langle i \rangle} x_k^{\langle i \rangle} + E^{\langle i \rangle} r_k^{\langle i \rangle}, \tag{5}$$

where $F^{\langle i \rangle} \triangleq F_{\mathcal{I}_u^{\langle i \rangle} \mathcal{I}_x^{\langle i \rangle}}$ and $E^{\langle i \rangle} \triangleq E_{\mathcal{I}_u^{\langle i \rangle} \mathcal{I}_r^{\langle i \rangle}}$ and $x_k^{\langle i \rangle} \triangleq x_{\mathcal{I}_x^{\langle i \rangle}}$, $u_k^{\langle i \rangle} \triangleq u_{\mathcal{I}_u^{\langle i \rangle}}$ and $r_k^{\langle i \rangle} \triangleq r_{\mathcal{I}_r^{\langle i \rangle}}$ for $i \in \mathbb{N}_{[1,m]}$.

The dynamics of the different subsystems are described by the set of difference equations:

$$\Sigma^{\langle i \rangle} : x_{k+1}^{\langle i \rangle} = A^{\langle i \rangle} x_k^{\langle i \rangle} + B^{\langle i \rangle} r_k^{\langle i \rangle} + d_k^{\langle i \rangle}, \tag{6}$$

where $A^{\langle i \rangle} \triangleq A_{\mathcal{I}_x^{\langle i \rangle} \mathcal{I}_x^{\langle i \rangle}}$, $B^{\langle i \rangle} \triangleq B_{\mathcal{I}_x^{\langle i \rangle} \mathcal{I}_r^{\langle i \rangle}}$ and $d_k^{\langle i \rangle}$ is a disturbance term to compensate for the unmodeled dynamics due to neglected state couplings between the subsystem $\Sigma^{\langle i \rangle}$ and its neighbours. The gains $F^{\langle i \rangle}$ are chosen so that the subsystems $\Sigma^{\langle i \rangle}$ are open-loop stable (with $r_k \equiv 0$ and $d_k \equiv 0$).

Assumption 2. In addition to Assumption 1, for every $i \in \mathbb{N}_{[1,m]}$ the feedback gain $F^{\langle i \rangle}$ stabilises subsystem $\Sigma^{\langle i \rangle}$.

Various methodologies have been proposed for the computation of such sparse stabilising gains [19,20].

Let us define $\mathcal{J}_x^{\langle i \rangle} \triangleq \mathbb{N}_{[1,n_x]} \backslash \mathcal{I}_x^{\langle i \rangle}$, and $\mathcal{J}_r^{\langle i \rangle} \triangleq \mathbb{N}_{[1,n_r]} \backslash \mathcal{I}_r^{\langle i \rangle}$. The vectors $\tilde{x}^{\langle i \rangle} \triangleq x_{\mathcal{J}_x^{\langle i \rangle}}$ and $\tilde{r}^{\langle i \rangle} \triangleq r_{\mathcal{J}_r^{\langle i \rangle}}$ will be referred to as *neglected* states and references. The pair $(\tilde{A}^{\langle i \rangle}, \tilde{B}^{\langle i \rangle})$ with $\tilde{A}^{\langle i \rangle} \triangleq A_{\mathcal{I}_x^{\langle i \rangle} \mathcal{J}_x^{\langle i \rangle}}$ and $\tilde{B}^{\langle i \rangle} \triangleq B_{\mathcal{I}_x^{\langle i \rangle} \mathcal{J}_r^{\langle i \rangle}}$ will be used to describe the effect of the neglected states and references on the system $\Sigma^{\langle i \rangle}$.

Then the ULC comprises m subcontrollers which produce the reference signals $r_k^{\langle i \rangle}$ so as to keep the state $x^{\langle i \rangle}$ and the reference $r^{\langle i \rangle}$ inside the polytope:

$$\mathcal{Z}^{\langle i \rangle} \triangleq \{[\begin{smallmatrix} x \\ r \end{smallmatrix}] \in \mathbb{R}^{n_x^{\langle i \rangle} + n_r^{\langle i \rangle}} : H_x^{\langle i \rangle} x + H_r^{\langle i \rangle} r \leq K^{\langle i \rangle}\}, \tag{7}$$

where $H_x^{\langle i \rangle} \in \mathbb{R}^{q_i \times n_x^{\langle i \rangle}}$, $H_r^{\langle i \rangle} \in \mathbb{R}^{q_i \times n_r^{\langle i \rangle}}$, and $K^{\langle i \rangle} \in \mathbb{R}^{q_i}$. The overall set of constraints is then defined as $\mathcal{Z} \triangleq \{[\begin{smallmatrix} x \\ r \end{smallmatrix}] \in \mathbb{R}^{n_x + n_r} : (x^{\langle i \rangle}, r^{\langle i \rangle}) \in \mathcal{Z}^{\langle i \rangle}, \forall i \in \mathbb{N}_{[1,m]}\}$.

Let $A_0^{\langle i \rangle} \in \mathbb{R}^{n_x^{\langle i \rangle} \times n_x}$ be the matrix obtained by collecting the rows of A with indices in $\mathcal{I}_x^{\langle i \rangle}$ and setting to zero the elements in the columns $\mathcal{I}_x^{\langle i \rangle}$. Similarly, we construct $B_0^{\langle i \rangle} \in \mathbb{R}^{n_x^{\langle i \rangle} \times n_r}$ by collecting from B the rows indexed by $\mathcal{I}_x^{\langle i \rangle}$ and then zeroing the columns whose index is in $\mathcal{I}_r^{\langle i \rangle}$. Then, it holds that: $x_{k+1}^{\langle i \rangle} = A^{\langle i \rangle} x_k^{\langle i \rangle} + B^{\langle i \rangle} r_k^{\langle i \rangle} + A_0^{\langle i \rangle} x_k + B_0^{\langle i \rangle} r_k$. Additionally, let us define the set $\mathcal{Z} \triangleq \{(x,r) : (x^{\langle i \rangle}, r^{\langle i \rangle}) \in \mathcal{Z}^{\langle i \rangle}, \forall i \in \mathbb{N}_{[1,m]}\}$, which is a polytope and can be written in the form $\mathcal{Z} = \{(x,r) : H_x x + H_r r \leq K\}$. Let the reference vector $r^{\langle i \rangle}$ be constrained in the set:

$$\mathcal{R}^{\langle i \rangle} \triangleq \{r^{\langle i \rangle} \in \mathbb{R}^{n_r^{\langle i \rangle}} : (H_x^{\langle i \rangle} G^{\langle i \rangle} + H_r^{\langle i \rangle}) r^{\langle i \rangle} \leq K^{\langle i \rangle} - \Delta K^{\langle i \rangle}\},$$

where $G^{\langle i \rangle} \triangleq (I - A^{\langle i \rangle})^{-1} B^{\langle i \rangle}$ is the reference-to-state static gain for $\Sigma^{\langle i \rangle}$ and $\Delta K^{\langle i \rangle} \geq 0$. We assume that the reference signals $r_k^{\langle i \rangle}$ retain the tracking error $\Delta x_k^{\langle i \rangle} \triangleq x_k^{\langle i \rangle} - G^{\langle i \rangle} r_k^{\langle i \rangle}$ in the set:

$$\mathcal{E}^{\langle i \rangle} = \{\Delta x^{\langle i \rangle} \in \mathbb{R}^{n_x^{\langle i \rangle}} : H_x^{\langle i \rangle} \Delta x^{\langle i \rangle} \leq \Delta K^{\langle i \rangle}\}. \tag{8}$$

Notice that $\Delta x_k^{\langle i \rangle} \in \mathcal{E}^{\langle i \rangle}$ if and only if $(x_k^{\langle i \rangle}, r_k^{\langle i \rangle}) \in \tilde{\mathcal{E}}^{\langle i \rangle}$ where: $\tilde{\mathcal{E}}^{\langle i \rangle} \triangleq \{(x^{\langle i \rangle}, r^{\langle i \rangle}) \in \mathbb{R}^{n_x^{\langle i \rangle} + n_r^{\langle i \rangle}} : x^{\langle i \rangle} - G^{\langle i \rangle} r^{\langle i \rangle} \in \mathcal{E}^{\langle i \rangle}\}$. If we set $z^{\langle i \rangle} \triangleq G^{\langle i \rangle} r^{\langle i \rangle} = A^{\langle i \rangle} z^{\langle i \rangle} + B^{\langle i \rangle} r^{\langle i \rangle}$, then the dynamics of $\Sigma^{\langle i \rangle}$ can be described in terms of $\Delta x^{\langle i \rangle} = x^{\langle i \rangle} - z^{\langle i \rangle}$ as follows:

$$\Delta x_{k+1}^{\langle i \rangle} = A^{\langle i \rangle} \Delta x_k^{\langle i \rangle} + d_k^{\langle i \rangle}, \tag{9}$$

where, under the assumptions that $(x_k^{\langle i \rangle}, r_k^{\langle i \rangle}) \in \mathcal{Z}^{\langle i \rangle}$ and $\Delta x_k^{\langle i \rangle} \in \mathcal{E}^{\langle i \rangle}$ for all $k \in \mathbb{N}$ and $i \in \mathbb{N}_{[1,m]}$, the disturbance $d_k^{\langle i \rangle}$ is drawn from the polytope:

$$
\mathcal{D}^{\langle i \rangle} = \left\{ d^{\langle i \rangle} \in \mathbb{R}^{n_x^{\langle i \rangle}} \;\middle|\; \begin{array}{l} \exists r \in \mathbb{R}^{n_r}, \exists x \in \mathbb{R}^{n_x}, \text{s.t.:} d^{\langle i \rangle} = A_0^{\langle i \rangle} x + B_0^{\langle i \rangle} r, \\ \text{and } \forall j \in \mathbb{N}_{[1,m]} : (x^{\langle j \rangle}, r^{\langle j \rangle}) \in \mathcal{Z}^{\langle j \rangle} \cap \tilde{\mathcal{E}}^{\langle j \rangle} \end{array} \right\}. \tag{10}
$$

The size of this polytope determines how strongly the i-th subsystem is dynamically coupled with its neighbours.

Let $\Omega^{\langle i \rangle}(0)$ be the maximal robustly positive invariant (RPI) set for (9) under the constraints $\Delta x^{\langle i \rangle} \in \mathcal{E}^{\langle i \rangle}$ and for $d_k^{\langle i \rangle} \in \mathcal{D}^{\langle i \rangle}$ for all $k \in \mathbb{N}$. Let $\Omega^{\langle i \rangle}(0)$ have the minimal representation $\Omega^{\langle i \rangle}(0) = \{x \in \mathbb{R}^{n_x^{\langle i \rangle}} : H_0^{\langle i \rangle} x \leq K_0^{\langle i \rangle}\}$, counting $n_0^{\langle i \rangle}$ inequalities. Under Assumption 2 this set exists and is a finitely generated polytope.

The complexity of the computation of a maximal RPI set for the overall large-scale system can prove preventive even for offline computations. Note, however, that the computation of the maximal RPI sets is done in a decentralised fashion. For $r \in \mathcal{R}^{\langle i \rangle}$ we define the sets $\Omega^{\langle i \rangle}(r) \triangleq \{x \in \mathbb{R}^{n_x^{\langle i \rangle}} : x - G^{\langle i \rangle} r \in \Omega^{\langle i \rangle}(0)\}$.

The following theorem is the main result of this section and provides an invariance result for hierarchical multi-rate control systems.

Theorem 3. *For all $i \in \mathbb{N}_{[1,m]}$ let $x_0^{\langle i \rangle} \in \Omega^{\langle i \rangle}(r^{\langle i \rangle})$ and assume that $r_k^{\langle i \rangle} = r^{\langle i \rangle} \in \mathcal{R}^{\langle i \rangle}$ for all $k \in \mathbb{N}$. Then $(x_k^{\langle i \rangle}, r_k^{\langle i \rangle}) \in \mathcal{Z}^{\langle i \rangle}$ for all $k \in \mathbb{N}$ and $i \in \mathbb{N}_{[1,m]}$.*

2.3   Computation of Maximum Reference Variations

Assume that a set of fixed reference rates $N^{\langle i \rangle}$ for $i \in \mathbb{N}_{[1,m]}$ is given. In this section we will compute upper bounds on the element-wise variations of the reference rates $r^{\langle i \rangle}$ so that $(x_k^{\langle i \rangle}, r_k^{\langle i \rangle})$ satisfies the prescribed constraints (7). For every subsystem $i \in \mathbb{N}_{[1,m]}$ we formulate the problem of determining the minimum element-wise change in the reference signal that may lead the initial state $x_{\nu N}^{\langle i \rangle}$ outside $\Omega^{\langle i \rangle}(r^{\langle i \rangle, \nu})$; the problem is stated as follows:

$$
\mathbb{P}_N^{\langle i \rangle} : \rho^{\langle i \rangle}(N) \triangleq \min_{r^1, r^2, x_0, d_0, \dots, d_{N-1}} \|r^1 - r^2\|_\infty, \tag{11a}
$$

subject to:

$$
r^1, r^2 \in \mathcal{R}^{\langle i \rangle}, \; x_0 \in \Omega^{\langle i \rangle}(r^1), \tag{11b}
$$

$$
d_j^{\langle i \rangle} \in \mathcal{D}^{\langle i \rangle}, \forall j \in \mathbb{N}_{[0,N-1]}, \tag{11c}
$$

$$
(A^{\langle i \rangle})^N x_0 + \Gamma_N^{\langle i \rangle} r^2 + \sum_{j=0}^{N-1} (A^{\langle i \rangle})^{N-j-1} d_j^{\langle i \rangle} \notin \Omega^{\langle i \rangle}(r^2), \tag{11d}
$$

where $\Gamma_N^{\langle i \rangle} \triangleq \sum_{j=0}^{N-1} (A^{\langle i \rangle})^j B^{\langle i \rangle}$. The above optimisation problem can be formulated as a MILP.

The value function of (11)a enjoys a very useful property: it is non-decreasing with respect to N. If $\mathbb{P}_N$ is infeasible for some N, this implies that for all $r^{\nu-1}, r^\nu \in \mathcal{R}$ it is $x^{\nu+1} \in \Omega(r^\nu)$ whenever $x^\nu \in \Omega(r^{\nu-1})$. In this case we set $\rho(N) = \infty$.

The following theorem states the conditions under which the constraints are satisfied in closed-loop. Note that, except for the last consequence of the theorem, no convergence of the system's trajectories to some constant value is assumed or required. This suggests that a purely cost-driven approach can be applied where the system's trajectories move in an oscillatory manner leading to an economically profitable performance determined by the optimisation of a performance criterion in a receding horizon fashion [8,9].

Theorem 4. *Let F be a (decentralised) asymptotically stabilising gain satisfying Assumption 2. Assume that for every subsystem $i \in \mathbb{N}_{[1,m]}$ there is a $\sigma^{\langle i \rangle} > 0$ so that the references $r^{\langle i \rangle,\nu}$ produced by the upper-layer controllers satisfy the following rate constraint at all time instants $\nu \in \mathbb{N}$:*

$$\|r^{\langle i \rangle,\nu} - r^{\langle i \rangle,\nu-1}\|_\infty \leq \rho^{\langle i \rangle}(N^{\langle i \rangle}) - \sigma^{\langle i \rangle}, \tag{12a}$$

$$r^{\langle i \rangle,\nu-1}, r^{\langle i \rangle,\nu} \in \mathcal{R}^{\langle i \rangle}. \tag{12b}$$

Let $x_0^{\langle i \rangle} \in \Omega^{\langle i \rangle}(r^{-1,\langle i \rangle})$ for all $i \in \mathbb{N}_{[1,m]}$. Then the linear system (1) with the feedback control law (2) satisfies the constraints $\begin{bmatrix} x_k \\ r_k \end{bmatrix} \in \mathcal{Z}$ for all $k \in \mathbb{N}$. Additionally, if $\lim_{k \to \infty} r_k = r$ with $r \in \mathcal{R}$, then $\lim_{k \to \infty} x_k = Gr$.

The ULC control action can be computed by a model predictive control strategy where any optimality criterion can be used so long as the constraints (12) are satisfied.

Theorem 5. *Let Assumption 2 hold true, $\mathcal{R}^{\langle i \rangle}$ be a nonempty compact set and T_L be fixed. If $\Omega^{\langle i \rangle}(0)$ is of full affine dimension, then there is a $N_\star^{\langle i \rangle} \in \mathbb{N}$ so that $\rho^{\langle i \rangle}(N_\star^{\langle i \rangle}) = \infty$.*

Proof. For the sake of simplicity let us assume that $\mathcal{D}^{\langle i \rangle} = \{0\}$. Since $\Omega^{\langle i \rangle}(0)$ has full affine dimension and contains the origin in its interior, there is an $\epsilon > 0$ so that $\epsilon \mathcal{B}_\infty \subsetneq \Omega^{\langle i \rangle}(0)$. The compactness or $\mathcal{R}^{\langle i \rangle}$ implies that there is a $\delta > 0$ so that $\mathcal{R}^{\langle i \rangle} \subseteq \delta \mathcal{B}_\infty$. Since $A^{\langle i \rangle}$ is strictly Schur, the limit $\lim_{N \to \infty} \Gamma_N^{\langle i \rangle}$ exists and is equal to $G^{\langle i \rangle}$. This implies that there is a $N_1^{\langle i \rangle} \in \mathbb{N}$ so that for all $N \geq N_1^{\langle i \rangle}$ it is $\|\Gamma_N^{\langle i \rangle} - G^{\langle i \rangle}\|_\infty \leq \epsilon/2\delta$. For $z \in \mathcal{R}^{\langle i \rangle}$ we have $\|(\Gamma_N^{\langle i \rangle} - G^{\langle i \rangle})z\|_\infty \leq \|\Gamma_N^{\langle i \rangle} - G^{\langle i \rangle}\|_\infty \cdot \|z\| \leq \epsilon/2$, or what is the same $\Gamma_N^{\langle i \rangle} z \in G^{\langle i \rangle} z \oplus (\epsilon/2)\mathcal{B}_\infty$ for all $z \in \mathcal{R}^{\langle i \rangle}$. We can, hence, infer that $\Gamma_N^{\langle i \rangle} \mathcal{R}^{\langle i \rangle} \subseteq G^{\langle i \rangle} \mathcal{R}^{\langle i \rangle} \oplus (\epsilon/2)\mathcal{B}_\infty$.

Because of Assumption 2 and because of the compactness of $\mathcal{R}^{\langle i \rangle}$, there exists a $N_2 \in \mathbb{N}$ so that for all $N \geq N_2$ it is $(A^{\langle i \rangle})^N x_0 \in (\epsilon/2)\mathcal{B}_\infty$ for all $x_0 \in \mathcal{R}^{\langle i \rangle}$. Because of (11)d, for $\mathbb{P}_N^{\langle i \rangle}$ to be infeasible for some N it is necessary and sufficient that for all $r^1, r^2 \in \mathcal{R}^{\langle i \rangle}$ and $x_0 \in \Omega^{\langle i \rangle}(r^1)$ it is $(A^{\langle i \rangle})^N x_0 + \Gamma_N^{\langle i \rangle} r^1 \in \Omega^{\langle i \rangle}(r^2)$, which can be equivalently written as $\Gamma_N^{\langle i \rangle} \mathcal{R}^{\langle i \rangle} \subseteq \Omega^{\langle i \rangle}(\mathcal{R}^{\langle i \rangle}) \ominus (A^{\langle i \rangle})^N \mathcal{R}^{\langle i \rangle}$. For

$N \geq N_\star^{\langle i \rangle} \triangleq \max\{N_1, N_2\}$ this inclusion is satisfied if $G^{\langle i \rangle} \mathcal{R}^{\langle i \rangle} \oplus (\epsilon/2)\mathcal{B}_\infty \subseteq$
$\Omega^{\langle i \rangle}(\mathcal{R}^{\langle i \rangle}) \ominus (\epsilon/2)\mathcal{B}_\infty$ from which we have $G^{\langle i \rangle} \mathcal{R}^{\langle i \rangle} \subseteq \Omega^{\langle i \rangle}(\mathcal{R}^{\langle i \rangle}) \ominus \epsilon\mathcal{B}_\infty$, but by
definition $\Omega^{\langle i \rangle}(r) = \{G^{\langle i \rangle} r\} \oplus \Omega^{\langle i \rangle}(0)$, thus $\Omega^{\langle i \rangle}(\mathcal{R}^{\langle i \rangle}) = G^{\langle i \rangle} \mathcal{R}^{\langle i \rangle} \oplus \Omega^{\langle i \rangle}(0)$ and
a condition for infeasibility is: $G^{\langle i \rangle} \mathcal{R}^{\langle i \rangle} \subseteq G^{\langle i \rangle} \mathcal{R}^{\langle i \rangle} \oplus (\Omega^{\langle i \rangle}(0) \ominus \epsilon\mathcal{B}_\infty)$, which is
true since $\Omega^{\langle i \rangle}(0) \ominus \epsilon\mathcal{B}_\infty$ is non-empty.   □

3   Control of a System of Interconnected Tanks

3.1   System Dynamics and Decomposition

The proposed methodology is tested on Johansson's quadruple-tank process [21]
where the control objective is to track given (possibly time-varying, piece-wise
constant) references s_1 and s_2 for the levels of tanks 1 and 2, namely h_1 and h_2,
as in Fig. 2 by manipulating the inflows q_a and q_b. Constraints are imposed on
the maximum flow that can be achieved by each pump and on the upper and
lower allowed levels of water in the tanks.

The system is subject to state and input constraints and its dynamics is
described in [22] by the system of continuous-time nonlinear equations

$$S_1 \frac{dh_1}{dt} = -a_1\sqrt{2gh_1} + a_3\sqrt{2gh_3} + \gamma_a q_a, \tag{13a}$$

$$S_2 \frac{dh_2}{dt} = -a_2\sqrt{2gh_2} + a_4\sqrt{2gh_4} + \gamma_b q_b, \tag{13b}$$

$$S_3 \frac{dh_3}{dt} = -a_3\sqrt{2gh_3} + (1 - \gamma_b)q_b, \tag{13c}$$

$$S_3 \frac{dh_4}{dt} = -a_4\sqrt{2gh_4} + (1 - \gamma_a)q_a. \tag{13d}$$

The maximum allowed level for tanks 1 and 2 is set to 1.36 m and for tanks 3
and 4 to 1.30 m. The minimum allowed level in all tanks is 0.2 m. The maximum
flows are $q_{a,max} = 3.26\,\text{m}^3/\text{h}$ and $q_{b,max} = 4\,\text{m}^3/\text{h}$; no negative flows are possible.
The values of the other parameters of the system are $a_1 = 1.31 \cdot 10^{-4}\,\text{m}^2$, $a_2 = 1.51 \cdot 10^{-4}\,\text{m}^2$, $a_3 = 9.27 \cdot 10^{-5}\,\text{m}^2$, $a_4 = 8.82 \cdot 10^{-5}\,\text{m}^2$, $S_1 = S_2 = 0.06\,\text{m}^2$, $S_3 = S_4 = 0.20\,\text{m}^2$, and $\gamma_a = \gamma_b = 0.5$. The nonlinear system is linearised about the
steady state $u^0 = (2.6, 2.6)'\,\text{m}^3/\text{h}$ and $x^0 = (0.6545, 0.4926, 0.7852, 0.8583)'$ m
and discretised with sampling period $T_s = 10\text{s}$. We define the discrete-time state
vector $x_k = (h_{1,k}, h_{2,k}, h_{3,k}, h_{4,k})'$ which comprises the levels of the four tanks,
the discrete-time input vector $u_k = (q_{a,k}, q_{b,k})'$ of manipulated variables which
are the two flows, and the discrete output $y_k = x_k$. The linearised discrete-time
system is written in the form of (1).

3.2   Centralised Versus Decentralised Control

We consider that the lower control layer operates at sampling time $T_s = 10\,\text{s}$.
The overall system is partitioned into two subsystems with $\mathcal{I}_x^{\langle 1 \rangle} = \{1, 4\}$, $\mathcal{I}_x^{\langle 2 \rangle} = \{2, 3\}$ and $\mathcal{I}_u^{\langle 1 \rangle} = \{1\}$, $\mathcal{I}_u^{\langle 2 \rangle} = \{2\}$. The system is controlled by means of the

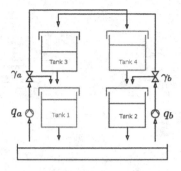

Fig. 2. Johansson's quadruple-tank process where the two sub-systems are denoted with different colours (Color figure online).

proposed decentralised hierarchical control methodology which is compared to its centralised hierarchical variant. Reference commands from the upper layer controller are computed so that they minimise a quadratic cost function. In particular, the ULC for subsystem 1 solves the following minimisation problem at the ULC sampling time instant ν:

$$J^{(1)\star}(x^{\nu}) = \min_{\{r_1^{\nu+j}\}_{j=0}^{N-1}} \sum_{k=0}^{N-1} (h_1^{\nu+k} - s_1)^2 + \lambda(r_a^{\nu+k} - r_a^s)^2, \qquad (14)$$

subject to the (linearised) system dynamics, measurements from the system, the requirement $r^{\nu+k} \in \mathcal{R}$ for all $k = 0, \ldots, N-1$, and the bounds on the maximum reference variation that accrue from Theorem 4. In what follows, the weight λ is fixed to 0.01. Then, the solution of problem 14 yields an optimal sequence of references $\{r_1^{\nu+k,\star}\}_{k=0}^{N-1}$, the first one of which – namely $r_1^{\nu,\star}$ is applied to the corresponding controlled LLC system in a receding horizon fashion. The ULC controller for sub-system 2 works in an analogous fashion where the minimisation problem becomes $J^{(2)\star}(x^{\nu}) = \min_{\{r_2^{\nu+j}\}_{j=0}^{N-1}} \sum_{k=0}^{N-1} (h_2^{\nu+k} - s_2)^2 + \lambda(r_b^{\nu+k} - r_b^s)^2$, subject to the corresponding constraints. According to Theorem 4 the closed-loop system will satisfy the prescribed constraints.

For the decentralised control case, the dependence of the maximum reference change $\rho^{(i)}$ on N is presented in Fig. 3. The reference rate $N = 40$ was selected for which $\rho^{(1)}(N) = 0.0034$ and $\rho^{(2)}(N) = 0.0063$ for the decentralised control system and $\rho(N) = 0.0035$ for the centralised control approach. The maximum reference variation $\rho^{(i)}(N)$ for the two subsystems is presented in Fig. 3. Notice that for $N \geq N^{\star} = 42$, it is $\rho^{(2)}(N) = \infty$. Vectors $\Delta K^{(i)}$ in (8) were chosen to be $\Delta K^{(i)} = cK^{(i)}$, with $c = 0.5$.

The controlled trajectories of the tank levels are presented in Figs. 4 and 5. The tank levels h_1 and h_2 are steered towards four different set-points and the set-point values are kept constant for 5.55 h. In order to quantify the performance of the three controllers, we use the following index introduced by Alvarado et al. [22] for the same system:

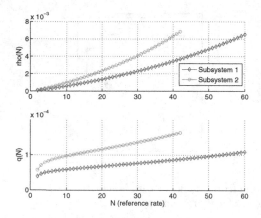

Fig. 3. The functions $\rho^{\langle i \rangle}(N)$ and $q^{\langle i \rangle}(N) \triangleq \rho^{\langle i \rangle}(N)/N$ for the two subsystems.

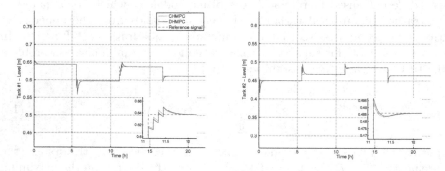

Fig. 4. The level in tank 1 and 2: comparison between centralised hierarchical MPC (CHMPC, green) and decentralised hierarchical MPC (DHMPC, blue). The dashed red line represents the set-point s_1. The inset shows the convergence of the tank level to the desired set-point in the interval 11 to 12.2 h (Color figure online).

$$J = \sum_{k=0}^{N_s-1} (h_{1,k}-s_{1,k})^2 + (h_{2,k}-s_{2,k})^2 + \kappa((q_{a,k}-q_{a,k}^s)^2 + (q_{b,k}-q_{b,k}^s)^2), \qquad (15)$$

where $\kappa = 0.01$ and $q_{a,k}^s$ and $q_{b,k}^s$ are the steady-state values of the input variables that correspond to the set-point defined by s_1 and s_2, and $N_s = 8000$ (22 h) is the simulation horizon. The values of the performance index J are presented in Table 1.

The maximal robust positive invariant sets $\Omega^{\langle i \rangle}(0)$, $i \in \{1, 2\}$ for the decentralised control case were computed offline in 1.97 s and 2.19 s and their minimal representations involved 5 and 4 inequalities respectively. The maximal positive invariant set $\Omega(0)$ for the centralised control system was computed in 0.60 s and its minimal representation comprised 12 linear inequalities. The associated MILPs $\mathbb{P}_N^{\langle i \rangle}$ as in (11) were solved offline in 2.12 s for subsystem 1 and 2.27 s for subsystem 2 on average. The corresponding centralised computation required

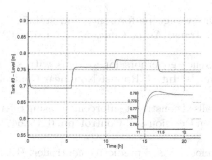 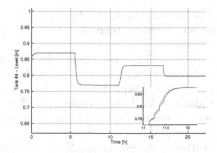

Fig. 5. The level in tanks 3 and 4: Closed-loop trajectories for CHMPC (green), and DHMPC (blue) (Color figure online).

Table 1. Performance of a decentralised and a centralised controller for Johansson's system.

Controller	$\tau_{s,1}$ (h)	$\tau_{s,2}$ (h)	J
DHMPC	0.1674	0.1500	0.1495
CHMPC	0.1146	0.1458	0.1516

6.33 s on average. All reported computation times were measured in MATLAB 2013a running on a Mac OS X machine, 2.66 GHz Intel Core 2 Duo, 4 GB RAM.

References

1. Jamshidi, M., Meyers, R.A.: Controls, Large-Scale Systems, Encyclopedia of Physical Science and Technology, 3rd edn, pp. 675–686. Academic Press, New York (2003)
2. Findeisen, W., Bailey, F.N., Brdys, M., Malinowski, K., Tatjewski, P., Wozniak, A.: Control and Coordination in Hierarchical Systems. IIASA International Series, vol. 9. Wiley, Chichester (1980)
3. Ishii, T., Yasuda, K.: Hierarchical decentralised autonomous control in super-distributed energy systems. IEEE Trans. Electr. Electron. Eng. **2**(1), 63–71 (2007)
4. Scattolini, R.: Architectures for distributed and hierarchical model predictive control - a review. J. Process Control **19**, 723–731 (2009)
5. Bakule, L.: Decentralised control: an overview. Ann. Rev. Control **32**(1), 87–98 (2008)
6. Ocampo-Martinez, C., Puig, V., Bovo, S.: Decentralised MPC based on a graph partitioning approach applied to the Barcelona drinking water network. In: Proceedings of 18th IFAC World Congress, pp. 1577–1583, Milano (2011)
7. Ocampo-Martinez, C., Barcelli, D., Puig, V., Bemporad, A.: Hierarchical and decentralised model predictive control of drinking water networks: application to Barcelona case study. IET Control Theor. Appl. **6**(1), 62–71 (2012)
8. Sampathirao, A.K., Grosso, J.M., Sopasakis, P., Ocampo-Martinez, C., Bemporad, A., Puig, V.: Water demand forecasting for the optimal operation of large-scale drinking water networks: The Barcelona Case Study. In: 19th IFAC World Congress, pp. 10457–10462, Cape Town (2014)

9. Angeli, M., Amrit, R., Rawlings, J.B.: On average performance and stability of economic model predictive control. IEEE Trans. Auto. Cont. **57**(7), 1615–1626 (2012)
10. Gilbert, E.G., Kolmanovsky, I.: Fast reference governors for systems with state and control constraints and disturbance inputs. Int. J. Robust Nonlinear Control. **9**(15), 1117–1141 (1999)
11. Kalabić, U.V., Kolmanovsky, I.V.: Decentralised constraint enforcement using reference governors. In: 52nd IEEE Conference on Decision and Control, pp. 6415–6421, Firenze (2013)
12. Scattolini, R., Schiavoni, N.: A multirate model based predictive controller. IEEE Trans. Aut. Contr. **40**(6), 1093–1097 (1995)
13. Picasso, B., De Vito, D., Scattolini, R., Colaneri, P.: An MPC approach to the design of two-layer hierarchical control systems. Automatica **46**(5), 823–831 (2010)
14. Heidarinejad, M., Liu, L., de la Peña, D.M., Davis, J.F., Christofides, P.D.: Multirate Lyapunov-based distributed model predictive control of nonlinear uncertain systems. J. Process Control **21**(9), 1231–1242 (2011)
15. Barcelli, D., Bemporad, A., Ripaccioli, G.: Hierarchical multi-rate control design for constrained linear systems. In: 49th IEEE Conference on Decision and Control, pp. 5216–5221 (2010)
16. Barcelli, D., Bemporad, A.: Decentralised model predictive control of dynamically-coupled linear systems: tracking under packet loss. In: 1st IFAC Workshop on Estimation and Control of Networked Systems, pp. 204–209, Venice (2009)
17. Alessio, A., Barcelli, D., Bemporad, A.: Decentralised model predictive control of dynamically coupled linear systems. J. Proc. Contr. **21**(5), 705–714 (2011)
18. Zhoujie, L., Martins, J.: Graph partitioning-based coordination methods for large-scale multidisciplinary design optimisation problems. In: 12th AIAA Aviation Technology, Integration, and Operations (ATIO) Conference, Indianapolis (2012)
19. Barcelli, D., Bernardini, D., Bemporad, A.: Synthesis of networked switching linear decentralised controllers. In: 49th IEEE Conference on Decision and Control, pp. 2480–2485, Atlanta (2010)
20. Šiljak, D.D.: Decentralised Control of Complex Systems. Academic Press, New York (1991)
21. Johansson, K.H.: The quadruple-tank process: a multivariable laboratory process with an adjustable zero. IEEE Trans. Contr. Syst. Tech. **8**(3), 456–465 (2000)
22. Alvarado, I., Limon, D., de la Peña, M., Maestre, J.M., Ridao, M.A., Scheu, H., Marquardt, W., Negenborn, R.R., De Schutter, B., Valencia, F., Espinosa, J.: A comparative analysis of distributed MPC techniques applied to HD-MPC four-tank benchmark. J. Process Control **21**, 800–815 (2011)

dbpRisk: Disinfection By-Product
Risk Estimation

Marios Kyriakou, Demetrios G. Eliades$^{(\boxtimes)}$, and Marios M. Polycarpou

KIOS Research Center for Intelligent Systems and Networks, University of Cyprus,
Nicosia, Cyprus
{kiriakou.marios,eldemet,mpolycar}@ucy.ac.cy
http://www.kios.org.cy

Abstract. This work describes a new open-source software platform, the **dbpRisk** software, for conducting simulation experiments in order to model the formation for disinfection by-product in drinking water distribution networks under various conditions and uncertainties. The goal is to identify the risk-level at each node location, contributing in the enhancement of consumer safety. The use of the **dbpRisk** software is demonstrated using a real water distribution network model from the Nicosia water transport network.

Keywords: Disinfection By-Products · Simulation · Risk evaluation · EPANET

1 Introduction

The goal of all water supply networks are to provide the consumers with adequate quantity of water, without compromising its quality. From the ancient to the present times, there has always been continuous development of water safety [12]; however, despite the technological progress, the distribution of healthy water is a challenge for all water suppliers worldwide. Water must be safe for human consumption and free from pathogenic micro-organisms, to prevent diseases and health problems [11]. Unfortunately water pollution is the primary cause of deaths and diseases in the world. To eliminate these risks, treatment is required before using the water, so that it is safe for human health [16]; this involves the water disinfection which effectively kills the bacteria and the micro-organisms existing within the bulk water.

Disinfection of drinking water can be considered to be the most important measure of the last century for the protection of public health. The deactivation of bacteria through disinfection has contributed in reducing water-borne diseases. Disinfection can be achieved with chemicals, such as Chlorine, Chloramines, Chlorine Dioxide and Ozone, that destroy the pathogen micro-organisms and produce safe drinking water. A result of disinfection chemical process is the production of Disinfection By-Products (DBP), such as trihalomethanes, haloacetic acids, bromate, and chlorite which can have negative effects on human health.

© Springer International Publishing Switzerland 2016
C.G. Panayiotou et al. (Eds.): CRITIS 2014, LNCS 8985, pp. 57–68, 2016.
DOI: 10.1007/978-3-319-31664-2_7

For instance, disinfectants react with bromides and/or with the natural organic matter that exists in the water source forming DBPs [22]. Also, the formation of DBPs may be due to anthropogenic contaminants which enter the drinking water sources and react with disinfectants [25]. Another parameter affecting the DBP creation is the water age, e.g. due to stagnation. The more time the disinfected water remains unconsumed, the higher the concentration of DBPs is [20]. Generally, the formation and production of DBPs depend on various chemical and environmental parameters, such as the pH, temperature which depend on the seasons, the injected chlorine dosage and the residues throughout the network, the Total Organic Carbon (TOC), the source water quality (e.g. if from desalination or from lake), the bromate concentration and water age [8,15,19,25].

Water distribution networks are responsible for transporting clean water to consumers. These are typically large-scale systems and are comprised of reservoirs, junctions, pumps, valves and pipes transporting and delivering the disinfected water to the consumers, via outflow nodes. From a hydraulics viewpoint, valves and pumps can be controlled automatically or manually, to regulate pressures within the network [3]. From a water quality viewpoint, the goal is to ensure that sufficient quantity of disinfected water is delivered to the consumers, and that a small quantity of disinfected residual is present in the consumption node, in accordance with EU regulations [21].

Chlorine disinfection is used in most drinking water networksdue to its low cost and effectiveness in neutralizing the dangerous micro-organisms under the safety conditions specified by the relevant agencies [21]. Chlorine is injected into the system at specific locations, in a gas-form (Cl_2) or as hypochlorite salts ($NaOCl$). At chlorine residual concentrations 0.03–0.06 mg/L, bacteria are deactivated in 20 min under normal conditions. Chlorine also reacts with natural organic matter and inorganic substances that exist in water [28]. This reaction is immediate and has as result the creation of chlorination by-products, such as the formation of trihalomethanes [25].

Trihalomethanes (THM) constitute an important category of chlorination by-products and their presences in drinking water is a clue of possible existence of other chlorinated organic compounds at lower concentrations [23]. Trihalomethanes are a group of four chemicals substances that are formed when the chlorine reacts with organic or inorganic matter of water. The trihalomethanes are chloroform, dibromochloromethane, bromodichloro-methane and bromoform [6]. The high concentration of THM has an impact in health, such as liver, kidney and problems in the central nervous system, as well as increased risk of cancer [14]. Depending on the different regulatory bodies, the Total Trihalomethane concentration should be below 0.08 mg/L (US Environmental Protection Agency) or 0.1 mg/L (European Union).

DBPs have been studied extensively during the last 40 years in order to understand and predict their dynamics in drinking water [7]. For instance, studies have utilized linear regression models in order to model the formation of DBPs [4,13]. Other research studies have proposed mechanistic or non-empirical kinetic models describing the formation of DBPs [1,8,17]. Furthermore, some studies have developed models considering the parameters affecting the THM dynamics, such as natural organic matter, initial dosage of chlorine, temperature, pH, total organic carbon, UV254, bromide [7,9,15]. A key issues is to balance the DBP risks associated with high chlorine concentration, versus the microbiological contamination risks associated with low chlorine concentration [25]. A substantial amount of research deals with different species of DBPs and refers to side effects on human health [25].

Water systems modelling is used extensively in research and has found applications in various commercial software. Modelling is mainly focused on the hydraulic dynamics, i.e. calculating the changes of flows and pressures within the distribution network, based on some estimated demands, whereas quality dynamics relate with the change in the concentrations of one or more chemical species. The open-source EPANET software is widely used in the academic community [24], and along with the Multi-Species eXtension Library (EPANET-MSX), complex chemical reactions may be simulated, along with their bulk-water and wall reactions [26].

The use of water quality modelling can be exploited for simulating and evaluating the DBP risk; for this, the EPANET(-MSX) modelling engine will be used. The contribution of this work is the design a software platform, the **dbpRisk** software, which is able to conduct simulations for modelling DBP formation under various conditions and uncertainties, in order to assign risk-levels and assist the decision makers in making more informed decisions for enhancing consumer safety. In addition, the software can be used as module of a Water Quality monitoring and control system which utilizes sensor measurements, simulation and control, to optimize the operation of the system to maintain a high level of water quality while reducing the DBP risk. In particular, the **dbpRisk** software interface is presented, based on Matlab, and is released under the open-source European Union Public Licence (EUPL) at https://github.com/ KIOS-Research/dbpRisk.

In Sect. 2, the problem formulation is presented, and in Sect. 3 the **dbpRisk** software is described. Section 4 presents a case-study on a real water distribution network and Sect. 5 concludes the paper.

2   Problem Formulation

This section presents the formulation of the problem for determining the high-risk areas in a water distribution network.

2.1   Quality Dynamics

In general, the overall chlorine decay dynamics in water flowing through a distribution system is as follows [5]:

$$\left(\frac{dC}{dt}\right)_{Total} = \left(\frac{dC}{dt}\right)_{Bulk} + \left(\frac{dC}{dt}\right)_{Wall} \tag{1}$$

The chlorine decay in the bulk water is typically described using a first-order kinetic model, such that [2,5].

$$\left(\frac{dC}{dt}\right)_{Bulk} = -K_b C \tag{2}$$

$$K_b = a[X_{TOC}]e^{(-b/T)} \tag{3}$$

where K_b is the bulk decay constant, C is the chlorine concentration, T is the temperature in Kelvin, X_{TOC} is the Total Organic Carbon (TOC) concentration in bulk water, and the constants $a = 1.8x10^6$ L/mg-h and $b = 6050$ K.

Some of the disinfectant substance also reacts with material at the pipe walls where the water moves. The pipe wall reaction rates are needed as well as the mass transfer limitations of the disinfectant from the bulk liquid to the wall. The dynamics for the wall reaction rate within a pipe p are as follows [5]:

$$\left(\frac{dC}{dt}\right)_{Wall} = -\frac{4K_{w_1}K_F C}{D_p(K_{w_1} + K_F)} = -\frac{K_w}{D_p}C \tag{4}$$

where K_F is the mass transfer coefficient, K_{w_1} is the wall reaction rate constant, K_w is the overall wall decay constant and D_p is pipe diameter. The mass transfer coefficient K_F will in general depend on the flow turbulence as well as the diameter of the pipe. A typical empirical relation for this parameter is

$$K_F = 1.6x10^{-4}\frac{R_e^{0.88}}{D_p} \tag{5}$$

where R_e is the Reynolds number.

Finally, a first-order chlorine decay dynamics modeling in pipes, neglecting spatial transport dynamics [5], is given by

$$\frac{dC}{dt} = -K_b C - \frac{K_w}{D_p}C. \tag{6}$$

According to various studies, Trihalomethanes kinetics can be modeled as follows [10,18,27]:

$$\frac{dX_{THM}}{dt} = \beta K_b C \tag{7}$$

where the reaction coefficients K_b, and the THM yield coefficient β was obtained by simulated distribution system data, in order to agree the results as much as possible to the real system.

Other relater water quality parameters can be modelled, such as the water age (X_{WA}) and the Total Organic Carbon (TOC) concentration X_{TOC} in the bulk water. Water age can be modelled using zero-order kinetics with a rate constant equal to 1; for example, each second the water becomes a second older [24]. TOC can be modelled following zero-order kinetics with a rate constant equal to 0, when it assumed to remain constant [26]:

$$\frac{dX_{WA}}{dt} = 1 \qquad \frac{dX_{TOC}}{dt} = 0. \tag{8}$$

2.2   Propagation Dynamics

In general, the propagation and reaction dynamics in water distribution networks are described by a set of hyperbolic partial differential equations, which can be discretized using some numerical scheme in order to facilitate computational solutions. Following the formulation in (Eliades and Polycarpou, 2010), let k be the discrete time with Δt time step, and let the state-space equations describing the substance propagation in a water distribution network segmented into N_x finite volume elements to be given by

$$x(k+1) = A(k; p_x)x(k) + R(p_x, p_c) \tag{9}$$

where $x(k)$ is the concentration of all substances in all finite volumes at time k, the state matrix $A(k; p_x)$ is time-varying and depends on the distribution network topology as well as to the hydraulic parameter set p_x which affects water flows, such as consumer demands, node elevations, as well as pipe lengths, diameters and roughness coefficients. Function R corresponds to the reaction dynamics of chlorine with organic substances to produce THM, which depends on the hydraulics parameter set p_x and the parameter set p_c. The parameters p_x, p_c are in general partially or nominally known, and the uncertainty in the knowledge of these parameters may affect the final solutions. To alleviate this problem, we may consider constructing a number of scenarios with the aim of capturing the variability in the real water distribution network. Let $\mathcal{P}$ be the finite set of all the different hydraulic and parameters considered. Each different hydraulic and parameters set corresponds to a scenario, and $\mathcal{P}$ is comprised of N_p scenarios. The intuition behind using different hydraulic scenarios, is to provide a more robust solution, which may be different from the solution computed if average parameter values were considered.

Let N be the number of consumption nodes in the network; for a simulation time $k \in K$, the estimated chlorine and THM concentration at each node is given by

$$\hat{Y}_C(k) = f_C(x, K; \mathcal{P}) \tag{10}$$

$$\hat{Y}_{THM}(k) = f_T(x, K, ; \mathcal{P}) \tag{11}$$

where f_C and f_T are quality dynamic simulators for estimating chlorine and THM concentrations respectively; in practice this is achieved through the use of the EPANET and EPANET-MSX libraries.

2.3   DBP Risk Modelling

Eventually, this problem relates to the question "Which areas in a large-scale water distribution network risk a higher disinfection by-product concentration?".

Let $L \in \{'blue/low', 'cyan/low - medium', 'green/medium', 'orange/medium - high', 'red/high'\}$ be the impact risk colour and level labels; for instance 'blue' corresponds to the lowest risk and 'red' to the highest risk. For N

network nodes, let $Z \in L^N$ be the disinfection by-product risk across all nodes, and let $f_L : \mathbb{R}^N \mapsto L^N$ be a function that maps the average estimated THM concentration within time K, to an impact metric in L. For the i-th node, the following are considered: $\hat{Y}^i_{THM}(k) \leq 30$ has low impact, $30 < \hat{Y}^i_{THM}(k) \leq 60$ has low-medium impact, $60 < \hat{Y}^i_{THM}(k) \leq 80$ has medium impact, $80 < \hat{Y}^i_{THM}(k) \leq 100$ has medium-high impact and $\hat{Y}^i_{THM}(k) > 100$ has high impact.

3   dbpRisk Software

The **dbpRisk** software is designed with the goal of providing a flexible and user-friendly tool for the academic as well as the professional community, making it easy to evaluate the DBP risk. The software is build upon the EPANET-Matlab-Class[1], an open development platform which incorporates methods to assist the simulation and the control of water distribution systems, utilizing Matlab's Class structures and the dynamic software libraries of the widely used EPANET engines as well as the EPANET-MSX for simulating multi-species reactions [24,26]. This tool is comprised of a set of functions which are based on the EPANET, along with other useful functions for visualization, simulation and data management.

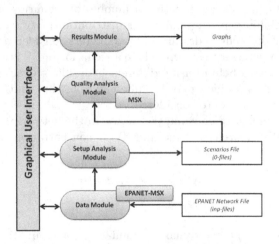

Fig. 1. The software architecture of the dbpRisk.

The dbpRisk has been designed in such a way as to a modular architecture for expandability, and its architecture is depicted in Fig. 1. First, the *Data Module* extracts all the network parameters from the EPANET input file provided, which includes the network topology, pipe lengths and diameters, roughness coefficients, node elevations and demands, characteristics of tanks, valves, pumps,

---

[1] The EPANET-Matlab-Class is released under an open-source EUPL license and is available at https://github.com/KIOS-Research/EPANET-Matlab-Class.

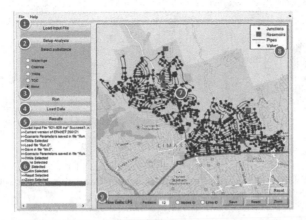

Fig. 2. The dbpRisk Graphical User Interface is comprised of the following parts: (1) the network loading buttons, (2) the setup analysis method, (3) the quality analysis method, (4) the load data button, (5) the results method, (6) the message box, (7) the water distribution network, (8) the legend for the different network elements, (9) the graph options

as well as quality parameters. These parameters are stored within an EPANET object which is created in Matlab, that will be used by the other modules. In addition, the water distribution network is plotted in the dbpRisk GUI Fig. 2. The *Setup Analysis Module* allows the user to select the parameter bounds and sampling method, for constructing the scenarios which will be used in the simulation module. These scenarios are stored in the *Scenarios* file (0-file). These scenarios are simulated in the *Quality Analysis Module* using the EPANET-MSX library to solve the different hydraulic scenarios, corresponding to the network flows, and then to solve the quality scenarios with respect to the scenarios. Finally, the *Results Module* calculate the impact risks and depicts this information, along with other graphs and frequency diagrams, on the **dbpRisk** GUI.

4   Case Study

The operation of the **dbpRisk** is demonstrated using on real model, the Nicosia transport network. This network is comprised of 395 junctions, 282 pipes, 2 tanks, 2 reservoirs and 122 valves.

In the following examples, unless otherwise stated, the following parameters are considered : temperature is 30°C with 5 % uncertainty; TOC has concentration $X_{TOC} = 1.5 \, \text{mg/L}$ in the main reservoir; the wall reaction coefficient is $K_w = 0.214 \, \text{m/day}$ and the parameter that used to model the individual THM formation is $\beta = 33.5 \, \text{mg/L}$. The network is loaded and the simulation parameters are specified, as in Fig. 3.

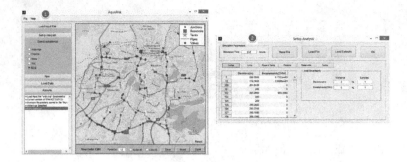

Fig. 3. The Nicosia water transport network and parameter setup.

4.1   Parameters Affecting the THM

Depending on the parameter we want to examine, as regards to the effect these might have on the THM concentration, we evaluate different scenarios with simulation duration of 9 days.

Effect of Chlorine Dose: In the first case, we introduce chlorine 1 mg/L and TOC is $X_{TOC} = 2.5$ mg/L in the Reservoirs. Water temperature is 20°C in each pipe and tank. A second scenario examines chlorine injection concentration 0.5 mg/L at the Reservoirs. The results are depicted in Fig. 4 where it is observed, as expected, that THM concentration is higher when chlorine dose is 1 mg/L.

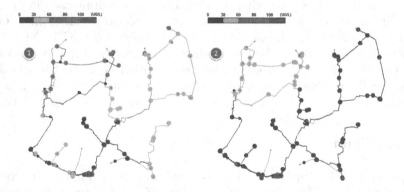

Fig. 4. DBP Risk: (1) Chlorine dose 1.0 mg/L, (2) Chlorine dose 0.5 mg/L.

Effect of Temperature: We introduce chlorine of 0.5 mg/L and TOC $X_{TOC} = 2.5$ mg/L in the Reservoirs. We create two scenarios, one with water temperature 20°C and one with water temperature 35°C. The results are depicted in Fig. 6 where it is observed that THM concentration is higher when temperature is 35°C. Another observation is that the variations of each species at the Latsia area with temperature 35°C and 15°C are depicted in Fig. 7 and in Fig. 5 correspondingly.

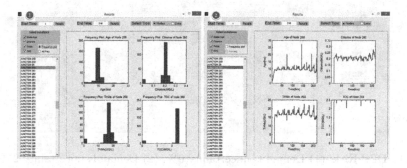

Fig. 5. Simulation results with temperature 15° at Latsia DMA: (1) Frequency plots (2) Chemical species time-series.

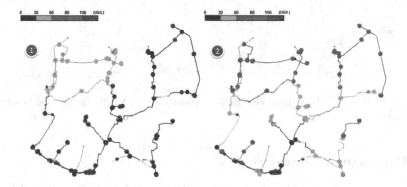

Fig. 6. DBP Risk: (1) Temperature 20°C, (2) Temperature 35°C.

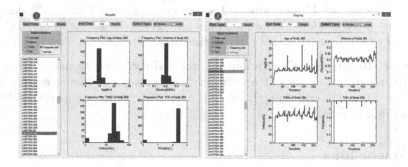

Fig. 7. Simulation results with temperature 35°C at Latsia DMA: (1) Frequency plots (2) Chemical species time-series.

Fig. 8. DBP Risk: (1) Demands uncertainty 0 %, (2) Demands uncertainty 25 %.

Fig. 9. DBP Risk: (1) Roughness coefficient uncertainty 0 %, (2) Roughness coefficient uncertainty 25 %.

4.2   Parameter Uncertainty

This section investigates the effects of uncertainty with respect to the DBP risk. As in the previous section, the simulation duration is 9 days. By considering uncertainties, it is possible to evaluate the sensitivity of each parameter affected, and to calculate upper and lower bounds of each chemical parameter.

Effect of Demand Uncertainty: Two scenarios with 0 % and 25 % demand uncertainty are considered. The reservoirs have $X_{TOC} = 1.5$ mg/L of TOC and 1 mg/L of Chlorine, with water temperature 20°C. Results are shown in Fig. 8.

Effect of Roughness Coefficients Uncertainty: Two scenarios with 0 % and 25 % roughness coefficient uncertainty are considered. The reservoirs have $X_{TOC} = 1.5$ mg/L and 1 mg/L of Chlorine, with water temperature 20°C. Results are shown in Fig. 9.

5   Conclusions

In this work a new open-source software platform, the **dbpRisk** software, was described. This can be used for conducting simulation experiments in order to model the formation for disinfection by-product in drinking water distribution networks under various conditions and uncertainties, with the goal of identifying the risk-level at each node location and provide assistance to decision makers for making more informed decisions for enhancing consumer safety. A case study was demonstrated using the Nicosia water transport network. Future work will consider more detailed water quality models regarding the DBP formation, and in addition, incorporate epidemiological metrics in order to measure the risk in relation to the affected population.

Acknowledgments. This research work has been partially funded by the European Research Council (ERC) under the project ERC-2011-ADG-291508 "Fault-Adaptive Monitoring and Control of Complex Distributed Dynamical Systems"(FAULT-ADAPTIVE), and by the Cyprus Research Promotion Foundation through the Frame work Programme for Research, Technological Development and Innovation 2009–10 (DESMI 2009–2010), co-funded by the Republic of Cyprus and the European Regional Development Fund, under the project "UrbanDBP".

References

1. Adin, A., Katzhendler, J., Alkaslassy, D., Rav-Acha, C.: Trihalomethane formation in chlorinated drinking water: a kinetic model. Water Res. **25**(7), 797–805 (1991)
2. Ahn, J.C., Lee, S.W., Choi, K.Y., Koo, J.Y.: Application of EPANET for the determination of chlorine dose and prediction of THMs in a water distribution system. Sustain. Environ. Res. **22**(1), 31–38 (2012)
3. Alperovits, E., Shamir, U.: Design of optimal water distribution systems. Water Resour. Res. **13**(6), 885–900 (1977)
4. Amy, G.L., Chadik, P.A., Chowdhury, Z.K.: Developing models for predicting trihalomethane formation potential and kinetics. J. Am. Water Works Assoc. **79**(7), 89–97 (1987)
5. Arevalo, J.M.: Modeling free chlorine and chloramine decay in a pilot distribution system. ProQuest (2007)
6. Brown, D.: The management of Trihalomethanes in water supply systems preferred access arrangement. Ph.D. thesis, University of Birmingham (2009)
7. Chowdhury, S., Champagne, P., McLellan, P.J.: Models for predicting disinfection byproduct (DBP) formation in drinking waters: a chronological review. Sci. Total Environ. **407**(14), 4189–4206 (2009)
8. Clark, R.M., Sivaganesan, M.: Predicting chlorine residuals and formation of TTHMs in drinking water. J. Environ. Eng. **124**(12), 1203–1210 (1998)
9. Di Cristo, C., Esposito, G., Leopardi, A.: Modelling trihalomethanes formation in water supply systems. Environ. Technol. **34**(1), 61–70 (2013)
10. Elshorbagy, W.: Kinetics of THM species in finished drinking water. J. Water Resour. Plan. Manage. **126**(1), 21–28 (2000)
11. European Union. European Commission. Directorate-General for the Environment: Water is for Life: How the Water Framework Directive Helps Safeguard Europe's Resources. Publications Office of the European Union (2010)
12. Geldreich, E.E.: Microbial Quality of Water Supply in Distribution Systems. CRC Press, Boca Raton (1996)
13. Harrington, G.W., Chowdhury, Z.K., Owen, D.M.: Developing a computer model to simulate DBP formation during water treatment. J. Am. Water Works Assoc. **84**(11), 78–87 (1992)

14. Hsu, C.H., Jeng, W.L., Chang, R.M., Chien, L.C., Han, B.C.: Estimation of potential lifetime cancer risks for trihalomethanes from consuming chlorinated drinking water in Taiwan. Environ. Res. **85**(2), 77–82 (2001)
15. Hua, G., Yeats, S.: Control of trihalomethanes in wastewater treatment. Fla. Water Resour. J. **4**, 6–12 (2010)
16. Jesperson, K.: Safe drinking water act reauthorized. National Drinking Water Clearinghouse (1996)
17. Kavanaugh, M.C., Trussell, A.R., Cromer, J., Trussell, R.R.: An empirical kinetic model of trihalomethane formation: applications to meet the proposed THM standard. J. Am. Water Works Assoc. **72**(10), 578–582 (1980)
18. McDonnell, B.E.: Controlling disinfection by-products within a distribution system by implementing bubble aeration within storage tanks. Ph.D. thesis, University of Cincinnati (2012)
19. Nikolaou, A.D., Golfinopoulos, S.K., Arhonditsis, G.B., Kolovoyiannis, V., Lekkas, T.D.: Modeling the formation of chlorination by-products in river waters with different quality. Chemosphere **55**(3), 409–420 (2004)
20. Omar, N.A.J.: The Effects of Pipe Material and Age on the Formation of Disinfection By–Products (DBP) In Nablus Water Network. Ph.D. thesis, National University (2010)
21. Polycarpou, M.M., Uber, J.G., Wang, Z., Shang, F., Brdys, M.: Feedback control of water quality. IEEE Control Syst. **22**(3), 68–87 (2002)
22. Richardson, S.D., Postigo, C.: Drinking water disinfection by-products. In: Emerging Organic Contaminants and Human Health, pp. 93–137. Springer (2012)
23. Rook, J.J.: Formation of haloforms during chlorination of natural waters. Water Treat. Exam. **23**, 234–243 (1974)
24. Rossman, L.A.: Epanet 2: users manual. US Environmental Protection Agency, Cincinnati, OH, USA (2000)
25. Sadiq, R., Rodriguez, M.J.: Disinfection by-products (DBPs) in drinking water and predictive models for their occurrence: a review. Sci. Total Environ. **321**(1), 21–46 (2004)
26. Shang, F., Uber, J.G., Rossman, L.: Epanet multi-species extension users manual. National Risk Management Research Laboratory, Office of Research and Development, US Enviromental Protection Agency, Cincinnati, OH 45268 (2007)
27. Speight, V.: Probabilistic Modeling Framework for Assessing Water Quality Sampling Programs. Water Research Foundation (2009)
28. Valenti, C.C.: Modeling Disinfection By-product Formation in Distribution Systems and Consecutive Systems by Hold Studies and Bench Studies with an Investigation of Alternative Disinfection Practices. ProQuest (2008)

Gaussian-Process-Based Demand Forecasting for Predictive Control of Drinking Water Networks

Ye Wang$^{(\boxtimes)}$, Carlos Ocampo-Martínez, Vicenç Puig, and Joseba Quevedo

Automatic Control Department, Technical University of Catalonia,
Rambla Sant Nebridi, 10, 08222 Terrassa, Spain
{ywang,cocampo,vpuig}@iri.upc.edu, joseba.quevedo@upc.edu

Abstract. This paper focuses on water demand forecasting for predictive control of Drinking Water Networks (DWN) in the short term by using Gaussian Process (GP). For the predictive control strategy, system states in a finite horizon are generated by a DWN model and demands are regarded as system disturbances. The goal is to provide a demand estimation within a given confidence interval. For the sake of obtaining a desired forecasting performance, the forecasting process is carried out in two parts: the expected part is forecasted by Double-Seasonal Holt-Winters (DSHW) method and the stochastic part is forecasted by GP method. The mean value of water demand is firstly estimated by DSHW while GP provides estimations within a confidence interval. GP is applied with random inputs to propagate uncertainty at each step. Results of the application of the proposed approach to a real case study based on the Barcelona DWN have shown that the general goal has been successfully reached.

Keywords: Gaussian process · Water demand forecasting · Drinking Water Networks · Double-Seasonal Holt-Winters · Predictive control

1 Introduction

Water demand forecasting has been discussed and explored in the past decades for long-term and short-term forecasts. Short-term demand forecasting plays a significant role in the optimal operational control of Drinking Water Networks (DWN). To manage DWN, which are complex and large-scale systems, obtaining an accurate model of water demand is of great significance. In the model predictive control (MPC) strategy for DWN, water demands can be regarded as disturbances, being necessary to obtain the water demand evolution over a given prediction horizon.

As electricity demand forecasting, water demand forecasting is strongly influenced by meteorological factors, such as temperature and humidity. Even though other factors related to water demand evolution can be considered, it is still difficult to forecast water demand taking into account meteorological factors

© Springer International Publishing Switzerland 2016
C.G. Panayiotou et al. (Eds.): CRITIS 2014, LNCS 8985, pp. 69–80, 2016.
DOI: 10.1007/978-3-319-31664-2_8

depending on time as well. In other words, if the temperature is chosen as a factor for forecasting water demands, the forthcoming information is probably from weather forecast. As a result, the other factors are not always available and water demand is usually characterized as a time series model.

Gaussian Process (GP) regression model has been treated as the state-of-the-art regression methodology and applied in many different real cases such as electricity forecasting [9,16] and disturbance forecasting in greenhouse temperature control system [13], among other fields. There are some other methodologies for electricity forecasting that have been discussed in the past decades, such as artificial neural networks [5,8]. These algorithms have also been employed for the water demand forecasting [1,11]. The superiority of GP regression comes from the use of the Bayesian Inference theory, which is able to update parameters of GP model in real time. In a GP model, it is assumed that the regression variables have a multivariate Gaussian distribution.

The idea of combining MPC and GP was proposed by [10]. It is suggested that GP could be an approach to model and forecast system disturbances and then being used to implement to MPC for a real system. The main difficulty of only applying GP to forecast system disturbances is that multiple-step ahead forecasts are required. At each step, some previous values will be used as testing inputs of GP regression model in order to obtain the estimation but probably some inputs are unknown at current time. If unknown values are replaced by estimates from GP at previous steps, the next estimation would be more inaccurate. Hence, modelling demand is divided into two parts: expected and stochastic parts.

Exponential smoothing methods are originally used to manipulate financial market and economic data and then widely applied to time series data [3,7]. Together with complementary components of level, trend and seasonality, a short-term forecasting can be performed. Double-Seasonal Holt-Winters (DSHW) is an extended exponential smoothing method with two seasonalities. It is suitable for forecasting water demand with daily and weekly period at hourly time scale. Unlike GP regression, DSHW for multiple-step ahead forecasts is only based on the last known value that is regarded as the initial value.

Leading to a combined forecasting method, a quite proper mean estimation for expected water demand is forecasted by using DSHW. The stochastic water demand is found by subtracting expected water demands. The random inputs with a Gaussian distribution are considered as the testing inputs for GP [14]. The uncertainty propagation is carried out during multiple-step forecasts as well.

The main contribution of this paper consists in proposing a new algorithm denoted *DSHW-GP* to forecast short-term water demand for the purpose of incorporating it into an MPC-based closed-loop control topology. The advantage of this approach is to make use of accurate forecasting by DSHW as the expected part to avoid the drawback of GP for multiple-step ahead. After applying this approach, the forecasting uncertainty evolution of demand over the MPC prediction horizon will be used for propagating uncertainty of system states. Going even further, a robust MPC controller can be designed to deal with uncertainty propagation of system states being alternative to the one proposed in [18].

The reminder of this paper is structured as follows. In Sect. 2, the proposed approach including detailed equations of DSHW and GP for regression and the DSHW-GP algorithm are presented. In Sect. 3, a real case study based on the Barcelona DWN is used for testing the proposed methodology in this paper and simulation results are also shown. Finally, main conclusions are drawn in Sect. 4.

2 Proposed Approach

2.1 MPC Framework and DWN Control-Oriented Model

Figure 1 shows the general MPC closed-loop scheme for DWN. In the labelled *Real scene* block, measurement sensors in the DWN are often influenced by disturbances. Current system states are estimated by the observer that depends on measurements obtained from the system sensors. In the *MPC configuration* block, a DWN model including system disturbances is required, which will be used to predict both the system states and outputs over a given time horizon. The general MPC controller design for DWN can be found in [12].

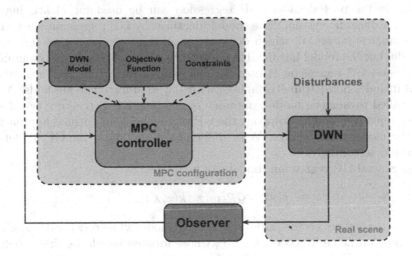

Fig. 1. Model Predictive Control (MPC) scheme for DWN

The control-oriented model for DWN considered in this paper is described by the following set of linear discrete difference-algebraic equations for all time instant $k \in \mathbb{N}$ [6]:

$$\mathbf{x}_{k+1} = \mathbf{A}\mathbf{x}_k + \mathbf{B}\mathbf{u}_k + \mathbf{B}_d\mathbf{d}_k, \tag{1a}$$

$$0 = \mathbf{E}_u\mathbf{u}_k + \mathbf{E}_d\mathbf{d}_k, \tag{1b}$$

where $\mathbf{x}_k, \mathbf{u}_k, \mathbf{d}_k$ denote the state vector, the manipulated flows through actuators and the demanded flow as additive measured disturbances, respectively.

Moreover, (1a) describes the dynamics of storage tanks and (1b) presents the static relations within the DWN at network nodes.

Assumption 1. *The water demands over the MPC prediction horizon H_p from the current time k are decomposed as*

$$\hat{\mathbf{d}}_{k+i} = \bar{\mathbf{d}}_{k+i} + \varSigma_{\mathbf{d}_{k+i}} \quad i = 1, 2, \ldots, H_p, \tag{2}$$

where $\bar{\mathbf{d}}_{k+i}$ is the vector of expected water demand, and $\varSigma_{\mathbf{d}_{k+i}}$ is the vector of probabilistic independent uncertainty forecasting, i.e., stochastic demand.

As aforementioned, the expected demand $\bar{\mathbf{d}}_{k+i}$ could be forecasted by using DSHW, and the stochastic demand $\varSigma_{\mathbf{d}_{k+i}}$ could be forecasted by using GP. Moreover, the GP could also generate a confidence interval considering the demand forecasting errors.

2.2   GP Regression with Uncertainty Propagation

GP is regarded as a supervised learning algorithm widely used for different domains in the past decades. GP regression can be used for identifying the model of a dynamic system. The model identified by GP regression is so called *non-parametric model* [4], which does not mean there are no parameters inside the model but the model has flexible parameters that can be adapted from input data. Hence, GP regression is used for the state-of-the-art regression methods [4] and includes non-parametric model with Bayesian inference methods. As for the so-called parametric model, parameters impose a fixed structure or value in advance upon the model. However, the GP regression is an optimal approach to make the model more flexible. With different training data, the GP model can be adapted accordingly.

The general GP regression model can be defined as

$$f(\mathbf{z}) \sim \mathcal{GP}(m(\mathbf{z}), k(\mathbf{z}, \mathbf{z}')), \tag{3}$$

where $\mathbf{z}$ is the feature vector (inputs) of the GP model while $m(\mathbf{z})$ and $k(\mathbf{z}, \mathbf{z}')$ are mean and covariance functions for GP, whose formats should be firstly defined with some certain parameters called *hyperparameters*. These hyperparameters can be selected by using Bayesian Inference methods with training data. Usually, GP is used for modelling and forecasting a set of random variables [15]. The mean function is usually null. Then, the GP model is rewritten in the following form:

$$f(\mathbf{z}) \sim \mathcal{GP}(\mathbf{0}, k(\mathbf{z}, \mathbf{z}')). \tag{4}$$

The forecasts of GP can be performed with noises, i.e., $y = f(\mathbf{z}) + \epsilon$. It is assumed that the noise ϵ obeys a Gaussian distribution $\epsilon \sim \mathcal{N}(0, \sigma_n^2)$. The joint distribution of the observation outputs y and the testing outputs $\mathbf{f}_*$ is defined as

$$\begin{bmatrix} y \\ \mathbf{f}_* \end{bmatrix} \sim \mathcal{N} \left(\mathbf{0}, \begin{bmatrix} K(\mathbf{z}, \mathbf{z}) + \sigma_n^2 I & K(\mathbf{z}, \mathbf{z}_*) \\ K(\mathbf{z}_*, \mathbf{z}) & K(\mathbf{z}_*, \mathbf{z}_*) \end{bmatrix} \right), \tag{5}$$

where $\mathbf{z}_*$ is a set of testing inputs and I denotes the identity matrix of suitable dimensions. Moreover, $K(\mathbf{z}, \mathbf{z})$, $K(\mathbf{z}, \mathbf{z}_*)$, $K(\mathbf{z}_*, \mathbf{z})$ and $K(\mathbf{z}_*, \mathbf{z}_*)$ are covariance matrices. The detailed definitions of covariance matrices can be found in [16].

Deriving the conditional distribution, it is possible to arrive at the key forecasting expression for the GP regression as

$$\mathbf{f}_* \mid \mathbf{z}, \mathbf{y}, \mathbf{z}_* \sim \mathcal{N}\left(m(\mathbf{f}_*), k(\mathbf{f}_*)\right), \tag{6}$$

where $m(\mathbf{f}_*)$ and $k(\mathbf{f}_*)$ are posterior mean and covariance functions, respectively, which are given as

$$m(\mathbf{f}_*) \triangleq K(\mathbf{z}_*, \mathbf{z})[K(\mathbf{z}, \mathbf{z}) + \sigma_n^2 I]^{-1} \mathbf{y}, \tag{7a}$$

$$k(\mathbf{f}_*) \triangleq K(\mathbf{z}_*, \mathbf{z}_*) - K(\mathbf{z}_*, \mathbf{z})[K(\mathbf{z}, \mathbf{z}) + \sigma_n^2 I]^{-1} K(\mathbf{z}, \mathbf{z}_*). \tag{7b}$$

For selecting the feature vector, the candidate feature variables come from previous target variables in a time series model. For the time series data, previous N data $(d(k-1), \ldots, d(k-N))$ from current time k are chosen as the feature vector.

For multiple-step ahead forecasts, the difficulty of applying the aforementioned method is that the previous real demand is unknown at each step ahead. One solution is provided by using a random inputs as feature vector that obeys a Gaussian distribution [14]. In this way, uncertainty could be propagated during the process of multiple-step ahead forecasts. The testing inputs are $\mathbf{z}_* \sim \mathcal{N}(\mu_{\mathbf{z}_*}, \Sigma_{\mathbf{z}_*})$, whose definitions can be found in [14]. Performing a Taylor expansion around $\mathbf{z}_*$ in (7a) and (7b), the final forecasts are shown as

$$m(\mu_{\mathbf{z}_*}, \Sigma_{\mathbf{z}_*}) = m(\mathbf{f}_*), \tag{8a}$$

$$k(\mu_{\mathbf{z}_*}, \Sigma_{\mathbf{z}_*}) = k(\mathbf{f}_*) + \frac{1}{2}\mathbf{Tr}\left\{ \left. \frac{\partial^2 k(\mathbf{z}_*)}{\partial \mathbf{z}_* \partial \mathbf{z}_*^T} \right|_{\mathbf{z}_* = \mu_{\mathbf{z}_*}} \Sigma_{\mathbf{z}_*} \right\}$$

$$+ \left. \frac{\partial m(\mathbf{z}_*)}{\partial \mathbf{z}_*}^T \right|_{\mathbf{z}_* = \mu_{\mathbf{z}_*}} \Sigma_{\mathbf{z}_*} \left. \frac{\partial m(\mathbf{z}_*)}{\partial \mathbf{z}_*} \right|_{\mathbf{z}_* = \mu_{\mathbf{z}_*}}, \tag{8b}$$

where $\mathbf{Tr}$ denotes the trace operator. Moreover, the first and second order derivatives are computed as

$$\left. \frac{\partial m(\mathbf{z}_*)}{\partial \mathbf{z}_{*d}} \right|_{\mathbf{z}_* = \mu_{\mathbf{z}_*}} = \left[-\frac{1}{2l^2}(\mathbf{z}_d - \mu_{\mathbf{z}_{*d}}) K(\mu_{\mathbf{z}_*}, \mathbf{z}) \right]^T K^{-1}(\mathbf{z}, \mathbf{z}) \mathbf{y}, \tag{9a}$$

$$\left. \frac{\partial^2 k(\mathbf{z}_*)}{\partial \mathbf{z}_{*d} \partial \mathbf{z}_{*e}^T} \right|_{\mathbf{z}_* = \mu_{\mathbf{z}_*}} = -2\left(-\frac{1}{2l^2}\right)^2 \left\{ M(\mathbf{z}_{*d})^T K^{-1}(\mathbf{z}, \mathbf{z}) M(\mathbf{z}_{*e}) \right.$$

$$\left. + [(\mathbf{z}_d - \mu_{\mathbf{z}_{*d}})(\mathbf{z}_e - \mu_{\mathbf{z}_{*e}}) K(\mu_{\mathbf{z}_*}, \mathbf{z})]^T K^{-1}(\mathbf{z}, \mathbf{z}) K(\mu_{\mathbf{z}_*}, \mathbf{z}) \right\}$$

$$+ 2\left(-\frac{1}{2l^2}\right) K(\mu_{\mathbf{z}_*}, \mathbf{z})^T K^{-1}(\mathbf{z}, \mathbf{z}) K(\mu_{\mathbf{z}_*}, \mathbf{z}) \delta_{de}, \tag{9b}$$

$$M(\mathbf{z}_{*i}) = (\mathbf{z}_i - \mu_{\mathbf{z}_{*i}}) K(\mu_{\mathbf{z}_*}, \mathbf{z}), \tag{9c}$$

where l is a parameter of covariance function and $\mathbf{z}_d \in \mathbb{R}^d$ and $\mathbf{z}_e \in \mathbb{R}^e$ are different column vectors of input data. Further detailed calculations can be found in [14].

2.3   Double-Seasonal Holt-Winters

The exponential smoothing method was firstly introduced by R. G. Brown in 1956 and later improved by C. C. Holt and P. R. Winters with trend and seasonal components, which is called *Holt-Winters* (HW) method. This method is usually applied to time series data in order to generate short-term forecasts [3].

Simple exponential smoothing did not consider the time series data with tendency and periodicity. HW method contains these two features but only with one period in an additive or multiplicative way. Afterwards, it is extended the single period to double multiplicative seasonality [17]. This method is the so-called *Double-Seasonal Holt-Winters* (DSHW).

Some comparisons with several exponential smoothing methods have been discussed in [2] and it is concluded that DSHW method can provide forecasting results with more robustness and accuracy.

The DSHW model for water demand is built as follows:

$$\hat{d}(k + j|k) = (L(k) + jT(k))S_1\left(k + j - \left[\frac{j}{s_1}\right]s_1\right)S_2\left(k + j - \left[\frac{j}{s_2}\right]s_2\right), \quad (10)$$

where $L(k), T(k), S_1(k), S_2(k)$ denote *level, trend* and *two seasonalities*, respectively: $S_1(k)$ is the first season s_1 while $S_2(k)$ is the second season s_2 and j is the forecasting index within a given horizon. To compute these components, the following expressions are used:

$$L(k) = \alpha\frac{d(k)}{S_1(k - s_1)S_2(k - s_2)} + (1 - \alpha)(L(k - 1) + T(k - 1)), \quad (11\text{a})$$

$$T(k) = \gamma(L(k) - L(k - 1)) + (1 - \gamma)T(k - 1), \quad (11\text{b})$$

$$S_1(k) = \delta_1\frac{d(k)}{L(k)S_2(k - s_2)} + (1 - \delta_1)S_1(k - s_1), \quad (11\text{c})$$

$$S_2(k) = \delta_2\frac{d(k)}{L(k)S_1(k - s_1)} + (1 - \delta_2)S_2(k - s_2), \quad (11\text{d})$$

where $\alpha, \gamma, \delta_1, \delta_2$ are smoothing parameters that can be obtained by using least-squared methods with given training data. In principle, a collection of training dataset in two suitable periods should be achieved at initial forecasting time k_{ini}.

2.4   DSHW-GP Approach

In this paper, the proposed DSHW-GP approach is shown in Algorithm 1. Since both of DSHW and GP forecasting models need to be trained before forecasting, it is assumed that a collection of past data is available. Meanwhile, the DSHW loop can be run with past data in a certain time in order to obtain the training data for GP loop. In this approach, the effectiveness and efficiency are both considered. Assuming the periodicity of the water demand with period Δ_p, due to the accuracy of the DSHW method, the calculation process can be reduced to be executed each $2\Delta_p$, which will be partially chosen as estimations of expected water demand with the horizon of Δ_p. Hence, H_p is considered equal to Δ_p in this case.

Algorithm 1. DSHW-GP Algorithm

1: $n \leftarrow$ Simulation Days
2: $k \leftarrow$ Current hour
3: **for** $i \leftarrow 1 : n$ **do**
4:      $tdd \leftarrow$ Get past a set of real demands   ▷ DSHW Loop
5:      Training DSHW by tdd with two periods (s_1, s_2)
6:      $dm \leftarrow dshw(k, 2\Delta_p)$: $2\Delta_p$-step ahead at time k
7:      **for** $j \leftarrow 1 : \Delta_p$ **do**   ▷ GP Loop
8:          $dmp \leftarrow$ Past a set of estimations of DSHW
9:          $dsto \leftarrow d_{total}$ - dmp
10:         Training GP model with $dsto$
11:         $mean, cov, lb, ub \leftarrow GP(k+j, \Delta_p)$ ▷ Prediction by GP with random inputs
12:         $\mathbf{d}(i,j) \leftarrow dm(j : j + \Delta_p - 1) + mean$
13:         $\Sigma_{\mathbf{d}(i,j)} \leftarrow cov$
14:         $\mathbf{dlb}(i,j) \leftarrow lb$
15:         $\mathbf{dub}(i,j) \leftarrow ub$
16:     **end for**
17:     $k \leftarrow k + \Delta_p$
18: **end for**

Remark. For daily forecasts, DSHW loop is only executed at the first hour of a day with training data. The forecasting results include $2\Delta_p$ demand estimations that will be regarded as the expected demand of hourly forecasts. The procedure is as follows: at time k, expected estimations are selected from $k + 1$ to $k + \Delta_p$. At time $k + 1$, expected estimations are selected from $k + 2$ to $k + \Delta_p + 1$. Until time $k + \Delta_p$, expected estimations are selected from $k + \Delta_p + 1$ to $k + 2\Delta_p$. The DSHW loop is executed daily while the GP loop is executed hourly. The total estimation contains two parts coming from selected DSHW and GP loops, respectively. The total mean estimation is the sum of results from DSHW and GP. Upper and lower forecasting bounds are produced by GP.

3 Case Study: Barcelona Drinking Water Network

3.1 Case-Study Description

The proposed approach is applied to the case study of Barcelona DWN. The Barcelona DWN supplies 237.7 hm^3 water to approximately 3 million consumers every year, covering a 424 km^2 area. The entire network is composed of 63 storage tanks, 3 surface sources, 7 underground sources, 79 pumps, 50 valves, 18 nodes and 88 water demands. The topology of Barcelona DWN is described in

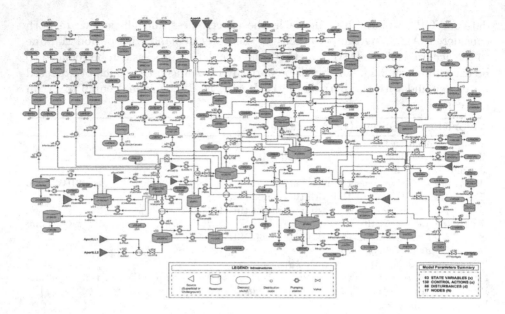

Fig. 2. Barcelona DWN topology

Fig. 2. Currently, AGBAR[1] is in charge of managing the entire network through a supervisory control system with sampling period of one hour. It is necessary to forecast the water demands of the whole network within an MPC strategy with a prediction horizon of 24 h. The improved forecasts of water demands could lead to obtain huge economic benefits. The quality of gathered real data has much influence on demand forecasting results due to unexpected noise from sensors. After comparing and selecting different sets of real data, the real water demand data of *C10COR* during the year 2013 will be used to illustrate the proposed approach. Similar results can be obtained in case of other water demands of the case study.

3.2   Results

Looking into the dataset of real water demands available, there are approximately one year's data available. From this set of data, the daily and weekly periods can be clearly observed. For the simulation in this paper, one month and half data set is divided into the testing data set and the remaining data set is used for the validation. The simulation is running for a scenario of two days (48 h). Comparing the forecasts and real values of water demands, the error measurements are calculated by using the key performance indicators (KPIs) defined as

---

[1] AGBAR: Aguas de Barcelona, S. A. Company which manages the drinking water transport and distribution in Barcelona (Spain).

Mean Squared Error (MSE):

$$MSE = \frac{1}{n} \sum_{t=1}^{n} (R_t - P_t)^2, \tag{12}$$

Mean Absolute Error (MAE):

$$MAE = \frac{1}{n} \sum_{t=1}^{n} | R_t - P_t |, \tag{13}$$

Symmetric Mean Absolute Percentage Error (SMAPE):

$$SMAPE = \frac{100}{n} \sum_{t=1}^{n} \frac{| R_t - P_t |}{R_t + P_t}, \tag{14}$$

where R_t denotes real value of the drinking water demand from validation data and P_t denotes the forecasting mean value of the water demand obtained by the DSHW-GP algorithm. In terms of MSE and MAE, they are representing the difference between the actual observation and the observation values forecasted by the model. Moreover, SMAPE is an accurate measurement based on percentage errors, which are adapted to compute time-series data. In this case study, $\Delta_p = 24\,\mathrm{h}$.

According to hourly-scale forecasts repeated 48 times, KPIs are shown in the Fig. 3. Plots of MSE and MAE show that they are varying in a small interval (no more than 1). SMAPE belongs to the range between 0 % and 100 %. If the practical value of SMAPE is near 0 %, the forecasting results are quite accurate. In this case, the general SMAPE is between 6 % and 9 % (never greater than 10 %).

The forecasting result for each step ahead is a Gaussian distribution. The confidence interval (CI) can be obtained as follows.

$$\mathbf{d}_k \in \left[\bar{\mathbf{d}}_k - \frac{c}{\sqrt{P}} \Sigma_{d_k}^{1/2}, \bar{\mathbf{d}}_k + \frac{c}{\sqrt{P}} \Sigma_{d_k}^{1/2} \right], \tag{15}$$

where P is the number of samples, which is equal to 1 in terms of one-step ahead forecast. Moreover, c denotes the critical value with respect to a confidence level, such as 95 % or 98 %. The calculation of this level is done by means of the inverse standard probability density function, which is shown as

$$c = \Phi^{-1} \left(1 - \frac{\alpha}{2} \right), \tag{16}$$

where c is the critical value with respect to the confidence level $\left(1 - \frac{\alpha}{2} \right)$.

In many applications of GP, confidence level is chosen between 90 % and 100 % since a large number could imply that some unexpected noises gathered by using different sensors stay inside the confidence interval. Hence, the critical values are

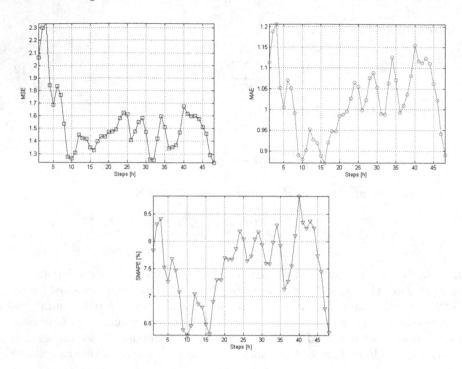

Fig. 3. Error measurements: MSE, MAE and SMAPE

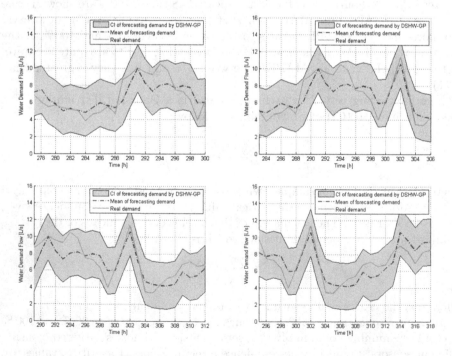

Fig. 4. A sequence of simulation results

around 2 when the confidence levels are chosen inside the aforementioned interval. Figure 4 shows a sequence of selected simulation results in 48-step forecasts. The gray area denotes the confidence interval with critical value equal to 2.

The real demand is approximately around the mean estimation in Fig. 4. Sometimes the mean estimation does not perfectly match the real demand since the latter probably contains some unexpected noisy measurements from sensors. In terms of GP, the challenge is how to select a proper feature vector for a real case and get the accurate testing inputs. In this case study, the goal of this work has been properly reached and the real water demands are inside the confidence interval.

4 Conclusions

In this paper, the DSHW-GP algorithm has been proposed and applied to the water demand forecasting for DWN management. DSHW and GP have their own strengths and drawbacks. The approach of DSHW-GP takes advantages of two methods while avoids drawbacks of both of them. The DSHW is used for modelling expected part of water demand while GP is used for modelling stochastic part of water demand. This approach is tested in the Barcelona DWN. Results show that it is useful for forecasting water demand in a short term achieving a confidence interval at the same time. The forecasting results can be applied to robust MPC to consider for the possible worst-case demand scenario.

Further work is focused on applying this approach to an MPC-based closed-loop scheme. The mean and bounds of demand forecasting obtained by using the DSHW-GP algorithm will be used to compute estimates of system states in order to design a robust MPC controller. Besides, the demand forecasting method can be used for guaranteeing a reliable supply in the water networks by means of avoiding unexpected uncertainties in a short-term future.

Acknowledgments. This work is partially supported by the research projects CICYT SHERECS DPI-2011-26243 and ECOCIS DPI-2013-48243-C2-1-R, both of the Spanish Ministry of Education, by EFFINET grant FP7-ICT-2012-318556 of the European Commission and by AGAUR Doctorat Industrial 2013-DI-041. Ye Wang also thanks China Scholarship Council for providing postgraduate scholarship.

References

1. Bakker, M., Vreeburg, J.H.G., van Schagen, K.M., Rietveld, L.C.: A fully adaptive forecasting model for short-term drinking water demand. Environ. Model. Softw. **48**(0), 141–151 (2013)
2. Blanch, J., Quevedo, J., Saludes, J., Puig, V.: Short-term demand forecasting for operational control of thebarcelona water transport network. In: Conferencia Nacional de Jóvenes Profesionales del Agua deEspaña, pp. 1–10. Barcelona (2010)
3. Christiaanse, W.R.: Short-term load forecasting using general exponential smoothing. IEEE Trans. Power Apparatus Syst. **90**(2), 900–911 (1971)

4. Deisenroth, M.P.: Efficient reinforcement learning using Gaussian processes. Ph.D. thesis, Karlsruhe Institute of Technology (2010)
5. Fung, Y., Rao Tummala, V.: Forecasting of electricity consumption: a comparative analysis ofregression and artificial neural network models. In: 2nd International Conference on Advances in Power SystemControl, Operation and Management, vol. 2, pp. 782–787 (1993)
6. Grosso, J.M., Ocampo-Martínez, C., Puig, V., Joseph, B.: Chance-constrained model predictive control for drinking water networks. J. Process Control **24**(5), 504–516 (2014)
7. Harrison, P.J.: Exponential smoothing and short-term sales forecasting. Manage. Sci. **13**(11), 821–842 (1967)
8. Hayati, M., Shirvany, Y.: Artificial neural network approach for short term load forecasting for illam region. World Acad. Sci. Eng. Technol. **22**, 280–284 (2007)
9. Lourenco, J.M., Santos, P.J.: Short-term load forecasting using a gaussian process model: the influence of a derivative term in the input regressor. Intell. Decis. Technol. **6**(4), 273–281 (2012)
10. Maciejowski, J.M., Yang, X.: Fault tolerant control using gaussian processes and model predictivecontrol. In: 2013 Conference on Control and Fault-Tolerant Systems (SysTol), pp. 1–12. Nice (2013)
11. Msiza, I.S., Nelwamondo, F.V., Marwala, T.: Water demand prediction using artificial neural networks and support vector regression. Digital Intell. **3**(11), 1–8 (2008)
12. Ocampo-Martínez, C., Puig, V., Cembrano, G., Quevedo, J.: Application of MPC strategies to the management of complex networks of the urban water cycle. IEEE Control Syst. Mag. **33**(1), 15–41 (2013)
13. Pawlowski, A., Guzman, J.L., Rodriguez, F., Berenguel, M., Normey-Rico, J.E.: Predictive control with disturbance forecasting for greenhousediurnal temperature control. In: The 18th IFAC World Congress, pp. 1779–1784. Milano (2011)
14. Quinonero-Candela, J., Girard, A., Rasmussen, C.E.: Prediction at an uncertain input for gaussian processes and relevancevector machines application to multiple-step ahead time-series forecasting. Technical report, University of Glasgow, Department of ComputingScience (2002)
15. Rasmussen, C.E., Williams, C.K.I.: Gaussian Processes for Machine Learning. ISBN 026218253X. the MIT Press, Massachusetts Institute of Technology (2006)
16. Samarasinghe, M., Al-Hawani, W.: Short-term forecasting of electricity consumption using gaussian processes. Master's thesis, University of Agder (2012)
17. Taylor, J.W.: Short-term electricity demand forecasting using double seasonalexponential smoothing. J. Oper. Res. Soc. **54**(8), 799–805 (2003)
18. Wang, Y.: Model predictive control for drinking water networks based on gaussian processes. Master's thesis, Technical University of Catalonia (2014)

Graph-Based Hydraulic Vulnerability Assessment of Water Distribution Networks

Michalis Fragiadakis, Savvas Xanthos, Demetrios G. Eliades,
Anastasis Gagatsis, and Symeon E. Christodoulou[✉]

University of Cyprus, 1 Panepistimiou Ave., P.O.Box 20537, 1678 Nicosia, Cyprus
mfrag@mail.ntua.gr,
{xanthos.savvas,eliades.demetrios,schristo}@ucy.ac.cy,
anastasis.gagatsis@gmail.com
http://www.ucy.ac.cy

Abstract. Presented herein is a methodology for the seismic and hydraulic assessment of the reliability of water distribution networks (WDN) based on general seismic assessment standards, as per the American Lifelines Alliance (ALA) guidelines, localized historical records of critical risk-of-failure metrics, and hydraulic simulations using adapted EPANET models. The proposed reliability assessment incorporates data of past non-seismic damage, the vulnerabilities of the network components against seismic loading, hydraulic modeling, and the topology of a WDN. The network reliability is assessed using Graph Theory and Monte Carlo simulation (MCS), coupled with a hydraulic analysis.

Keywords: Vulnerability · Water Distribution Networks · Hydraulic modeling

1 Introduction

Lifeline systems, such as water distribution networks, are of critical importance to the uninterrupted provision of services and thus to the resiliency of a city, where 'resilience' refers to a system's capacity to quickly and effectively recover from a catastrophic event.

A number of previous studies have assessed the vulnerability of WDN, but seldom have the non-seismic, the hydraulic performance and the system-component interactions been considered in evaluating the seismic vulnerability of such systems. This paper combines data on historical non-seismic performance of WDN and their components by use of survival analysis, simulation and a graph-based shortest-path algorithm to holistically evaluate network vulnerability. The intent is, firstly, to propose a methodology for assessing the vulnerability of a WDN using available everyday measurements and, secondly, to extent the methodology of the ALA guidelines [1] with localized knowledge on the performance and vulnerability of such networks under normal operating conditions.

© Springer International Publishing Switzerland 2016
C.G. Panayiotou et al. (Eds.): CRITIS 2014, LNCS 8985, pp. 81–87, 2016.
DOI: 10.1007/978-3-319-31664-2_9

2 Vulnerability of Water Distribution Networks

2.1 Component, Network and Hydraulic Vulnerability

Vulnerability assessment of WDN encompasses as a minimum, (1) component; (2) network (topology and connectivity) and (3) operations (hydraulic) analysis. Most of the related research work focuses on component analysis i.e. the estimation of either the probability of failure or of the time-to-failure for pipe segments. The component-based approach, though, does not provide vulnerability metrics on a node-to-node basis (topology) and it does not incorporate the hydraulic model of the network.

In terms of non-seismic assessment of WDN, most studies in literature are primarily on deterioration modeling, showing a relationship between failure rates and the time of failure (age of pipes). Recent studies introduced additional risk factors, citing the importance of the network operating conditions, of the number of previously observed breaks (NOPB) [2,3], and of the network topology [4,5]. In terms of seismic vulnerability, the ALA guidelines [1] relate it to several failure parameters, proposing empirical vulnerability functions based on the peak ground velocity (PGV) and the permanent ground deformation (PGD). The reliability procedures proposed by [1] are amended in [6,7], and localized by use of topological and historical data on a network's previous performance (such as the NOPB and the survival curves per pipe).

Hydraulic vulnerability is a more complex issue. In the simplest case, the network performance is measured by the probability that it fails to deliver water from its sources (inflow vertices) to every house connection (outflow vertices). If such, rather simplified, network performance definition is adopted, the performance of the network can be quickly evaluated using methods based on Graph Theory and MCS. Alternatively, if failure is defined with respect to hydraulic quantities, then hydraulic analysis of the network is required. Such analysis could either be conducted post a failure-event investigation on selected network configurations, or coupled directly within the WDN reliability analysis as shown in Fig. 1(a), providing hydraulic results for all iteration steps of the MCS analysis.

2.2 Proposed Strategy for Overall Vulnerability Assessment

Seismic Vulnerability. The vulnerability curves suggested in [1] are combined with available and localized survival curves, with each pipe's survival probability (as deduced by use of clustering underlying risk factors such as the NOPB, Fig. 1(b)), then used to adjust the vulnerability curves proposed by the ALA.

Consider, for example, the real-life network shown in Fig. 2(a) consisting of multiple district metered areas (DMA) and with its non-seismic performance as shown in Fig. 2(b). The region in question is mapped as a graph and a MCS, with an assumed seismic load of Mw = 7.0, is performed to produce the failure probabilities and thus the network reliability at every network node. The result is then mapped as a spatial risk plot ('heatmap') identifying the network areas of high failure risk (Fig. 3(a)). In this case the areas of concern seem to be limited

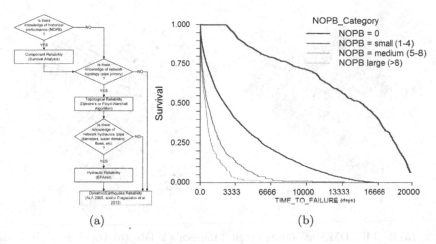

(a)   (b)

Fig. 1. (a) Proposed reliability analysis procedure. (b) Survival curves for asbestos cement (AC) pipes, as a function of the number of previous breaks (NOPB).

to three areas which, on closer inspection, are related to areas of open-ended pipe pathways (orphan nodes). The horizontal allocation of risk is actually shown to be highly sensitive to open-ended network topologies.

The situation changes drastically once the NOPB risk factor is included in the analysis (Fig. 3(b)) by use of the algorithm proposed by [6,7]. The inclusion of a network's non-seismic performance increases the pipes' risk of failure and thus alters the network reliability. The increased network vulnerability is the direct outcome of the increased pipe vulnerabilities, as impacted by their performance prior to the seismic event. The probability of failure is now highly sensitive to the condition of each network element, as manifested and influenced by their non-seismic performance over time (survival analysis), and introduced in the risk analysis by means of the proposed adjustments to [1].

Hydraulic Vulnerability. The region of choice encompasses three DMA regions, has a range of elevation from 15–65 m, a total consumer demand of approximately 10 K and an average daily consumption of 200 L/day/capita. The EPANET real-time hydraulic simulation consists of 450 junctions (nodes), 621 pipes with diameter of 100 mm and 1 reservoir with a total head of 90 m. All pipes are given a constant friction factor and the friction loss is calculated by the Hazen-Williams equation.

The use of EPANET as a hydraulic analysis tool for seismic simulation analysis poses several challenges, especially when the dynamic link library is utilized in a multiple iteration vulnerability assessment application [6,7]. No-flow sub networks often result in negative pressures at nodes where base demand is expected and hence the simulation stops. Moreover whilst the MCS is performed, pipe failure could either signify that a selected pipe (link) would be completely decommissioned from the network (closed while experiencing catastrophic failure) or

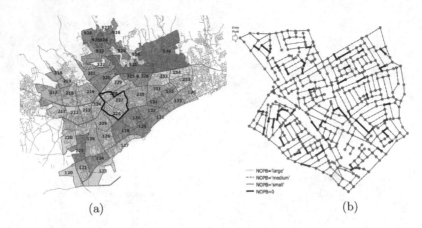

(a)   (b)

Fig. 2. (a) Real-life DMA as adapted from Limassol's WDN. (b) Topology of the DMA network considered, in a disturbed state ($NOPB \geq 0$ for every pipe).

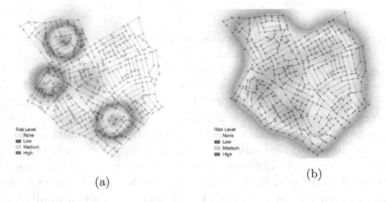

(a)   (b)

Fig. 3. Spatial analysis (heatmap) of studied network's reliability, (a) based on the ALA guidelines (seismic effects are considered, with Mw = 7.0); (b) based on survival curves and considering the effects of the NOPB risk factor.

would still be connected but experiencing water leak (pressure loss) that is not known in advance based on the type of failure the pipe experienced. In both cases, the network description file would need to be adjusted and a new network file created for each iteration point without any assurance that the adjusted file would provide converged results. Hence, the steps proposed by the reliability analysis shown in Fig. 1 were followed, with the hydraulic analysis step completed selectively on a smaller sub group of scenarios as a standalone step on converged simulation results as those illustrated in Fig. 4. Initial MCS results for the undisturbed network are shown in Fig. 5 with an elevation map of the region and flow path analysis for the boundary conditions described earlier.

As per the proposed outline of steps (Fig. 1), EPANET's dynamic link was incorporated within the existing code that performs the MCS and resulting

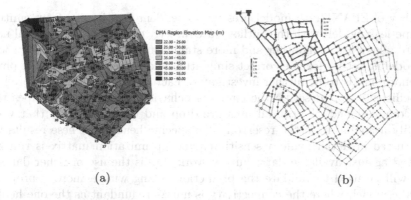

(a)   (b)

Fig. 4. Real-life DMA as adapted from Limassol's (Cyprus) WDN. (a) Elevation map of simulated region, (b) Undisturbed analysis based on EPANET and initial conditions described in Sect. 2.2. (*Elevation of each node is shown in figure (b) in meters (m)*)

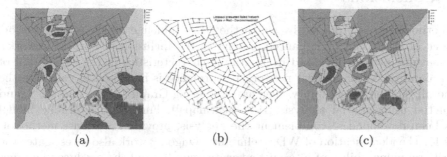

(a)   (b)   (c)

Fig. 5. (a) Total head of system (m) prediction by EPANET hydraulic simulation in Fig. 4(a); (b) MC identification of failed pipes within the network; (c) Total Head of System (m) considering the effects of the NOPB risk factor as described in Fig. 4(b) (color figure online).

heatmaps as shown in Fig. 5. At each MCS step, several pipes are given a failure condition as shown in Fig. 5(b) and the EPANET library is then called and the adjusted domain solved for all hydraulic quantities. Figure 5(a) and (c) depict the preliminary results of the system's total head for the seismic scenario described in Fig. 4. Blue contours (zero demand availability) match well with the spatial results obtained from the MCS identifying regions of high probability of failure and thus zero supply to the demand regions.

It should be noted that the simulation stability was greatly improved by the alternate representation of the demand at the nodes. If demand was assigned for each node explicitly, a separate step in the iteration loop would require the identification of nodes that were unreachable either due to the assumption that their neighboring links were decommissioned, or if the only available flow path was at a much lower elevation. The subsequent step is a rather cumbersome and also complex process with high likelihood of divergence. The built-in capability of EPANET to model pressure-dependent flow issuing from emitters (i.e. pipe-leak model) with the outflow rate directly dependent on the local node pressure allows for a smoother and more stable simulation. The overall process and modeling set-up for the correct simulation and representation of the physical scenario needs to be further investigated. Factors that could be explored are the coefficients that describe the emitters behavior, the number of pipes that are decommissioned, the overall pressure drop and the assumption that water is readily available from the reservoir at a specific head etc. These results will be discussed in detail while a sensitivity and optimization matrix is run and validated against available data. Future work entails the use of richer datasets which will be used to validate the predictions along with a more appropriate hydraulic model, where the connectivity is not as redundant as the one here in which connectivity is always assumed at each node.

3   Conclusions

A methodology is proposed by which the ALA guideline on the seismic performance of WDN can be enhanced, to enable the inclusion of both a network's non-seismic performance and its hydraulic characteristics in the calculation of its reliability. Available past network performance is first used to calculate the generalized pipe vulnerability, then assessed using Graph Theory and MCS, and depicted using spatial analysis (risk 'heatmaps'). Further, a hydraulic model has been developed to complement the analysis, providing a robust methodology for the identification of WDN reliability. Ongoing work also investigates the effects on vulnerability of intermittent water supply (and the produced hammer effects), which in turn have been the cause of an increase in leakage incidents in the network in study.

Acknowledgments. The work presented herein is part of the NIREAS-IWRC research project, which is co-funded by the European Regional Development Fund and the Republic of Cyprus through the Cyprus Research Promotion Foundation (Grant No. NEA YPODOMI/STRAT/0308/09).

References

1. American Lifelines Alliance. Seismic Guidelines for Water Pipelines. ASCE-FEMA, USA (2005)
2. Christodoulou, S.E., Deligianni, A.: A neurofuzzy decision framework for the management of water distribution networks. Water Resour. Manag. **24**(1), 139–156 (2010)
3. Christodoulou, S.E.: Water network assessment and reliability analysis by use of survival analysis. Water Resour. Manag. **25**, 1229–1238 (2011)
4. Pinto, J., Varum, H., Bentes, I., Agarwal, J.: A theory of vulnerability of water pipe network (TVWPN). Water Resour. Manag. **24**(15), 4237–4254 (2010)

5. Yannopoulos, S., Spiliotis, M.: Water distribution system reliability based on minimum cut-set approach and the hydraulic availability. Water Resour. Manag. **27**(6), 1821–1836 (2013)
6. Fragiadakis, M., Christodoulou, S., Vamvatsikos, D.: Reliability assessment of water distribution networks under seismic loads. Water Resour. Manag. **27**(10), 3739–3764 (2013)
7. Fragiadakis, M., Christodoulou, S.: Seismic reliability assessment of urban water networks. Earthq. Eng. Struct. Dyn. **43**(3), 357–374 (2013)

Sensor Data Validation and Reconstruction in Water Networks: A Methodology and Software Implementation

Diego García, Joseba Quevedo, Vicenç Puig$^{(\boxtimes)}$, and Miquel Àngel Cugueró

Intelligent/Advanced Control Systems (SIC/SAC),
Universitat Politècnica de Catalunya (UPC), Terrassa (Barcelona), Catalunya, Spain
{diego.garcia,joseba.quevedo,vicenc.puig,miquel.angel.cuguero}@upc.edu
http://sac.upc.edu

Abstract. In this paper, a data validation and reconstruction methodology that can be applied to the sensors used for real-time monitoring in water networks is presented. On the one hand, a validation approach based on quality levels is described to detect potential invalid and missing data. On the other hand, the reconstruction strategy is based on a set of temporal and spatial models used to estimate missing/invalid data with the model estimation providing the best fit. A software tool implementing the proposed data validation and reconstruction methodology is also presented. Finally, results obtained applying the proposed methodology on raw data of flow meters gathered from a real water network are also included to illustrate the performance of the proposed approach.

Keywords: Data validation · Data reconstruction · Time series

1 Introduction

Water networks are Critical Infrastructure Systems (CIS) geographically distributed and decentralized, involving a large number of sensors for real-time monitoring and efficient and safe operation of these networks.

However, in real water network operation, problems affecting the communication system between sensors and data loggers, or in the telecontrol system itself, often arise generating missing data during certain periods of time. The data recorded by these sensors are sometimes uncorrelated so data coming from healthy sensors cannot be used to replace unhealthy sensor missing data, which therefore must be replaced by a set of estimated data. Another common problem in such systems is the lack of sensor reliability (due to e.g. offset, drift or breakdowns) producing false flow data readings. These unreliable data must also be detected and replaced by estimated data, since sensor data are used for several network water management tasks, namely: planning, investment plans, maintenance operations, billing/consumer services and operational control. Furthermore, SCADA and telemetry systems generate extremely heterogeneous data.

© Springer International Publishing Switzerland 2016
C.G. Panayiotou et al. (Eds.): CRITIS 2014, LNCS 8985, pp. 88–93, 2016.
DOI: 10.1007/978-3-319-31664-2_10

A methodology to validate and reconstruct missing/invalid sensor data, previously introduced in [5], is applied here to data coming from flow meters in the Catalonia water transport network. In this paper, the main contribution is a software tool implementing this methodology that is able to properly handle raw sensor data (including storage, querying and visualization).

The structure of the paper is as follows: Sect. 2 introduces the proposed sensor validation and reconstruction methodology. Section 3 describes a software tool that implements the proposed methodology. Section 4 illustrates the application of the proposed methodology and the software tool to a real water network. Finally, Sect. 5 draws the main conclusions achieved.

2 Methodology

The methodology presented here is designed to validate and reconstruct invalid and missing sensor data. This methodology is detailed in the next sections.

2.1 Sensor Data Validation

The sensor data validation methodology is inspired in the Spanish AENOR-UNE norm 500540. The methodology applies a set of consecutive validation tests to a given dataset to finally assign a certain quality level depending on the tests passed. The six different quality levels are the following:

- Level 0: This level allows to detect data acquisition and communication errors.
- Level 1: Any sensor has an operational measurement interval. Any value above or beyond this interval is invalidated by this level.
- Level 2: The trend level takes into account the data changes over time. This allows to detect unexpected changes in the data.
- Level 3: This level allows to check the variables in a given unit, e.g. a flow meter cannot measure a non-zero value if the valve located at the same pipe is totally closed.
- Level 4: This level evaluates the sensor's measurements against an estimated data given by a time series model based on historical data [3].
- Level 5: This level checks the correlation between different neighboring sensors [4].

2.2 Sensor Data Reconstruction

Time Series Models (TSM) and Spatial Models (SM) are used to reconstruct missing and invalid data. The former are based on time series' features such as seasonality, trend and periodicity, in order to estimate future values based on hystorical behavior. Two TSMs are used in the proposed methodology/tool: an exponential smoothing Holt-Winters model and a generalized ARIMA model.

On the one hand, a spread method for time series modelling because of its simplicity and performance is the Holt-Winters (HW) approach [2,6]. There are various approaches for this method, e.g. additive or damped trend, additive or multiplicative seasonality, single or multiple seasonality. Here, good performance is achieved with the additive single seasonality approach, with estimated value for a forecasting horizon ℓ as follows

$$\hat{y}_{TS1}(k) = \bar{R}(k - \ell) + \ell\bar{G}(k - \ell) + \bar{S}(k - L) \tag{1}$$

where $\bar{R}$ is the level component, $\bar{G}$ is the trend component, $\bar{S}$ is the seasonal component and L is the season (daily here) periodicity.

On the other hand, the generalized, well known and useful ARIMA model for time series [1] is described for hourly-sampled data by the following difference equation, which describes a periodicity of one day (24 h)

$$\hat{y}_{TS2}(k) = -a_1 y(k - 1) - a_2 y(k - 2) - a_3 y(k - 3) - ... - a_{24} y(k - 24), \tag{2}$$

Alternatively, SM are linear regression models relating different spatially dependant measurements in the system, stated as follows

$$\hat{y}_s(k) = a y_f(k) + b. \tag{3}$$

where a and b are the parameters of the model to be calibrated.

Furthermore, the Mean Squared Error (MSE) is the model accuracy measure. The model with the lowest MSE over the m-estimations previous to k is the selected candidate to estimate the invalid/missing k-sample.

3   Software Implementation

The architecture of the software tool implemented is depicted in Fig. 1. There are two main components: the *Data Management Web* application and the *Validation and Reconstruction* tool[1]. The Data Management component is a web application. Thus, it allows the access to the data from everywhere. The Validation and Reconstruction component is implemented in Matlab.

3.1   Data Management Web Application

This module provides a user-friendly tool allowing to import and export data so that stored data is available to all the registered users. In order to focus the efforts on the data intrinsic values and not on how to access them, the tool provides three main services:

– Data importation from different sources (e.g. CSV, Excel, Access).
– Data exportation of a determined time period in three different formats: CSV, Excel and SAC format[2].
– Interactive data visualization.

---

[1] Both software tools are proprietary software.
[2] SAC format is a binary Mat-file containing a defined data structure.

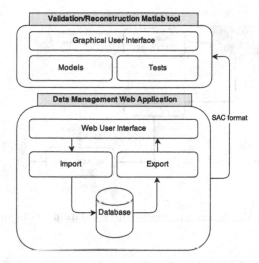

Fig. 1. Software architecture diagram.

This data management component is implemented using Django[3] web framework, providing a Web User Interface implemented in HTML and JavaScript in order to interact with the Import and Export Python modules. The Import and Export modules handle the operations of saving and querying data against the Postgresql Database server.

3.2 Validation and Reconstruction Matlab Tool

The Validation and Reconstruction methodologies (described in Sects. 2.1 and 2.2) are implemented in Matlab.

This tool applies the presented methodologies to the data in three different stages: Calibration, Validation and Reconstruction. Figure 2 shows the data flow between these stages. Calibration stage uses historic data to learn and estimate the parameters required by the tests and models described in Sects. 2.1 and 2.2. Calibration stage runs only once, in order to initialize the paramaters required by the following stages. Validation stage implements the methodology of Sect. 2.1. Finally, Reconstruction stage implements the methodology described in Sect. 2.2.

4 Results

In this section, some results obtained from the Validation and Reconstruction Matlab Tool applying the methodology described here to data coming from a real water network, are presented. The dataset is composed by hourly sampled data coming from a flow meter "A" installed in the Catalonia water transport

---

[3] Django is a free open source web framework. Its primary goal is to facilitate the creation of complex, database-driven websites.

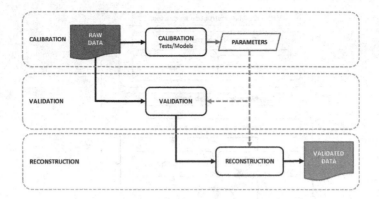

Fig. 2. Validation and reconstruction data flow diagram.

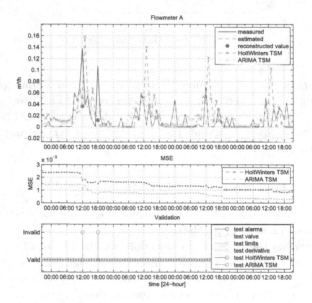

Fig. 3. Results of the validation and reconstruction methodology on the flow meter "A".

network, managed by Aigües Ter Llobregat (ATLL) company. Figure 3 shows four consecutive days of measurements gathered by the flow meter "A". As it may be seen, two peaks, at 12:00 and 18:00, in the first day that they do not fit the daily flow pattern shown in the following days. Thus, these two peaks are invalidated by the ARIMA model. Finally, these two samples are reconstructed by the model having the lowest MSE, which is also the ARIMA model.

5 Conclusions

In this paper, a data validation and reconstruction framework is introduced to overcome the sensor problems arising in CIS, such as water networks. A validation strategy based on a set of data quality tests allows to detect suspicious erroneous data. Then, a reconstruction scheme is defined using Temporal and Spatial Models to provide an estimation based on the model having best fit. In addition, a software tool is described to provide a homogeneous and accessible database by a user-friendly interface, to easily apply the methodology presented here. Finally, some results obtained using data from a real network are presented using the software described, proving the ability of the methodology to detect and reconstruct anomalous data.

Acknowledgements. This work is partially supported by CICYT SHERECS DPI-2011-26243 of the Spanish Ministry of Education, by EFFINET grant FP7-ICT-2012-318556 of the European Commission and by AGAUR Doctorat Industrial 2013-DI-041. The authors also wish to thank the support received by the company ATLL in the development of this work.

References

1. Blanch, J., Puig, V., Saludes, J., Quevedo, J.: Arima models for data consistency of flowmeters in water distribution networks. In: 7th IFAC Symposium on Fault Detection, Supervision and Safety of Technical Processes, pp. 480–485 (2009)
2. Makridakis, S., Wheelwright, S., Hyndman, R.: Forecasting methods and applications. Wiley, New York (1998)
3. Quevedo, J., Blanch, J., Puig, V., Saludes, J., Espin, S., Roquet, J.: Methodology of a data validation and reconstructions tool to improve the reliability of the water network supervision. In: International Conference of IWA Water Loss, Sao Paolo, Brazil (2010)
4. Quevedo, J., Blanch, J., Puig, V., Saludes, J., Roquet, J., Espin, S.: Methodology to determine the drinking water transport network efficiency based on interval computation of annual performance. Revista Automática e Instrumentación **408**, 44–49 (2009)
5. Quevedo, J., Chen, H., Cugueró, M.A., Tino, P., Puig, V., García, D., Sarrate, R., Yao, X.: Combining learning in model space fault diagnosis with data validation/reconstruction: application to the barcelona water network. Eng. Appl. Artif. Intell. **30**, 18–29 (2014). http://www.sciencedirect.com/science/article/pii/S0952197614000153
6. Winters, P.R.: Forecasting sales by exponentially weighted moving averages. Manag. Sci. **6**(52), 324–342 (1960)

Critical Infrastructure Online Fault Detection: Application in Water Supply Systems

Constantinos Heracleous[1]([⊠]), Estefanía Etchevés Miciolino[2], Roberto Setola[2], Federica Pascucci[3], Demetrios G. Eliades[1], Georgios Ellinas[1], Christos G. Panayiotou[1], and Marios M. Polycarpou[1]

[1] Department of Electrical and Computer Engineering,
KIOS Research Center for Intelligent Systems and Networks,
University of Cyprus, Nicosia, Cyprus
{heracleous.constantinos,eldemet,gellinas,christosp,mpolycar}@ucy.ac.cy
[2] Complex Systems and Security Lab, University Campus Bio-Medico of Rome,
Rome, Italy
{e.etcheves,r.setola}@unicampus.it
[3] Roma Tre University, Rome, Italy
pascucci@dia.uniroma3.it

Abstract. In this paper we first introduce a testbed that is able to emulate the operation and common faults of a water supply system, as well as its interaction with a SCADA system. Then we implement an online fault detection algorithm based on a fault diagnosis architecture for nonlinear uncertain discrete-time systems, that we apply and test with the testbed. We finally present some experimental results illustrating the effectiveness of this approach.

Keywords: Critical infrastructures · Water supply systems · Fault detection · Testbed · Modelling · Discrete-time systems

1 Introduction

Everyday life in modern societies relies heavily on the reliable operation and intelligent management of critical infrastructures, such as electric power systems, water systems, telecommunication networks, transportation systems etc. [12]. When critical infrastructures fail, the consequences may be tremendous, in view of societal, health, and economic aspects, leaving the developed countries around the world searching for ways to improve critical infrastructures protection, reduce their vulnerabilities and increase their resilience [1,11].

This work was partially supported by the Prevention, Preparedness and Consequence Management of Terrorism and other Security-related Risks Programme European Commission - Directorate - General Home Affairs under the FACIES project, and by the European Research Council Advanced Grant FAULT-ADAPTIVE (ERC-AdG-291508).

© Springer International Publishing Switzerland 2016
C.G. Panayiotou et al. (Eds.): CRITIS 2014, LNCS 8985, pp. 94–106, 2016.
DOI: 10.1007/978-3-319-31664-2_11

The design, control, and fault monitoring of such critical systems is also becoming increasingly more challenging as their size, complexity, and interactions are steadily growing [13]. To support human operators with the control tasks and the increasing employment of automatic process management systems, sophisticated monitoring devices have been developed, which have led the way to fault diagnosis methodologies that can improve the systems reliability and fault tolerance.

Various fault diagnosis methodologies, suitable for detecting, isolating, identifying, and accommodating a fault, have been proposed in the literature, for various systems and formulations, such as continuous and discrete, centralized and decentralized, linear and nonlinear [3,5,9]. More recently, intelligent fault diagnosis methodologies have been proposed, which combine model-based analytical redundancy and on-line approximation models, such as neural networks, to detect faults and to learn the unknown fault dynamics [6,14,19,20].

In this paper we address the problem of critical infrastructure fault diagnosis, using as an application a water supply system. We first introduce a testbed able to emulate the operation and common failures of a critical infrastructure, and then we implement and apply a fault diagnosis methodology for online detection of incipient faults in the system. Specifically, the testbed emulates a scaled version of a city water supply system, that is monitored and controlled by a SCADA (supervisory control and data acquisition) system. This testbed has the ability to emulate several scenarios where faults can be introduced. The online fault detection method, which is designed as an algorithm, continuously monitors the system, by receiving online data from the SCADA system. In the case that a physical fault occurs, it can be detected and an alarm is automatically given to the operator. The development of the testbed, the online fault detection algorithm and the practical application of the fault diagnosis architecture to a critical infrastructure are the main contributions of this paper.

In the following sections, we first give some elementary background for the water supply systems and then we describe the testbed set-up. Next, we derive the mathematical model for the testbed and then we discuss the online fault detection method that we apply to the testbed system. Finally, we present some experimental results that illustrate the effectiveness of this approach.

2   Water Supply Systems

In developed countries around the world water supply systems are critical infrastructures responsible for providing uninterrupted and good quality water to the people. In general, water supply systems are divided into two parts, the water transmission network and the water distribution network [15,16]. The water transmission network is responsible for transporting raw water from the sources (e.g., water dams, rivers) to the water treatment plants for cleaning and improving the water quality. The treated water is then transported with pipelines to the water storage facilities near the consumers areas. The distribution network follows next, and is responsible for providing good quality water at adequate volumes, from the storage facilities to the point where it is delivered to the consumers, based on the daily water demand [8]. Water distribution networks consist mainly of many underground pipes, that run through the city, so that consumer premises can connect to and receive water.

Water supply systems unfortunately can suffer from failures, that can compromise their healthy operation and reduce their reliability and performance. Specifically, water supply systems can suffer from structural and associated hydraulic faults such as pipe faults, pump and valve faults, tank aging, illegal connections etc., which can cause water leakages and pressure loss, and subsequently interrupt the water supply [10,17]. Water quality failure is another problem in water supply systems, that can occur due to chemical and microbiological contamination of water, resulting in significant adverse health effects for the consumers [7]. Finally, water supply monitor and control systems (i.e., SCADA) can also fail, due to hardware/software faults, cyber attacks, power outages etc., which can also reduce significantly the system reliability and performance.

A good approach for reducing the likelihood of all the aforementioned failures is by carrying out prognostic analysis and taking necessary preventive measures [10]. Unfortunately, this is very hard to achieve in such a large scale complex system, where failures can occur due to many unpredictable events. This leads to the need for efficient fault detection schemes, since the consequences of a fault can be reduced significantly if the detection is fast enough to allow necessary actions to be taken. One way to achieve fast fault detection is by using model-based online fault detection techniques that can monitor the system and give an alarm in the event of a fault. To explore the effectiveness and applicability of such approach we developed a testbed for emulating a scaled-down version of a water supply system for a small fictional city as we discuss in the subsections that follow.

2.1 Example of a City Water Supply System

The fictional city "Highlake", shown in Fig. 1, has two residential areas and an industrial area, as well as a water supply system for the city's water needs. The water supply system receives good quality water from the nearest pumping station and consists of water storage facilities and water distribution networks in each area. Specifically, there are five water tanks, two at each residential area and one at the industrial area, and all are situated at the highest point of each area, enabling gravity-based delivery of the water by the distribution networks.

Water tanks 1 and 2 are the city's main tanks providing water not only to residential area 1, but also to the other water tanks of the city. These two tanks can store up to $20000 \, \text{m}^3$ of water that is supplied by two main pipelines (one for each tank) from the closest pumping station. Finally, there is a direct connection between the two tanks, controlled by a valve, which can be used as needed (e.g., due to the failure of one of the main pipelines).

Water tanks 3 and 4 provide, through the distribution network, water to residential area 2. The two tanks can store up to $15000 \, \text{m}^3$ of water that they

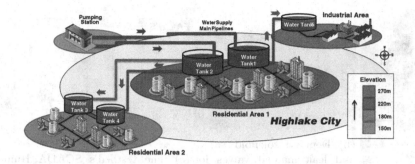

Fig. 1. Water supply system of "Highlake" city.

receive from tanks 1 and 2 with two pipelines (see Fig. 1). The water flow to tanks 3 and 4 is controlled by valves, while there is also a direct connection between the two tanks, which can be used as needed. Water tank 5, through the distribution network, provides water to the industrial area. This tank can store up to $7000\,\text{m}^3$ of water that receives from tank 1 through a pipeline with the help of a pump, due to the elevation difference between the two areas.

Finally, a SCADA system is used for monitoring and controlling Highlake's water supply system. The SCADA system receives data from various sensors installed at different points in the system and can control the valves and pumps accordingly, so that the users can have uninterrupted, good quality water at a reasonable pressure to their premises.

2.2 Testbed for Emulating the Water Supply System of a City

A scaled-down version of Highlake's water supply system was implemented as a testbed within the framework of the EU co-funded project FACIES [2]. The general objective of the testbed was to emulate the operation of a water supply system, such as following a daily water demand curve [8], filling the tanks so as to avoid any water shortages, as well as interacting with a SCADA system. Moreover, the testbed also emulated some of the common faults of the water supply systems, such as leaks and pump and valve faults, allowing the study of the system under these faulty conditions.

To meet all of these objectives many parts and components have been selected, tested, and finally connected together properly to form the testbed as shown in Fig. 2a. The testbed consists of five cylindrical-shape tanks fitted with level sensors. Specifically, two 25 L tanks are used for residential area 1, two 10 L tanks for residential area 2, and one 10 L tank for the industrial area. Also, one 125 L rectangular shape tank is used as a reservoir. The tanks were placed at specific heights into a steady structure, with all the connections between them as described in Sect. 2.1.

The testbed is also equipped with four water pumps, three for emulating the pumping station, providing water from the reservoir to the residential area 1 tanks, and one pump that provides water from tank 1 to tank 5. Also, many

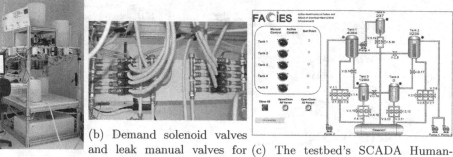

(a) Testbed   (b) Demand solenoid valves and leak manual valves for residential area 1   (c) The testbed's SCADA Human-Machine Interface (HMI)

Fig. 2. The testbed for emulating Highlake's water supply system.

on/off solenoid valves have been installed in the testbed for emulating the city's water demand. Specifically, the output of each tank is connected to a manifold with a number of solenoid valves attached (see Fig. 2b). Depending on how many valves are opened and closed at each time instance, the total water demand for the city is emulated. A few manual valves have also been installed to all the manifolds and other places as well, for emulating pipe and tank leakages.

A commercial SCADA system was also setup for the testbed with the appropriate HMI (Human-Machine Interface) (see Fig. 2c) allowing the user(s) to interact with the system. The SCADA system can communicate with the testbed's PLC (Programmable Logic Controller) via the Modbus protocol and receive sensor readings and send commands to the pumps and valves. The testbed status is always available through the HMI, while every variable value is saved in the SCADA database.

3   Testbed System Mathematical Model

In this section we derive the mathematical model for the testbed system that was described in Sect. 2.2. We consider the testbed as a nonlinear uncertain discrete-time dynamic system:

$$x(k+1) = f(x(k), u(k)) + \eta(x(k), u(k), k) \tag{1}$$

where $x \in \mathbb{R}^n$ and $u \in \mathbb{R}^m$ denote the state and input vectors, respectively, $f : \mathbb{R}^n \times \mathbb{R}^m \mapsto \mathbb{R}^n$ represents the nominal healthy dynamics and $\eta : \mathbb{R}^n \times \mathbb{R}^m \times \mathbb{N} \mapsto \mathbb{R}^n$ the modelling uncertainty [6]. Note that n is the number of level sensors fitted to the tanks (i.e., $n = 5$), while m is the number of inputs to the model representing the pumps' flow rates and the valves' control signals (i.e., $m = 3 + 9 = 12$).

The testbed system, depicted in Fig. 3, consists of five cylindrical tanks denoted by T_i, $i = 1, \ldots, 5$. The tanks T_1 and T_2 represent the tanks at residential area 1. They have cross-section area $A_1 = 0.0573 \, \text{m}^2$ and water levels

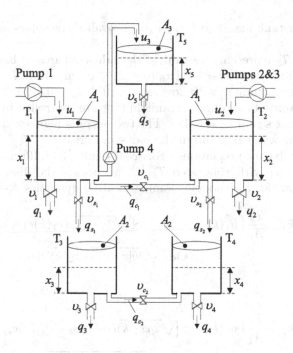

Fig. 3. Testbed system diagram.

x_1 and x_2 respectively ($0 \leq x_1, x_2 \leq 0.4\,\mathrm{m}$). The two tanks have a direct connection between them, controlled by an on/off valve with input signal $v_{c_1} = 0, 1$ (close valve $\Rightarrow v_{c_1} = 0$, and open valve $\Rightarrow v_{c_1} = 1$), while the water flow rate between them is denoted by q_{c_1}. The supply flow rates of the pumps, filling T_1 and T_2, are denoted by u_1 and u_2, respectively ($0 \leq u_1, u_2 \leq 1.5 \cdot 10^{-4}\,\mathrm{m}^3/\mathrm{s}$). Both tanks have multiple outputs through manifolds (see Fig. 2b) that regulate the output flow rates q_1 and q_2, thus emulating the water demand in residential area 1. Specifically, each manifold on tanks T_1 and T_2 has four on/off valves controlled by the input signals v_1 and v_2 respectively. The signals are discrete (i.e., $v_1 = v_2 = 0, 1, 2, 3, 4$) and determine how many valves are open on each tank manifold (e.g., $v_1 = 2 \Rightarrow$ two of the four valves are open on T_1 manifold). Finally, as can be seen in Fig. 3, both tanks T_1 and T_2 have one more output that is used for supplying tanks T_3 and T_4 with water. Both outputs are controlled by on/off valves with discrete input signals v_{s_1} and v_{s_2} ($v_{s_1} = v_{s_2} = 0, 1$), while the flow rate for each output is denoted by q_{s_1} and q_{s_2}.

Tanks T_3 and T_4 represent the tanks at residential area 2. They have cross-section area $A_2 = 0.0346\,\mathrm{m}^2$ and water levels x_3 and x_4, respectively ($0 \leq x_3, x_4 \leq 0.35\,\mathrm{m}$). The two tanks also have a direct connection between them controlled by an on/off valve with input signal $v_{c_2} = 0, 1$, while the water flow rate between them is denoted by q_{c_2}. Both tanks have multiple outputs through manifolds that regulate the output flow rates q_3 and q_4, thus emulating the water demand in residential area 2. Specifically, each manifold on tanks T_3 and T_4 has three on/off valves, controlled by the input signals v_3 and v_4 respectively. The signals are discrete (i.e., $v_3 = v_4 = 0, 1, 2, 3$) and determine how many valves are open at each tank manifold (e.g., $v_3 = 3 \Rightarrow$ all three valves are open on T_3 manifold).

Finally, tank T_5 represents the tank at the industrial area. It has cross-section area $A_3 = 0.0707\,\mathrm{m}^2$ and water level x_5 ($0 \le x_5 \le 0.2\,\mathrm{m}$). Tank T_5 receives water from tank T_1, using pump 4, with flow rate u_3 ($0 \le u_3 \le 0.85 \cdot 10^{-4}\,\mathrm{m}^3/\mathrm{s}$). Tank T_5 also has two outputs through a manifold that are controlled by on/off valves with discrete input signal $v_5 = 0, 1, 2$. The two outputs regulate the flow rate q_5 that emulates the water demand in the industrial area.

By using the balance equations, Torricelli's rule [4,18,19] and the forward Euler discretization with time step T_s [6], we obtain the discrete-time state Eqs. (2)–(6) below, for the model's nominal healthy dynamics $f(\cdot)$.

$$x_1(k+1) = x_1(k) + \frac{T_s}{A_1}\Big(u_1(k) - u_3(k) - S\big[\sqrt{2gx_1(k)}(v_1(k)c_1 + v_{s_1}(k)c_{s_1})$$
$$+ v_{c_1}(k)c_{c_1}\sqrt{2g|x_1(k) - x_2(k)|}\mathrm{sign}(x_1(k) - x_2(k))\big]\Big) \tag{2}$$

$$x_2(k+1) = x_2(k) + \frac{T_s}{A_1}\Big(u_2(k) - S\big[\sqrt{2gx_2(k)}(v_2(k)c_2 + v_{s_2}(k)c_{s_2})$$
$$- v_{c_1}(k)c_{c_1}\sqrt{2g|x_1(k) - x_2(k)|}\mathrm{sign}(x_1(k) - x_2(k))\big]\Big) \tag{3}$$

$$x_3(k+1) = x_3(k) + \frac{T_s S}{A_2}\Big(v_{s_1}(k)c_{s_1}\sqrt{2gx_1(k)} - v_3(k)c_3\sqrt{2gx_3(k)}$$
$$- v_{c_2}(k)c_{c_2}\sqrt{2g|x_3(k) - x_4(k)|}\mathrm{sign}(x_3(k) - x_4(k))\Big) \tag{4}$$

$$x_4(k+1) = x_4(k) + \frac{T_s S}{A_2}\Big(v_{s_2}(k)c_{s_2}\sqrt{2gx_2(k)} - v_4(k)c_4\sqrt{2gx_4(k)}$$
$$+ v_{c_2}(k)c_{c_2}\sqrt{2g|x_3(k) - x_4(k)|}\mathrm{sign}(x_3(k) - x_4(k))\Big) \tag{5}$$

$$x_5(k+1) = x_5(k) + \frac{T_s}{A_3}\Big(u_3(k) - v_5(k)c_5 S\sqrt{2gx_5(k)}\Big) \tag{6}$$

The state vector is denoted as $x \triangleq [x_1\ x_2\ x_3\ x_4\ x_5]^T$, and the input vector as $u \triangleq u_p \cup u_v$, where $u_p \triangleq [u_1\ u_2\ u_3]^T$ denotes the pumps' water supply flow rates and $u_v \triangleq [v_1\ v_2\ v_3\ v_4\ v_5\ v_{c_1}\ v_{c_2}\ v_{s_1}\ v_{s_2}]^T$ denotes the valves' control signal vector. The cross-section area of the restrictions is $S = 3.167 \cdot 10^{-5}\,\mathrm{m}^2$ (in this case is specified as the cross-section area of the pipes), while the gravity acceleration is $g = 9.81\,\text{m/s}^2$. Finally, the values for the various discharge coefficients [4], that have been determined experimentally are $c_1 = c_2 = 0.68$, $c_3 = c_4 = 0.4$, $c_5 = 0.7$, $c_{s_1} = c_{s_2} = 0.62$, and $c_{c_1} = c_{c_2} = 0.37$.

The uncertainty $\eta(\cdot)$ in the model (see Eq. (1)) is caused by several factors such as parameter uncertainty, unmodelled dynamics, and so on. The uncertainty will be considered bounded at all times by a function $\bar{\eta}(\cdot)$ that can be found experimentally.

4 Online Fault Detection

The consequences of an accidental or malicious fault can be reduced significantly if the fault is detected early and necessary action is taken within a minimum amount of time after the detection [10]. For this reason, we apply a fault detection (FD) method that can monitor the testbed system, by receiving data online from the SCADA system and signaling an alarm in the event of a fault.

We use the fault detection approach proposed in [6], that deals with the discrepancy between the sensor readings x_i and the estimated values $\hat{x}_i$ derived from the system model for each component i. In this approach, the modelling uncertainty, represented by the vector η in Eq. (1), is considered as unstructured and possibly an unknown nonlinear function, which is always bounded by some known functional $\bar{\eta}$. Because of that, a threshold error $\bar{e}_i(k)$ can be found, for each component i at each time instance k, and the decision on the occurrence of a fault (detection) is made when the magnitude of at least one of the estimation error components, $e_i(k) = x_i(k) - \hat{x}_i(k)$, exceeds its corresponding threshold, i.e., $|e_i(k)| \geq \bar{e}_i(k)$. To apply the approach proposed in [6] for online fault detection in a critical infrastructure system, using input data from the infrastructure's SCADA system, we design Algorithm 1.

Algorithm 1. Online Fault Detection algorithm

 1: **procedure** $\text{FD}(\hat{x}(0), \bar{e}(0))$ ▷ use as input the initial values for $\hat{x}$ and $\bar{e}$
 2:     $k \leftarrow 0,\ t \leftarrow \text{timer}$ ▷ t denotes a timer that starts at 0 s
 3:     **repeat every** $t = k \cdot T_s$ ▷ repetition of the loop with period T_s
 4:         $x(k) \leftarrow x_{db_{\text{last}}}$ ▷ obtain from DB the last recorded values of the sensors
 5:         $u(k) \leftarrow u_{db_{\text{last}}}$ ▷ obtain from DB the last recorded values of the inputs
 6:         $e(k) \leftarrow x(k) - \hat{x}(k)$ ▷ state estimation error calculation
 7:         **if** $|e(k)| > \bar{e}(k)$ **then**   ▷ comparison for fault detection
 8:             Alarm - Fault Detected
 9:         **end if**
10:         $\hat{x}(k+1) \leftarrow \lambda(\hat{x}(k) - x(k)) + f(x(k), u(k))$ ▷ FD estimator dynamics
11:         $\bar{e}(k+1) \leftarrow \lambda\bar{e}(k) + \bar{\eta}(x(k), u(k), k)$ ▷ FD estimation error threshold
12:         $k \leftarrow k + 1$
13:     **until** FD turn off
14: **end procedure**

Once the FD procedure is called, it runs a loop with period T_s (T_s has to be long enough to ensure that all steps of the loop can be executed). At each iteration for each time instance k, the algorithm runs queries to the SCADA database to get the last recorded readings from the sensors and the input values from the controller (lines 4–5). Then, the state estimation error $e(k)$ is calculated (line 6) and its magnitude $|e(k)|$ is compared with the estimation error threshold $\bar{e}(k)$. If the condition $|e(k)| > \bar{e}(k)$ is true, then a fault is detected and an alarm is given to the operator (lines 7–9). The algorithm then calculates the values of the estimation states for the next iteration time instance $k + 1$ using the FD estimator dynamics (line 10), where $0 \leq \lambda < 1$ and vector f denotes the model's nominal healthy dynamics [6]. The estimation error threshold for the next iteration time instance $k + 1$ is subsequently calculated (line 11), where $\bar{\eta}(\cdot)$ is a known function that bounds the modeling uncertainty $\eta(\cdot)$. Finally, the time instance k increases, and once the timer $t = k \cdot T_s$, the algorithm repeats again.

In the following subsections we discuss the application of the algorithm to the testbed and then present some experimental results to illustrate the effectiveness of this approach.

4.1   Application to the Testbed System

Before using the online fault detection algorithm, we first design a meaningful scenario for the testbed system. Since the testbed emulates the water supply system of a city, we consider a daily water demand curve [8] that the testbed must follow in each experimental run. The target water daily demand curve is shown in Fig. 4, where the 24 h are scaled down to 360 s (6 min), which will also be the length of each run. The solenoid valves that emulate the water demand at each area, are opened and closed at predefined time instances, so that the emulated total water demand of the city (sum of the demand in all areas) follows closely the target water demand curve (see Fig. 4). To avoid any water shortages, the water supply pumps and valves have certain rules and, depending on the water level at each tank, the proper action is taken, either to supply a certain tank with water, or to stop and avoid overflow.

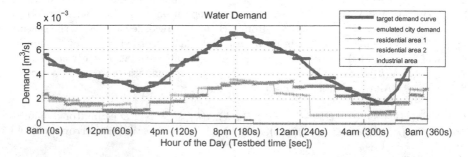

Fig. 4. Daily water demand curve the testbed follows at each run.

The online fault detection algorithm was implemented for the testbed system and since there are five water level sensors, one for each tank, we utilize five fault detection (FD) components. For the FD estimator dynamics we use the model's nominal healthy dynamics (Eqs. 2–6) while for the modelling uncertainty $\eta(\cdot)$ we found the bounding function $\bar{\eta}(\cdot)$ through experimental data when the system was always healthy. Specifically, for each component $i = 1, \ldots, 5$ the bounding function is $\bar{\eta}_i(x(k), u(k), k) = a_i$ where $a_i \in \mathbb{R}^+$.

4.2 Experimental Results

In this section we present some experimental results to illustrate the effectiveness of the approach with the testbed system. In all the experimental runs the same scenario (see Fig. 4) was used, with the FD loop period set to $T_s = 1\,\mathrm{s}$ and the filter constant $\lambda = 0.9$, while we use the uncertainty bound values found experimentally with the current T_s and λ settings. In each experimental run we introduce to the testbed a certain fault, such as leak, pump, or valve fault, at a specific time instance and we rely on the FD component(s) for the detection of the fault.

In Fig. 5, a leak fault was introduced at $t = 180\,\mathrm{s}$ to Tank 3 through the water demand flow rate q_3 (see Fig. 3). The leak is estimated to be around 6 % of the flow rate q_3 at the specific time. The fault is detected by the FD component #3 of Tank 3 at $t = 186\,\mathrm{s}$, about 6 s after the fault.

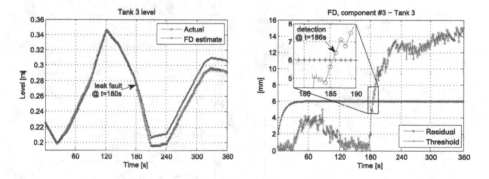

Fig. 5. Time-behaviors of signals related to Tank 3 when a leak fault is introduced at time $t = 180\,\mathrm{s}$.

In Fig. 6 a pump fault was introduced at $t = 225\,\mathrm{s}$, shutting down Pump 1, that supplies water to Tank 1. Just before the fault, the pump was on, supplying water to Tank 1 with flow rate $1.5 \cdot 10^{-4}\,\mathrm{m}^3/\mathrm{s}$. The fault is detected by the FD component #1 of Tank 1 at $t = 227\,\mathrm{s}$, about 2 s after the fault.

Finally, in Fig. 7 a valve fault was introduced at $t = 200\,\mathrm{s}$, keeping the valve between Tanks 2 and 4 (i.e., v_{S2}, see Fig. 3) always closed. Just before the fault the valve was open, with Tank 2 supplying water to Tank 4. The fault is detected by the FD component #4 of Tank 4 and the FD component #2 of Tank 2 at $t = 204\,\mathrm{s}$ and $t = 210\,\mathrm{s}$ respectively.

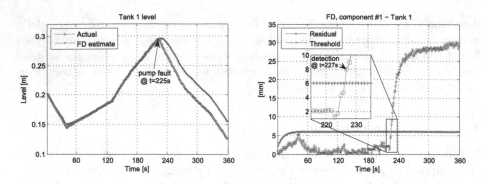

Fig. 6. Time-behaviors of signals related to Tank 1 when a pump fault is introduced at time $t = 225$ s.

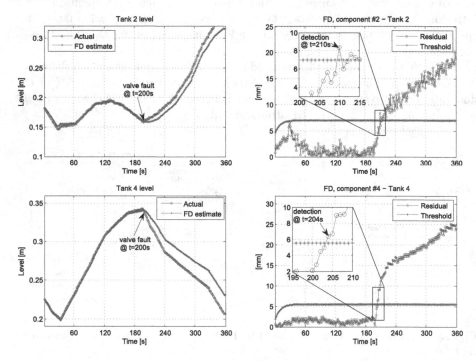

Fig. 7. Time-behaviors of signals related to Tank 2 and Tank 4 when a valve fault is introduced at time $t = 200$ s.

5   Conclusions and Future Work

In this paper we have implemented and tested an online fault detection approach for critical infrastructures based on a proposed fault diagnosis architecture for nonlinear uncertain discrete-time systems. A testbed has been developed, to emulate the operation and common faults of a critical infrastructure (i.e., a water supply system), as well as its interaction with a SCADA system. We have also presented some experimental results that illustrate the effectiveness of this approach with the testbed.

In the future, we plan to implement, apply, and test fault isolation and accommodation approaches suitable for critical infrastructures. Moreover, we plan to compare, with the help of the testbed, various fault diagnosis architectures and explore ways for cyber attack detection as well.

References

1. Council directive (2008/114/EC) on the identification and designation of European critical infrastructures and the assessment of the need to improve their protection. Off. J. Eur. Union **345**, 75–86 (2008)
2. EU Project FACIES: Online identification of Failure and Attack on interdependent Critical InfrastructurES (2012). http://facies.dia.uniroma3.it/
3. Blanke, M., Kinnaert, M., Lunze, J., Staroswiecki, M.: Diagnosis and Fault-Tolerant Control, 2nd edn. Springer, Heidelberg (2006)
4. Borutzky, W., Barnard, B., Thoma, J.: An orifice flow model for laminar and turbulent conditions. Simul. Model. Pract. Theory **10**(3–4), 141–152 (2002)
5. Chen, J., Patton, R.: Robust Model-Based Fault Diagnosis for Dynamic Systems, 3rd edn. Springer, New York (1999)
6. Ferrari, R.M.G., Parisini, T., Polycarpou, M.: A fault detection and isolation scheme for nonlinear uncertain discrete-time sytems. In: 2007 46th IEEE Conference on Decision and Control, pp. 1009–1014 (2007)
7. Gray, J.: Water contamination events in UK drinking-water supply systems. J. Water Health **6**(1), 21–26 (2008)
8. Herrera, M., Torgo, L., Izquierdo, J., Pérez-García, R.: Predictive models for forecasting hourly urban water demand. J. Hydrol. **387**(1–2), 141–150 (2010)
9. Isermann, R.: Supervision, fault-detection and fault-diagnosis methods – an introduction. Control Eng. Pract. **5**(5), 639–652 (1997)
10. Islam, M., Sadiq, R., Rodriguez, M.J., Najjaran, H., Francisque, A., Hoorfar, M.: Water distribution system failure: a framework for forensic analysis. Environ. Syst. Decisions **34**(1), 168–179 (2014)
11. Lindström, M., Olsson, S.: The European programme for critical infrastructure protection. In: Olsson, S. (ed.) Crisis Management in the European Union, pp. 37–59. Springer, Heidelberg (2009)
12. Moteff, J., Parfomak, P.: Critical Infrastructure and Key Assets: Definition and Identification. Tech. report, Congressional Research Service (2004)
13. Polycarpou, M., Ellinas, G., Kyriakides, E., Panayiotou, C.: Intelligent health monitoring of critical infrastructure systems. In: Complexity in Engineering, COMPENG 2010, pp. 18–20 (2010)
14. Polycarpou, M.: Stable learning scheme for failure detection and accommodation. In: Proceedings of the 1994 IEEE International Symposium on Intelligent Control, pp. 315–320 (1994)
15. Ratnayaka, D.D., Brandt, M.J., Johnson, M.: Water Supply, 6th edn. Butterworth-Heinemann, Boston (2009)
16. Smet, J., Wijk, C. (eds.): Small Community Water Supplies: Technology, People and Partnership. IRC International Water and Sanitation Centre (2002)
17. Tabesh, M., Soltani, J., Farmani, R., Savic, D.: Assessing pipe failure rate and mechanical reliability of water distribution networks using data-driven modeling. J. Hydroinformatics **11**(1), 1–17 (2009)

18. White, F.M.: Fluid Mechanics, 7th edn. Mcgraw-Hill, New York (2011)
19. Zhang, X., Polycarpou, M., Parisini, T.: A robust detection and isolation scheme for abrupt and incipient faults in nonlinear systems. IEEE Trans. Autom. Control **47**(4), 576–593 (2002)
20. Zhang, Y., Jiang, J.: Bibliographical review on reconfigurable fault-tolerant control systems. Ann. Rev. Control **32**(2), 229–252 (2008)

Power and Energy System Security

An Attack Analysis of Managed Pressure Drilling Systems on Oil Drilling Platforms

Thomas Richard McEvoy and Stephen D. Wolthusen[✉]

Norwegian Information Security Laboratory, Department of Computer Science,
Gjøvik University College, Gjøvik, Norway
{richard.mcevoy,stephen.wolthusen}@hig.no

Abstract. Oil rig systems are frequently assumed to be isolated from external networks, securing them from malicious software attacks. Integrated operations and media and device mobility undermine this assumption. A successful attack on a drilling operation could be devastating in human, environmental, economic and reputational terms. Several threat sources can easily be identified. We therefore propose the use of Causal Bayesian Networks to analyse probable attack strategies on a managed pressure drilling (MPD) system, where the attacker aims to maximise impact, while minimising attribution. Our results can be used to inform company representatives and operators of likely risks and highlight requirements for the successful diagnosis and recovery of well control incidents stemming from cyber causes.

1 Introduction

A well control incident on an oil rig may can have devastating effects for implicated organisations [1–3]. Advanced control systems allow the exploitation of difficult-to-drill oil fields while improving drilling safety [4–6]. However, limited work has been devoted to the *security* of such systems. Oil rig systems are often considered to be isolated from external threats. Integrated operations and device and media mobility render this assumption fallacious [7–9][1].

We propose the use of Causal Bayesian Belief Networks as a means of analysing this exposure. These are readily accessible to non-experts and provide an economical means of representing well states under attack, taking account of human, physical and cyber factors. Scenarios may be analysed dynamically and update "on the fly" in the light of new evidence. Simplistic worst case scenario analysis is also replaced by a probability distribution over outcomes, allowing a granular response.

Our analysis shows that attackers may not need to create dramatic well control incidents to cause severe production losses. Correlating events in relation to well control incidents is already difficult without having to account for maliciously altered sensor signals or actuator settings, making detection and correct

---

[1] Anecdotal evidence from private conversation indicates that >80 % of malicious software found on oil rigs arrives through mobile devices and removable media.

© Springer International Publishing Switzerland 2016
C.G. Panayiotou et al. (Eds.): CRITIS 2014, LNCS 8985, pp. 109–121, 2016.
DOI: 10.1007/978-3-319-31664-2_12

diagnosis the critical problem. It appears relatively straightforward for attackers to avoid cyber attribution by creating events which are ambiguous in detection terms, but have the potential for severe, even permanent losses. This puts a priority on researching detection and correlation methods which consider the potential presence of malicious software. It also shows the need to make drilling crew aware of the possibility of cyber attacks and the need to take account of "man in the loop" problems in planning detection and alerting systems.

We discuss related work in Sect. 2 with a brief description of managed pressure drilling in Sect. 3. We set out our approach to attack analysis in Sect. 4. Section 5 describes our model, while, in Sect. 6, we provide our analysis in part, summarising our findings with further discussion and conclude, detailing our on-going and future work in Sect. 7.

2   Related Work

We refer to a standard text, e.g., [10] for well control fundaments. These also show the difficulty of well incident detection. A complete description of managed pressure drilling may be found in [11,12]. Generally, automatic control systems are regarded as safer and more reliable for drilling remote, or difficult to exploit, oil fields. Managed pressure drilling (MPD) represents one approach [5]. As a result, extensive literature can be found on the performance, safety and reliability of such mechanisms, e.g, [4,13]. But cyber security in relation to well control does not seem to have been studied explicitly.

Oil field security became a subject of concern to governments, following 9/11 and the first Gulf war. Attention was primarily on physical security. Harbour [14] gives an example of a physical security assessment approach, based on the probability of key events along an event pathway. We seek to provide an equivalent cyber-physical security analysis. Some work has been done on risk assessment in relation to cultural and organisational issues and oil rigs can not longer be treated as isolated networks [7,15]. Radmand et al. [16] address the more specific issue of the use of wireless sensors on board oil rigs, pointing out that little is done to address known security issues with such systems, relying on notional physical isolation. The authors are not aware of any openly published research on attacks specific to control processes.

A general introduction to risk analysis can be found in [17]. Bayesian Belief Networks (BBN) have been used for risk analysis in other engineering related disciplines [18] and Causal Bayesian methods were proposed for information security risk analysis in [19]. Causal BBN are discussed in [20]. Attack trees including attack-defence (attack-countermeasure) trees, Petri nets, and process algebrae represent other forms of dynamic attack-defense modeling [21–23] which contrast with static analysis techniques that fail to take account of dynamic characteristics in the environment.

3   Managed Pressure Drilling

The aim of well control is to maintain pressure in the borehole above formation pore pressure to prevent an influx, or *kick*, of hydrocarbons and below formation fracture pressure, preventing damage to the well bore, subsequent loss of pressure, and a kick. Either situation, if mishandled, can lead to a, potentially very damaging, blowout. Moreover, managing pressure prevents other problems such as well ballooning, stuck pipes, collapsed formations, or drill head twist off [10,11]. The most common causes of kicks are alterations in the geological formation (e.g., diapirism[2] and improperly controlled pipe movement. Equation 1 summarises the control aims, noting that well formation instability may also lead to *stuck pipe* [11].

$$p_{pore} < p_{well.instab} < BHP_s < p_{diff.sticking} < p_{lost.circ} < p_{fracture} \qquad (1)$$

Conventionally, pressure is controlled by managing the density of drilling mud in the drill hole. Mud weight is managed using solids control equipment. Detection and response are operator-centric [10]. Automated methods, such as managed pressure drilling (MPD), are becoming more popular since they improve on manual pressure management techniques, particularly where the drilling window is narrow or the formation is weak. In managed pressure drilling (MPD), the drill hole is closed, converting control to a closed vessel inventory problem [13,24]. Mud density is kept constant and pressure is controlled using an automated choke and a back pressure pump with two PLCs being used, one to control the pumps and choke manifold and the other to provide sensor information to the operator [25]. Both ongoing drilling operations and kicks can be managed by this approach [26]. Mud logging [10,27] is used to take various measurements of drilling characteristics such as rate of penetration (ROP), density of cuttings, gas and temperature. Measurements can be taken topside or in the borehole. These measurements can indicate issues in the bore hole such as kicks and provide an accurate borehole history which enables forecasting of issues. Mud logging crew play an important supplementary role in warning drilling crew about potential well control problems.

Historically, manual monitoring of key control instrumentation (e.g. pump activity, kill and choke line pressure, mud or trip tank levels, hydrocarbon levels and the size of chips) were used to detect issues. Such methods may still be employed on a contingency basis. However, monitoring was (and is) distributed, difficult to correlate, and results can frequently be ambiguous (Fig. 1).

Moreover, human factors and production pressures on operations may influence decisions on responses to readings. But, once initiated, responses to drilling incidents are codified in a *well control matrix* which is created prior to commencing operations [10,28], based on the expert knowledge of the geologists and engineers with executive oversight. Each rig will have its own distinct set of planned responses. Clearly, automating analysis and control where possible has increased the safety and reliability of operations under normal circumstances [24,25,27].

---

[2] Extrusion of a salt bed into a sedimentary layer.

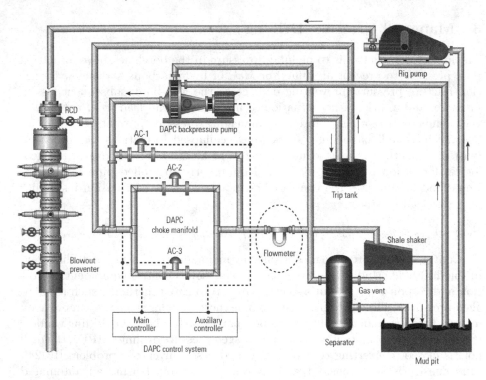

Fig. 1. Automated dynamic annular pressure control (from [25])

Results can also be fed into safety systems, e.g., altering set points where alarms will sound, providing a holistic approach to well management. But this approach does not preclude ambiguous or difficult to diagnose situations and other aspects such a production pressures may influence management and crew decisions resulting in circumstances which can cause *system accidents* [29], but, in general, there is some confidence in the literature in this approach.

4   Problem and Approach

Confidence in such systems is misplaced, if their *security* is left unconsidered. MPD limits the time window during which manual intervention can allow recovery. Risk assessments are a traditional way of analysing and demonstrating potential security issues. But such assessments frequently focus solely on cyber events, tend to overemphasize confidentiality as a security characteristic, and do not allow for probable responses to events as they unfold, both human and mechanical – which is a weakness when considering industrial control and cyber-physical systems where such interactions are intrinsic to the system. This could lead to the results of such assessments being dismissed as unrealistic. Such methods, even ones explicitly incorporating countermeasures such as work by Roy *et al.* [30] also tend to be difficult to access for non-experts. Our problem is how to realistically and economically portray the potential consequences of various attacks including interactions with the physical system, and hence focus defence efforts appropriately?

We argue that Causal Bayesian Belief Networks [20] provide an economical way of codifying and storing such an assessment. It allows us to consider interventions, fixing a variable state in order to understand its effect on an overall probability distribution. It also allows us to consider chains of events, enabling us to represent agent interactions. This follows causal reasoning and captures expert opinion as well as evidence from simulations and tests in a single analysis and its results are readily accessible to non-experts, such as senior decision-makers in organisations. In the following we demonstrate this method in an example attack – selected from four cases related to pressure related negative well bore conditions[3]. We assume the attacker also wishes to avoid cyber attribution (for example, to be able to repeat the attack). The complete study allows us to identify the attackers goals and to consider defensive strategies in advance.

5   Model

A *Causal Bayesian Network* is a directed acyclic graph (DAG) G where nodes represent variables with an assigned probability distribution over their states, linked by causal intuition. Adjacent nodes represent conditional dependence. Non-adjacent nodes represent conditional independence. Each node represents a table capturing conditional probability distributions over dependent variables. A Causal Bayesian Network is distinct from a Bayesian Belief Network because it allows one or more *interventions* whereby a node can be set to a specific value $do(X \quad x)$ which may represent assumptions or interventions by the analyst to reduce scope, when considering a causal chain of events. Hence the probability distribution P_x over the DAG G represents a subset of complete probability distribution. It represents only those states induced by the intervention $X = x$. These nodes are marked in a diagram of the graph by a double-circled node. Since a Causal Bayesian Network carries information about conditional independence and interventions, it reduces the number of states under consideration when dealing with probabilities, achieving considerable economies during analysis. We make the following environmental and adversary assumptions:

- The formation has a narrow drill window, making both under- and over-pressure easy to achieve in a short period – see Sect. 3
- Normal drilling activity is in progress
- Drilling is at depth, rather than in shallow gas sands
- The attacker will aim to disrupt operations on a long-term basis
- The attacker wishes to avoid attribution
- The attacker is has prior knowledge of the well formation
- The sensors are all operational within normal parameters, with the exception of those directly controlling the managed drilling pumps and telemetry.

---

[3] The complete study is available on request.

We assume that the attack will be carried out by autonomous malicious mobile code (similar to, e.g., Stuxnet or earlier work), imported to the rig by a mobile device or removable media. The code on will seek out the target PLCs or RTUs, possibly using a coordinated approach [9,21] to affect the main pump, the back pressure pump, and the automated choke controllers or their telemetry.

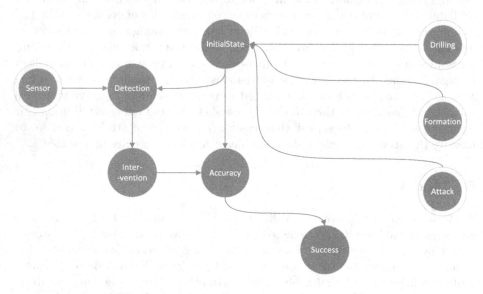

Fig. 2. Attack graph causal Bayesian network

The attack commences when the attacker affects the set point, forces the PLC output [31], or alters the control logic of the system and conceals the resulting (direct) telemetry — regarding backpressure pump speed (used to calculate pressure) and choke pressure readings — from the operator.

$$do(AttackType = UnderPressureAttack, Severe) \tag{2}$$
$$do(AttackType = UnderPressureAttack, Mild) \tag{3}$$
$$do(AttackType = OverPressureAttack, Mild) \tag{4}$$
$$do(AttackType = OverPressureAttack, Severe) \tag{5}$$

In our attack analysis, we considered four types of attack shown in Eqs. 2 to 5; these aims should be compared with the possible well-bore states in Eq. 1. Other attacks such as chronic pressure variations can also be considered using the same approach. From Fig. 2, we consider the probable initial well condition as this cannot be determined directly. Consequently, we have to determine the probability that the operating crew will consider other evidence (in isolation) than the control signals from the MPD system in determining the well condition, how easy this is to achieve, and whether or not to respond with an intervention, depending on their view of the reliability of the MPD rig. The accuracy of their diagnosis, in turn, determines the potential for damage and the likelihood of a successful intervention, where the use of automated MPD requires feedback or more sophisticated controls such as model-following control laws may further obscure adversary intervention.

The attack graphs are similar in each case — see Fig. 2. To illustrate the approach, we provide the analysis and results for Eq. 3 in Sect. 6 and discuss our conclusions regarding the stable characteristics of the model. The probabilities represent expert opinion, in this case drawn from the literature. Specific studies would be needed for individual rigs.

6   Analysis and Discussion

In Eq. 3, we consider a situation where the well pressure has dropped so that the pressure profile is wavering between sufficient and insufficient pressure to prevent a formation influx. The situation, improperly handled, could lead to a blowout or collapsed formation.

The attacker's assumed prior knowledge of the well bore condition allows us to apply a Gaussian distribution to the selected pressure set, shown in Table 1. We also show that error margins for less well prepared attacker would be greater. We regard these values as relatively invariant for any attack, i.e., the attacker will achieve his attack aim 68 % of the time.

Table 1. Initial well condition

	Kick	Instability	BHPs
Prepared attack	0.16	0.68	0.16
Unprepared attack	0.25	0.50	0.25

The attack should present itself as a series of chronic small-scale influxes, unless it unintentionally causes a kick. MPD sensor equipment is very sensitive to bore hole pressure changes (±2.5 %). While beyond the scope of this paper, however, we note that conventional methods are up to 10 times less accurate [32]. Drilling crews with a knowledge of the rig are almost as capable of detecting an influx by sight or smell as the use of traditional gauges [10]. Moreover, such manual approaches are not necessarily sensitive to potential gauge failure, or malicious action, and interpretation may suffer from confirmation bias. The mud logging crew acts as a backup to the drilling crew. They take account of MPD readings, but also use additional information about borehole conditions (see Sect. 3). However, their tests are oriented towards detecting situations associated with physical changes in well bore behavior such as increase in ROP (rate of penetration) which will not be present in the case of an attach. Hydrocarbons are difficult to detect in mud flow, even under the microscope, and, without the usual additional signs, may pass unnoticed. Furthermore, the use of oil-base muds may make an attack harder to detect as the gas is more easily dissolved in the mud and pressure would have to lower considerably before an obvious sign of an influx such as *bubble-out* occurs[4]. This is particularly dangerous where a kick is occurring as it means there is limited time to prevent a more serious blow out.

Hence if the drilling crew is deprived of accurate sensory information by the MPD PLC, the attacker has considerable scope for pressure manipulation. Ambiguous signals are already known to produce delayed crew responses, which may be exacerbated by poor communication on the rig floor [10]. A lack of other obvious physical signs bodes poorly for early or accurate detection. Table 2 shows our resulting belief regarding detection probabilities[5]. It may take further damage, e.g. a stuck pipe, to alert the crew to the situation.

Table 2. Condition detection

Actual condition	Detected condition		Conditional probability
Kick	Kick	0.50	0.08
	Instability	0.25	0.04
	BHPs	0.25	0.04
Instability	Kick	0.35	0.24
	Instability	0.35	0.24
	BHPs	0.30	0.20
BHPs	Kick	0.01	0.00
	Instability	0.09	0.01
	BHPs	0.90	0.14

Because oil rigs use a well control matrix to determine responses to anomalous events, given an event is "detected", a codified response will be implemented. The response is quasi-deterministic in nature. However, the danger is that the crew trust the automated MPD system to deal with the problem rather than intervening themselves, or rather that the well control matrix is codified with this response — without suitable additional checks to ensure all sensor information is accurate. The *damage* potential is a result of the *intervention* strategy selected compared to the actual well *condition* (Table 3).

If the correct intervention is selected *and* the maliciously subverted MPD is bypassed during the intervention, the potential for long term damage to production is reduced. An incorrect intervention is likely to worsen the situation as is relying on the MPD to resolve the problem. For example, reacting to well ballooning as though it is a kick can result in damage to the formation. However,

---

[4] Bubbles of gas appear in the mud flow.
[5] Probabilities are calculated by taking the product of the posteriors of the preceding nodes with the priors of the current node.

Table 3. Recovery attempt

	Intervention	Cond. Prob	Non-intervention	Cond. Prob
Kick	0.95	0.30	0.05	0.02
Instablity	0.50	0.15	0.50	0.15
BHPs	0.00	0.00	1.00	0.39

there is a degree of uncertainty over the effects of any intervention. Even accurately selecting the appropriate response may not result in a successful outcome. Table 4 below shows the analysis outcomes.

Table 4. Damage potential

	Kick condition	Instability condition	BHPs condition
Kick intervention	0.05	0.21	0.05
Kick non-intervention	0.00	0.01	0.00
Instability intervention	0.02	0.10	0.02
Instability non-intervention	0.02	0.10	0.02
BHPs intervention	0.00	0.00	0.00
BHPS non-intervention	0.06	0.26	0.06

Table 5 shows the likely outcomes of the mild underpressure attack. In non-technical terms, given an attacker will normally succeed in creating such a condition, the crew will intervene, leading to non-productive time, around 35 % of the time. They will fail to intervene, when they should, around 17 % of the time.

Table 5. Probable consequence

	Successful	Cond. Prob.	Unsuccessful	Cond. Prob.
Accurate kick	0.94	0.05	0.06	0.00
Inaccurate kick	0.50	0.13	0.50	0.05
Accurate instability	0.94	0.19	0.06	0.01
Inaccurate instability	0.35	0.03	0.65	0.06
Accurate BHPs	0.94	0.06	0.06	0.00
Inaccurate BHPs	0.06	0.02	0.94	0.31

Inaccurate diagnosis followed by unsuccessful intervention (or non-intervention, respectively) is intuitively the worst outcome and features worryingly high in the probabilities for this example attack (42 %) – reflecting our belief that the crew is effectively blinded to the well bore conditions by this (and any) kind of cyber attack and hence unlikely to respond correctly.

Table 6. Attack analysis summary

Attack	Attack weighting
Severe underpressure	0.43
Mild underpressure	0.42
Mild overpressure	0.49
Severe overpressure	0.47

We use this as one of the salient characteristics for attack selection, shown in Table 6. Mild overpressure attacks with the aim of creating differential sticking score highest. It is also worth noting that overpressure attacks carry the highest likelihood of accurate diagnosis allowing a successful outcome for the crew as well due to the complications of dealing with stuck pipe conditions. So the result is somewhat unintuitive because detection (*of a negative condition*) is easier in this case and intervention a given, but it reflects the penalties of inaccurate detection and intervention for this condition. Indeed, a kick intervention for a stuck pipe would be likely to cause mechanical damage, due to friction from expanding mud, both to the drill string and the rotating control device and the blowout preventer (BOP). A Macondo-like situation could also result, pushing the drill string out of true and making it impossible to close the BOP [1]. The other salient attack selection characteristic is failure to attribute the negative well bore condition to a cyber attack. Stuck pipe is more likely to be attributed to physical causes whereas failure to maintain well bore pressure above pore pressure would cause, in our opinion, further attention to be paid to the pressure maintenance and monitoring systems and could reveal anomalies thrown up by the attack. Again, the attacker seems likely to select this form of attack on this basis as well as its higher potential for permanent damage to exploitation efforts.

7   Conclusion and Future Work

Managed pressure drilling is an example of an automated control system in oil wells, offering advantages in terms of safety and reliability. Like other control systems, however, it is also vulnerable to attack and suffers from limited sensor redundancy. Using Causal Bayesian Networks, we demonstrate how a set of probable attacks on sensors and PLC (actuator) systems could lead to desirable (for the attacker) negative outcomes. The analysis demonstrates relative stability in the nodes of the belief network. The key factor is the (in-)ability of the crew to detect the attack, showing the need for greater awareness and, key, mechanisms to signal sensor anomalies.

In future work, we will address the question of accurate detection in the face of potentially unreliable subsets of sensors, whilst parallel efforts concentrate on establishing minimal requirements for observability and controllability for the number and placement of sensors.

References

1. Read, C.: BP and the Macondo Spill: The Complete Story. Palgrave Macmillan, New York (2011)
2. Bea, R.: Final Report on the Investigation of the Macondo Well Blowout. Technical report, Deepwater Horizon Study Group, Department of Civil and Environmental Engineering, University of California Berkeley, Berkeley, CA, USA, March 2011
3. Hempkins, W.B., Kingsborough, R.H., Lohec, W.E., Nini, C.J.: Multivariate statistical analysis of stuck drillpipe situations. SPE Drill. Eng. 2(3), 237–244 (1987)
4. Dunn-Norman, S., Erickson, K.T., Cetinkaya, E.K., Stanek, F.K., Miller, A.: SCADA system trends in deepwater developments. In: Rio Oil & Gas Expo and Conference, Rio de Janeiro, Brazil, Brazilian Institute of Oil, Gas and Biofuels, pp. 1–8, October 2000
5. Skogdalen, J.E., Utne, I.B., Vinnem, J.E.: Developing safety indicators for preventing offshore oil and gas deepwater drilling blowouts. Saf. Sci. 49(8–9), 1187–1199 (2011)
6. Zengkai, L., Yonghong, L., Ju, L.: Availability and reliability analysis of subsea annular blowout preventer. Adv. Inf. Technol. Comput. Sci. 25, 73–76 (2013). Special Issue: Proceedings of the 2nd International Conference on Energy (ICE 2013), Beijing, China
7. Johnsen, S.O., Aas, A., Qian, Y.: Sector-specific information infrastructure issues in the oil, gas, and petrochemical sector. In: Lopez, J., Setola, R., Wolthusen, S.D. (eds.) Critical Infrastructure Protection. LNCS, vol. 7130, pp. 235–279. Springer, Heidelberg (2012)
8. Falliere, N., O Murchu, L., Chien, E.: W32.Stuxnet Dossier. Technical Report Version 1.4, Symantec, Cupertino, CA, USA, February 2011
9. Langner, R.: To Kill a Centrifuge: A Technical Analysis of What Stuxnet's Creators Tried to Achieve. Technical report, The Langner Group, Hamburg, Germany, November 2013
10. Aberdeen Drilling Schools & Well Control Training Centre: Well Control for the Rig-Site Drilling Team. Aberdeen Drilling Schools, Aberdeen, UK, March 2002
11. Mæland, M.: Managed Pressure Drilling: The Solaris Prospect – HPHT Exploration Well. Master's thesis, Department of Petroleum Engineering and Applied Geophysics, Norwegian University of Science and Technology, Trondheim, Norway, June 2013
12. Aarsnes, U.J.F.: Reduced Order Observer Design for Managed Pressure Drilling. Master's thesis, Department of Engineering Cybernetics, Norwegian University of Science and Technology, Trondheim, Norway, June 2013
13. Breyholtz, O., Nygaard, G., Nikolaou, M.: Automatic control of managed pressure drilling. In: Proceedings of the 2010 American Control Conference (ACC 2010), Baltimore, MD, USA, pp. 442–447. IEEE Press, June 2010
14. Harbour, J.L.: Assessing offshore vulnerabilities and counter-response capabilities using RapidOps. In: Oceans 2002, Biloxi, MS, USA, vol. 2, pp. 1176–1179. IEEE Press, October 2002

15. Dynes, S., Kolbe, L., Schierholz, R.: Information security in the extended enterprise: a research agenda. In: Hoxmeier, J.A., Hayne, S. (eds.) Proceedings of the 13th Americas Conference on Information Systems (AMCIS 2007), Keystone, CO, USA, p. 330. Association for Information Systems, August 2007
16. Radmand, P., Talevski, A., Petersen, S., Carlsen, S.: Taxonomy of wireless sensor network cyber security attacks in the oil and gas industries. In: Proceedings of the 24th IEEE International Conference on Advanced Information Networking and Applications (AINA 2010), Perth, Australia, pp. 949–957. IEEE Press, April 2010
17. Peltier, T.R.: Information Security Risk Analysis, 3rd edn. CRC Press, Boca Raton (2010)
18. Trucco, P., Cagno, E., Ruggeri, F., Grande, O.: A Bayesian Belief Network modelling of organisational factors in risk analysis: a case study in maritime transportation. Reliab. Eng. Syst. Saf. **93**(6), 845–856 (2008)
19. Kondakci, S.: A causal model for information security risk assessment. In: Proceedings of the Sixth International Conference on Information Assurance and Security (IAS 2010), Atlanta, GA, USA, pp. 143–148. IEEE Press, August 2010
20. Pearl, J.: Causality: Models, Reasoning, and Inference, 2nd edn. Cambridge University Press, Cambridge (2009)
21. McEvoy, T.R., Wolthusen, S.: Agent interaction and state determination in SCADA systems. In: Butts, J., Shenoi, S. (eds.) Critical Infrastructure Protection: Proceedings of the Sixth Annual IFIP Working Group 11.10 International Conference on Critical Infrastructure Protection. International Federation for Information Processing Advances in Information and Communication Technology, vol. 390, pp. 99–109. Springer, Heidelberg (2012)
22. Wu, R., Li, W., Huang, H.: An attack modeling based on hierarchical colored petri nets. In: Proceedings of the 2008 International Conference on Computer and Electrical Engineering (ICCEE 2008), Phuket, Thailand, pp. 918–921. IEEE Press, December 2008
23. Arnold, F., Hermanns, H., Pulungan, R., Stoelinga, M.: Time-dependent analysis of attacks. In: Abadi, M., Kremer, S. (eds.) POST 2014 (ETAPS 2014). LNCS, vol. 8414, pp. 285–305. Springer, Heidelberg (2014)
24. Godhavn, J.M., Pavlov, A., Kaasa, G.O., Rolland, N.L.: Drilling seeking automatic control solutions. In: Proceedings of the 18th IFAC World Congress, Milano, Italy, pp. 10842–10850. International Federation of Automatic Control, August 2011
25. Elliot, D., Montilva, J., Francis, P., Reitsma, D., Shelton, J., Roes, V.: Managed pressure drilling erases the lines. Oilfield Rev. **23**(1), 14–23 (2011)
26. Zhou, J., Stamnes, O.N., Aamo, O.M., Kaasa, G.O.: Switched control for pressure regulation and kick attenuation in a managed pressure drilling system. IEEE Trans. Control Syst. Technol. **19**(2), 337–350 (2011)
27. Ablard, P., Bell, C., Cook, D., Fornasier, I., Poyet, J.P., Sharma, S., Fielding, K., Lawton, L., Haines, G., Herkommer, M.A., McCarthy, K., Radakovic, M., Umar, L.: The expanding role of mud logging. Oilfield Rev. **24**(1), 24–41 (2012)
28. Pavel, D., Grayson, B.: MPD powers static pre-drill modeling with dynamic capacity. Drill. Contractor **68**(6), 110–113 (2012)
29. Perrow, C.: Normal Accidents: Living with High Risk Technologies. Princeton paperbacks, Princeton University Press, Princeton (1984)
30. Roy, A., Kim, D.S., Trivedi, K.S.: Attack Countermeasure Trees (ACT): towards unifying the constructs of attack and defense trees. Secur. Commun. Netw. **5**(8), 929–943 (2012)

31. Sandaruwan, G.P.H., Ranaweera, P.S., Oleshchuk, V.A.: PLC security and critical infrastructure protection. In: Proceedings of the 8th IEEE International Conference on Industrial and Information Systems (ICIIS 2013), Kandy, Sri Lanka, pp. 81–85. IEEE Press, December 2013

32. Burgess, T., Starkey, A.A., White, D.: Improvements for kick detection. Oilfield Rev. **2**(1), 43–51 (1990)

The Effect of Branch Parameter Errors to Voltage Stability Indices

Vedran Kirincic[1(✉)], Markos Asprou[2], Petros Mavroeidis[2], and Elias Kyriakides[2]

[1] Faculty of Engineering, University of Rijeka, Vukovarska 58, Rijeka, Croatia
vedran.kirincic@riteh.hr
[2] KIOS Research Center for Intelligent Systems and Networks and the Department of Electrical and Computer Engineering, University of Cyprus, 1678 Nicosia, Cyprus
{asprou.markos,petros.mavroeidis,elias}@ucy.ac.cy

Abstract. Errors in the values of network parameters stored in the control center may affect the important application of voltage stability monitoring. This paper investigates the effect of branch parameters errors to voltage stability monitoring, using the state vector obtained by the state estimator. In particular, the state vector is used for calculating a voltage stability index that indicates the most critical branch (the one that first reaches its active power transfer limit). The states of the power system are estimated under various scenarios of possible errors in the reactance of the critical branch and then are used for the calculation of the voltage stability index. The case studies are performed using the IEEE systems with 14 and 39 buses and it is shown that the calculated value of the stability index depends on the error in the branch parameters, the power system structure and the contingency leading to voltage instability.

Keywords: Voltage stability monitoring · Branch parameter error · State estimation · Synchronized measurement technology · Phasor measurement unit · Power systems

1 Introduction

The advent of synchronized measurement technology has triggered a renewed interest in voltage stability monitoring. The fast reporting rate and the time stamping of the synchronized phasor measurements in combination with advances in ICT infrastructure enable increased capabilities in the monitoring of voltage stability [1]. The development of better voltage stability monitoring and enhancement tools has become urgent due to the transformation of

This work was co-funded by the European Regional Development Fund and the Republic of Cyprus through the Research Promotion Foundation (Project PENEK/0311/42 for the state estimation part and Project PROSELKYSH/NEOS/0311/34 for the stability part.

© Springer International Publishing Switzerland 2016
C.G. Panayiotou et al. (Eds.): CRITIS 2014, LNCS 8985, pp. 122–134, 2016.
DOI: 10.1007/978-3-319-31664-2_13

power systems, as a result of deregulation, renewable energy integration and the tighter financial environment. The consumer demand is increasing without analogous investments in infrastructure, the power market is adopting a competitive structure, and power systems are moving towards the smart grid paradigm with the main vehicle being further renewable integration. The occurrence and impact of several recent blackouts [2] have further shifted attention and funding towards the development of tools for the voltage stability monitoring that incorporate synchronized phasor measurements provided mainly by phasor measurement units (PMUs).

There are a number of approaches for assessing the voltage stability of a power system [3]. Traditional methods include the PV curve and VQ curve methods, as well as methods based on the singularity of the power flow Jacobian matrix at the point of bifurcation [4]. Innovative approaches include the use of decision trees [5], artificial neural networks [6], and statistical methods, such as k-nearest neighbors [7]. In [8] a research work on the application of synchronized measurement technology for monitoring the stability in a power system and taking necessary control actions in a coordinated manner to avoid an unstable scenario is reported. Other approaches consider the Thevenin equivalent, a critical analysis of which is made in [9]. From the system operator's point of view, quantitative metrics, such as voltages stability indices, are needed. A review of such indices can be found in [10], while an analysis of the advantages and disadvantages of distributed vs centralized approaches can be found in [11]. An emulation to assess the computational burden and the applicability of an algorithm monitoring small-signal stability can be found in [12].

The accuracy of the assessment of the voltage stability of a power system, by any of the above methods, depends on the accuracy of the information regarding the operating state of the system. The state estimator is the main source of providing this information and its accuracy is of paramount importance since its output is used as input in many functions of the power system control center. The accuracy of the state estimator is considerably improved by the use of synchronized phasor measurements in its measurement vector. Although the use of only synchronized phasor measurements in a linear state estimator would be the ideal scenario, such a case is not yet realistic since the PMUs are installed incrementally in the power system measurement layer and thus the power systems are partially observable by PMUs. Therefore, the use of both synchronized and conventional measurements (power flows, power injections and voltage magnitudes) is the most appropriate solution for the application of the synchronized measurement technology in state estimator. Such a state estimator scheme is called hybrid [13].

In this work, the hybrid state estimator proposed in [13] and the linear state estimator explained in [14] are used to estimate the states of each bus and the power flows at each branch. Further, a stability index is used locally for each branch to determine the distance until reaching instability. This mixed strategy, which incorporates a central state estimator and a distributed computation of voltage stability, serves two purposes. On one hand, the state estimator filters measurements errors and accounts for the probability of no power measurement device in the critical branch. In addition, it is an application already running in the SCADA room. On the other hand, the additional computational time needed for voltage stability indices at individual branches is minimal and the requirement of an enhanced monitoring of voltage stability is satisfied, as all branches are monitored. The above concepts are analyzed in detail in the following sections and applied to the IEEE 14 and 39 bus systems [15,16]. The paper is organized as follows. Section 2 describes the state estimation theoretical background, while Sect. 3 provides the used voltage stability detection methodology. In Sect. 4, the simulated case studies are explained. In Sects. 5 and 6, the obtained results are demonstrated and discussed. The paper concludes in Sect. 7.

2 State Estimation Theoretical Background

The state estimator provides the power system states (i.e., buses voltage magnitude and angle) in consecutive time intervals of 30 s to 5 min, using measurements from dispersed substations, such as real/reactive power flows, real/reactive power injections, and voltage magnitudes. The full observability of the power system by the available measurements for obtaining a unique solution by the state estimator is a prerequisite. The most widely used formulation for the power system state estimator is the Weighted Least Squares (WLS) where the objective is the minimization of function $J(\mathbf{x})$ as:

$$J(x) = [z - h(x)]R^{-1}[z - h(x)] \tag{1}$$

By taking the derivative of $J(\mathbf{x})$ over $\mathbf{x}$ and applying Taylor series the following Gauss Newton iterative scheme is obtained:

$$x^{k+1} = x^k + [G(x^k)]^{-1}H^T(x^k)R^{-1}[z - h(x^k)] \tag{2}$$

where $\mathbf{H}(\mathbf{x})$ is the Jacobian matrix and is equal to $\partial h(x)/\partial x$, $\mathbf{G}(\mathbf{x})$ is the gain matrix, given by $H^T(x)R^{-1}H(x)$, and $\mathbf{R}$ is the measurement error covariance matrix. It is to be noted that the iterative procedure stops when the element of Δx^{k+1} (the difference of $\mathbf{x}$ between two consecutive iterations) with the absolute maximum value is smaller than a predefined threshold.

As it is aforementioned, the use of voltage and current phasor measurements in the state estimator measurement vector improves the accuracy of the state estimator and such state estimator formulation is called hybrid. However, one should be careful with the inclusion of the current phasor measurements in the hybrid state estimator measurement vector, since their inclusion maybe detrimental in the performance of the state estimator [17]. More specifically, the elements of the Jacobian matrix that correspond to the current phasor measurements may become undefined during the iterative procedure. Therefore, many approaches have been proposed in the literature for overcoming this problem. In this paper, the hybrid state estimator proposed in [13] is used for estimating the power system states. In this hybrid state estimator formulation the current phasor measurements are transformed to pseudo flow measurements as:

$$P_{ij_{pseudo}} = V_i I_{ij} \cos(\theta_i - \theta_{ij}) \tag{3}$$

$$Q_{ij_{pseudo}} = V_i I_{ij} \sin(\theta_i - \theta_{ij}) \tag{4}$$

Therefore, the measurement vector of the hybrid state estimator is formed as:

$$z = \begin{bmatrix} P_{fl} & P_{fl}^{pse} & P_{inj} & Q_{fl} & Q_{fl}^{pse} & Q_{inj} & \theta_V^{PMU} & V_{PMU} \end{bmatrix}^T \tag{5}$$

Further, in this work a linear state estimator is also used for tracking the dynamics of the power system states in case of a fault, exploiting the fast reporting rate of the PMU measurements. Although the current situation in the deployment of the PMUs does not allow the application of a linear state estimator, this will not be the case in the near future since the electric utilities install more and more PMUs, and therefore the power systems will be fully observable by PMUs. The formulation of a linear state estimator implies the transformation of the voltage and current phasor measurements from polar to rectangular form. Therefore, the measurements of the PMUs can be expressed as a function of the rectangular power system states as [14]:

$$z = Hx + e = \begin{bmatrix} V_r^{meas} \\ V_i^{meas} \\ I_r^{meas} \\ I_i^{meas} \end{bmatrix} = \begin{bmatrix} \partial V_r/\partial V_r & \partial V_r/\partial V_i \\ \partial V_i/\partial V_r & \partial V_i/\partial V_i \\ \partial I_r/\partial V_r & \partial I_r/\partial V_i \\ \partial I_i/\partial V_r & \partial I_i/\partial V_i \end{bmatrix} \begin{bmatrix} V_r \\ V_i \end{bmatrix} + e \tag{6}$$

where V_r, V_i, I_r, I_i are the real and imaginary parts of the bus voltage phasors and the branch current phasors respectively when they are expressed in rectangular form.

Based on the WLS framework the minimisation of function $J(x)$ will result in the non-iterative estimation procedure of the state vector:

$$x = (H^T R^{-1} H)^{-1} H^T R^{-1} z \tag{7}$$

3   Voltage Stability Detection Methodology

An analysis of voltage stability monitoring approaches has been presented in the introductory section. These may vary from just considering higher and lower thresholds for voltage values to applying complex computational schemes. This work is based on power margins and voltage stability indices. In [10,18], a thorough comparison of several voltages stability indices available in the literature is given. The indices were used to monitor online voltage stability margins in a power system using PMUs. The method proposed in [19,20] starts from determining the sending and receiving ends of the branch, depending on the active power flow direction. With respect to the pi-model of the network branch given in Fig. 1 in which the branch parameters R and L are the series resistance and inductance, the parameters G and C are the shunt conductance and capacitance, a is the off-nominal tap position of transformer (in the case of the transmission line $a = 1$), and $z_V = z_V \angle \varphi_V$ is the load impedance, knowing the voltage

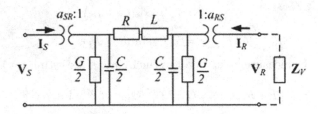

Fig. 1. The pi-model of the network branch with the tap modeling and load impedance

$V_S = V_S\angle\varphi_{V_S}$ and the current $I_S = I_S\angle\varphi_{I_S}$ phasors at the sending end, the receiving end voltage $V_R = V_R\angle\varphi_{V_R}$ and the current $I_R = I_R\angle\varphi_{I_R}$ phasors are obtained:

$$V_R = \left(\frac{V_S}{a_{SR}}K - I_S a_{SR}Z\right)a_{RS} \qquad (8)$$

$$I_R = \frac{1}{a_{RS}}\left[\left(\frac{V_S}{a_{SR}}K - I_S a_{SR}Z\right)D - \frac{V_S}{a_{SR}Z}\right] = \frac{1}{a_{RS}}\left[V_R D - \frac{V_S}{a_{SR}Z}\right] \qquad (9)$$

where $\mathbf{Z}$, $\mathbf{K}$ and $\mathbf{D}$ are given as:

$$Z = Z\angle\varphi_Z = R + j\omega L = R + jX \qquad (10)$$

$$K = K\angle\varphi_K = 1 + \frac{1}{2}\left[RG - \omega^2 LC + j\omega\left(CR + LG\right)\right] \qquad (11)$$

$$D = D\angle\varphi_D = \frac{1}{Z} + \frac{G}{2} + j\omega\frac{C}{2} \qquad (12)$$

The apparent power at the receiving end is calculated using the voltage and current phasors, while the active power at the receiving bus is obtained as the real part of the apparent power:

$$S_R = V_R I_R^* = V_R\left[\frac{1}{a_{RS}}\left(V_R^* D^* - \frac{V_S^*}{a_{SR}Z^*}\right)\right] = \left(\frac{V_R}{a_{RS}}\right)^2 D e^{j(-\varphi_D)}$$
$$- \frac{V_S V_R}{a_{SR}a_{RS}Z}e^{j\left(\varphi_Z + \varphi_{V_R} - \varphi_{V_S}\right)} \qquad (13)$$

$$P_R = \left(\frac{V_R}{a_{RS}}\right)^2 D\cos\left(\varphi_D\right) - \frac{V_S V_R}{a_{SR}a_{RS}Z}\cos\left(\varphi_Z + \varphi_{V_R} - \varphi_{V_S}\right) \qquad (14)$$

The operating characteristic of the network branch is obtained by expressing the receiving end voltage magnitude V_R as the function of the sending end voltage magnitude V_S, the receiving end active power P_R, the load impedance angle φ_{Z_V} and the branch parameters:

$$V_{R_{1,2}} = \sqrt{\frac{P_R M}{\cos\left(\varphi_{Z_V}\right)K} + \frac{V_S^2}{2K^2} \pm \sqrt{\left(\frac{P_R M}{\cos\left(\varphi_{Z_V}\right)K} + \frac{V_S^2}{2K^2}\right)^2 - \left(\frac{P_R Z}{\cos\left(\varphi_{Z_V}\right)K}\right)^2}} \qquad (15)$$

where $M = R\cos(\varphi_{Z_V} + \varphi_K) + \omega L \sin(\varphi_{Z_V} + \varphi_K)$. The maximum transferrable active power is derived by equating the internal root of the given expression to zero:

$$P_{R\max_{1,2}} = \frac{-V_s^2 \cos(\varphi_{Z_V})(M \mp Z)}{2a_{s_R}^2 K(M^2 - Z^2)} = \frac{-V_s^2 \cos(\varphi_{Z_V})}{2a_{s_R}^2 K(M \pm Z)} \quad (16)$$

After considering the smaller of two solutions for $P_{R\max_{1,2}}$, the power stability transfer margin $P_{R\text{margin}}$ is introduced by subtracting the actual power at the receiving end from the obtained maximum power. The stability indices (SI_j), as proposed in [21,22], are calculated for each network branch j. The lower the SI_j is, the closer the receiving bus is to its marginally stable operation point, with the lower margin left. The SI for the whole system is obtained by finding the minimum in the set of j buses:

$$SI = \min\{SI_j\} = \min\left\{\frac{P_{Rj\max} - P_{Rj}}{P_{Rj\max}} = \frac{P_{Rj\text{margin}}}{P_{Rj\max}}\right\} \quad (17)$$

The described approach is simple to implement and requires minimal computational effort, so it can be used for online applications.

4 Case Studies

The impact of the network branch parameter errors on the calculation of power margins and SI was analyzed using the standard IEEE test systems with 14 and 39 buses. The static and dynamic data for the test systems were modeled in the PowerWorld simulator [23]. The values computed in PowerWorld are considered as the actual values while the measurements used as inputs for the state estimators (implemented in Matlab) are created by adding Gaussian noise to the actual values. The standard deviation values, according to the type of measurement, are shown in Table 1.

Table 1. Maximum measurement uncertainties

Measurement type	Maximum measurement uncertainty
Real/reactive power flow and injection (p.u.)	3/100
Voltage magnitude PMU (p.u)	0.02/100
Current magnitude PMU (p.u)	0.03/100
Phase angle PMU (degrees)	0.54

The noisy measurements were processed by the state estimator to derive the power system state vector, which includes the voltage phasors for all the buses assuming a fully observable power system. In the first case, a consecutive load increase was assumed in the IEEE 14-bus system. More specifically, the active

Table 2. Placement of measurements in the IEEE 14-bus system

Measurement type	Measurement location
Flow measurement location (bus # - bus #)	1–2, 4–9, 4–5, 5–6, 6–12, 6–13, 7–8, 7–9, 13–14
Injection measurements location (bus #)	1, 2, 3, 4, 6, 9, 10, 11, 12, 13, 14
PMU location (bus #)	2, 6, 9

Table 3. Placement of measurements in the IEEE 39-bus system

Measurement type	Measurement location
PMU location (bus #)	2, 6, 9, 10, 11, 14, 17, 19, 20, 22, 23, 25, 29

power of the load at bus #2 was increased from the initial value of 10 MW to the final value of 1000 MW in 100 time steps. The states of the IEEE 14-bus system were provided by the hybrid state estimator and the types and the locations of conventional and synchronized measurement units for rendering the IEEE 14-bus system observable are tabulated in Table 2. It is to be noted that the locations of the PMU measurements were chosen for maximizing the accuracy of the hybrid state estimator, according to the methodology proposed in [24]. In the second case study, a dynamic scenario was simulated in the IEEE 39-bus system with a more severe change of the power system state. A generator outage at bus #39 was simulated in $t_{OUTAGE}=1$ s, with the total simulation time of $t_{TOTAL}=20$ s. The transient stability results for each time instant were put into the linear state estimator, which was able to track the fast system dynamics. The output of the linear state estimator was then used to determine the active power margins and SI. The locations of PMUs for having full power system observability are tabulated in Table 3. These locations that are determined using the methodology proposed in [25], are the optimal in terms of minimizing the number of PMUs needed for rendering the power system observable.

As it is aforementioned, the main purpose of this paper is the investigation of the dependency of the voltage stability monitoring scheme on the branch parameter errors. The literature review reveals that the branch parameter values stored in the databases could vary from the real ones as high as 30 % of their nominal values [26, 27]. Therefore simulations are performed for different levels of parameter errors of the critical branches. In this paper, it is assumed, without loss of generality, that the erroneous parameter of the network branches is only the reactance.

The first simulated scenario for both test systems is performed without errors in branch reactances, in order to identify the critical branch and use it as a base case for the subsequent scenarios. After the lowest value of the SI was found, the offset of $\pm 5\%$, $\pm 10\%$ $\pm 20\%$ and $\pm 30\%$ was added in further simulations to the reactance of the critical branch. Additionally, for the IEEE-39 bus test system in each of the simulated cases, the time difference (t_{DIFF}) and the active power margin difference (PM_{DIFF}) between the case without parameter errors (base case) and for the case with erroneous parameters are calculated. The time difference corresponds to the instances at which power margins start decreasing rapidly. The power margin difference is the difference in power margins at the time instant when the power margin for the case with a branch error starts decreasing rapidly.

5   Results

In the case of the IEEE 14-bus system where a consecutive load increase at bus #2 is assumed, the critical branch is the one connecting buses #1 and #2 (the receiving end). Figure 2 shows the active power flow, limit and margin, considering a $\pm 30\%$ error in the critical branch reactance. It can be observed that when the active power flow in Fig. 2(a) reaches the maximum active power value, the active power margin in Fig. 2(b) drops to zero. Also, the receiving end voltage magnitude in Fig. 2(c) continuously decreases as the load value increases. In Fig. 2(d) the stability index decreases as the system approaches instability. The dotted and dashed lines represent the results obtained with $\pm 30\%$ error in the critical branch reactance, respectively. It can be observed that in the case of $+30\%$ error, the calculated power margin is lower than the actual one, while in the case when -30% error in the critical branch reactance is assumed, the calculated power margin is larger than the actual one. Instability is detected for all cases at the same time with differences in SI being rather small. However, the latter is misleading as SI is relatively insensitive to power margin differences due to the large value of the denominator, P_{max}. The effect of the critical branch parameter error is more apparent when considering power margin differences instead of SI, Fig. 2(b). For instance, if the trigger of remedial actions was based on a threshold of the power margin then the error in the branch parameter would lead in different triggering times. In addition, for a given change in the load an error in branch parameter could lead either to false alarm or no detection of a potentially dangerous operating point regarding voltage stability.

In the scenario performed in the IEEE 39-bus system, a generator outage at bus #39 was assumed. The critical branch is the one connecting buses #26 (the receiving end) and #29. Figure 3 shows the active power flow, limit and margin, considering as well a $\pm 30\%$ error in the #26–#29 branch reactance. After the generator outage, the critical branch maximum power continuously decreases until it becomes equal to the actual power flow (Fig. 3(a)). As the system approaches instability, the power margin in Fig. 3(b) and the receiving bus voltage in Fig. 3(c) also decrease. Finally, the zero value of SI in Fig. 3(d) indicates that the system reached instability. Again, the dotted and dashed lines represent the results obtained with the $\pm 30\%$ error in the critical branch reactance, respectively. It is evident that the value of the -30% error results in higher power margin than the actual power margin value (without branch parameter error), while the $+30\%$ error gives lower power margin than the actual power margin value.

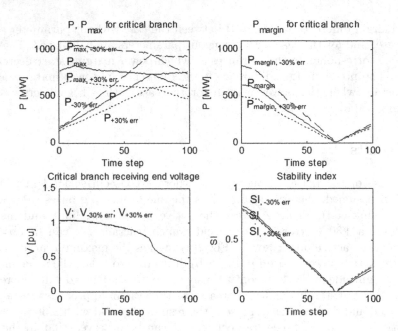

Fig. 2. Active power (flow, limit and margin), the receiving end voltage and *SI* for the IEEE 14-bus system without error (solid line) and with the ±30 % (+dotted, -dashed) error in the branch reactance

In order to study the effect of the branch reactance error to power margins and *SI* in detail, additional simulations are performed for the already described case scenario in the IEEE 39-bus system, with the errors of ±5 %, ±10 % ±20 % and ±30 % in the reactance of the critical branch. Figure 4 presents the power margin for the critical branch. In Table 4 t_{DIFF} and PM_{DIFF} are given for each of the simulated cases.

Table 4. Time difference (t_{DIFF}) and power margin difference (PM_{DIFF}) between the base case and the cases with error in the branch reactance for the IEEE 39-bus system

Error [%]	±5	±10	±20	±30	Error [%]	±5	±10	±20	±30
t_{DIFF} [s]	0.16	0.56	1.20	1.88	PM_{DIFF} [MW]	−21	−46.1	−82.6	−115.1
	−0.48	−0.82	−1.70	−2.84		21	58.7	129.2	226.8

Positive values of branch parameter errors lead to positive values of t_{DIFF} and negative values of PM_{DIFF} and vice versa. From the obtained results, it is clear that the negative error in branch reactance results in the larger absolute values of t_{DIFF} and PM_{DIFF} for all the simulated cases. In addition, for negative

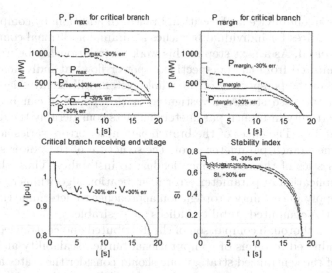

Fig. 3. Active power (flow, limit and margin), the receiving end voltage and *SI* for the IEEE 39-bus system without error (solid line) and with the ±30 % (+dotted, -dashed) error in the branch reactance

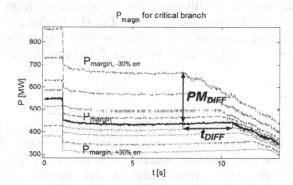

Fig. 4. The power margin for critical branch in the IEEE 39-bus system for the base case and for the cases with ±5 %, ±10 %, ±20 % and ±30 % error in the branch reactance

errors, a non linear dependence of both t_{DIFF} and PM_{DIFF} on the branch parameter error size is observed.

6 Discussion

The methodology presented in this paper uses a central state estimator to derive the states of the system, and a distributed monitoring scheme by calculating the voltage stability indices for the critical branch. The reason for the latter is that the state estimator acts like a filter to possible errors introduced by individual measurements and to account for the fact that it is probable not to have a power measurement device in the critical branch. In addition, by computing voltage stability indices for individual branches a minimal additional computational time is introduced. As a next step in this work the relationship between voltage stability monitored from the perspective of power flows at individual lines and monitored from the perspective of the whole system will be investigated.

Based on the case studies investigated in this paper it can be concluded that the uncertainty in branch parameters impacts considerably the detection of voltage instability. The effect of the branch parameter errors varies according to the sign of the branch parameter error, the structure of the power system and the characteristics of the contingency leading to instability. Thus, the development and application of parameter error identification algorithms or algorithms that would apply uncertainty propagation approaches to determine the standard deviation of the computed stability indices are desirable.

Moreover, a thorough comparison of the distributed and centralized strategies could be conducted in terms of computational burden-scalability and accuracy. In the case of the centralized strategy one should consider the states as obtained by the state estimator for assessing voltage instability, while in the distributed strategies the direct use of PMU measurements can be considered. The use of a state estimator (centralized approach) even in a power system fully observable by PMUs is beneficial since it can filter possible measurement errors. On the other hand, in case of not full observability by PMUs, the tracking of fast evolving contingencies that lead to power system voltage instability is not feasible using state estimator, but it could be using local raw PMU measurements if exist.

7   Conclusion

This paper investigates the effect of branch parameter errors to voltage stability monitoring. The input in the voltage stability monitoring methodology is given by a state estimator and various scenarios with respect to possible errors in branch parameters when the state estimator was executed are considered. Based on the active power flow margin, the stability index is obtained indicating the most critical branch that reaches its power transfer limit. The case studies were performed using the IEEE systems with 14 and 39 buses.

The calculated value of the stability index depends on the error in the branch parameters, which could negatively affect the system operator's ability to initiate proper actions to retain the system stability. Further, the system operator may not be able to apply the proper remedial action at the right time using incorrect information about the available transfer margin.

References

1. Novosel, D., Madani, V., Bhargava, B., Khoi, V., Cole, J.: Dawn of the grid synchronization. IEEE Power Energy Mag. **6**(1), 49–60 (2008)
2. Kirschen, D., Bouffard, F.: Keeping the lights on and the information flowing. IEEE Power Energy Mag. **7**(1), 50–60 (2009)

3. Van Cutsem, T., Vournas, C.: Voltage Stability of Electric Power Systems. Kluwer, Norwell (1998)
4. Kundur, P.: Power System Stability and Control. McGraw-Hill, New York (1994)
5. Diao, R., et al.: Decision tree-based online voltage security assessment using PMU measurements. IEEE Trans. Power Syst. **24**(2), 832–839 (2009)
6. Chakrabarti, S., Jeyasurya, B.: Multicontingency voltage stability monitoring of a power system using an adaptive radial basis function network. Int. J. Electr. Power Energy Syst. **30**(1), 1–7 (2008)
7. Adamiak, M.G., et al.: Wide area protection-technology and infrastructures. IEEE Trans. Power Deliv. **21**(2), 601–609 (2006)
8. Vittal, V., et al.: A tool for on-line stability determination and control for coordinated operations between regional entities using PMUs. PSERC (2008)
9. Wang, Y., Pordanjani, I.R., Li, W., Xu, W., Chen, T., Vaahedi, E., Gurney, J.: Voltage stability monitoring based on the concept of coupled single-port circuit. IEEE Trans. Power Syst. **26**(4), 2154–2163 (2011)
10. Salehi, V., Mohammed, O.: Real-time voltage stability monitoring and evaluation using synchrophasors. In: Proceedings of North American Power Symposium (NAPS) (2011)
11. Kamwa, I., Grondin, R., Hebert, Y.: Wide-area measurement based stabilizing control of large power systems-a decentralized/hierarchical approach. IEEE Trans. Power Syst. **16**, 136–153 (2001)
12. Interrante, J., Aggour, K.S.: Applying cluster computing to enable a large-scale smart grid stability monitoring application. In: High Performance Computing and Communication and IEEE 9th International Conference on Embedded Software and Systems (IIPCC-ICESS) (2012)
13. Asprou, M., Kyriakides, E.: Enhancement of hybrid state estimation using pseudo flow measurements. In: Proceedings of IEEE Power and Energy Society General Meeting, pp. 1–7 (2011)
14. Asprou, M., et al.: The use of a PMU-based state estimator for tracking power system dynamics. In: IEEE Power and Energy Society General Meeting (2014)
15. Christie, R.: Power system test archive. http://www.ee.washington.edu/research/pstca
16. Pai, M.A.: Energy Function Analysis for Power System Stability. Kluwer, Boston (1989)
17. Abur, A., Gomez-Exposito, A.: Power System State Estimation: Theory and Implementation. Springer, New York (2004)
18. Salehi, V., et al.: Laboratory-based smart power system, part II: control, monitoring, and protection. IEEE Trans. Smart Grid **3**(3), 1405–1417 (2012)
19. Nguegan, Y., et al.: Online monitoring of the electrical power transfer stability and voltage profile stability margins in electric power transmission systems using phasor measurement units data sets. In: Power and Energy Engineering Conference (2009)
20. Nguegan, Y.: Real-time identification and monitoring of the voltage stability margin in electric power transmission systems using synchronized phasor measurements. Ph.D. thesis, Department of Electrical Engineering, Kassel University, Kassel, Germany (2009)
21. Gong, Y., Schulz, N., Guzman, A.: Synchrophasor-based real-time voltage stability index. In: Proceedings of IEEE PES Power Systems Conference and Exposition (PSCE), pp. 1029–1036 (2006)
22. Gong, Y.: Development of an improved on-line voltage stability index using synchronized phasor measurement, Ph.D. thesis, Mississippi State University (2005)

23. PowerWorld corporation. http://powerworld.com
24. Asprou, M., Kyriakides, E.: Optimal PMU placement for improving hybrid state estimation accuracy. In: IEEE PowerTech, Norway (2011)
25. Chakrabarti, S., Kyriakides, E.: Optimal placement of phasor measurement units for power system observability. IEEE Trans. Power Syst. **23**(3), 1433–1440 (2008)
26. Kusic, G.L., Garrison, D.L.: Measurement of transmission line parameters from SCADA data. IEEE PES Power Syst. Conf. **1**, 440–445 (2004)
27. Bockarjova, M., Andersson, G.: Transmission line conductor temperature impact on state estimation accuracy. In: IEEE Power Tech, pp. 701–706 (2007)

CFD Simulation of Contaminant Transportation in High-Risk Buildings Using CONTAM

Andreas Nikolaou and Michalis P. Michaelides$^{(\boxtimes)}$

Department of Electrical Engineering, Computer Engineering and Informatics,
Cyprus University of Technology, 30 Archbishop Kyprianos Street,
3036 Lemesos, Cyprus
michalis.michaelides@cut.ac.cy

Abstract. In this work we study the problem of airborne contaminant transportation in high-risk buildings using CFD methods. The main contribution of this work is the design and evaluation of two building case studies using CONTAM coupled with the CFD0 Editor: (i) a conceptual office building with a large conference room surrounded by four smaller offices and (ii) the Pefkios Georgiades amphitheater which is a real building housed at the Cyprus University of Technology in Lemesos. For both case studies, a large number of scenarios were performed involving the transportation of a dangerous contaminant from various locations inside the building and recommendations were provided as to the number and locations of sensors that would guarantee prompt detection to ensure the safety of the people. A comparison of CFD to multi-zone and a study regarding the total computational time of CFD with respect to the grid size were also performed.

Keywords: High-risk buildings · Critical infrastructure protection · Contaminant transportation · CFD · CONTAM · Sensor placement

1 Introduction

High-risk buildings belong to Critical Infrastructures, which according to the European Council Directive 2008/114/EC are defined as those systems which are essential for maintaining the societal and economic well-being of the people, and in case their operation would be disrupted or destroyed, the state would fail in maintaining those functions [1]. These include governmental buildings and ministries, utilities, schools, airports and hospitals. In these buildings the indoor air quality can be compromised as a result of an accident or terrorist attack, affecting the health and the safety of its occupants. A possible type of terrorist attack is the release of some airborne chemical, biological or radiological agent in the building interior [2]. Under these safety-critical conditions, through various controls of the Air Handling System (AHS), the contaminant should be either diluted or completely removed (if possible) from the building zones with a quick and effective way, while at the same time ensuring minimum exposure for the

© Springer International Publishing Switzerland 2016
C.G. Panayiotou et al. (Eds.): CRITIS 2014, LNCS 8985, pp. 135–146, 2016.
DOI: 10.1007/978-3-319-31664-2_14

occupants. Thus, the placement of the sensors that will detect the presence of the contaminant becomes of paramount importance in order to have an effective emergency system.

For deciding where to place the sensors, we need to simulate a large number of scenarios by varying the source characteristics (position, evolution rate, onset time) in order to observe the dynamics of the contaminant transportation inside the building. For airborne contaminants, as the ones considered in this work, their transportation is primarily affected by the building airflows which can be calculated using multi-zone models or Computational Fluid Dynamics (CFD). Multi-zone models, represent a building as a network of well-mixed zones. Temperature, humidity, air velocity and pollutant concentration are assumed uniform within one zone. CFD modeling, on the other hand, involves numerically solving the conservation equations of mass, momentum, energy and species concentrations by dividing the space into a finite number of discrete cells and then using an iterative procedure to achieve a converged solution. It can provide the spatial distributions and temporal evolution of air pressure, velocity, temperature, humidity, contaminants, and turbulence intensity. The degree of accuracy of the method comes at the expense of high computational overhead and depends on the correct representation of the boundary conditions, the solution grid, and the level of transient characteristics [3]. CONTAM [4] is a multi-zone simulation software developed by the US National Institute of Standards and Technology (NIST), with which the user can easily create the building outline and specify the zone volumes, the openings, the environmental conditions, as well as the contaminant sources present, to compute airflows and simulate contaminant concentrations in the different building zones. In a recent release in 2011, CONTAM introduced the capability of including a single CFD zone inside a multi-zone building simulation using the CFD0 Editor - see [5]. This enables the detailed modeling of a zone when the well-mixed multi-zone assumption is not appropriate (i.e., for large open spaces) thus capturing the local distribution of air and contaminant properties in the specific zone.

The main contribution of this work is the design and evaluation of two building case studies using CONTAM coupled with the CFD0 Editor: (i) a conceptual office building with a large conference room surrounded by four smaller offices and (ii) the Pefkios Georgiades amphitheater which is a real building housed at the Cyprus University of Technology in Lemesos. Note that the Pefkios amphitheater is used for both academic purposes and for hosting a number of other important presentations with subjects ranging from business to politics, making it a critical infrastructure. The office building served as an evaluation platform for experimenting with the CFD capabilities of CONTAM, while the Pefkios Georgiades was a great chance to apply the methods in a real building setting. The CFD0 Editor was used for the 3-D design of one of the building zones in each scenario; the conference room in the first and the amphitheater in the second. Attention was paid to details, including the shape, the volumes, the airflows and the various furniture and appliances inside the CFD zone in order for the simulation to be as realistic as possible. For both buildings case studies, a large number of scenarios were investigated involving dangerous contaminant sources introduced in different locations inside the CFD zone. Each of the scenarios was simulated using CFD methods for producing detailed airflow information and contaminant concentrations in the zone of interest. Based on the simulation results of the scenarios investigated, recommendations were provided as to where to place the sensors in order to provide fast detection and ensure the safety of the people.

The problem of simulating contaminant transportation in buildings for detecting the presence of dangerous contaminants has received significant interest from the research community over the last decade using both CFD [6,7], as well as multi-zone models [3,8,9]. In this work, we use a CFD zone inside a multi-zone setting to construct and evaluate a realistic model of the Pefkios Georgiades amphitheater, in order to provide recommendations for placing the sensors inside.

The rest of this paper is organized as follows. In Sect. 2, we describe the design and evaluation of the office building case study while the Pefkios Georgiades amphitheater case study is analyzed in Sect. 3. Finally, Sect. 4 concludes the paper and discusses future work.

2   Office Building Scenario

In this section, we examine a conceptual office building composed of four small offices and a big conference room in the middle. We assume that natural ventilation is the dominant source of air-movement inside the building with the wind blowing from the west causing a pressure of 1 Pa on the wall exterior. Figure 1 shows the office outline as constructed on CONTAM, with the various rooms (zones) labeled together with the resulting pressures and airflows depicted with red and green lines respectively. The conference room in the middle with dimensions $10 \times 4 \times 3$ m was simulated as a CFD zone using a grid mesh of $42 \times 30 \times 24$ cells in the X,Y and Z directions respectively. The 3-D design constructed using CFD0 Editor includes a table surrounded by 9 chairs, a bookshelf and a projector as shown in Fig. 2.

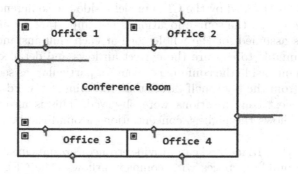

Fig. 1. Office building outline on CONTAM

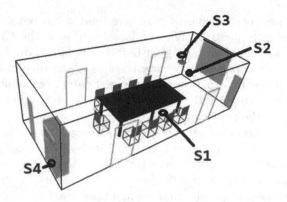

Fig. 2. 3D design of conference room.

Using the designed office building, four different scenarios were simulated and analyzed, involving a Carbon Monoxide (CO) source introduced at different locations inside the conference room with a continuous emission rate of 1000 gr/h. More specifically, we investigated the four following source location scenarios shown in Fig. 2: (i) under the conference table (S1); (ii) next to projector screen (S2); on the projector (S3); and (iv) on the bookshelf (S4). Some representative results for S4 are shown in Fig. 3(a) and (b), depicting the resulting airflows and contaminant concentration contour plots in the conference room respectively, for the slice corresponding to $Z = 1$ at time $t = 00:04:30$ (HH:MM:SS).

The average concentration time series for the same scenario (S4) is portrayed in Fig. 4 for the various office zones using both multi-zone and CFD simulation for the conference room. Note from the figure the large difference between the CFD results and the Multi-Zone (MZ) measurements for the various zones. In particular, for the MZ the only significant concentration in observed in the conference room reaching a steady state value of 420 ppm, whereas using the CFD model the conference room average concentration is smaller than 100 ppm while the largest concentrations are observed in Office 3 and Office 4 reaching values of 550 and 300 ppm respectively after 30 min. This difference is the result of the detailed analysis performed by the CFD model inside the conference room. Note that for the MZ model the source location is not important because a uniform concentration is assumed for the whole zone at each time instant. This makes the MZ model unable to capture the correct airflows and detailed propagation of the contaminant inside the conference room. In particular, as seen in Fig. 3(a) strong airflows from the bookshelf direct the contaminant towards Offices 3 and 4 where the largest concentrations were observed. This is also confirmed by Fig. 3(b) which shows the highest concentrations around the bookcase and the door to Office 3.

In summary, the MZ method can provide erroneous results in situations where we model large building spaces with complex airflows. The CFD method is in general a more accurate, realistic and trusted solution for these cases and should

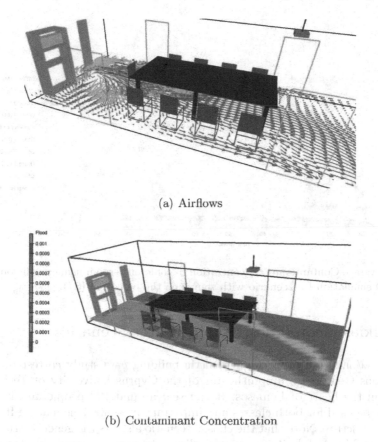

(a) Airflows

(b) Contaminant Concentration

Fig. 3. Conference room scenario with CO source on bookshelf (S4).

be preferred whenever possible. The only drawback of CFD is the computational time needed to perform the simulation that is far greater than MZ. The computational time of CFD simulations is further investigated in the next section.

Regarding sensor placement, the intuitive solution is to place the sensors in specific building areas that receive high contaminant concentration in order to ensure the prompt detection of the contaminant. In the four different scenarios simulated, however, there wasn't any overlap between the sources' regions of influence (regions with high contaminant concentration). So there was not a possible location that a sensor could be installed in order to detect the contaminant coming from more than one source so the only possibility was to install four different sensors, one for each case. Note however, that this is because the chosen scenarios were (i) limited in number and (ii) selected to be as different from each other as possible. For correctly solving the sensor placement problem, a large number of scenarios need to be considered in order to adequately cover the possible source characteristics (location, onset time, release rate) as well as the changing environmental conditions affecting the contaminant propagation.

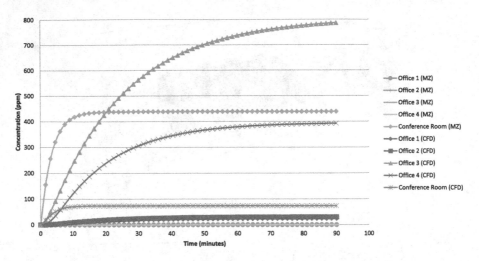

Fig. 4. Average Contaminant concentration in conference room using multi-zone (MZ) and CFD simulation for scenario with source on the bookshelf (S4).

3 Pefkios Georgiades Amphitheater Scenario

In this section, we investigate a realistic building case study corresponding to the Pefkios Georgiades amphitheater of the Cyprus University of Technology located in the heart of Lemesos. It can seat around 120 people and it is currently being used for both classes and important presentations making it a Critical Infrastructure. Note that the chosen scenario also fits the general structure of many other high-risk buildings (i.e., parliaments, shopping malls, theaters, cinemas or stadiums) containing a large covered open-space area with forced ventilation. Figure 5 shows the 3-D design of the amphitheater using the program CFD0 Editor (Fig. 5(a)), the outline of the surrounding spaces and boundaries sketched using CONTAM (Fig. 5(b)), as well as a comparison of the sketched and real amphitheater (Fig. 5(c)). The amphitheater has dimensions $16 \times 15 \times 6$ m and was simulated as a CFD zone using a grid mesh of $120 \times 140 \times 60$ cells in the X,Y and Z directions respectively. Note that the actual shape of the amphitheater is oval but CONTAM (and the CFD0 Editor) does not have the ability to draw such shapes so it was needed to use a staircase approximation as shown in Fig. 5(b). We assumed forced ventilation as a result of the AHS with flows primarily originating from air ducts on the floor (Fig. 5(e)) and returning through a large air duct above the main desk (Fig. 5(d)). Note that the current implementation of a CFD zone inside CONTAM does not support an AHS so fictitious floors were added above and below the amphitheater in order to simulate the presence of the air ducts. All airflows were measured using a flow meter (average value of 3 m/s for supply and 2.5 m/s for return) in order for the simulation to be as realistic as possible.

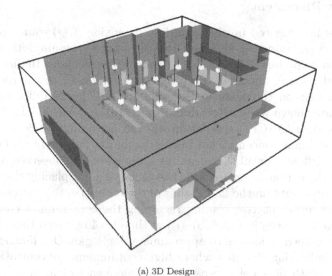

(a) 3D Design

(b) Outline of amphitheater

(c) Comparison between real and sketched amphitheater

(d) Air duct above main desk   (e) Air duct on the floor

Fig. 5. 3D design of amphitheater Pefkios Georgiades.

3.1   Sensor Placement

The scenarios investigated involve a carbon monoxide (CO) source of emission rate 500 g/min positioned at different locations inside the amphitheater. More specifically, we experimented with a CO source placed under the main desk in the front of the room, one near the projector at the back of the room and 24 different locations on the seats in the auditorium. The 26 different locations investigated are shown with yellow dots in Fig. 6(a). For each of these scenarios, the coupled CONTAM-CFD simulation was ran providing the detailed airflows and the contaminant concentration inside the amphitheater. In general, due to the resulting airflows, for all the scenarios investigated we observed an upwards movement of the contaminant towards the ceiling. So, for placing the sensors we decided to concentrate on the last Z-slice of the room (i.e. the one closest to the ceiling.) Some representative results, regarding the contaminant concentration at slice $Z = 60$ are shown in Fig. 6(b)–(d) at time $t = 40$ s. From these figures, we used simple geometrical shapes to approximate the Region Of Influence (ROI) of each source, indicating the area where high contaminant concentration (shown on the figures with pink color) was observed, enough to trigger a sensor. This resulted in a circular ROI for the sources placed near the amphitheater seats, a rectangular ROI for the source placed near the projector and a square ROI for the source placed under the main desk demonstrated in Fig. 6(b)–(d). Then by spatially superimposing the ROIs for all the different scenarios and finding the places where they overlap, we came up with 9 recommended sensor locations for covering all 26 different scenarios. These locations are indicated with purple dots in Fig. 6(a), together with the source ROI for the different scenarios investigated. So, with the 9 recommended sensors, it is possible to detect anyone of the contaminant sources investigated (and possibly many more) in 40 s or less.

In addition to CO, we also experimented with a Sarin source, a deadly contaminant that is classified as a weapon of mass destruction. In this scenario, the source of emission rate 500 g/min is placed not in the amphitheater, but in the air ducts of the building in order to simulate a possible terrorist attack. The idea is that the terrorist could have installed the container holding the dangerous substance (Sarin) into the air ducts at a time of low security measures and trigger the releasing mechanism using a remote control during an important event taking place at Pefkios. After simulating this scenario, due to the location of the air-vents and the resulting airflows, the contaminant was quickly spread inside the whole amphitheater. Therefore, the only possible measure for protecting the people inside the amphitheater, is installing sensors inside the supply ducts of the AHS and shutting down the ventilation system as soon as the contaminant is detected. At the same time, the building should be evacuated immediately.

3.2   Computational Time

The total computing time for the coupled CONTAM-CFD simulation can be divided into three parts [7]: (i) Multi-zone calls, (ii) Iterative exchange of boundary conditions and (iii) CFD calls. From these, CFD calls take up most of the

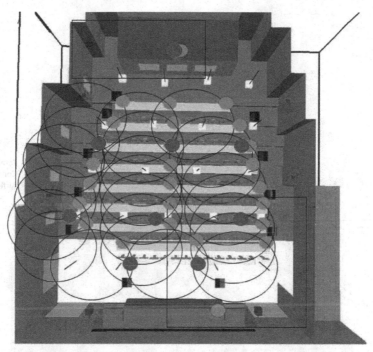

(a) Sensors (purple) and Sources (yellow)

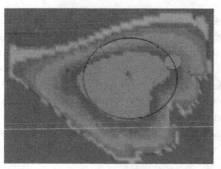

(b) ROI for seat scenario

(c) ROI for main desk scenario

(d) ROI for projector scenario

Fig. 6. Sensor placement in pefkios amphitheater (Color figure online).

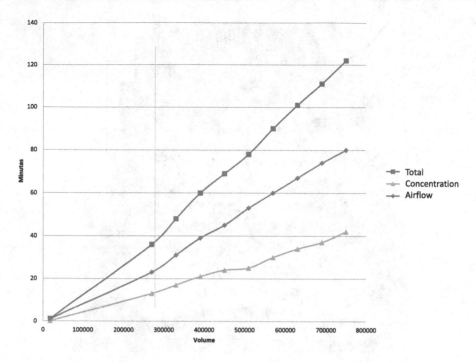

Fig. 7. Computing time vs. Number of grid cells

total computing time. However, there is one more important factor. It is the size of the 3-dimensional grid. Figure 7 shows the computing time for the same scenario using different grid sizes. The simulation has been performed by the following system: Microsoft Windows XP Professional x64 bit SP2, Intel Xeon CPU, X5660 @2,80 GHz, 2,79 GHz, 11,9 GB of RAM. The figure shows the computing time for performing the airflow calculations, the concentration calculations and the total time which is the sum of the two. From the plot, it becomes evident that the total time needed increases linearly with the grid resolution so in order to minimize computation time, we should use the minimum resolution that produces reasonable results.

For the investigated scenario, this minimum resolution is shown with the orange line in Fig. 7; below this critical point, the calculated airflows are no more representative of the real situation. This is mainly due to restrictions imposed by the specific building case study. In particular, the area of the air supply ducts on the floor and the return duct on the wall above the main desk, must be taken into consideration to determine the size of the grid in each axis. Another restriction has to do with the size of any other object restraining or changing the airflows (for example, the stairs of the amphitheater). Note, that such an analysis should be performed for each different building case study, in order to minimize the computational time without compromising the accuracy of the simulations. Of course, if simulation time and computing power are not an issue, one should select the highest grid resolution possible in order to achieve the most detailed and accurate results.

4   Conclusions and Future Work

In this work, two building case studies were designed using CONTAM that include a large zone which was simulated using CFD methods: (i) a conceptual office building and (ii) the Pefkios Georgiades amphitheater. For both case studies, a large number of scenarios were performed involving the transportation of a dangerous contaminant from various locations inside the CFD zone. For both scenarios, recommendations were provided as to the number and locations of sensors that would provide prompt detection to ensure the safety of the people. Moreover, for the office building scenario, a comparison was performed with multi-zone to highlight the differences and demonstrate the importance of using CFD simulation in large building spaces. Finally, for the Pefkios scenario, a study was performed concerning the computational time of the CFD simulation and the minimum grid resolution for obtaining adequate results.

In the future, we plan to investigate other critical buildings using CFD simulation software and provide recommendations as to where to place the sensors. Currently, our reasoning was based on the analysis of a limited number of scenarios that involved different source locations. In the future, we will also experiment by changing other source parameters (type, number, magnitude, evolution rate) as well as environmental conditions affecting the flows (wind speed, wind direction, temperature). Finally, this work would not be complete without the design of the control system responsible for making the right decisions at the right time. These involve automatically opening and closing doors and windows and controlling the status of the AHS following the detection of a contaminant in order to ensure the safety of the people.

References

1. Commission, E.: Council directive 2008/114/ec of 8 december 2008 on the identification and designation of european critical infrastructures and the assessment of the need to improve their protection. Official J. Eur. Union **L345**(23), 12 (2008)
2. Cousins, D., Campbell, S.D.: Protecting buildings against airborne contamination. Lincoln Lab. J. **17**(1), 131–152 (2007)
3. Chen, Y., Wen, J.: Sensor system design for building indoor air protection. Build. Environ. **43**(7), 1278–1285 (2008)
4. Walton, G., Dols, W.: CONTAM 2.4 user guide and program documentation. National Institute of Standards and Technology, Gaithersburg, MD 20899–8633, 2.4c edn. nISTIR 7251, October 2005
5. Wang, L., Dols, W., Chen, Q.: Using CFD capabilities of CONTAM 3.0 for simulating airflow and contaminant transport in and around buildings. HVAC&R Res. **16**(6), 749–763 (2010)
6. Arvelo, J., Brandt, A., Roger, R., Saksena, A.: An enhanced multizone model and its application to optimum placement of CBW sensors. ASHRAE Trans. **108**(2), 818–826 (2002)

7. Zhai, Z., Srebric, J., Chen, Q.: Application of CFD to predict and control chemical and biological agent dispersion in buildings. Int. J. Vent. **2**(3), 251–264 (2003)
8. Michaelides, M., Reppa, V., Christodoulou, M., Panayiotou, C., Polycarpou, M.: Contaminant event monitoring in multi-zone buildings using the state-space method. Build. Environ. **71**, 140–152 (2014)
9. Eliades, D., Michaelides, M., Panayiotou, C., Polycarpou, M.: Security-oriented sensor placement in intelligent buildings. Build. Environ. **63**, 114–121 (2013)

Detection and Management of Large Scale Disturbances in Power System

Antans Sauhats, Vladimir Chuvychin, Galina Bockarjova, Diana Zalostiba,
Dmitrijs Antonovs, and Roman Petrichenko[✉]

Institute of Power Engineering, Riga Technical University, Riga, Latvia
{sauhats,chuvychin,galina}@eef.rtu.lv,
{Diana.Zalostiba,Dmitrijs.Antonovs,Romans.Petricenko}@rtu.lv

Abstract. Recent blackouts of major power systems (PSs) clearly demonstrate the topicality of the blackout problem when rapid multiple tripping of vital PS elements leads not only to PS collapse but also essentially affects the operation of other critical infrastructures. To prevent such situations special types of automation such as PS splitting and frequency control automation are employed. Taking into account the drawbacks of existing devices the new methods and technical solutions to increase sustainability to such events are discussed.

Keywords: Power systems · Automation · Load shedding · Protection · Blackout prevention · Power system restoration

1 Introduction

Depletion of fossil energy resources, energy consumption growth, the electricity market liberalization, the increasing number of large cities and new structures, which are critical to the power supply interruptions, are factors, which threaten operational security and affect power system (PS) management and control, encountering new problems and challenges. Consequently there is an increasing risk of development of a severe emergency (or even blackout) leading to enormous losses [1–3].

Maintaining reliability and efficiency of power supply under numerous uncertainties is the main task being solved during power system operation. Based on the detailed blackout analysis (mainly shown in [4]) in the most cases the dangerous overload of transmission grid initiates the development of severe emergency situation (e.g. multiple line tripping, stability loss, voltage instability) which spreading in cascade-wise manner and giving the start to other emergency processes (e.g. oscillations/swings, frequency emergency); each of the emergency processes triggered by the overload and their aftereffects can cause outages of generating units and as a result a partial or complete PS blackout. The blackout analysis has shown that the most severe conditions for the generating unit (incl. boilers, turbines, reactors, pumps, generators) are asynchronous operation (AO) or out-of-step followed by PS uncontrolled splitting and frequency drop

© Springer International Publishing Switzerland 2016
C.G. Panayiotou et al. (Eds.): CRITIS 2014, LNCS 8985, pp. 147–152, 2016.
DOI: 10.1007/978-3-319-31664-2_15

emergency [3–5]. The process of blackout development is complicated, develops very rapidly, so personnel cannot adequately react on such events. For that reason protection should be fast-acting and preventive being oriented towards the complete automation of the process (in pre-emergency, emergency and after-emergency mode).

It should be noted that operation and control of modern PSs cannot exist without usage of information and communication systems. Erroneous operation or non-operation of such systems, e.g. due to cyber-attacks, make the system very labile and can misinform the operators about existing PS conditions thus causing development of PS collapse. Since the threats of PS blackout development will exist always and are hardly predictable the special protection schemes and systems such as out-of-step prevention and advanced automatic under frequency load shedding are efficient means to diminish the probability and aftereffects of severe emergency development.

2   Emergency Automation

Usually to prevent and eliminate AO the local protection and automation devices monitoring voltages and currents at selected transmission lines (TLs) are used. The main aim of such devices is to detect out-of-step during beginning of its development and to divide the PS grid into pre-determined areas. Evaluation of AO threats is based on the real-time information collected from a single TL terminal. The newest technology integrates Global Positioning System (GPS) receivers providing for synchronised phasors measurements [6] over multiple grid locations ensuring accuracy of better than one microsecond [7].

To detect AO the various local and wide-area systems can be used (given in details in [7]). As shown by [6,7], wide-area systems with remote synchronised measurements may be realised using measurement of phasors (i.e. complex of fundamental frequency AC system voltages and currents). The configuration consists of two or more phasor measurement units (PMU), which provide synchronized real-time information regarding the state of the system using GPS. The data provided by the PMUs are sent to an appropriate control unit (or concentrator). The platform is based on powerful digital processor, and is capable of receiving data from a large number of PMUs and verifying the data integrity. The platform provides high performance communication links to other components like substation automation or power plant automation. However, localised systems are widely accepted for the real-time control in PSs, especially taking into consideration high costs of global systems and taking into account the possibility of complete system damage in case of failure of communication channels, concentrator, or GPS.

The proposed solution uses elements of both the above mentioned methods. The AO recognition is carried out by local devices, but to increase their efficiency communication channels, synchronized measurements and information from remote substations are used. The real-time synchronised measurements of voltage phasors are compared between two key substations (Bus 1 and Bus 2 in Fig. 1) located within a transmission corridor in question. The automation is able to keep working state in case of GPS and/or communication channels failure. Additionally, two remote voltage phasors are simulated in the same timeframe reaching for relevant locations (Gen1 and Gen2 in Fig. 1).

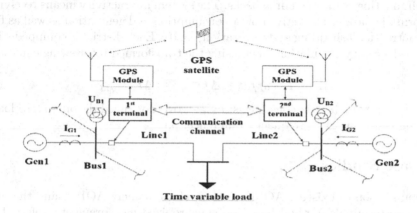

Fig. 1. Simplified diagram of terminals connection in power system.

In case of AO in power system the angle δ between simulated voltages (Gen1 and Gen2 in Fig. 1) increases till 180°. The terminal operates when the following requirements are met: angle δ has reached its limit value; angle changes with a sufficiently high rate $(d\delta/dt)$; voltage circuits are in serviceable condition; currents and voltages are symmetrical; communication channels are in operation condition.

The practical usage of fiber optic channels with multiplexors technology realization has showed that different types of problems (incl. protection blocking due to communication channels time delay deviation from its nominal value) occur during data transferring process [8]. To avoid the time delay asymmetry influence on the protection system functionality, the measurement synchronization method should be applied. The GPS disciplined clock can be used as the source of the external synchronization signal. Sharing of communication channels and GPS allow to make the channels control and data validation.

As result of AO protection relays action PS is divided into several parts. The imbalance between produced and consumed energy occurs resulting in a frequency deviation. To restore frequency automatic under-frequency load shedding (UFLS) or/and spinning reserve are used. The main goal of UFLS is to gradually shed portions of the load when the system frequency reaches values lower than allowed.

Existing UFLS automation has drawbacks, which limit adaptability of emergency automation to a change under-frequency situation. UFLS tripping frequency settings are calculated for a particular power system. Load shedding value is considered at the rated value. In practice this value is not a constant but variable one. Thus, implying rated values as the load shedding which can be different from real one, improper frequency behaviour takes place.

The authors propose a new method for smart under-frequency load shedding system (SUFLS) based on the integration of interactive information channels (IICs) and taking into account current load level in the each pre-defined district thus eliminating mentioned drawbacks. The system interactivity means receiving of information about the active power consumption and generation as well as full load control (load shedding and restoration) [9,10]. Each district is equipped with a power deficiency calculation block using the transformed rotor swing equation:

$$\Delta P = T_J \cdot df/dt + \Delta f/k_{gov} + \Delta f \cdot k_{load} \tag{1}$$

where T_J – rotor's inertia constant, s; k_{gov} - governor speed droop; k_{load} - load-damping constant; Δf - frequency difference, p.u.

3   Case Studies

The comparison of existing AO protection relays, namely AOP-A and the proposed two terminals method based on synchronized measurements, referred to as AOP-B, is presented and analysed using the Latvian PS transmission grid model [7]. The Latvian PS is interconnected with neighbouring networks of Lithuania, Estonia and Russia. Generators connected to the grid loss their stability and various transient groups are formed after simulation of the complex unstable conditions that emerged from the fault. Each unstable group will require either controllable splitting of the grid or tripping of unstable machines. However, further analysis is concentrated on inter-system observations under this complex instability pattern, in particular Latvia to Russia connection. Suitability of AOP-B in comparison with AOP-A is confirmed by a verification study performed in ETAP. Figure 2 compares phasors angle values for corresponding system locations as modelled by AOP-A and AOP-B (changes in time during AO) versus ETAP simulation results for the same buses (generators).

The comparison of presented graphs brings to the conclusion that settings are chosen properly and performance of the new proposed method and device is in line with requirements.

The simplified PS model (5 CHP generators connected via TLs) has been used to analyse and compare results of UFLS and SUFLS operation. The system consists of 5 districts with one CHP in each and is equipped with interactive information channels. The operation of proposed automation has been tested at cascade emergency situation (using Matlab Simulink software) when power instant deficiency at the fifth and the third district was simulated. The assumed active power deficiency value is 28.6 % (at t = 0 s) and 20.0 % (at t = 160 s) respectively. Figure 3 shows the behaviour of the PS frequency using the existing UFLS and the proposed SUFLS. The red dashed lines show UFLS settings.

As seen from Fig. 3, in case of UFLS application three steps of load shedding were activated when the first deficiency occurs at t = 0 s. Then frequency restoration is simulated using slow-acting under-frequency load shedding with

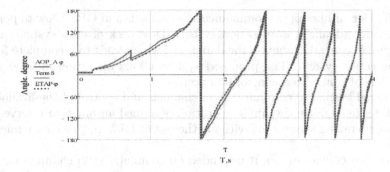

Fig. 2. Case study: AOP-A (red) and AOP-B (green) modelled angles (black) in comparison with system instability - grid maintenance case (angles in degrees) (Color figure online).

one frequency and different time settings (UFLS2) [11]. When the second emergency situation occurs at t = 160 s, three already disconnected steps cannot be used for UFLS therefore frequency hovers at low level. In case of SUFLS operation the deep drop of frequency isn't observed. SUFLS automation chooses the optimal variant of disconnected load at the first and the second occurrences of active power deficiency. As result of SUFLS operation, frequency does not drop below 49.56 Hz.

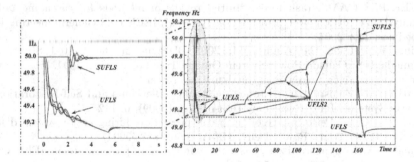

Fig. 3. Frequency behavior at cascade type of emergency situation (Color figure online).

4   Conclusions

1. The likelihood of blackout development can not be reduced to zero, but PSs automatic means, particularly automation for prevention and elimination of generators asynchronous mode and under-frequency load shedding, can significantly minimize consequences and scale of the disaster and accelerate the recovery process.

2. Application of fiber optic communication channels and GPS allow to perform technically advanced automation system. Drawback of such systems is the presence of central elements, the damage of which leads to a complete failure of the entire system. The proposed system allows operation in local mode after loss of centralized control function.
3. Functional testing of communication channels and control of the availability of GPS signals allow the implementation of named automation reserve algorithms operating separately, without the use of GPS and/or communication channels.
4. The central control makes it depended on communication channels decreasing reliability. To improve the situation the same approach of application of reserve (simplified) algorithm can be used performing assigned task with less precision.

Acknwoledgement. Development of this paper has been co-financed by the European Social Fund within the project "Exploration and Solving of Energy Systems' Strategic Development and Management Technically-Economic Problems", project agreement No. 2013/0011/1DP/1.1.1.2.0/13/APIA/VIAA/028.

References

1. McCalley, J., et al.: Probabilistic security assessment for power system operations. In: IEEE PES General meeting Proceedings. Task Force on Probabilistic Aspects of Reliability Criteria, vol. 1, pp. 212–220 (2004)
2. IEEE PES CAMS, task force, "Initial review of methods for cascading failure analysis in electric power transmission systems", IEEE PES General meeting Proceedings, July 2004
3. Final Report on the August 14, 2003 Blackout in the United States and Canada. U.S.-Canada Power System Outage Task Force, April 2004. http://www.nrcan-rncan.gc.ca/media/docs/final/finalrep_e.htm
4. Barkans, J., Zalostiba, D.: Protection Against Blackouts and Self-Restoration of Power Systems. RTU Publishing House, Riga (2009). p. 142
5. Patel, S., et al.: Performance of generator protection during major system disturbances. IEEE Trans. Power Deliv. **19**(4), 1650–1662 (2004)
6. Phadke, A.G.: Synchronized phasor measurements in power systems. IEEE Comput. Appl. Power **6**(2), 10–15 (1993)
7. Antonovs, D., et al.: Protection scheme against out-of-step condition based on synchronized measurments. In: 18th PSCC 2014 Conference Proceedings, Wroclow, Poland, 18–22 August 2014
8. Utans, A., et al.: Experimental testing of the quality of relay protection communication channels. In: The 5th International Conference on Electrical and Control Technologies, Lithuania, Kaunas, pp. 253–256, 6–7 May 2010
9. Bruno, S., et al.: Load control through smart-metering on distribution networks. In: IEEE Bucharest Power Tech Conference, Bucharest, Romania, 29 June - 2 July 2009
10. Lemmen, H.: "SMART Transmission System" presentation. In: IEEE Smart Grid World Forum, Brussels, Belgium, 2–3 December 2010
11. Berkovich, M., Gladishev, V.: Power System's automation, Energoatomizdat (1991) (in Russian)

Impact of a Surface Nuclear Blast
on the Transient Stability
of the Power System

Christopher L. Barrett[1], Virgilio Centeno[2], Stephen Eubank[1],
Cansin Yaman Evrenosoğlu[2], Achla Marathe[1], Madhav V. Marathe[1(✉)],
Chetan Mishra[2], Henning Mortveit[1], Anamitra Pal[1], Arun Phadke[2],
James Thorp[2], Anil Vullikanti[1], and Mina Youssef[1]

[1] Network Dynamics and Simulation Science Laboratory,
Biocomplexity Institute of Virginia Tech,
Blacksburg, VA 24061, USA
{cbarre04,eubank,amarathe,marathe,henning.mortveit,
anam86,vsakumar,myoussef}@vt.edu
[2] Bradley Department of Electrical and Computer Engineering,
Virginia Tech, Blacksburg, VA 24061, USA
{vcenteno,yamanc,chetan31,aphadke,jsthorp}@vt.edu

Abstract. In this chapter, we study the consequences of an improvised nuclear detonation (IND) to the sub-transmission and distribution systems of Washington D.C. in the Eastern Interconnection (EI). We briefly discuss the geographical location of the blast and the interconnection of the power utility serving this area, with the neighboring power utilities. Analysis of the grid with respect to steady state stability as well as transient stability is performed to understand the impact of loss in load as a result of the blast. The steady state analysis alone does not offer a complete understanding of the loss of the neighboring substations. The transient stability analysis shows that for the simulated event, the system stabilizes approximately 7 s after the occurrence of the event. The stability of the system can be attributed to the fact that the drop in load was relatively small compared to the generation capacity of the EI.

Keywords: Eastern interconnection · Stability analysis · Improvised nuclear detonation

1 Introduction

Modern power system has become the backbone for a large number of other networks such as the communications network, transportation network, and the Internet. This dependency has considerably increased the risks caused by a disruption in the power network on the other networks. Tracking the flows of the power network is one way in which the power network's impact on other networks can be estimated. Therefore, it becomes necessary to study the statics as

© Springer International Publishing Switzerland 2016
C.G. Panayiotou et al. (Eds.): CRITIS 2014, LNCS 8985, pp. 153–158, 2016.
DOI: 10.1007/978-3-319-31664-2_16

well as the dynamics of severe contingencies on the power system flows. This study summarizes the possible static and dynamic impacts of a 10kT surface nuclear blast [1] in downtown Washington D.C. on the sub-transmission and distribution power grid located in the vicinity of the city.

The power grid is a large critical infrastructure and analyzing its security against mass destruction events is a relevant topic for study. Many large cities, including Washington D.C., are located within the EI and a large blast caused by terrorist attacks can cause instability of the city's sub-transmission system and distribution system [2–4]. Such disruptive events can also lead to cascading failures that span large geographical areas.

In this chapter, we perform a preliminary investigation illustrating the stability of the EI due to a hypothetical 10KT ground burst of a dirty bomb in the downtown of Washington D.C.; see [3,4] for a description of the scenario. The goal of the study is to develop a generic procedure that can be applied to other regions for similar analysis. Barrett et al. [2] investigated the geographical distribution model of damage probability in Washington D.C. which revealed the most vulnerable locations due to the blast. Loads that are located in those vulnerable areas are removed from the grid. We first investigate the steady state power flow after the blast takes place. But a steady state analysis does not account for the possibility of losing loads/generators and transmission line trips occurring during the transients that follow. Therefore, we also study the dynamical response of the entire system with a special focus on the blast area. Analysis of this scenario reveals that although few neighboring machines trip, the rest of the system stabilizes within a short time interval. This indicates that the system (in general) is robust in handling such exigencies.

The chapter is organized as follows: Sect. 2 discusses the structure of the EI and the utilities serving the blast area. Section 3, examines the steady state power flow of the grid after the blast. The dynamical response analysis supported by numerical simulation is presented in Sect. 4 followed by a discussion in Sect. 5. The conclusions and the future work directions are discussed in Sect. 6.

2   System Overview

The Eastern Interconnection (EI) has approximately 54,740 buses, 51,780 transmission lines, 6,290 generators and 32,780 loads based on a 2011 Summer Base Case model that was used for the study. It is composed of 135 areas. Washington D.C. is located in the East-Central region of the EI. The electric service provider (ESP), ESP1, is the utility that caters to the power requirements of the major portions of the city. The key generating stations under ESP1 are G1, G2, G3, G4, and G5.[1] In addition, ESP2 provides power to a small area. The neighboring utilities are ESP3, ESP4, ESP5, and ESP6. By neighbors, it is meant that these utilities are directly connected to ESP1 and ESP2 and they share power with one of the two through one or more tie-lines.

---

[1] The electric service provider companies and the generating stations names have been anonymized.

In steady state, power enters the city from the North (469MW), South (577MW), West (449MW), East (457MW), and North-East (141MW), respectively. To understand the dynamics of the blast and determine its effects on the stability of the grid, behavior of generators and associated controls are also analyzed.

3   Steady State Power Flow Analysis

There are three types of damaged zones: Least Damage Zone (LDZ), Moderate Damage Zone (MDZ) and Severe Damage Zone (SDZ). Six substations located in the severe damage zone of the blast are removed and the transmission and distribution lines connecting them to the rest of the system are disconnected. This results in a load drop equivalent to approximately 1400 MW. We first investigate the steady state power flow. The loss of large load leads to reducing the overall active and reactive power generation. The simulation shows that this results in a new steady state operating condition for the grid. The active generated power and reactive generated power are reduced by 0.13 % and 1.435 %, respectively. Meanwhile, the active load and reactive load are reduced by 0.116 % and 0.114 %, respectively. The drop in loads correspond to the power that was being supplied from the six substations that got destroyed. The drop in generation occurred in the generators that were present in the moderate and least damage zones.

The steady state power flow analysis does not provide any other information on the new operating condition. For example, further drop in generation, or a distributed reduction in generation across the neighboring areas is expected, but it cannot be observed by only performing a steady state analysis. Moreover, steady state analysis does not show that some generators or loads might be disconnected from the grid due to the dynamical response after the blast. Therefore, detailed dynamical analysis based on transient stability analysis is needed to understand, accept, or reject the steady state analysis.

4   Transient Stability Analysis

The dynamic analysis of the system is done through a study of progressive scenarios in PSS/E [5] using python programming for automation. Study of each scenario helps design the next scenario, thus successively building the time-line. The first scenario contains only the initial effect of the actuating event (the blast). The second scenario studies this event plus the immediate response of the grid to that event. Proceeding in a similar way, the final scenario captures all the events that are expected to occur in the real system over a period of time. The aim of the overall study is to analyze the impact of the blast on system dynamics by emulating real system behavior. For example, in the first scenario a line may become overloaded at some point in time and so in the next scenario it will be tripped to model the response of the protection system. For analyzing system behavior, the output of generators feeding to the affected loads are analyzed. The rule of thumb is that the generators that were directly supplying the load will be affected the most [6].

4.1 Scenario 1

The scenario under study is the complete loss of six substations located in the severe damage zone due to the blast occurring at time $= 1$ s with the system in steady state before that. The plots for rotor angles of the key generating stations in the ESP1 area (G1, G2, G3, G4 and G5) and one generating station of ESP2 area (G7) are shown in Fig. 1. The simulations are run for 100 s. These angles are relative to the rotor angle of the G6 generator which is in the ESP2 area and is farthest from the region affected by the blast and thus expected to be minimally affected by it.

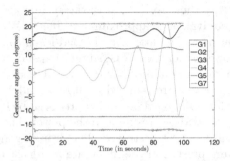

Fig. 1. Rotor angle plots of key ESP1 generators for Scenario 1. The angles are plotted relative to the G6 generator. The G4, G2 and G1 generators show growing oscillations.

From the plot, it is clearly visible that the rotor angle in light blue (G4) and the one in dark green (G2) have considerable oscillations with respect to the others, with the maximum being at G4. Also the magnitudes of the oscillations are slowly increasing indicating that the generators will lose synchronism. Moreover, since the generating stations closer to G4 (like G2 and G1) have relatively bigger swings compared to the ones which are further away (like G5), there is an indication that some disturbance occurred at G4 after the outage event which spread to other buses. The rule of thumb used here is that the closer the source, the larger is the magnitude of the oscillations at that place [6].

On further analyzing the machines at G4 individually, we find that the exciters of those machines are the cause of the oscillations. For proving this hypothesis, the rotor angle response of all the key generators with respect to G6 station as before is plotted (Fig. 2) but this time the exciters are removed from the G4 generators from the start. It is observed that unlike earlier, the G4 generator (light blue) has not lost synchronism and there are no swings observed. The inference drawn from this analysis is that after the outage event at 1 s, the generators at G4 would lose synchronism and thus trip at approximately 5 s (when the oscillations started to grow in Fig. 1) due to their exciter malfunction. This will serve as the next scenario.

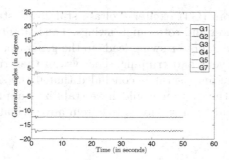

Fig. 2. Rotor angle response of key ESP1 generators with exciters removed at G4 from the start. The angles are plotted relative to the G6 generator. In the absence of the exciters at G4, generators G4 and G2 do not have growing oscillations.

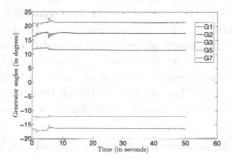

Fig. 3. Rotor angle plots of key ESP1 generators for Scenario 2. The angles are plotted relative to the G6 generator. After some initial oscillations following the blast, the system stabilizes at a new equilibrium point.

4.2 Scenario 2

The scenario under study is the loss of damaged substations at time = 1 s followed by tripping of G4 generators at time = 5 s. From Fig. 3, it is observed that apart from the small, sustained oscillations/distortions in the rotor angles approximately 30 s onwards, the rest of the system is stable. The stability can be attributed to the fact that a load drop of 1.4 GW is very small in comparison to the capacity of the EI (approximately 723 GW). The cause of the oscillations that occurred from 30 s onwards was attributed to numerical errors in the simulation building up over-time.

5 Discussion

The blast in the downtown of Washington D.C. results in the loss of a large load in the ESP1 area. Initially, as anticipated, the frequency of the system begins to rise since the generation is larger than the load. The turbo governor action of the generators then tries to bring the frequency back to normal. However, one of ESP1 generators (G4) exciter (voltage stabilizer) starts to malfunction introducing heavy power and rotor angle swings. The inability of the governor to keep up with the output power swing leads to the generator losing synchronism around 4 s after the event and tripping. The system then runs smoothly afterwards. Thus, from the analysis it is concluded that if the simulated event had happened in reality, the system would have stabilized approximately 7 s after the initiating event and then would be free from any oscillations (Fig. 3).

6   Conclusions

This chapter studies the consequences of a hypothetical nuclear blast on the power grid of Washington D.C. It discusses the overall network structure of the power grid in DC and the neighboring areas that are connected with the power utilities serving the city. Both steady state and dynamical response analysis of the transient stability of the grid are performed to study the loss in load caused by the blast. The steady state analysis alone does not offer a complete understanding of the loss of the neighboring substations. The dynamic analysis shows that for the simulated event, the system stabilizes approximately 7 s after the occurrence of the event. The stability of the system can be attributed to the fact that the drop in load was small in comparison to the capacity of the EI.

Acknowledgments. Authors thank members of the Network Dynamics and Simulation Science Laboratory for their helpful suggestions and comments. This work has been partially supported by DTRA Grant HDTRA1-11-1-0016, DTRA CNIMS Contract HDTRA1-11-D-0016-0001, NSF ICES Grant CCF-1216000, NSF NetSE Grant CNS-1011769 and DOE Grant DE-SC0003957. The content is solely the responsibility of the authors and does not necessarily represent the official views of the NSF, DOE and DoD DTRA.

References

1. National Security Staff, Interagency Policy Sub-coordination committee for preparedness and response to Radiological and Nuclear threats. Planning guidance for response to a nuclear detonation (2010)
2. Barrett, C., Eubank, S., Evrenosoğlu, C.Y., Marathe, A., Marathe, M., Phadke, A., Thorp, J., Vullikanti, A.: Effects of hypothetical improvised nuclear detonation on the electrical infrastructure, In: Proceedings of the International ETG-Congress: Security in Critical Infrastructures Today, Germany, Berlin, November 2013
3. Buddemeier, B.R., Valentine, J., Millage, K.K., Brandt, L.D.: National capital region: key response planning factors for the aftermath of nuclear terrorism. Technical report, Lawrence Livermore National Lab (2011)
4. Wein, L.M., Choi, Y., Denuit, S.: Analyzing evacuation versus shelter-in-place strategies after a terrorist nuclear detonation. Risk Anal. **30**(6), 1315–1327 (2010)
5. PSSE Transmission System Planning. http://w3.usa.siemens.com/smartgrid/us/en/transmission-grid/products/grid-analysis-tools/Pages/grid-analysis-tools.aspx
6. Kundur, P.: Power System Stability and Control. McGraw-Hill, New York (1994)

Building an Integrated Metric for Quantifying the Resilience of Interdependent Infrastructure Systems

Cen Nan[1], Giovanni Sansivini[1(✉)], and Wolfgang Kröger[2]

[1] Reliability and Risk Engineering Group, ETH Zürich, Zürich, Switzerland
{cnan,sansavig}@ethz.ch
[2] ETH Risk Center, ETH Zürich, Zürich, Switzerland
wkroeger@ethz.ch

Abstract. Resilience is a dynamic multi-faceted term and complements other terms commonly used in risk analysis, e.g., reliability, availability, vulnerability, etc. The importance of fully understanding system resilience and identifying ways to enhance it, especially for infrastructure systems our daily life depends on, has been recognized not only by researchers, but also by public. During last decade, researchers have proposed different methods and frameworks to quantify/assess system resilience. However, they are tailored to specific disruptive hazards/events, or fail to properly include all the phases such as mitigation, adaptation and recovery. In this paper, an integrated metric for resilience quantification with capabilities of incorporating different performance measures is proposed, which can be used to quantify the performance of interdependent infrastructure systems in a more comprehensive way. The feasibility and applicability of the proposed metric will be tested using an electric power supply system as the exemplary system with the help of advanced modelling and simulation techniques. Furthermore, the discussion related to the effects of interdependencies among systems on their resilience capabilities is also included in this paper.

Keywords: Interdependent Critical Infrastructure · Resilience

1 Introduction

Critical infrastructures (CIs) are the systems so vital to any country that their incapacity or destruction would have a debilitating impact on the health, safety, security, economics and social well-being [1]. CIs have always been complicated, but in recent years, they have witnessed growing interconnectedness and complexities, which have turned them into a so-called "Systems-of-Systems" (SoS) [2]. These unforeseen interdependencies may provide the tolerance to attacks and failures if well managed (positive impact). However, on the other hand, these interdependencies might also be a source of threat, creating new unknown risks, e.g., the risk of cascading failures, which makes CIs more vulnerable (negative impact). Interdependency can be of different types: physical, geospatial,

© Springer International Publishing Switzerland 2016
C.G. Panayiotou et al. (Eds.): CRITIS 2014, LNCS 8985, pp. 159–171, 2016.
DOI: 10.1007/978-3-319-31664-2_17

informational, logical (see [1] for more details about the definition and dimensions of term interdependency). To better understand the performance of these infrastructure systems, especially their behaviors during and after the occurrence of disturbances (e.g., natural hazards or technical failures), a great effort has been devoted by researchers in recent years with emphasis on different phases and aspects, e.g., availability assessment during the initial loss phase, evaluation of restoration efforts during recovery phase, etc. However, these assessments are challenged by the diversity of the physical flow in the infrastructure systems, by the lack of comparable quantification indexes, and by the multiplicity of loss scenarios. A unifying method to analyze and strengthen system performance as responses to disturbances is still missing. To this aim, resilience analysis is a proactive way to enhance the ability of the infrastructure systems, to prevent/avoid damage before disturbance events, to mitigate losses during the events, and to improve recovery capability after the events [3]. The term resilience can be interpreted as the ability of the system or SoS to withstand a change or a disruptive event by reducing the initial negative impacts (absorptive capability), by adapting itself to them (adaptive capability) and by recovering from them (restorative capability). In this paper, these capabilities are referred as three essential resilience features: enhancing any of them will enhance system resilience. They focus on the system response during and after the occurrence of disruptive events. It is important to further understand and find ways to quantify these capabilities that contribute to characterization of the system resilience performance [4]. Absorptive capability refers to an endogenous ability of the system to reduce the negative impacts caused by disruptive events and minimize consequences. In order to quantify it, robustness can be used, which is defined as strength of the system to resist initial impacts [5]. Adaptive capability refers to an endogenous ability of the system to adapt to disruptive events through its self-organization capabilities in order to minimize consequences. It is a dynamic ability of the system to adjust its behaviors throughout the recovery period. Restorative capability refers to an exogenous ability of the system to be repaired by external actions throughout the recovery period. Both adaptive and restorative capabilities describe the systems ability during the recovery phase, and it is not straightforward to distinguish their effects on system performance. Therefore, the simultaneous quantification of both capabilities is given same indicators, i.e., rapidity ($RAPI$) and performance loss (PL). Resilience is a dynamic multi-faceted term and its assessment should cover all the phases, e.g., disruption and recovery phase, and include all the essential resilience features using an integrated metric. Most of existing methods for resilience quantification lack the ability to cover all the phases, and to include all resilience capabilities within all integrated metric and even overlap with other concepts such as robustness, vulnerability, fragility etc. [6,7]. Furthermore, these methods rely on the modeling approaches that partially capture the complex behaviour of interdependent infrastructure systems. Therefore, the major goal of this paper is to develop a generic resilience metric that can incorporate all essential resilience features and characterize resilience as the system ability, mainly for resilience quantification.

2   An Integrated Resilience Metric

Resilience is a complex concept that can not to be adequately addressed considering one single system capability [8]. One solution is to develop corresponding measures assessing various essential resilience features (i.e. absorptive, adaptive and restorative capability) in different phases, and then integrate them into a unique resilience metric. Figure 1 provides a general illustration of these essential resilience features. The y-axis represents the measurement of performance (MOP). Examples of MOP include the availability of critical facilities, the number of customers served, the connectivity of a network, the level of economic activities, etc. The selection of an appropriate MOP depends on the specific service provided by the CI under analysis. For generality, in the following wo assume that the value of MOP is normalized between 0 and 1 where 0 is total loss of operation and 1 is the target MOP value in the steady phase.

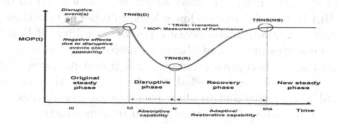

Fig. 1. System resilience transitions and phases

The first phase is the original steady phase $(t < t_d)$, in which the system performance assumes its target value. The second phase is the disruptive phase $(t_d \leq t < t_r)$, in which the system performance starts dropping until reaching the lowest level at time t_r. During this phase, the system absorptive capability can be assessed by developing appropriate measures. As discussed in Sect. 1, Robustness (R) is one measure to assess this capability, which represents the minimum MOP value. This measure is able to identify the maximum impact caused by disruptive events; however, it is not sufficient to reflect the ability of the system to absorb the impact. Two additional complementary measures are further developed: Rapidity $(RAPI_{DP})$ and Performance Loss (PL_{DP}) during disruptive phase. In [5], the term rapidity is referred as the capability to meet priority and achieve goals in a timely manner in order to contain losses and avoid future disruption. This term can be quantified mathematically as the slope of performance level as average rapidity. To improve the accuracy of the estimation of this measure, the method of ramp detection is adopted. In general, a ramp is a change with a large enough amplitude and over a relatively short period [9]. According to [10], a ramp is assumed to occur if the difference between the measured value at the initial and final points of a time interval t is greater than a predefined ramping threshold value. The system rapidity can then be calculated as the average of slope of each ramp. Compared to the calculation of the average rapidity, this method is more comprehensive in term of capturing the system performance during different phases. The performance loss, using the system illustrated in Fig. 1 as an example, can be interpreted can be quantified as the area of the region bounded by the graph of the MOP before and after occurrence of negative effects caused by disruptive events, which can also be referred as the system impact area. A new measure, i.e. the time averaged performance loss ($TAPL$), is introduced. Compared to the measure PL, it encompasses the time of appearance of negative effects due to disruptive events up to full system recovery and provides a time-independent indication of both adaptive and restorative capabilities as responses to the disruptive events. A system that experiences less performance loss has larger resilience. The third phase is the recovery phase ($t_r \leq t < t_{ns}$), in which the system performance starts increasing until the new steady level. During this phase, the system adaptive and restorative capability can be assessed by developing appropriate measures: $RAPI_{RP}$ and PL_{RP}. As shown in Fig. 1, the newly attained steady level may equal to the previous steady level. But it may also reach a lower level. In order to take these situations into consideration, a quantitative measure Recovery Ability (RA) is developed. Although the measures introduced above are useful in assessing system behaviour during and after disruptive events, an integrated metric with the ability of combining these measures is needed in order to assess the system resilience with an overall perspective and to allow comparisons among different systems and system configurations. Therefore, a general resilience metric (GR) is further developed. This metric differs from existing ones in that it is time-dependent and able to incorporate all three essential capabilities. Furthermore, it is not system-specific. The resilience metric builds on the quantification of the system capabilities and is calculated as:

$$
\begin{aligned}
GR &= f(R, RAPI_{DP}, RAPI_{RP}, TAPL, RA) \\
&= R \times (\frac{RAPI_{RP}}{RAPI_{DP}}) \times (TAPL)^{-1} \times RA = R \times \left(\frac{\frac{|\sum_{i=1}^{K_{RP}} \frac{MOP(t_i)-MOP(t_i-\Delta t)}{\Delta t}|}{K_{RP}}}{\frac{|\sum_{i=1}^{K_{DP}} \frac{MOP(t_i)-MOP(t_i-\Delta t)}{\Delta t}|}{K_{DP}}} \right) \\
&\times \left(\frac{\int_{t_d}^{t_{ns}} [MOP(t_0) - MOP(t)]dt}{t_{ns} - t_d} \right)^{-1} \times \left| \frac{MOP(t_{ns}) - MOP(t_r)}{MOP(t_0) - MOP(t_r)} \right|
\end{aligned} \tag{1}
$$

where $TAPL$ represents time average performance loss; K_{DP} and K_{RP} represent number of detected ramps in disruptive phase and recovery phase; MOP(t0) represents performance level at original steady phase. The metric GR provides an integrated way to measure the system resilience by considering all essential capabilities. This approach of measuring system resilience is neither model nor domain specific. For instance, historical data can also be used for the resilience analysis. It only requires the time series data that represents system output during whole time period. In this respect, the selection of the MOP is very important. GR is dimensionless and it is most useful in a comparative manner.

For instance, it can be used to compare the resilience of various systems to same disruptive event. More resilient systems result in higher GR value. It can also be used to compare resilience of same system under different disruptive events. Higher GR value indicates that the system is more resilient to certain disruptive events. Furthermore, the GR value can be used to compare and engineer resilience of a system to a specific disturbance under different mitigation and protection strategies. An effective alternative increases the GR value.

3   Case Study

Electric power systems are among the most prominent representatives of infrastructure systems and the need for their reliable and resilient performance during disruptive events is essential [11]. In this section, the Swiss high-voltage electric power supply system (EPSS) is selected as an exemplary application to demonstrate the feasibility and applicability of the proposed integrated resilience metric with the help of advanced modelling and simulation techniques.

3.1   Modelling EPSS Using a Multi-layer Approach

The modeling of CI is a whole research field by itself. Modeling an entire infrastructure (i.e. EPSS) as a whole is usually impractical [12]. Choosing relevant subsystems and modeling them efficiently for the intended purposes seems more promising. For each subsystem, appropriate modeling approaches can be identified, which fully represent its behavior and functionalities. Motivated by this concept, a multi-layer modeling approach is developed (see [13] for more details about this approach). Within this approach, EPSS is viewed as made of three interrelated subsystems corresponding to different infrastructure layers, i.e. system under control (SUC), operational control system (OCS), and social system (SS). Both SUC and OCS can be regarded as technical parts of infrastructure systems. The major responsibility of OCS is to control and monitor corresponding SUC, e.g., SCADA systems. In this paper, the SCADA system is used as an example of the OCS. The SS represents the non-technical part of infrastructure systems, which is generally related to social factors that have influences on the overall system performance. A two-layer agent-based modelling approach has been developed to simulate the SUC. In total, 585 agents are created to represent corresponding components, i.e. transmission lines, generators and loads (see [14] for more details). Similar to the modelling approach used to model the SUC, a failure-oriented two-layer agent-based modelling approach is developed to model the SCADA system. In total, 587 agents are created to represent corresponding components of the SCADA system, i.e. FCDs (Field level Control Devices), FIDs (Field level Instrumentation Devices), and RTUs (Remote Terminal Units) (see [15] for more details). In order to model SS, i.e. human operator performance in this case, CREAM (Cognitive Reliability Error Analysis Method) combined with the agent-based modelling and fuzzy logic is implemented. During the simulation, if there is a request for the operator take actions (e.g., handle an alarm), the performance shaping factors (PSFs) will be assessed based on current simulation environment, e.g., time of day, simultaneous goals, etc., and corresponding human error probability (HEP) ([0,1]) will then be calculated (see [15] for more details). The lower HEP value indicates better performance by human operators. To decide whether or not there is an error by human operators, it is necessary to set a threshold value (HEP_A) representing the maximum acceptable HEP value. If a calculated HEP is more than HEP_A, then it is assumed that a human error occurs (the human action fails to perform). The higher HEP_A indicates less human errors. All the developed models of three subsystems are integrated in a high level architecture (HLA)-compliant experimental simulation platform.

3.2 Design of Experiment

Although little damages caused by natural hazards have been observed throughout last century in Switzerland, historical records reveal that hazards such as earthquakes and winter storms were the cause of significant damage in at least 9 events over the past 1000 years [16]. According to [17], the estimated frequency of natural hazards, i.e. winter storms, which have the potential to result in the simultaneous disconnection of 20 transmission lines, is about $6E^{-4}$ to $7E^{-4}$ per year. The impact of this disruptive event will result in large negative effects, and should not be underestimated even if the frequency of its occurrence is relatively low. Therefore, in this paper, it is assumed that a winter storm impacts central region of Switzerland, where power transmission lines are located; as a result of this event, 17 transmission lines are disconnected. To simulate the performance of the infrastructure system under study (EPSS) subjected to the disruptive event, all three models (SUC, SCADA, SS) are included in the experiment. The number of available transmission lines (components of SUC) and the number of available RTUs (components of SCADA) are selected as the measure of performance (MOP) respectively. It is assumed that the disruptive event occurs at time 3 h. At the t = 3 h, 17 predefined transmission lines within the region are disconnected due to the storm. In order to model the quasi-simultaneous disconnection of the affected lines, it is assumed that the interval between disconnections of two lines follows a normal distribution N(35,3) seconds. The sudden disconnection of a transmission line will be first detected by the corresponding RTU component of the SCADA system and an alarm will be sent to the control center, which is referred as the abnormal line disconnection alarm in this experiment. After receiving the alarm, repair actions will be determined by the operators in the control center to restore the disconnected lines. It is assumed that the general response time ($Response_G$) for this type of alarm follows a normal distribution N(80,5) seconds. The sudden disconnections of many transmission lines could also overwhelm the operators in control center, possibly resulting in the delay of response and repair actions. In order to simulate this situation, the formula below is used to calculate actual response time ($Response_A$):

$$Response_A = delayfactor * Response_G$$

$$delayfactor = \begin{cases} weightingfactor * (HEP - HEP_A) + 1 & if(HEP \geq HEP_A) \\ 1 & if(HEP < HEP_A) \end{cases} \quad (2)$$

In this experiment, weighting factor is set to 100. It is assumed that repair actions for the abnormal disconnected lines are always performed successfully and the repair time is assumed to follow exponential distribution with the mean value equal to $MTTR$ (mean time to repair). The sudden disconnections of transmission lines could also overload other transmission lines, especially their neighbouring ones [18], and have the potential for knock-on effects with cascading consequences. If a transmission line is overloaded, an overload alarm will be generated and sent to the operator in the control center, which is referred as the overload alarm in this experiment. If the operator recognizes this alarm and handles it successfully $(HEP < HEP_A)$, the corrective actions will be performed, i.e. power load re-dispatch. However, if no action is taken after a certain time past the overload alarm, it is considered that the operator has failed to react to the overload alarm $(HEP \geq HEP_A)$, and the protection devices, e.g., circuit breakers, will automatically disconnect the overloaded line to prevent permanent damages to the infrastructure. In general, abnormal line disconnection alarms are generated when the system is in disruptive phase $(t_d \leq t < t_r)$ and the handling of this alarm completes when the system is in recovery phase $(t_r \leq t < t_{ns})$. The disconnection of transmission lines of SUC also has negative effects on its interlinked SCADA system, i.e. service interruption of RTUs. In this experiment, it is assumed that a RTU component of the SCADA system has two power supply sources: its monitored/control transmission line(s) and its own battery. Therefore, a RTU component is assumed to be out of power supply if its connected transmission line(s) is (are) all disconnected and its battery is fully depleted. In this case study, different feasible strategies are also developed and tested, each of which mainly focuses on the enhancement of a specific system resilience capability in different phases. For example, the improvement of the efficiency of line reparation enhances the restorability capability during recovery phase, the improvement of the human operator performance enhances the adaptive capability during recovery phase, and the improvement of RTU battery capacity (RBC) enhances the absorptive capability during disruptive phase. The target system for each strategy also varies: SUC is the target system for strategy 1 and 2, and SCADA is the target system for strategy 3. In order to demonstrate feasibility of the proposed method and the applicability of the resilience improvement strategies, various simulation experiments are developed. In total, 18 experiments are set for strategy 1 and 2, resulting from the combination of the varying parameters in the two strategies targeting $HEP_A \in (0.03, 0.3, 1)$ and $MTTR(h) \in (0.5, 1, 1.5, 2, 2.5, 3)$; 6 experiments are set for strategy 3 $(RBC(m) \in (5, 10, 15, 20, 25, 30))$. The selection of values of these parameters is based on the experience and knowledge of the target systems (i.e. SUC and SCADA). The number of simulation runs (N) for each scenario is determined by the coefficient of variation (CV) of the resilience measure of the corresponding target system. CV is defined as the ratio of the standard deviation σ to the mean μ. In this

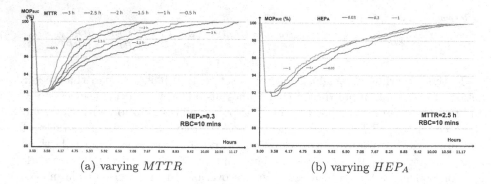

(a) varying $MTTR$ (b) varying HEP_A

Fig. 2. The average system performance under different experiments

simulation, $\mathrm{CV}(GR_{TargetSystem}) \leq 0.13$ is the criteria to determine the number of runs for each computer experiment which are needed to estimate system resilience.

3.3 Simulation Results

SUC and SCADA: SUC is the target system for strategy 1 and 2. Figure 2(a) shows the performance of SUC following the disruptive event under various simulation scenarios related to strategy 1, in which the $MTTR$ varies from 0.5 h to 3 h (HEP_A is set to 0.3 and RBC is set to 10 min). In Fig. 2(a), the y-axis denotes the MOP_{SUC} (i.e. the number of connected lines) and the x-axis denotes the time. At time t = 3 h, the disruptive event is triggered. After about 12 min, the MOP value reaches its lowest level, i.e. 92.1 %. The MOP value then increases as the result of the repair actions. As shown in Fig. 2(a), as $MTTR$ value increases, the time for the SUC to reach new steady state (t_{ns}, recovery time) also increases. For instance, t_{ns}=6.4 h when $MTTR$ is set to 0.5 h, while $t_{ns} = 11.4$ h when $MTTR$ is set to 3 h. It seems that strategy 1 has a strong impacts on the restorability capability of SUC during the recovery phase.

Similar results are also observed in Fig. 2(b), in which HEP_A value varies from 0.03 to 1 for strategy 2 (MTTR is set to 2.5 h and RBC is set to 10 min). As shown in Fig. 2(b), as HEP_A value increases, the time for the SUC to reach new steady state (t_{ns}, recovery time) increases. Furthermore, system robustness R also increases as HEP_A value increases. The R value equals 91.6 % when HEP_A is set to 0.03 and increases to 92.1 % when HEP_A is set to 1. Compared to the results shown in Fig. 2(a), improvement of human operator performance seems to have impacts not only on the system adaptive and restorability capability during recovery phase, but also on the absorptive capability during disruptive phase, although the impacts on the latter are less significant. The overall simulation results for strategy 1 and 2 are summarized in Table 1, including the coefficient of variation for each measure. As shown in Table 1, Strategy 1 has little impact on the absorptive capability of the target system (SUC). All the metrics related

Table 1. Summary of the overall simulation results for different computer experiments related to strategy 1 and 2

$MTTR$	HEP_A	$GR(SUC)$	Disruptive Phase			Recovery Phase	
			R	PL_{DP}	$RAPI_{DP}(/h)$	PL_{RP}	$RAPI_{RP}(/h)$
0.5 h	0.03	16.33	0.916	0.026	0.443	0.09	0.292
	0.3	19.15	0.921	0.0076	0.446	0.079	0.315
	1	20.82	0.921	0.0075	0.451	0.079	0.323
1 h	0.03	15.90	0.916	0.027	0.437	0.14	0.273
	0.3	18.67	0.921	0.0073	0.458	0.12	0.299
	1	20.40	0.921	0.0073	0.457	0.12	0.296
1.5 h	0.03	14.98	0.916	0.026	0.446	0.18	0.278
	0.3	16.29	0.921	0.0072	0.467	0.15	0.293
	1	19.26	0.921	0.0072	0.453	0.16	0.292
2 h	0.03	14.04	0.916	0.026	0.441	0.22	0.260
	0.3	15.98	0.921	0.0072	0.466	0.18	0.295
	1	18.03	0.921	0.0072	0.473	0.17	0.291
2.5 h	0.03	13.76	0.916	0.026	0.447	0.24	0.272
	0.3	15.74	0.921	0.0075	0.457	0.20	0.282
	1	17.16	0.921	0.0072	0.466	0.23	0.282
3 h	0.03	13.73	0.916	0.026	0.448	0.27	0.25
	0.3	14.86	0.921	0.0072	0.466	0.28	0.266
	1	16.38	0.921	0.0075	0.449	0.28	0.267

to this capability, i.e. R, PL_{DP}, $RAPI_{DP}$, do not vary significantly for results of case studies with same HEP_A value but different $MTTR$ value. The R value remains unchanged, while the difference among values of PL_{DP} and $RAPI_{DP}$ is relatively low. Strategy 1 is able to enhance system restorative capability as well as adaptive capability more significantly than the absorptive capability. The PL_{DP} value rises from 0.09 to 0.27 when $MTTR$ value increases from 0.5 to 3 h (the HEP_A value is set to 0.03), indicating that the performance of the target system is less impacted during recovery phase if the efficiency of the repair actions is improved. A similar trend can also be observed in other cases ($HEP_A = 0.3$ and 1). Furthermore, this strategy also has positive effects on the value of $RAPI_{RP}$, which increases from 0.25 to 0.292 (1/h), when $MTTR$ value increases from 0.5 to 3 h and the HEP_A value is set to 0.03, indicating that less time is needed to recover to a new steady state. Strategy 2 has positive impact on the adaptive capability as well as on the restorative capability. This positive impact is stronger when the operator performance improves from poor level (HEP_A=0.03) to average/acceptable level (HEP_A=0.3). For instance, PL_{RP} value drops from 0.14 to 0.12 when HEP_A value increases from 0.03 to 0.3 ($MTTR$ is set to 1 h in this case). Compared to the strategy 1, strategy 2 is able

Table 2. Summary of the overall simulation results of strategy 3

RBC(min)	GR(SCADA)	Disruptive Phase			Recovery Phase	
		R	PL_{DP}	$RAPI_{DP}(/h)$	PL_{RP}	$RAPI_{RP}(/h)$
5	28.65	0.9400	0.017	0.485	0.411	0.138
10	29.97	0.9404	0.017	0.499	0.400	0.134
15	30.80	0.9412	0.014	0.513	0.391	0.120
20	32.45	0.9423	0.013	0.496	0.382	0.100
25	35.00	0.9473	0.004	0.455	0.401	0.110
30	38.85	0.9484	0.004	0.467	0.393	0.120

to enhance the absorptive capability more significantly. For example, if HEP_A is set to 0.3, the PL_{DP} value drops to the range [0.0072, 0.0076], indicating that performance of SUC is less impacted during disruptive phase if the human operator performance is improved. A similar trend is also observed for R, which increases from 91.6 % to 92.1 % when the HEP_A value is increased from 0.03 to 0.3. However, similar to its impacts on resilience capabilities during recovery phase, this strategy also becomes less efficient in enhancing the absorptive capability when the operator performance reaches an average/acceptable level. Both improvement strategies have positive impacts on the enhancement of resilience capabilities of the target system. Improving repair efficiency is more efficient in enhancing the system adaptive and restorative capability during the recovery phase. On the other hand, improving human operator performance is more efficient in enhancing the system absorptive capability during the disruptive phase. However, in order to assess whether these strategies are able to enhance the overall resilience capability, the integrated resilience metric must be quantified. According to Table 1, when both strategies are performed simultaneously, the resilience of SUC can be enhanced significantly, indicating 51.6 % increase of GR_{SUC} value from 13.73 to 20.82 when $MTTR$ value decreases from 3 h to 0.5 h and HEP_A increases from 0.03 to 1. SCADA is the target system for strategy 3. The overall simulation results for strategy 3 are summarized in Table 2. As shown in Table 2, during the disruption phase, strategy 3 has positive impact on the enhancement of the system robustness, and moreover the performance loss of the SCADA also decreases significantly, indicating that the performance of the SCADA system is less impacted during disruptive phase. For instance, the PL_{DP} equals to 0.017 when RBC is set to 5 min, while this measurement drops to 0.004 when RBC is set to 30 min. Compared to its strong impacts on the enhancement of absorptive capability, the impact of this strategy on the adaptive and restorative capability of the system during recovery phase is unclear. PL_{RP} value remains at the range of [0.382, 0.411] and $RAPI_{RP}$ value remains at the range of [0.1, 0.138].

Effects of Interdependencies: In this case study, the two analyzed systems (i.e. SCADA and SUC) are dependent on each other for their operations. SCADA

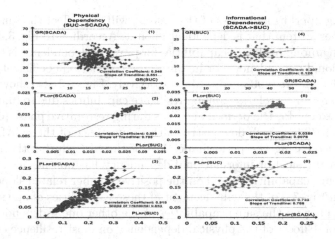

Fig. 3. Comparisons of effects of physical and informational dependency

is dependent upon SUC for the power supply (physical dependency), while SUC is dependent upon SCADA for the transmission of control actions and measurements (informational dependency). Interdependencies among systems may have direct impacts on resilience capabilities. These effects are apparent when considering the resilience improving strategies. For example, strategy 1 and 2 target SUC and directly improve its resilience as shown in this section. On the other hand, the same strategies also improve the resilience of SCADA system due to its physical dependencies with SUC. The effects of interdependency on resilience capabilities can be estimated by cross-comparing the performances of the two interdependent systems. Comparisons of impacts of dependencies on resilience capabilities using PL value in different phases and GR value as examples are illustrated in Fig. 3.

The effects of physical dependency between SUC and SCADA are shown in the left insets of Fig. 3 using simulation results related to strategy 1 and 2 (N=329), and effects of informational dependency between SCADA and SUC are shown in the right insets of Fig. 3 using simulation results related to strategy 3 (N=97). The trendline represents linear correlation. The effects of the interdependency on resilience capabilities and on overall system resilience can be quantified in terms of the degree of correlation measured by the correlation coefficient (Pearson's r) and the coupling strength measured by the slope of the trendline. Both two metrics of the two types of dependencies are also listed in Fig. 3. The implicit assumption is that the effects of interdependencies can be approximately described by a linear relationship. The correlation coefficient indicates a measure of the linear correlation between two groups of variables, giving a value between +1 and −1 inclusive, where 1 and −1 is total positive and negative correlation respectively, 0 is no correlation. In this paper, this measurement is used to indicate the extent to which resilience capabilities are dependent with each other. Higher values indicate that actions affecting the capability, e.g., performance loss of the system, will also affect the same capability of the other system that is dependent upon it. According to Fig. 3, the degree of correlation among resilience capabilities for physical dependency is larger than for informational dependency. For instance, the correlation coefficient values for PL_{DP} and PL_{RP} are 0.996 and 0.918 respectively. Figure 3 also shows the relative weak degree of correlation among resilience capabilities due to informational dependency except for the performance loss during restorative phase (correlation coefficient = 0.733), which demonstrates the importance of the SCADA system in terms of decreasing the performance loss of the SUC during the restorative phase. Either physical or informational dependency has non-negative effects on all the resilience capabilities based on the positive number related slope of trend-lines listed in Fig. 3, i.e. the enhancement of these capabilities of one system has a positive impact on the same capabilities of the other one if dependency exists between them. Effects of the physical dependency on most resilience capabilities are stronger than of the informational dependency, except for the performance loss during restorative phase. Although the degree of correlation among overall system resilience due to both types of dependencies is moderate according to the correlation coefficient, the corresponding value of slope of trendline shows that the coupling due to physical dependency is much stronger than for informational dependency (0.5507 vs 0.128). Therefore, the effects of enhancing the resilience of one system have a much more significant impact on an interdependent system in case physical dependencies are present. The quantification of the effects of interdependency is conditioned on the selection of the disruptive event (i.e. winter storm), of the measure of performance, and of the different strategies.

4 Conclusion

This paper proposes a generic integrated metric assessing resilience of interdependent infrastructure systems, which is time-dependent and able to incorporate all essential resilience features. In order to verify the feasibility of the proposed metric, the performance of an EPSS after the occurring of a natural hazard, e.g., a winter storm, is analyzed. The final simulation results demonstrate the effectiveness of these strategies and their impacts on the overall resilience capability with the help of the resilience metric. The simulation results also show how tightly two systems within EPSS are interdependent with each other and indicate the strength of the impacts of two types of dependencies on the resilience capability.

References

1. Kröger, W., Zio, E.: Vulnerable Systems. Springer, New York (2011)
2. Eusgeld, I., Kröger, W., Sansavini, G., Schläpfer, M., Zio, E.: The role of network theory and object-oriented modeling within a framework for the vulnerability analysis of critical infrastructures. Reliab. Eng. Syst. Saf. 94(5), 954–963 (2009)

3. Madni, A.M., Jackson, S.: Towards a conceptual framework for resilience engineering. IEEE Syst. J. **3**(2), 181–191 (2009)
4. Fiksel, J.: Designing resilient, sustainable systems. Environ. Sci. Technol. **37**(23), 5330–5339 (2003)
5. Bruneau, M., Chang, S.E., Eguchi, R.T., Lee, G.C., O'Rourke, T.D., Reinhorn, A.M., Shinozuka, M., Tierney, K., Wallace, W.A., von Winterfeldt, D.: A framework to quantitatively assess and enhance the seismic resilience of communities. Earthq. Spectra **19**(4), 733–752 (2003)
6. Francis, R., Bekera, B.: A metric and frameworks for resilience analysis of engineered and infrastructure systems. Reliab. Eng. Syst. Saf. **121**, 90–103 (2014)
7. Alessandri, A., Filippini, R.: Evaluation of resilience of interconnected systems based on stability analysis. In: Hämmerli, B.M., Kalstad Svendsen, N., Lopez, J. (eds.) CRITIS 2012. LNCS, vol. 7722, pp. 180 190. Springer, Heidelberg (2013)
8. McDaniels, T., Chang, S., Cole, D., Mikawoz, J., Longstaff, H.: Fostering resilience to extreme events within infrastructure systems: Characterizing decision contexts for mitigation and adaptation. Global Environ. Change **18**(2), 310–318 (2008)
9. Ferreira, C., Gama, J., Miranda, V., Botterud, A.: Probabilistic ramp detection and forecasting for wind power prediction. In: Billinton, R., Karki, R., Verma, A.K. (eds.) Reliability and Risk Evaluation of Wind Integrated Power Systems, pp. 29–44. Springer, New York (2013)
10. Kamath, C.: Understanding wind ramp events through analysis of historical data.In: Transmission and Distribution Conference and Exposition, IEEE PES, pp. 1–6. IEEE (2010)
11. Bilis, E.I., Kröger, W., Nan, C.: Performance of electric power systems under physical malicious attacks. IEEE Syst. J. **7**(4), 854–865 (2013)
12. Filippini, R., Silva, A.: Resilience analysis of networked systems-of-systems based on structural and dynamic interdependencies, vol. 7, pp. 5899–5908 (2012)
13. Nan, C., Sansavini, G.: Proposing a multi-layer modeling framework for complex infrastructure systems. In: Conference Proceedings ESREL, pp. 2051–2058 (2015)
14. Schläpfer, M., Kessler, T., Kröger, W.: Reliability analysis of electric power systems using an object-oriented hybrid modeling approach. arXiv preprint arXiv:1201.0552
15. Nan, C., Eusgeld, I., Kröger, W.: Analyzing vulnerabilities between scada system and suc due to interdependencies. Reliab. Eng. Syst.Saf. **113**, 76 93 (2013)
16. Bilis, E., Raschke, M., Kroeger, W.: Seismic response of the swiss transmission grid.In: Conference Proceedings ESREL, pp. 5–9 (2010)
17. Raschke, M., Bilis, E., Krger, W.: Vulnerability of the swiss electric power transmission grid against natural hazards. In: Conference Proceedings ICASP11, pp. 1407–1414 (2011)
18. Lachs, W.R.: Transmission-line overloads,: real-time control. In: Generation, Transmission and Distribution, IEE Proceedings C, vol. 134, pp. 342–347. IET (1987)

Calculation of Cyber Security Index in the Problem of Power System State Estimation Based on SCADA and WAMS Measurements

Irina Kolosok[✉] and Liudmila Gurina

Energy Systems Institute, Lermontov Street, 130, 664033 Irkutsk, Russia
{kolosok,gurina}@isem.sei.irk.ru
http://www.sei.irk.ru

Abstract. State estimation is an important procedure providing reliable quality information for control of electric power system (EPS). The paper focuses on the possible consequences of cyber attacks on the state estimation results. To measure the impact of cyber attacks on the state estimation results we introduce an index of cyber security which is determined on the basis of a set of characteristics that define the accuracy of the state estimation results. Since these characteristics are not deterministic the cyber security index is estimated by the method of fuzzy sets. The index of cyber security makes it possible to reveal the most vulnerable facilities in electric power system and develop a strategy for the improvement of their cyber security. The suggested strategy implies the use of PMU measurements coming from WAMS in addition to SCADA measurements.

Keywords: State estimation · SCADA · PMU · Cyber attack · Cyber security index · Bad data detection · Test equation method

1 Introduction

An attribute of the smart grid is stability of the network towards physical and cyber intrusion. Developing the conceptual smart grid models and projects, researchers nowadays, pay great attention to the issue of cyber security.

State estimation (SE) is a mathematical data processing method which is widely used for calculation of power system state variables on the basis of measurements [1,2]. The measurements used for SE include mainly the measurements received from SCADA. These measurements may contain large errors or bad data. Bad data can essentially distort the SE results. Bad data detection and suppression of their influence on the estimates of the electric power system state variables are the most pressing issues to be coped with when solving the problem of state estimation. The reasons of bad data can be both random factors related to a failure in the data collection system, personnel errors, etc. and

© Springer International Publishing Switzerland 2016
C.G. Panayiotou et al. (Eds.): CRITIS 2014, LNCS 8985, pp. 172–177, 2016.
DOI: 10.1007/978-3-319-31664-2_18

deliberate impacts (cyber attacks) on the system of data collection and transfer, databases and state estimation software.

In order to assess the capability of a sophisticated technical system to resist the impact of cyber attacks the authors of [3] introduce the notion of cyber security level of the system with the cyber security index being its numerical characteristic.

This paper makes an attempt to determine the cyber security index for the problem of state estimation, since this index characterizes the extent to which the state estimation results are protected from potential errors in the measurement data when SCADA systems are affected by cyber attack. To determine the cyber security index we suggest the use of a set of characteristics which define the accuracy of the state estimation results. Since these characteristics are not deterministic the cyber security index is estimated by the method of fuzzy sets. The index of cyber security makes it possible to reveal the most vulnerable facilities in electric power system and develop a strategy for the improvement of their cyber security. The suggested strategy implies the use of PMU measurements coming from WAMS in addition to the measurements obtained from SCADA.

The paper consists of five sections. The first section is an introduction to the problem. The second section describes the EPS state estimation problem and test equation method to solve the problem of bad data detection and state estimation. Cyber security index in the state estimation problem is determined by the theory of fuzzy sets in the third section. Section four demonstrates the proposed solution with a case study. The main conclusions are drawn in the fifth section.

2   State Estimation Based on SCADA and WAMS Data

The SE problem consists in calculating the EPS steady-state conditions by measurements received from SCADA and WAMS. Consideration is given to cyber security of the power system state estimation problem, therefore SCADA and WAMS systems have been chosen to analyze the impact of cyber attacks.

A method based on test equations has been devised at Energy Systems Institute Siberian Branch of the Russian Academy of Sciences to solve the state estimation problem [2]. A mathematical statement of the SE problem is reduced to the objective function minimization

$$J = (\bar{y} - \hat{y})^T R^{-1} (\bar{y} - \hat{y}) \tag{1}$$

subject to constraints in the form of test equations that relate only state variables measured y:

$$w(y) = 0. \tag{2}$$

In (1) $\hat{y}$- a vector of measurement variables estimates, R - a diagonal matrix of weighting coefficients, whose elements are inverse to measurement variances.

The test equation method makes it possible to perform a priori bad data detection. For a priory detection of bad data the test equation discrepancies are calculated. High discrepancies in the test equations

$$| \, w_k \, (\bar{y}) \, | \, > \, d_k, \tag{3}$$

where d_k is a threshold that depends on statistical properties of normal measurement errors are indicative of the presence of bad data in the measurement vector components $\bar{y}$ in the k - th test equation.

The algorithms for logical rules have been developed to detect bad data among the measurements entering into the test equations with large discrepancies [2]. The test equation method has proved to be very efficient, however its application causes a number of problems associated usually with insufficient redundancy of measurements. In some cases the logical rules do not notice bad data, or incorrectly reject valid measurements or only identify the groups that include erroneous measurements.

3   Determination of a Cyber Security Index in the state Estimation Problem

There are several vulnerable points in the architecture of SCADA systems, which can be used for cyber attacks. These can be direct damage of RTU communication channels between RTU and control center; damage of software located on the servers of power system control center, including the state estimation software and databases in the control center. In this paper we will analyze cyber security of the state estimation procedure when modeling the false data injection attacks against the RTU units installed at the nodes of the calculation scheme.

The calculations were made for two variants of measurements supplied to the scheme. In the first variant we used only SCADA measurements that came via telemetry channels from RTU. In the second variant, PMU measurements were added to SCADA measurements to eliminate critical measurements and critical sets.

3.1   Selection of Indicators for the Determination of Cyber Security Index

It was necessary to select a set of indicators whose values when compared with the admissible limits under cyber attacks will make it possible to determine the cyber security level.

The algorithm for validation of measurements by the test equation method is used to divide all the measurements into 4 groups: (1) valid; (2) erroneous; (3) doubtful; (4) unchecked or critical [2].

The quality of the state estimation results is determined by the value of the objective function (1) at the point of solution. If the value $J(\hat{y})$ exceeds the value $\chi_{1-\alpha}^2 (m-n)$, where α is a specified probability of the type 1 error in the test of hypothesis on distribution $J(\hat{y})$, this is indicative of the presence of bad data in the measurements.

The analysis of modeled cyber attacks on measurement systems (SCADA, WAMS) shows that for solving the state estimation problem the indicators which possess the highest information content and characterize the performance of the bad data detection method implemented in the state estimation procedure and the accuracy of the obtained estimates are: ν_φ – the ratio of the objective function value (1), calculated by the measurements of node at the point of solution, to the value $\chi^2_{1-\alpha}(m-n)$; ν_e – the ratio of the number of correctly detected bad data to the number of bad data at the i-th node; ν_r – the ratio of the number of bad data identified as valid to the number of measurements of the i-th node; ν_d – the ratio of the number of erroneous measurements identified as doubtful to the number of measurements of the i-th node.

3.2 Determination of State Estimation Cyber Security Index on the Basis of Fuzzy Sets Theory

The cyber security index of the state estimation procedure is determined under the conditions of uncertainty due to the impossibility of predicting cyber attacks, the input data are stochastic and the calculated indicators are of random character. Therefore, it is impossible to strictly formalize this problem and solve it by strict mathematical methods. Thus, the theory of fuzzy sets was applied to determine the index of cyber security and level that corresponds to it [4]. Each selected characteristic is defined by a linguistic variable (LV) $\{x, T, U, G, M\}$, where x – name of variable, T – term-set, each element of which is represented by a fuzzy set on the universal set U; G – syntax rules, generating the names of terms; M – semantic rules setting the membership functions of fuzzy terms generated by syntax rules G [5]. For each term of linguistic variable we construct a membership function. The aggregate of membership functions of linguistic variables will make it possible to calculate the cyber security index on the basis of α - levels. While determining the cyber security index, on the basis of assessment of the used measurements validity, detection of bad data in them, and, accordingly accuracy of a solution to the state estimation problem we chose the following security levels: high $\alpha \geq 0.75$; average $0.25 \leq \alpha \leq 0.75$; low $\alpha < 0.25$. Bearing in mind the critical significance of each chosen indicator and designating the cyber security index as ρ_ν, we obtain

$$\rho_\nu = \min\{\mu_{\tilde{A}_1}(A_1), ..., \mu_{\tilde{A}_i}(A_i), ..., \mu_{\tilde{A}_n}(A_n)\}. \tag{4}$$

For the linguistic variables we take the enumerated above indicators – ν_φ, ν, ν_r and ν_d. The membership function is calculated by the method of paired comparisons [5].

4 Case Study

The cyber security index of state estimation was determined on the basis of the scheme of a real section of electric power system that contains 7 nodes and 7 branches (Fig. 1).

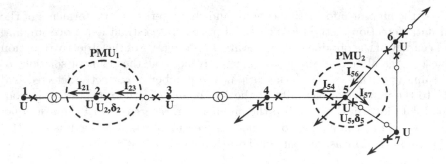

Fig. 1. Test scheme. SCADA measurements: × – active power, ○ – reactive power, U – voltage

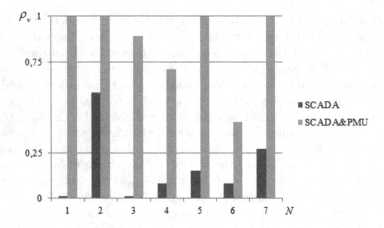

Fig. 2. Cyber security indices for the state estimation based on the SCADA and WAMS data (N – number of the node)

To collect the statistical data on the state estimation results we performed multiple modeling of measurements by adding noise to the steady state calculation results under the assumption that the measurement errors have normal distribution $N\left(0, \sigma_y^2\right)$. Then, we modeled the failures of individual RTUs by adding the measurements of bad data of various magnitude (from $\pm 10\sigma$ to $\pm 20\sigma$) to the measurements from these RTUs, made state estimation, and used average values as input data for the calculation of cyber security index.

According to the technique described in Sect. 4, we determined the membership functions of the linguistic variables ν_r, ν_d, ν_φ and ν_e based on the results of bad data detection and state estimation by SCADA measurements only.

The values of cyber security index ρ_ν are determined as the minimum values from all membership functions μ_ν for each node of the studied scheme and are shown in Fig. 2.

To assess the quality of power system state estimation on the basis of SCADA and WAMS data for the case of cyber attacks, we placed PMUs at nodes 2 and 5 of the considered scheme (Fig. 1).

Figure 2 show that when the SCADA measurements are used alone, the cyber security index has the value which does not exceed the maximum level. After the placement of two PMUs at nodes 2 and 5 the cyber security index increased noticeably and reached a secure level for most of the nodes in the network.

The research shows that the most reliable results in bad data detection can be obtained by using the robust criteria of estimation. This is one of the directions to improve the cyber security of the state estimation.

5   Conclusions

1. The procedure of bad data detection in the state estimation of electric power system decreases considerably the probability of distortion of the calculation model of the current state in case of cyber attack on the SCADA system.
2. To improve the effectiveness of the methods for the verification of data used in the state estimation of electric power system it is necessary to increase the redundancy of SCADA measurements, supplement the SCADA measurements with the PMU measurements obtained from WAMS, combine various bad data detection methods (a priori, a posteriori, robust), and use the criterion of maximum probability of bad data detection when placing PMUs.

Acknowledgement. The research was done as part of the integration project 01201369131 of the Siberian Branch of the Russian Academy of Sciences and supported by grant 4711.2014.8 of Leading Scientific School of the Russian Federation.

References

1. do Coutto Filho, B.M., do Silva, A.M.L., Falcao, D.M.: Bibliography on power system state estimation (1968–1989). IEEE Trans. Power Syst. **10**, 229–240 (1990)
2. Gamm, A.Z., Kolosok, I.N.: Test equations and their use for state estimation of electrical power system. In: Scientific Proceedings of Power, Electrical Engineering of Riga Technical University. RTU, Riga, pp. 99–105 (2002)
3. Sandberg, H., Teixeira, A., Johansson, K.J.: On security indices for state estimation in power network. In: Preprints of the First Workshop on Secure Control System, CPSWEEK 2010 (2010)
4. Kerin, U., Krebs, R., Lerch, E.: Power system application tool for on-line security investigations. Internationaler ETG-Kongress 2013, Germany, Berlin, 05–06 November 2013 (2013)
5. Bogatyrev, L.L., Manusov, V.Z., Sodnomdorzh, D.: Mathematical modeling of power system operating conditions under uncertainty. Publishing House of MSTU, Ulan-Bator, p. 348 (1999) (in Russian)

Factors Influencing Oscillations within Meshed HVDC Grids and Implications for DC Voltage Control

Anne-Katrin Marten[1]([✉]), Dirk Westermann[1], Lorenzo Vento[2], and Patrick Favre-Perrod[2]

[1] Department of Power System, TU Ilmenau, Gustav-Kirchhoff-Str. 1, 98693 Ilmenau, Germany
{anne-katrin.marten,dirk.westermann}@tu-ilmenau.de
[2] College of Engineering and Architecture Fribourg, University of Applied Science of Westerm Switzerland, Boulevard de Prolles 80, 1700 Fribourg, Switzerland
Patrick.Favre-Perrod@hefr.ch

Abstract. Since meshed HVDC grids are discussed for offshore wind farms interconnection and onshore long distance transmission use, there is also a research focus on operation of such new type of grids. A major aspect is DC voltage control. Tests on a low voltage meshed HVDC mock-up system showed oscillatory behavior using state of research DC voltage control characteristics. This paper presents an analysis of influencing factors for these oscillations and proposes improvements for the DC voltage control characteristic, for the operation management and shows that converter parameters can invoke oscillations.

Keywords: DC voltage control · Meshed HVDC/MTDC grids · Operation management · Stability

1 Introduction

With an increasing proportion of renewable energy generation in offshore wind farms or huge solar power plants (e.g. in deserts), the distance between consumption and generation increases significantly. A suitable solution for the transmission problem is considered to be an HVDC system. Due to reliability reasons the vision of a meshed HVDC system comes up e.g. in Asia or Europe [1]. The control of DC energy balance is solved for point-to-point connections by one converter controlling active power infeed and the other controlling DC voltage [2]. This method needs to be adapted for meshed HVDC grids covering a lot of GW with remote converter stations since power flows are divided automatically all over the system according to the power infeed and consumption of converters.

Since important physical values for the determination of system state, stability and power flow in AC systems do not exist in DC grids, voltage is the most important variable. Power flows as well as the system state are defined by

© Springer International Publishing Switzerland 2016
C.G. Panayiotou et al. (Eds.): CRITIS 2014, LNCS 8985, pp. 178–189, 2016.
DOI: 10.1007/978-3-319-31664-2_19

actual DC node voltages. If there is an energy lack DC voltage decreases and vice versa. Thus, it seems to be suitable to control DC voltage at all converter nodes (or at least at more than one in order not to overload this converter and the connected AC system with DC grids balancing power) with respect to the requirements at the AC point of common coupling and a given power reference value for the converter. Thereby balancing energy distribution to more than one converter is ensured.

Some voltage control methods have been developed and described in literature. The essence is summarized in [3–5]. In general a centralized voltage control is possible if the HVDC grid covers a small amount of power, since balancing power will be small as well. This can be extended with a decentralized backup so that other converters participate in DC voltage control as well if a certain voltage margin is left, i.e. in a case where the central voltage controller cant cover the whole balancing power. The stress for a single AC point of common coupling can be prevented in general if the voltage control is distributed to all converters or even some converters of a DC grid.

In general three different DC voltage control methods exist: Voltage droop control, constant voltage and voltage margin control [3]. All three can be summarized as voltage droop control according to (1) while constant voltage control has a droop constant $k_{DC,i} \to 0$ and constant power control has a droop constant $k_{DC,i} \to \infty$. $P_{conv,i}$ is the power reference given to the inner converter control, $P_{conv,ref,i}$ is the power reference provided by e.g. a schedule, $U_{DC,i}$ and $U_{DC,conv,ref,i}$ is the measured voltage and reference voltage respectively.

$$P_{conv,i} = P_{conv,ref,i} - \frac{1}{k_{DC,i}}(U_{DC,i} - U_{DC,conv,ref,i}) \tag{1}$$

Voltage droop control can be extended by a voltage dead band or low droop band, to give respect to a given converter power reference value (see Fig. 1). Since voltage droop control is the only option with significant and limited droop it is supposed to be the most suitable for DC voltage control.

To test several HVDC operations and control methods a downscaled HVDC mockup was built (see Sect. 2). It was found that undamped oscillations of the

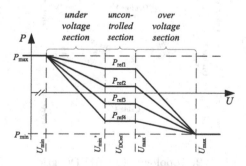

Fig. 1. Dead band voltage droop control characteristic for DC voltage control.

transmitted power occurred in the system. Its basic operation was realized by using a dead band voltage droop control characteristic as shown in Fig. 1. This paper describes the mockup structure and measured oscillations in Sect. 2. Afterwards the oscillation causing factors on the equipment side as well as on the control side have been identified using a software simulation. For complexity reduction a point-to-point (P2P) topology was simulated. The results including suggestions for improvement are presented in Sect. 3.

2   Low Voltage Test System

A reduced scale model of a meshed HVDC grid was configured at the laboratory of power systems of the University of Applied Sciences of western Switzerland. The scaling factors for the hardware model is shown in Table 1.

Table 1. Scale of the mockup system and its maximum ratings.

	Scale	Maximum value
Voltage	$10^3 : 1$	800 V
Current	$10^3 : 1$	6 A
Power	$10^6 : 1$	4.8 kW

2.1   Structure

The model represents a meshed HVDC grid with 4 Converters and 6 lines so, that it results in 4 meshes (see Fig. 2). It includes overhead (OH) lines as well as cables. For hardware simulations the converters are connected to an interconnected ac system. For the purpose of this paper it can be assumed that there are no restrictions given by the ac connection points.

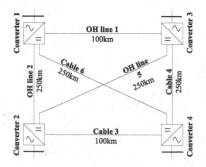

Fig. 2. Topology of the HVDC grid.

2.2   Measurements

Since it was intended to split the balancing power of the DC grid to more than one converter, for the first operation tests of the grid a dead band voltage droop control was applied to all converters. It was found that there can result undamped oscillations between the converters. Those oscillations can also occur within a P2P connection when the dead band droop control is used. In order to make a root cause analysis of the oscillation a P2P connection has been analyzed in a first step. As a test scenario the converter power reference value has been set to 1.1 kW for converter 1 and −0.6 kW for converter 2. The corresponding line parameters (R and L) are given in Table 2 as well as the converters DC link capacity C_{LE}. Figures 3 and 4 show the measured voltage at both converters DC nodes of the connection and the line current using the described test scenario. It can be seen that the voltage at the converter nodes is oscillating against each other and in consequence the current is oscillating as well. The oscillation parameters are given in Table 3 and show the oscillation frequency, the minimum and maximum value of the converter node DC voltages, the minimum and maximum line current as well as the differences between the minimum and maximum of each value.

The measurements have been repeated with an inductance twice as large than the original with the result of a smaller oscillation frequency of 30 Hz and larger oscillation amplitudes of voltages and line current ($\Delta(U_{max}, U_{min}) = 26$ V, $\Delta(I_{max}, I_{min}) = 2.5$ A).

It is important to avoid such significant oscillations in real transmission HVDC grids for similar reason as AC power system oscillations are avoided e.g. by power system stabilizers (PSS) that can damp AC oscillations [7]. This reason is a blocking of transmission capability due to oscillations and thus sub optimal

Table 2. Line parameters for test scenario.

	$R[\Omega]$	$L[mH/]$	$C_{LE}/2[\mu F]$
Line 1	3	51	700

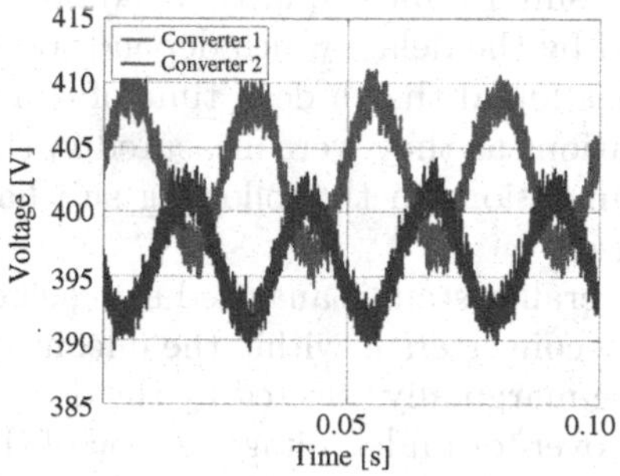

Fig. 3. Voltage measurement on a point-to-point connection with a constant power reference value.

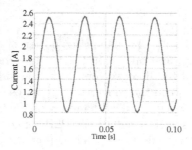

Fig. 4. Line current measurement on a P2P connection with a constant power reference value.

Table 3. Oscillation parameters.

	Maximum, Minimum	Δ(max,min)	Frequency
U_{conv1}	395 V, 410 V	15 V	40 Hz
U_{conv2}	390 V, 402 V	12 V	40 Hz
I	0.8 A, 2.5 A	1.7 A	40 Hz

power flows or non optimal use of physical transmission capacity. Additionally an increased equipment stress can be caused as well as oscillation propagation from the DC into the AC system via the converter due to its voltage control characteristic. Thus, oscillations of that kind within the DC grid, maybe also spreading to the AC system causing different negative effects, have to be avoided or well damped.

3   Oscillation Causing Factros

The investigated grid was modeled using Matlab Simulink in order to reproduce the converter behavior. The $p-v-$characteristic was extended with a dead time and a delay (Fig. 5). The dead time represents delay due to communication, computing time, measured value acquisition and processing. Converter time constants are represented by the delay, which depends on the internal converter control parameters. It was found that a dead time of 4 ms and a delay of 10 ms result in the same oscillations as they were measured in the physical model. For all physical tests and simulations in the following subchapters a characteristic as shown in Fig. 1 was used.

The stability of the overall system is analyzed using eigenvalues (EVs). When the operating point of the converters is within the uncontrolled section of the $p-v-$characteristic, EVs are marginally affected by the delay and dead time. If the operating point is on the over- or undervoltage section of the $p-v-$characteristic the time delay causes an EV shift closer towards the imaginary axis. However, the biggest influence on the EV shift has the considered due to the dead time.

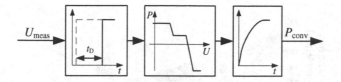

Fig. 5. Line current measurement on a P2P connection with a constant power reference value.

It was found that in the asymptotically stable system the two converter operating points are on the uncontrolled section (dead band) of its $p - v$–characteristic, i.e. no correction by the voltage control method is necessary. If the system is marginally stable (undamped oscillation with $P_{conv} < P_{max}$) exactly one of the two converter operating points is on the over- or undervoltage section of the $p - v$–characteristic while the other is in the uncontrolled section. Finally the unstable system state is characterized in that way that both converter operating points are oscillating simultaneously on the over- or undervoltage section of the $p - v$–characterstic, between the minimum and maximum converter power while both signals are phase shifted by 180°. Thus the system is only bounded due to the converter power limits.

3.1 Dead Time and Delay

Thus, delay and especially dead time have the most significant impact on the system stability/oscillations. For each HVDC system a dead time limit can be defined. For values below that limit there is no influence on the oscillation. This limit is dependent on the line inductances and system capacitances values. If these values are increased the critical dead time increases as well. This effect is exemplarily shown for two different node capacity values and its impact on the oscillation frequency in Fig. 6.

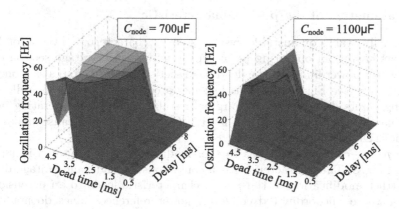

Fig. 6. Current oscillation frequency as a function of converters dead time and delay for two node capacity values.

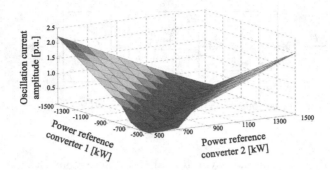

Fig. 7. Current oscillation amplitude as a function of power reference values of a P2P connection.

3.2   Converter Reference Value

If the reference values for the converters are well matched, no converter will leave the dead band or at least will stay close to the dead band e.g. if losses are not well considered during converter power reference value calculation. The worse the reference values are matched the more the operating points will reach outside the dead band. If this fact is combined with a delay and dead time both converters oscillate with even higher amplitudes the worse the reference values are matched (see Fig. 7).

Consequently, in real systems one needs to have one instance that calculates converter power reference values with special attention to $p - v-$characteristic coordination. This is valid for P2P connections as well as for multi terminal HVDC grids if more than one converter controls DC voltage. Converter reference values do not affect oscillation frequency, i.e. if the converter reference values are not well matched (including system losses) the oscillation frequency will be the same - independent of the difference in the absolute power reference values.

3.3   Parameters of the $p - v-$characteristic

A marginally stable or unstable system state is characterized by one or both converters having an operating point on the under-/ overvoltage section or at the converter power limits. If the dead band section is modified to a section with a small droop (see Fig. 8) and thus becomes a controlled section as well, some operating points do not reach a marginally stable or unstable operating point. Thus small power imbalances in the HVDC system do not cause undamped oscillations as it is illustrated in Fig. 8.

The $p - v-$characteristic was further modified as it is proposed in [8] and shown in Fig. 8. This characteristic is a continuous undead band voltage droop. This further modification of the $p - v-$characteristic leads to an extension of the area where uncoordinated converter power reference values do not cause marginally stable or unstable oscillations (see Fig. 9).

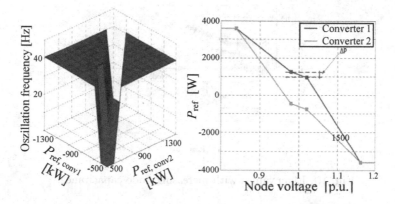

Fig. 8. Oscillation frequency (left) as a function of power reference values of a P2P connection with a undead band DC voltage control (right).

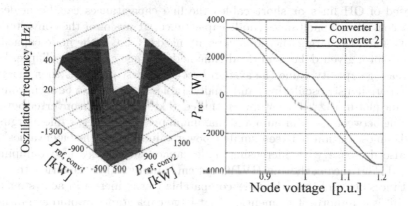

Fig. 9. Oscillation frequency (left) as a function of power reference values of a P2P connection with a continuous undead band DC voltage control (right).

3.4 Line Parameters

An HVDC system including converter and line capacitances as well as line inductances and resistances can be compared to an LC pi-section. The resonance frequency of a line is given by:

$$f_R = \frac{1}{2\pi\sqrt{LC}} \tag{2}$$

As simulations confirm, the oscillation frequency decreases with increasing inductances and capacitances with a negligible impact of the resistances.

If the oscillation amplitude is considered there is a negligible impact of the resistance if the line inductance or capacity exceeds a certain value. For smaller values the resistance has a significant impact. Hence the oscillation amplitude becomes smaller the higher the line resistance will be.

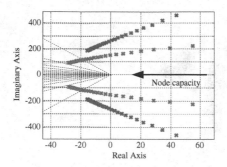

Fig. 10. Eigenvalues with increasing node capacitance.

If two or three level voltage source converters (VSC) are considered they have a significant impact on the overall system capacity. Regarding systems composed of OH lines or short cables the line capacitances can be neglected against converter capacitances (node capacitance). The slower the converter and its control are, the larger the node capacity needs to be. If the node capacity is too small for a given delay and dead time node voltage can even collapse. With an increasing capacity value the system become at first unstable, then marginal stable (continuously oscillating) and finally stable. This can also be seen from the eigenvalue plot in Fig. 10. Unstable in this context means that converter power is oscillating between its minimum and maximum possible values, while marginally stable is an oscillation between smaller power values. Since the eigenvalues' real parts also decrease with increasing node capacitance values also damping is increased. This means that an HVDC system is more stable the larger the node capacitances are and thus they are comparable to the inertia in ac systems. At this point it is important to mention that large capacitances would significantly feed fault currents even if this topic is out of scope of this paper.

The necessary size of node capacitance to stabilize the system do not exclusively depend on delay and dead time constants of the converters but also on the line inductances since its comparable behavior to an LC resonator. The eigenvalue dependence on the line inductance is shown in Fig. 11 for an increasing value. This eigenvalues can contribute to oscillations if a certain inductance value is exceeded and if further increased cause instabilities until an extreme value is reached. When the value is increased even further the eigenvalue can becomes stable again even if the eigenvalue can still cause undamped oscillations. If the unstable line inductance values are combined with large capacity values, the eigenvalues move back towards the stable complex plane.

3.5   Line Length and Types

For comparative analysis different line technology parameters shown in Table 4 are used which are over head lines (OH line), XLPE cables and gas insulated lines (GIL).

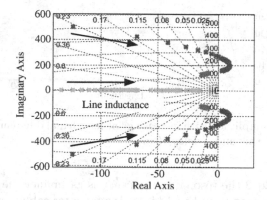

Fig. 11. Eigenvalues with increasing line inductance.

Table 4. Line parameters of different line technologies.

	R'[mΩ/km]	L'[mH/km]	C'[nF/km]
OH line [6]	28	0.86	13.8
Cable [9]	19	0.73	183
GIL [9]	9.4	0.22	54

As it is explained before resistances, inductances and capacitances of the DC grid have a fundamental impact on the oscillation behavior. With an increasing line length these parameters change as well. Thus the oscillation frequency (see Fig. 12) and amplitude (see Fig. 13) decreases with increasing line length. Since the distributed line inductance L' and resistance R' are the smallest when considering GILs they have the highest oscillation frequency. Even if the difference between R' and L' of cable and OH line technology is significant the difference in oscillation frequency is very low since cables' C' is much higher than that of OH lines. Very low line resistances of high temperature superconducting cable technology is very low there would result a very low damping effect and due to smaller line capacitances a less stable system behavior (see Fig. 10).

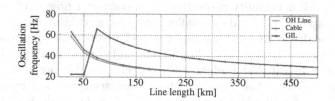

Fig. 12. Oscillation frequency with increasing line length and different line technologies with a dead time of 4 ms and a delay 10 ms.

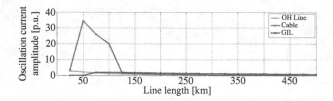

Fig. 13. Oscillation amplitude with increasing line length and different line technologies with a dead time of 4 ms and a delay 10 ms.

According to Eq. 2 the resonance frequency is as smaller the bigger L and C becomes. As can be seen from Fig. 13 there is a peak for cables around 50 km line length and a small peak for GIL between 100 and 150 km which indicate the resonance points. The resonance point for the OH line occurs for shorter distances and cannot be seen in Fig. 13. Since the converter induced DC link capacitors (700 μF each) and especially the DC inductance of the converters (0.55 H each, PWM converter) are major compared to the line parameters they have a significant impact. At the resonance point of the cable setup both converter operating points lie on the over- or undervoltage section of the $p - v$−characteristic. However, an onshore HVDC overlay grid will be mainly built up with OH lines due to its faster installation time and lower costs. Short sections will probably be realized with one of the underground technologies (GIL or cable) due to environmental or visual reasons.

4   Conclusion

As worldwide several efforts are made towards a meshed HVDC overlay grid to transmit remotely generated renewable electricity to centers of load, suitable operation methods need to be developed. To determine the ac systems state, its stability and power flows several variables are necessary. In DC grids the necessary measure is reduced to a single one which is DC node voltage. Thus it is essential for system stability and operation to have an adequate control method for DC node voltages. Even if several methods are presented in literature, voltage droop control seems to be the most reasonable one, more than ever if it is extended by a functionality respecting given converter power reference values (integrated voltage dead band or smaller droop for a certain voltage band).

A reduced scale HVDC grid was build at the University of Applied Sciences of Western Switzerland to test several operation and control methods. During the first tests it was found that undamped and even unstable oscillations between converters can occur. This paper identifies oscillation causing factors on the equipments side as well as on the control side. For the analysis of influencing factors, a P2P topology is simulated. Afterwards the identified improvements have been applied to a meshed HVDC system with the same positive effects. The following impact factors have been found: dead time and delay of the inner converter control, inconsistent converter power reference values, parameters and shape of $p-v-$characteristic for DC node voltage control, equipment parameters (capacitances and inductances) as well as line length and type. The biggest impact was identified by the delay time of the inner converter control combined with DC grid capacitances (converter output and lines) and secondly the shape of the $p-v-$characteristic since oscillations occur when converter operating points change between piece wise linear defined sections. Thus the system behavior was approved using an undead band voltage droop control and the most significant impact was achieved using a continuously defined undead band voltage droop control.

References

1. DESCERTEC Foundation and Japan renewable Energy Foundation: Asian Super Grid for Renewable Energies. http://www.desertec.org/press/press-releases/1203 10-01-asian-super-grid-for-renewable-energies-desertec-foundation-signs-memo randum-of-understanding/
2. Thepparat, P.: Analysis of the combined and coordinated control method for HVDC transmission. Ph.D. thesis (2010)
3. Vrana, T.K., Beerten, J., Belmans, R., Fosso, O.B.: A classification of DC node voltage control methods for HVDC grids. Electr. Power Syst. Res. **103**, 137–144 (2013). Elsevier
4. CIGR WG B4.52: HVDC grid feasibility study (2011)
5. Beerten, J., Gomis-Bellmunt, O., Guillaud, X., Rimez, J., van der Meer, A., van Hertem, D.: Modeling and control of HVDC grids: a key challenge for future power system. In: 18th Power Systems Computation Conference (2014)
6. Kundur, P.: Power System Stability and Cotrol. McGraw-Hill, New York (1994)
7. Eremia, M., Shahidehpour, M.: Handbook of Electrical Power System Dynamics - Modelling, Stability and Control. Wiley, Hoboken (2013)
8. Marten, A.-K., Westermann, D.: A novel operation method for meshed HVDC over-lay grids and corresponding steady state and dynamic power flow calculation principle. In: 10th IET International Conference on AC and DC Power Transmission, ACDC 2012 (2012)
9. Koch, H.: Gas-Insulated Transmission Lines. Wiley, West Sussex (UK) (2012)

Security and Recovery Policies

Public-Private Partnership: The Missing Factor in the Resilience Equation. The French Experience on CIIP

Danilo D' Elia[✉]

University of Paris VIII Vincennes-Saint Denis, Paris, France
deliadanilo@gmail.com

Abstract. Critical information infrastructure protection is a complex and multifaceted problem domain and continues to become more so. Because it is impossible to prevent the occurrence of all incidents, the CIIP should be approached in terms of resilience. However, governments are facing a key challenge in the implementation of resilience: the need of cooperation with the private sector. How to organize the public-private cooperation is arduous but geopolitics provides the tools to under-stand this kind of complex relationship. In analyzing the French case, this paper aims to see PPP through a new pathos: as a risk-mitigating factor.

Keywords: Cyber risk · Critical infrastructure protection · Public-private partnership · Resilience

1 Introduction

The terms of the political debate around Critical Information Infrastructure Protection (CIIP) are focused on a main point: the cooperation between public authorities and private sector is needed but its implementation is hard to achieve.

For many years, information security has been the exclusive domain of a closed community of people from military, academics, IT and telecom companies. The information revolution in the 90s radically changed the scale and the nature of the issue: people and engineered machines are now part of the same global environment made of information: the infosphere. Therefore, this revolution brings the problem of CIIP beyond traditional national defense circles and managing cyber risk of CIs calls for close cooperation between public-private players. Due to the deregulation process of many public sectors in the 80 s and the globalization of 90 s, the private sector is now owning or controlling the majority of CIs and is at the core of the ICT expertise. Thus both the corporate and the public authorities are facing shared threats as industrial espionage, organized crime and sabotage: no one can resolve those issues alone.

Over the past years, academics from security studies, economics and public policy have investigated initiatives launched to establish cooperation between public and private sector for CIIP. Based on the concepts borrowed from such

© Springer International Publishing Switzerland 2016
C.G. Panayiotou et al. (Eds.): CRITIS 2014, LNCS 8985, pp. 193–199, 2016.
DOI: 10.1007/978-3-319-31664-2_20

other disciplines as distributed security, we analyze the French case through the geopolitical approach based on the study of power rivalries between various actors and the conflicting perceptions used to reinforce or defy the established order [1]. What kind of rivalries are challenging the public-private cooperation and how the public authorities are dealing with that is the focus of this article. As preliminary note it is important to take into consideration that the original definition of PPP refers to a specific form of direct partnership developed in 80 s, but today it is used as a catch all label for all possible forms of cooperation [2]. Given that the article is not focusing on the institutional forms, we employ the PPP as synonymous of any kind of direct and indirect cooperation.

This article presents a new approach to PPP: we will first outline the difficulties of the cooperation. Then, the French case is analyzed. In conclusion, we argue that a well-defined spectrum of public-private cooperation can be seen as a risk mitigation tool affecting positively the infrastructures resilience.

2 The Cyber Resilience Equation or The Clash of Civilizations

The massive development and the penetration of ICTs into the society as a whole changed the rules of the game of CIIP and new rivalries raised. First, protection concept such as perimeter defense become no longer commensurate with contemporary requirements, thus a new thinking based on the shift from threat deterrence to risk management has emerged. In accordance with the concept of resilience, many cyber risk methods have been developed by information security experts (ISO 27000X series, or EBIOS in France). However their success is limited due to the rivalries and lack of common methodologies and tools between risk mangers & CISOs within the company [3]. As a result of this conflict, cyber risk is rarely fully integrated in organization's global risk management.

Moreover, protecting against the cyber threats has led to a contradictory practice and has revealed the schizophrenic conduct of national security authorities. In many countries, intelligence services and defense agencies are developing offensive capabilities for security interests: to achieve that, they exploit vulnerabilities in current operating systems and hardware or contribute to new vulnerabilities in widespread encryption systems. This situation makes the risk assessment more complex: backdoors could be identified and exploited by malicious actors and thus reduce the resilience of the entire system.

Finally, the implementation of public-private cooperation is complex because behind the oversimplified categories of public and private, various actors with conflicting representation and interests interface with each other. On the private side the players include infrastructure operators, maintenance firms, Industrial Control Systems (ICS) providers and security companies. With the emergence of CIIP issue, a main divergence appeared: the different culture between IT security (protection against intentional damages) and safety of operational technology-OT (protection against accidental events). Historically, confidentiality is not the main consideration in OT systems, and availability and integrity are by far the dominant concerns. On the other hand, OT systems frequently have little or no intrinsic security behavior. Here we come with the issue aforementioned: the need to develop a comprehensive approach of the cyber risk.

On the public side also, the presence of various players generates a fragmentation of the role of public sector: national intelligence, law enforcement, defense, emergency management, etc. Thus, four major challenges are undermining the implementation of PPP [2]: unclear delineation of role and responsibilities of players; lack of trust between partners, different languages (technological Vs bureaucratic), diverging interests (security Vs corporate benefits), and misplaced expectations (national security Vs multinational availability). Therefore the dialogue is inherently difficult.

3   The French Feedback Loop Process and Its Limits

In accordance with the objective to become a world power in cyber defence, France has launched numerous initiatives to ensure CIIP. Table 1 summarizes the main moves and highlights the global impact on cyber risk. If viewed broadly, these initiatives enable to move from a supposed high-level of risk (A) to a low-level of risk (B) and thus reducing the severity. In France the CIIP is historically organized as a cross-ministerial issue and the operators, according to the legal umbrella called *SAIV Framework (Secteurs d'activité d'importance vitale)*, bear the financial and operational burden based around five pillars: prevention, preparedness, detection response, mitigation and recovery. Due to space constraints, a complete analysis of moves cannot be covered at much length, thus we selected a critical initiative on the field of the PPP: the SCADA working group.

3.1   Bridging the Gap Between National Security and Operational Life of CIs

In 2009, a specialized agency in charge of the defence against cyber threat (French Network and Information Security Agency-ANSSI) was established and the strengthening of CIIP was defined as a major objective of cyber security strategy. Nevertheless, over the last years, several major attacks were disclosed and thus the 2013 White Paper on Defense and National Security defined the cyber security as an element of national sovereignty and the government imposed additional constraints to CIs[1].

The ongoing evolution of the SAIV framework shows that the traditional role of public authorities as rulemaker is still essential. On the other hand, the CIIP has to be thought as an adaptive process: standards are continually being

---

[1] Military Program Act 2014–2019 article 22, Defence Code Article L1332-6 and following. The measures include: mandatory cartography of the critical information systems, mandatory audits of information systems and networks by certified third parties; mandatory declaration of cyber incidents; implementation of certified sensors; more power to State authorities in order to take exceptional measures in case of a serious crisis.

established and updated, thus regulation needs to be reviewed over time to try to fit with new risks. However, due to the features of ICT environment, evolving much faster that standard setting process, regulation could be only a stopgap and is not a silver bullet solution. Here the PPPs play their crucial role: despite the enforcement of new standards, the public authorities defined the situation not satisfying. Thus the second step of French strategy was the identification of the missing bricks in order to better mitigate the risk. Particularly ICS security was identified as a main concern, thus ANSSI conducted a series of interviews in 2010 with CI operators, security suppliers and ICS vendors. The goal was to draw a shared understanding of the limits of the current security infrastructure, where best practices were to be found and the need of future requirements. In that way, the national authorities aim at establishing new standards and in parallel working with the industry to offer tailored solution for CIs.

Table 1. Cyber Resilience Equation- The French Case

Domain	Initiative	Description	Influencing
Security standard	Working group on ICS security	Working group established by the national authority on cyber security and bringing together all the stakeholders involved in CIIP. Focusing on: security standard, risk management and trusted solutions.	Countermeasures
			Vulnerability
			Impacts
	Military Program Act 2014-2019 article 22	Security Standards and legal measures to be imposed to CIs: mandatory cartography of the critical information systems; mandatory and regular audits of information systems and networks; mandatory declaration of cyber incidents; implementation of certified sensors.	Countermeasures
			Threats
			Impacts
Education & Training	French Centre of excellence for fight against cyber crime	The Centre is a PPP focusing on training and involving four companies (CEIS, Microsoft, Orange, Thales) three universities and the Gendarmerie.	Impacts
			Vulnerability
	Cyberdefence Cluster	Private company from telecom sector as well as from security and defense will jointly cooperate with the main research laboratories and MoD agencies in promoting innovation and training the future experts.	Countermeasures
			Vulnerability
	Chaire Thales Cyber Defense	Research Program founded by private sector in cooperation with the MoD. Focusing on cyber defense and developing courses and training for military.	Vulnerability
Awareness	Network of cyber defence reservists	Network of reservist made up of about 100 citizens helping in raising awareness, debating and suggesting, organising and establishing events that contribute to making cyber defence a national priority.	Vulnerability
	Awareness campaign led by DIRISI	In 2012 the Joint Direction of Infrastructure Networks and Information Systems (MoD) lunched an awareness campaign on cyber risk targeting CIs employees and managers.	Vulnerability
	Chaire Airbus Cyber strategy	Research centre founded by Airbus Foundation in cooperation with the Institute of Advanced Studies in National Defence. Focusing on geopolitics of cyber security.	Vulnerability
Trusted solutions	Industrial Cyber Plan	ANSSI is in charge to release a road map in order to boost the national cyber industrial base. The aim is to develop a sovereign industrial ecosystem and to develop a strategy in cooperation with the private sector.	Countermeasures
Information Sharing	French Club of Security Managers	The French Club of Security Managers is a non-profit organization allowing CIOs, risk manager to meet, work and exchange information.	Threats
	CERT- FR	French government CSIRT. As such, CERT-FR is the point of contact for all computer-related security incidents regarding France.	Vulnerability
Exercise	Piranet	Part of a series of national level crisis management exercises organised by the Prime Minister. The aim is to test the crisis prevention and management plans. More than 500 public & private participants.	Impacts

However, the differences of language and culture emerged again [4]. In 2011, ANSSI was aware of that and created a department fully dedicated to foster cooperation with CIs. In addition, permanent exchange platform (SCADA Working Group) was established with the main stakeholders from government (ANSSI and MoD) and industry (SCADA providers, national CIs and security suppliers) to establish best practices on supply chain risk management. In parallel, a twofold initiative has been launched. The certification process, led by ANSSI, for the rating audit companies as independent evaluators in order to state how well CIs have implemented the new framework. In addition, the standardization process refs also to trusted solutions and vendors. As showed by the Snowden affairs, a strong domestic ICT industrial base is a strategic advantage in cyber conflicts. The knowledge of software or hardware vulnerabilities could be exploited for both espionage and sabotage. ANSSI through the expertise acquired on-the-field of incident-response and recovery, is promoting and leading the development of trusted suppliers by the accreditation process.

These moves stress how cyber risk depends on so many variables that public and private players can impact only through a coordinated approach. The first important achievement is the mutual understanding of various interests and thus the convergence of opinions in adopting minimum security standards. In doing that, the SCADA WG reduces the gap between the government lack of technological path and the CIs lack of security path and contributes to better assess future needs for CIs. The outcomes of these initiatives could directly impact the risk factors: elaborating the secure design of new ICS leads to reduce the technical vulnerabilities. On the other hand, the implementation of trusted products, as the detection sensors, generates more countermeasures and a broader view of frequency and gravity of cyber attacks.

In that sense, the process launched in 2010 is a first important step to organize the public-private dialogue. However, a more in-depth analysis reveals important tensions that might be potentially damaging the implementation of the dialogue. On the private side, increasing critics have been heard condemning the regulatory-based approach without taking in account the market drivers. The primary interest of CI operators is to employ solutions broadly adequate for multinational plants. For security suppliers their concern is more for developing solutions able to be sold on the international market. Here is where corporate interests clash with national security and highlight the need of more international cooperation: since CIIP is defined as matter of national sovereignty, public powers are imposing new constraints to CIs and influencing the development of national technologies which should fulfill national standards. The consequences such as limitation of foreign investment and increasing cost to implement a multitude of national standards are relevant for private sector.

In conclusion, these dynamics underscore the need to find the balance between national sovereignty and global business interests. That leads to the question of the right scale of international cooperation: how to define a good partner? The European Union is the most appropriate level or it would be more valuable to establish a trusted group of partners on the basis of mutual acceptance of national standards? The issue is complex, and the debate is still ongoing in Europe.

4   Gaming the Future: Public-Private Debate and 3P Strategy

The implementation of CIP is never going to be simple, but the French case outlines several important insights. Due to the complexity of the CI resilience issue, the State needs to make a preliminary capability assessment (which capabilities are needed to be jointly developed with the private sector?), then various and interdependent initiatives should be established with the private sector. PPP and regulation, thus, are complementary measures of infrastructure resilience. On the one hand, the government's responsibility is to build the appropriate and continuously updated framework, both at national and international level. On the other hand, PPPs operate to address the missing bricks that need a cooperative approach: training, situational awareness of attacks, technical solutions, etc. As demonstrated by the evolution undertaken by ANSSI in 2009–2013, dealing with CI resilience means to be adaptive: being the policeman (conducting the inspection), the conventional rulemaker (helping CIs understand the measures to be implemented) or the facilitator (to develop the technical solution). Given that, the State takes on other important roles in enhancing the cyber resilience.

First of all, to open the debate on the balance between law enforcement, security and offensive capabilities. Keeping secret vulnerabilities or cracking encryption standards means increasing technical vulnerabilities for everyone. In that way, the State schizophrenia (promoting and implementing defenses while actively attacking) is no longer sustainable with the concept of resilience. However, the schizophrenia is also on the citizen's side: we accept that the State needs pre-emptive intelligence in order to anticipate the major threats to CIs. This situation pushes States to openly explain their activities - without revealing security recipes - to the citizens [5,6]. In addition, public power should establish a strategy of PPPs that will evolve as the risk evolves. The real question is not about what exactly is the role of government and private sector, but rather how the different pieces of public-private cooperation fit together in order to mitigate the risk. CIIP is neither a state nor a solution but a continuous process based on dialogue and demanding different levels of intervention from public and private. Therefore, a large and trusted spectrum of PPPs can act directly as a mitigation tool able to improve the national resilience.

With this new ethos of PPP, State and private sector can play an increasing role in reducing the overall impact of the cyber risk and improve the ability of organizations to defend itself against cyber threats. At this stage more detailed studies should follow on specific cases and since the CIIP topic includes transnational issues, further research on regional and international level of PPP should be encouraged.

Acknowledgments. This work is funded by Airbus Defense and Space-CyberSecurity and supported by the *Chaire Castex de Cyberstratégie*. Any opinions expressed in this publication are those of the author and do not necessarily reflect the views of *Airbus*.

References

1. Lacoste, Y.: La géographie ça sert d'abord à faire la guerre. La découverte, Paris (2014)
2. Dunn Cavelty, M., Suter, M.: The art of CIIP strategy: tacking stock of content and processes. In: Lopez, J., Setola, R., Wolthusen, S.D. (eds.) Critical Infrastructure Protection. LNCS, vol. 7130, pp. 15–38. Springer, Heidelberg (2012)

3. Douzet, F., Héon, S.: L'analyse du risque cyber, emblématique d'un dialogue nécessaire. Sécurité & Stratégie no. 14, La Document. Francaise, Paris, February (2014)
4. Meynet, S., et al.: SCADA/ICS security ANSSI Working Group. In: CESAR Conference (2013)
5. Omand, D.: Securing the State. Hurst, London (2010)
6. Schneier, B.: A fraying of the public/private surveillance partnership. www.schneier.com/blog/archives/11/a_fraying_of_th.html. Accessed 30 November 2013

Enterprise Security Analysis and Training Experience

Andres Ojamaa$^{(\boxtimes)}$ and Enn Tyugu

Institute of Cybernetics at Tallinn University of Technology,
Akadeemia tee 21, 12618 Tallinn, Estonia
{andres.ojamaa,tyugu}@cs.ioc.ee

Abstract. A holistic approach to security can be introduced by using a model that binds security measures with costs and security metrics. We describe exercises based on the graded security model, and supported by an expert system that are used for training both general managers and security experts. Trainees have to solve a number of problems under conditions that correspond to a realistic critical information infrastructure security planning situation, with the level of details depending on the expertise of trainees.

Keywords: Security training · Graded security · Security model

1 Introduction

We present an approach to teaching managers, where first a small number of basic concepts is explicitly introduced by defining a security model that includes cost considerations as an essential part of the model. These concepts are then used, based on the presented model, in a process that is close to real-life security design situations for making decisions and aided by an expert system. This process includes an abstract analysis section, followed by hands-on training that is usually the favorite usage of the model for the trainees. Performing the analysis of a security model that covers all the essential aspects of cybersecurity in a generalized way helps trainees to get a general picture of the enterprise security.

An expert system for teaching cybersecurity for trainees with different expertise levels was developed, and this expert system was based on a graded security model [4]. It has been used since 2010 in the courses Information and Cyber Security Assurance in Organizations and Foundations and Management of Cyber Security of the international masters program in cybersecurity at Tallinn University of Technology [9].

This paper summarises the basics of rational security design and the graded security model in Sects. 2 and 3, respectively. The security expert system used in the training process is introduced in Sect. 4, followed by the description of the training process in Sect. 5. References to related work are given in Sect. 6.

© Springer International Publishing Switzerland 2016
C.G. Panayiotou et al. (Eds.): CRITIS 2014, LNCS 8985, pp. 200–208, 2016.
DOI: 10.1007/978-3-319-31664-2_21

2   Rational Security Design

Security planning for an enterprise is aimed at finding a distribution of resources for security measures to achieve the best security solution under given conditions. This is called *rational security design*. Inputs for the rational security design are: *total amount of available money (maximal allowed costs), characterization of the secured system, security requirements*.

Finding a security solution assumes using a security metric that offers a possibility of comparing different solutions, and the possibility to express the quality of the solution by a numeric value. We use an *integrated security confidence* for this purpose that takes into account effects of taken security measures (see the following section). Although security planning will be performed as an optimization process, one can use mainly empirical data and expert knowledge. Therefore we call the result a *rational* and not necessarily an optimal solution.

Security planning may require solving several partial problems: evaluating costs required for implementing a selected solution, estimating the relative importance of any taken security solution, detecting similar security measures and collecting them in security measures groups, etc. The present set of exercises is intended to offer hands-on experience for solving these partial problems, as well as for constructing the complete solution.

3   Graded Security Policy and Model

The graded security policy uses a small number of security levels for characterizing each security aspect. As another approximation of reality in the model, we use a small number of security measures groups (about ten), instead of a large number of security measures (hundreds). These simplifications are useful in training, because they make the model comprehensible.

The security model describes how *security measures* are related to *security goals*, what are the *costs* to apply security measures, and what is the *confidence* for guaranteeing the respective *security level*. The concepts used in the graded security model are the following.

3.1   Security Goals

There are three common security goals (or security aspects) that must be achieved: *Confidentiality (C)*, *Integrity (I)*, *Availability (A)*.

Confidentiality guarantees that secured information will be accessible only to actors with the rights for using the information. *Integrity* means that secured information remains intact (can not be corrupted). *Availability* means that information can be accessed/used at any time when needed. It is possible to utilize more security goals—for example, in our expert system, one can use *Mission criticality* as an additional goal.

3.2   Security Class

A security goal can be achieved only to some level, and can practically never reach 100 %. Therefore each security goal has a *security level* that describes how strict the measures that are applied for achieving the goal must be. We use four security levels: *no requirements (0), low security level (1), medium security level (2), high security level (3)*. *Security class* is a tuple of security goals with respective security levels, e.g., *C0I3A3* denotes a security class with confidentiality *(C)* equal to *0*, integrity *(I) 3* and availability *(A) 3*.

3.3   Security Measures Group

A key component of the graded security model is the security measures group (SMG). It unites security measures with similar effects and is described by the parameters: security level l, cost of the security measures c, set of security measures to be taken m and security confidence p. The security level of SMG determines the values of other parameters of the group.

The four parameters l, c, m, p of a group are bound by the four tabulated functions: $c = f_1(l)$, $l = f_2(c)$, $m = f_3(l)$, $p = f_4(l)$ that are different for each group. These functions are given by the expert system, and they depend also on the environment (on a situation) where the security is applied. In our system, SMG as a component of the security model can be used as a black box, because the functions binding its parameters are hidden in the expert system.

A number of security measures groups may vary from one version of a model to another. In the present training environment we have the following groups: *personnel training, firewalls, encryption, antivirus software, segmentation, redundancy, backup, access control*, and *intrusion detection*.

The concepts presented here: security goals, security class, security metrics and security measures group constitute the basis of the security education for managers and experts. The security experts, but not the managers, should understand security groups in detail, including functional dependences between their parameters.

3.4   Security Metrics

When security measures are applied, each security measures group i gets a value p_i of *security confidence* that is a percent to which the security is guaranteed by measures of the group (practically always less than 100 %). *Overall security* (integral security confidence) s is a security metric that describes all security aspects of the secured system by means of one single value. This value is calculated as a weighted mean of security confidences of security measures groups:

$$s = \sum_i w_i p_i, \text{ where } \sum_i w_i = 1.$$

The weights w_i characterize importance of each group i in the overall security of system. They depend on a concrete situation and should be assigned by an expert before the usage of the model. Our expert system has also functionality for automatically assigning the weights w_i depending on the type and properties of the secured system.

There are other and more precise ways to define integral security metrics. In particular, the integral security can be calculated analogously to reliability of a system depending on structure of the system [3].

3.5   Security Model

A security model includes a component for each group, and shows also a security class and formulas for calculating costs. Figure 1 in the following section shows a model for 9 security measures groups.

4   Security Expert System

We apply an expert system developed in an earlier work [4] for building and using graded security models based on empirical data from banking practice. Two banks operating in Estonia, Swedbank and SEB, have been interested in this development and have cooperated with us in the development. The expert system is intended for building security models and solving security design problems: calculating the best distribution of given resources, checking reachability of security goals, planning the evolving security for several years, etc. Solving these problems in a training process will be discussed in the next section.

The expert system has been built on an open source visual programming platform CoCoViLa that provides advanced visual interface for applications [8]. Figure 1 shows a window of the expert system for specifying security models. A model is specified by selecting its components from the palette, putting them in the scheme of the model, and adjusting their parameters. Components have default values of parameters, but each of them has a popup window that can be used for adjusting properties of the component. A popup window "Properties" for the security class component is shown on the right side of the figure. It includes a string *C2I1A1M2* that is the security class value.

We can see nine components representing SMGs. Only two of them: *Encryption* and *User training* are presented in the extended way, so that the relation between their costs and confidences is visible. Components for security class and optimizer are also visible in the window. The latter is a control component for calculations, it includes also calculation of total costs and overall security.

There is a component for visualisation of the results, and it is bound with three SMGs: *Antivirus software, User training* and *Antivirus software*. Their security levels will be visualised in a results window as it is shown below. Standard connections between the components of the security model (between each group and the security class etc.) are established automatically, and are not visible. The scheme includes also two more components that are needed for adjusting

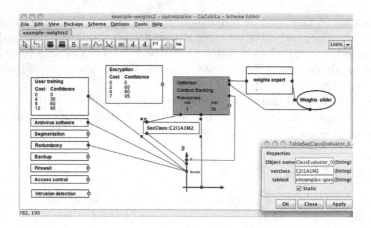

Fig. 1. Visual representation of security model is input for the expert system

the weights w_i for calculating the overall security: *Weights expert* and *Weights slider*.

The scheme in Fig. 1 describes a graded security model of a bank. It is easy to specify different security models, e.g., adding new security measures groups. As we know, the largest model developed so far contains 40 groups [3]. A library of models can be developed for different training situations that can cover essential situations.

The expert system provides full automation of calculations on the specified model. The results created by the visualization component are shown in a window shown in Fig. 2. This window can be viewed as an graphical dashboard representing the whole security situation of an enterprise. It shows the following:

- an overall security curve: the Pareto set of pairs (*costs, overall security*);
- security levels of the SMGs connected to the visualizer component for each value of costs;
- whether the specified security class can be achieved for given costs.

The main result is the topmost curve in the window. It represents a Pareto set consisting of best achievable overall security values for different values of costs. An optimization problem is solved for each point of the curve. This problem is finding a distribution of costs between the SMGs that gives the best value of the overall security for given costs.

The window shown in Fig. 2 includes more curves besides the overall security curve. These curves show the calculated security levels for three SMGs: *Antivirus software*, *Redundancy* and *User training*. To show security levels for some measures group, one has to connect the respective measures group with the *levels* port of the graph object in the scheme as it is shown in Fig. 1.

Colour of the topmost curve gives additional information for each value of costs: red—the requirements of the security class are unsatisfied, yellow—the

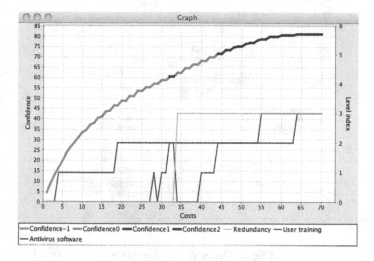

Fig. 2. A results window of the expert system (Color figure online)

requirements of the security class are partially satisfied, and blue—all requirements of the security class are satisfied, i.e., all security goals are achieved at
the required levels.

5   Training Process

Trainees are expected to solve a number of security design problems in the conditions that are close to a realistic security planning situation. A suggested order
of training steps for these problems is shown in Fig. 3. The first two are introductory steps. The third step—analysis of SMGs is an activity for experts. So are
the following two steps of adjustment of parameters. Default parameters given in
the expert system can be used in training of general managers. Calculating the
best distribution of resources is the main training activity. It is possible to concentrate on this activity immediately after introductory steps. Calculating the
evolving security continues the previous step and considers security as a process
continuing for several years. Checking the reachability of security goals is an
independent problem, but it can be solved by the same means as calculating the
best distribution of resources.

If a scheme from the scheme library is used, then the first five training steps
can be omitted, and one can immediately start solving the last three problems
that are training steps for managers as well as for security experts. Below are
described some steps of using the expert system.

The model-based security analysis is suitable for security training of people
with different level of experience. It relies on analytic capabilities of a person,
and it introduces the basics of security in the form of a security model. The
hands-on part of the training is performed using an expert system. The aim of
the presented security model and of set of exercises is to help the trainee to

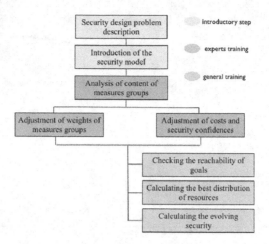

Fig. 3. Order of training steps

build his/her mental model of cybersecurity by combining (1) analytical app-roach where basic concepts and an explicit security mode are introduced, and (2) hands-on experience by solving security design problems with the help of an expert system.

6   Related Work

Graded security policy is the basis for security protection programs of nuclear security and anti-terrorist security of US Department of Energy [7,12], as well as for several European information assurance standards. In particular, German BSI-Standard 100-2 [2] and Estonian ISKE standard [1] are both based on the graded security policy. We adopt this policy in our expert system, and use the respective security model. Evolving security analysis that we use here has been investigated by Kivimaa et al. [5].

A popular way to teach security concepts is to give some hands-on experi-ence by targeted video games like CyberSiege [10] from the Naval Postgraduate School, or using games from the DISA online training catalogue, e.g., the well-known game CyberProtect [11]. These tools are intended for teaching security concepts for people with varied backgrounds and different levels of expertise. They introduce essential security measures by means of exercises in a more or less realistic situation, but give trainees only implicitly a partial security model. There are also more advanced and complex cyber security learning systems, such as CyberNEXS [6] from Leidos (SAIC). The latter is aimed at development of skills on expert level. CyberNEXS is probably the most advanced of the cyber-security training systems. It provides games for four scenarios: network defense, forensics, penetration testing (attacks) and capture the flag. We presented here a complementary approach to war games for teaching cybersecurity that is based on the analysis and usage of a security model.

7 Conclusion

We have proposed a model-based technique and software of security training. It relies on analytic capabilities of a person, and it introduces the basics of security in the form of a security model. The hands-on part of the training is performed using an expert system. The aim of the presented security model and of set of exercises is to help the trainee to build his/her mental model of cybersecurity by combining (1) analytical approach where basic concepts and an explicit security mode are introduced, and (2) hands-on experience by solving security design problems with the help of the expert system. Our four years teaching experience on masters level at Tallinn University of Technology [9] has validated the methodology.

Acknowledgements. The authors appreciate the support of the Estonian Academy of Sciences, the target funding project SF0140007s12 of Estonian Ministry of Education and Research, the European Regional Development Fund (ERDF) through Estonian Centre of Excellence in Computer Science (EXCS) project and the project No. 3.2.1201.13-0026 *Model-based Java software development technology*.

References

1. Estonian Information System Authority: Three-level IT baseline security system ISKE. https://www.ria.ee/iske-en
2. German Federal Office for Information Security (BSI): BSI-Standard 100-2 IT Grundschutz Methodology. https://www.bsi.bund.de/SharedDocs/Downloads/EN/BSI/Publications/BSIStandards/standard_100-2_e_pdf.pdf
3. Kivimaa, J., Kirt, T.: Evolutionary algorithms for optimal selection of security measures. In: Ottis, R. (ed.) Proceedigs of the 10th European Conferences on Information Warfare and Security, pp. 172–184. Academic Publishers, Reading, UK (2011)
4. Kivimaa, J., Ojamaa, A., Tyugu, E.: Graded security expert system. In: Setola, R., Geretshuber, S. (eds.) CRITIS 2008. LNCS, vol. 5508, pp. 279–286. Springer, Heidelberg (2009)
5. Kivimaa, J., Ojamaa, A., Tyugu, E.: Managing evolving security situations. In: Unclassified Proceedings of the MILCOM 2009, 18–21 October 2009. IEEE, Piscataway (2009)
6. Leidos: CyberNEXS Cyber Security Training. https://www.leidos.com/cybersecurity/solutions/CyberNEXS
7. Lobsenz, G.: DOE Adopts New "Graded" Terrorist Protection Policy (2008). http://pogoarchives.org/m/nss/energydaily-20080826.pdf
8. Modeling and Simulation Group at IoC: CoCoViLa model-based software development platform. http://www.cs.ioc.ee/cocovila/
9. Tallinn University of Technology: Cyber security master's programme. http://www.ttu.ee/studying/masters/masters_programmes/cyber-security/
10. Thompson, M., Irvine, C.: Active learning with the CyberCIEGE video game. In: Proceedings of the 4th Conference on Cyber Security Experimentation and Test, CSET 2011. USENIX Association, Berkeley (2011)

11. U.S. DoD, Defense Information Systems Agency: CyberProtect, version 1.1. http://iase.disa.mil/eta/
12. U.S. DoE, Office of Information Resources: DOE O 470.3B, Graded Security Protection (GSP) Policy. https://www.directives.doe.gov/directives/0470.3-BOrder-b/view

Using Programmable Data Networks to Detect Critical Infrastructure Challenges

Kyle J.S. White[✉], Dimitrios P. Pezaros, and Chris W. Johnson

School of Computing Science, University of Glasgow,
Glasgow G12 8QQ, Scotland, UK
mail@kylewhite.com,
{dimitrios.pezaros,christopher.johnson}@glasgow.ac.uk

Abstract. Critical infrastructures must be better protected against challenges to their data communications in the face of increasing numbers of emerging challenges, complexity and society's demand and intolerance of failures. In this paper, we present a set of challenges and their characteristics by reviewing reported incidents. Using domain specific attributes we discuss how these could be mitigated. We advocate the adoption of the latest programmable networking approaches in critical infrastructure networks and we present our proposed modular architecture with configurable monitoring and security components. Lastly, we show results from a network challenge simulation which highlights the benefits of our approach in providing rapid, precise and effective challenge detection and mitigation.

Keywords: Resilience · Security · Critical systems

1 Introduction

Data communication networks are playing an increasingly pivotal role in critical infrastructures. Society is becoming ever more reliant on critical infrastructures to manage a range of services including communications, power and transportation. It is therefore necessary that the underlying data networks of such infrastructures remain highly resilient and available in the face of emerging challenges. Data networks worldwide are becoming progressively interconnected and explicitly, critical infrastructures are becoming less isolated, e.g., EU Air Transportation systems are increasing their interconnectivity through an international Airport Collaborative Decision Making (A-CDM) system [2]. In this paper, we argue that critical infrastructure data networks are encountering a series of emerging challenges. We discuss the motivation for increasing data communication resilience and the domain specific attributes of critical infrastructures we can exploit, in Sect. 2. In Sect. 3, we review reported incidents within our focussed context of mission-critical Air Traffic Management (ATM) systems. By analysing these incidents and considering other possible scenarios, we have characterised a taxonomy of emerging challenges and their features. In order to

© Springer International Publishing Switzerland 2016
C.G. Panayiotou et al. (Eds.): CRITIS 2014, LNCS 8985, pp. 209–221, 2016.
DOI: 10.1007/978-3-319-31664-2_22

best take advantage of the attributes of critical network infrastructures (CNI), we argue for the introduction of the latest programmable networking approaches, specifically Software Defined Networking (SDN). SDN allows centralised, logical control of data traffic routing. This offers unique opportunities as event based code can be executed in response to real-time network behaviour, e.g. allowing the controller to enforce different policies depending on the traffic type. Using our domain specific knowledge and familiarity with SDN, we argue that the typical qualities of many CNIs can be exploited using tailored algorithms on SDN-based architectures that will allow them to better mitigate such challenges than would be possible in other data networks. We then present our vision of a modular architecture in Sect. 4 and discuss how it can be utilised to improve resilience. Our final contribution, in Sect. 5, is an initial experiment which highlights the benefits of our architecture, and SDN, when detecting and remediating against a flooding challenge, before concluding the paper.

2   Characteristics of Critical Network Infrastructures

Data networks within critical infrastructures have certain characteristics that hold true more predominately than for data networks in general. Firstly, they should be highly redundant with respect to both topology and services. Secondly, any changes are perceived as high risk. Finally, high availability and low latency are required. These three attributes converge neatly. To achieve high availability, there should be significant redundancy. Low latency requires over-provisioning and considerate routing strategies for queuing and congestion. To make changes to a system undermines the experienced reliability to date as unknown consequences can occur. Leaving the system unchanged is therefore perceived as the best means to maintain achieved levels of high availability. This means traffic patterns and topologies are relatively static in comparison with the ad-hoc, ever-changing behaviour of the legacy Internet. As technology is advancing and some changes are being made, such as reducing the relative isolation of critical infrastructures, it is now time to make further, protective, changes to safeguard critical infrastructure data network's resilience. As evidence for the increasing interdependency of systems we refer to the new EU networked system to directly share collaborative flight planning data among different systems and countries [2] and for a comprehensive overview of CNI's interdependencies in general, see [13].

The complexity of critical infrastructure communication networks is rising as they age. Current data networks are moving larger bandwidths of data traffic and systems are processing ever greater volumes of data. This trend continues as capacity improves and as demand increases for more knowledge of the system with more intelligent data correlations. Modern critical infrastructures often have diverse technologies integrated into the overall system. This has come from building improvements onto legacy components and adapting new technology to interface with existing protocols.

Fig. 1. Depiction of the layers of dependency in critical infrastructure systems

2.1   Energy and Communication Resilience

Critical infrastructures rely on power and communications in order to maintain mission-critical services. These two components are often interconnected with energy required to power communications and a communications network required to manage, monitor and control the power systems. Nearly all elements of critical infrastructures require both power and communications to perform their function. In Fig. 1, we present our view of the functional hierarchy of components required to effectively provide the services which comprise critical infrastructures. The pyramid requires the underlying components to be in place to offer the services at higher layers. We differentiate between energy the CI national grid supply, and the power required for an individual CI to function internally. Capacity, safety, security, automation and resilience engineering fall between basic needs and advancing current research. Systems integration, real-time processing and optimisation form the pinnacle of current CI research.

Given the relationship discussed above, power and communications can be categorised together. However, as we discuss in previous work [19], the challenges faced in communications resilience are greater. Power supplies are source-independent, with energy needs being met from mains, back-up generators and even fail-safe battery power in the worst case. Voltage spikes or brown outs can be mitigated using standard techniques such as Diesel Rotary Uninterruptible Power Supplies which convert the power to a steady, clean stream in terms of phase, harmonic distortion and consistent voltage. Communications resilience is a more sophisticated problem as it is time-critical for real-time applications and the content is source-dependent. Communication payloads are a complex, non-Poisson process of traffic load and arrivals. This implies high variability and unpredictable dynamics over long timescales. Traffic peaks can also be significant in terms of utilisation, even with substantial over-provisioning. Data packets are also susceptible to corruption, loss and delay. We therefore argue there is strong motivation to place a greater emphasis on communications resilience to ensure the same levels of reliability and availability as are present in power resilience.

3   Examples of CNI Challenges

Numerous challenges threaten the failure of critical infrastructures. We have defined a generalised taxonomy of characteristics for a series of accidental failures and malicious attacks which can be categorised together. We base this categorisation on the behaviour of the challenge in the data network, the characteristics of CNIs can be exploited to defend against such challenges and the existence of past incidents which are an instance of such a challenge or allude to the scenario being a possible, legitimate threat. The challenges in this partial taxonomy are representative because they have a similar manifestation but with different implications. There are also common attributes we can use to detect these challenges which we review after presenting our taxonomy. We consider:

- Flooding:
  - Distributed Flood
  - Centralised Flood
- Disconnectivity
- Oscillation
- Network Scan

Flooding: Network flooding is where a large amount of data overwhelms the available capacity of the network resources, e.g., in terms of physical bandwidth. Other types of flooding exist such as SYN flooding, where a large number of TCP flows are simultaneously sent to a remote server initiating the connection protocol. The server sends TCP SYN-ACK and awaits ACK replies for each of these flows, before running out of memory, thus stopping new connections being made. We distinguish between two types of flooding: *distributed* and *centralised*. Distributed floods are well-known for causing Distributed Denial of Service (DDoS) attacks, Flashcrowds and Botnets. These challenges have a distributed source address space and a concentrated destination address space. Centralised floods begin from a focussed point in the network and can have a single root cause. They may however propagate, such as a case of a broadcast storm, where network devices forward data packets to all connected devices, as instructed, resulting in an endless flow of traffic. Characteristics of this type of flooding are a concentrated source address space and a concentrated destination address space. These are well known challenges and many solutions exist to mitigate them in generic network environments [10].

Disconnectivity: Disconnectivity is where part of the network infrastructure is no longer available. This may be due to hardware, e.g., a physical link or switch going down or software misconfiguration of a firewall or routing table errors. The threat of failure from a disconnectivity challenge is independent of its cause. While it is important to rapidly diagnose and isolate the cause of the problem, in terms of overall system availability, it is more important to understand the impact of the challenge. Depending on where the disconnectivity arises, this may mean an alternative path between parts of the network experiences higher traffic levels as data is rerouted around the problem area or it may mean parts of the network are entirely isolated. Characteristics of this challenge will likely be a significant drop in traffic in some parts of the infrastructure, a similarly significant rise in traffic in other parts, as well as the potential creation of additional routing paths throughout the network.

Oscillation: Link redundancy is a core feature of mission-critical networks. Even in simple topologies, persistent routing oscillations can occur. This challenge makes understanding normal behaviour complex and is bad for stability, load balancing, reliability, predictability and fault detection [4]. It also degrades router performance and makes monitoring data harder to interpret. Finally, anomaly detection methodologies are also hampered since many rely on trends or sampling [1], and the characteristics of oscillation are bursty traffic conditions and routing table variability.

Network Scan: Network scans and other distributed attacks such as Exploits and Worms can be categorised together with common characteristics of a distributed destination address space, focussing on a limited set of destination ports. These challenges exploit network vulnerabilities and are malicious attacks. In traditional networks firewalls and network monitoring tools offer some protection against these attacks.

While distinct, there are common aspects to which can be used to optimally detect these challenges, particularly when in an SDN environment. The key aspect for this taxonomy is the desire to have both distributed and centralised knowledge to detect and mitigate the challenge. Flooding incidents require rapid identification of the source of the traffic. This can be achieved through a distributed alarms which recognise flood traffic, and centralised control which can determine if the event is localised, distributed or propagating throughout the network. Similarly, disconnectivity requires both distributed knowledge of local behaviour as well as a global perspective to determine where the cause is and whether any parts of the network are now completely isolated. Oscillation can occur at various scales or across local domains making it necessary to examine at both levels. Finally, network scans vary and depending on their nature may be obscured at either a local or global level. If a network scan is mounted in a distributed address space attacking the same port, this requires a centralised detection algorithm. However, if a port scan is targeting a concentrated destination address space and examining each of its ports, this can be handled locally.

3.1   Review of CNI Incidents

To provide evidence for our claims of the challenges facing critical infrastructures we explore recent incidents involving Air Traffic Transportation Systems. The following four incidents highlight the severity of the impact faced when challenges do undermine the resilience of ATM data networks and therefore the safety and security of the service which relies upon them.

In 2007, the US Customs and Border Protection computer systems at LAX suffered from a network outage [8]. The fault analysis concluded the single initial point of failure was caused by a malfunctioning Network Interface Card (NIC). This in turn caused data to overload the system. This system is not directly involved in ATM services however, the 10-hour-long issue caused delays and congestion affecting up to 17,000 passengers with new arrivals not being allowed to disembark, and international departure disruptions. Analysis suggests this incident had similar characteristics to a *centralised flooding* challenge which propagated throughout the network.

In 2008, a European airport ATM system experienced a similar incident caused by an intermittent faulty NIC. This fault and the subsequent error of automated network software designed to mitigate anomalous issues ultimately caused periods of complete airport closure due to safety concerns. The seven week period over which problems persisted included times where ATM lost track of planes or associated flight information [5]. This was a complex incident with multiple factors involved, however, the root cause gives further evidence to the threat faced from *flooding* challenges.

The FAA (Federal Aviation Administration) Telecommunications Infrastructure (FTI) experienced a four-hour outage in 2009 causing disruption for over 800 flights [3]. The incident was a series of cascading events which culminated in failure. Earlier scheduled maintenance led to a routing table being programmed incorrectly. This was inactive until it was restarted. Independently, alarms monitoring router utilisation had been inadvertently disabled for all routers. The lack of an alarm system compounded the routing error and a significant delay occurred while network engineers manually probed the network to localise the problem and eventually determine which router was at fault. Given a routing failure scenario such as this and the potential for human error due to manual programming, it is probable severe oscillation incidents can occur as well as significant flooding, in order to have router utilisation exceeding alarm thresholds.

Most recently, a fire caused disconnectivity at a core FAA PoP (Point of Presence) in Atlantic City in 2012 [12]. The building was evacuated and caused some air traffic and flight planning systems in the U.S. to become temporarily unavailable. The ATM service was significantly slowed. Back-up systems relied on telephones for communications. This incident was well-managed but highlights that despite high levels of redundancy, disconnectivity is a very real threat and the challenge of continuing operations seamlessly in the face of disrupted infrastructure connectivity cannot be guaranteed.

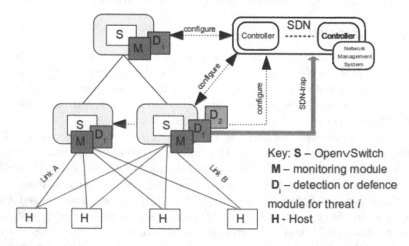

Fig. 2. Modular SDN architecture with distributed, configurable monitoring & security

4   Proposed CNI Architecture

In order to better tackle the threat of failure that the emerging challenges we have outlined present, we argue that the latest networking technologies should be introduced into ATM data networks. By applying SDN as the foundations for our proposed architecture, numerous advantages can be gained. We believe that by augmenting SDN functionality with our specific architecture, distributed algorithms can be tailored to exploit critical infrastructure attributes to better defend against a wide array of future challenges including those in our taxonomy. To begin, we will introduce the benefits of an SDN approach alone and then we will discuss our proposed additions which further increase resilience.

4.1   SDN for Critical Infrastructures

SDN is a networking approach which separates the data and control planes. The data plane handles the forwarding of network traffic to the correct destination space while the control plane handles the decision on how traffic should be routed. There is a single logical controller, which may be physically distributed, which sets control plane rules in the flow tables of switches. These rules match packets which arrive at the switch. If the information in the packet header matches a rule, the switch performs the associated action, e.g., forwards the packet on the data plane. If there is no match, the packet is sent to the controller which can decide to establish a new rule and install it on the switch. The controller can modify existing rules and actions can be set to discard, forward packets to their destination or send them to the controller to handle. There has been a great deal of work on various related aspects of network functionality in an SDN environment including anomaly detection techniques [9,20], integrating different approaches to monitoring and security services [16,17], network verification [6] and automatic failure recovery [7]. OpenFlow, a protocol specification which is layered on top of TCP, is the first standard communications interface defined between the control and forwarding layers of an SDN architecture. It relies on Open vSwitches with routing flow tables. The *POX* OpenFlow controller and others [14], allow operators to specify event-based functionality.

Of the many advantages SDN brings to a network operator, those of most specific interest to critical infrastructures include: vendor-independent centralised management and control; centralised and automated management of network devices allowing uniform policy enforcement thus reducing configuration errors and increasing network reliability and security; fine-grained control of varying services, users, devices and application policies; improved automation and management by using common APIs to manipulate the underlying network behaviour for provisioning systems and applications [11].

Crucially, SDN is vendor-independent and can therefore be used on a variety of different devices. This is advantageous since, as we discussed earlier, many of the CNIs comprise a mixture of legacy systems, conversion networking devices and differing manufacturer equipment. Further related work [15], which separates a physical network infrastructure into different logical networks could be of significant interest to critical infrastructures when it matures. SDN technology could allow changes to be test-deployed alongside operational CNIs in the same environment as a final safeguard before migration from the testbed to live deployment.

4.2 An SDN Architecture for ATM

While OpenFlow offers an excellent environment to explore some of the advantages of SDN we believe more can be achieved to aid safety and security through an SDN approach. With increasing bandwidths and data processing, anomaly detection is requiring faster processing in order to be effective in a real-time context. We propose that to achieve truly optimised, efficient anomaly detection for critical infrastructures, the processing of detection methodologies should be distributed. To achieve this, switches would require more resources, however we argue this is a realistic proposition for two reasons: the costs of computing components are reducing and with the separation of control and data planes through SDN there are far greater possibilities for distributing anomaly detection algorithms. We therefore believe the cost-benefit trade-off for this architecture is now in favour of distributed anomaly detection, particularly to exploit the environment of CNIs. In Fig. 2 we show our modular approach to an SDN architecture for critical infrastructures, which has centralised knowledge and distributed intelligence. Open vSwitches are configured by an SDN controller as standard. Hosts are connected to Open vSwitches by 2-fold physically redundant links: Links A & B. The novelty of our architecture comes from the configurable monitoring and security modules. These are pre-tested modules which can be deployed on-demand by network operators to perform a task given the current status of the network. This distributed approach allows network operators to have the freedom and control over their resources to respond to challenges as they emerge. When an incident unfolds, operators want to learn more in real time. This architecture offers them the ability to do that rapidly. If a given threat is presumed to be causing a problem in the network, security detection or defence modules specific to that threat can be deployed to a given switch to gain further information and attempt to self-heal. Similarly, if detailed performance information is desired prior to, for example, network upgrades, a suite of monitoring tools can be deployed throughout the network to learn about the localised behaviour in that part of the infrastructure. Figure 2, also details an SDN-trap. We define this as an asynchronous message from the switch to the controller which could be used to alert the controller that anomalous behaviour has been identified.

5 Flood Detection and Remediation Experiment

To prove the merits of our architecture we implemented a flooding detection and remediation experiment based on challenge characteristics and our domain specific knowledge. This experiment is designed to show the advantages and potential which can be leveraged for critical infrastructures using our SDN-based architecture and early feasibility results. We simulated a scale version of a major European Air Navigation Service Provider's (ASNP) secondary radar surveillance network. In Fig. 3, we show our experimental topology. The core of the network is a ring connecting switches S_1, S_2 and S_3. These switches represent the primary ATM locations throughout the country. H_1, H_2 and H_3 represent the subscribers to the surveillance data to, for example, display where aircraft are located on Air Traffic Controller displays. In reality these hosts are in fact large Local Area Networks (LANs) with their own layers of redundancy. In Fig. 3, the core ring network connecting switches S_1, S_2 and S_3 has a high bandwidth and shares the captured radar data from the distributed radar locations, represented here as H_4, H_5 and H_6. Each radar dish has a local switch which sends dual copies of the output data on the Red and Green links which represent the 2-fold physical redundancy in the network. Each switch is configurable through the centralised SDN controller.

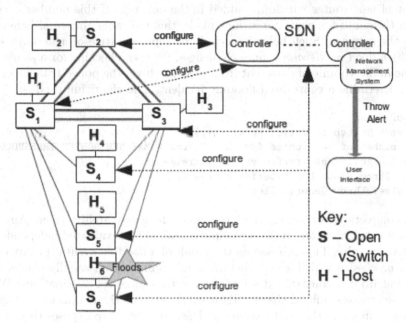

Fig. 3. Flooding experiment on scaled ANSP radar surveillance network topology

5.1 Methodology

To begin, standard operational traffic was initiated in the network with H_4, H_5 and H_6 sending their continual radar data to the core ring via the Red and Green links to S_1 and S_3, respectively. The operational traffic was modelled from recordings of live data which we analysed in our previous work [19]. As the standard traffic began, the POX controller performed its default behaviour, establishing flow table entries for the switches on the core ring, allowing their associated hosts to directly route traffic to each other. Flow table rules were also installed on the radar switches S_4, S_5 and S_6 to allow them to send traffic from their hosts to H_1 and H_3.

In our controller, we implemented a traffic metric polling for each switch to provide the number of flows, the number of bytes and the number of packets sent from that switch to each destination address. This polling was triggered by a timer event every five seconds. From our knowledge of surveillance networks and following the static characteristics of critical infrastructure data networks, we determined that new connections between pairs of devices which had never previously exchanged data is a relatively rare event in this domain. Once the network is established and the controller has installed flow table entries for standard operational traffic patterns, new connections to send data from e.g. H_4 to H_5, are unlikely. We exploited this characteristic to better detect a flooding challenge in the network. Every time a packet is sent to the controller and a new flow table entry is installed on a switch, we add this forwarding rule into a list of the latest added routes. Each time a timer event is called, we examine the number of new routes which are added in the network. If this number exceeds a given threshold for new connections made, this indicates abnormal behaviour within the network. Such behaviour could be representative of a *network scan*, *centralised flood* or *disconnectivity* challenges. By then checking for a significant increase in the volume of data sent from this switch via the polled traffic metrics, we can determine a centralised flooding incident. The algorithm used is:

```
On Timer Event:
  for each Switch in Latest Route Entries:
    if number of new routes for this Switch > MAX_NEW_ROUTES_THRESHOLD:
      if significant traffic volume increase:
        Throw Flood Characteristics Alert
      else: Throw Generic Alert
```

On completion of checking the latest route entries we archive them. Any new flow table entries created in the next time period will be evaluated independently of archived results. This is based on the profile of a flooding event typically being a rapid process in which a malfunction or misconfiguration rapidly causes data to be sent from a constrained set of sources to a large set destinations. When our system throws a flood characteristic event, we pass the details of the switch, its latest routes and the traffic volumes. The controller then exposes these alerts which can be collected by a network monitoring system and reviewed through e.g. a web based user interface such as KSWatch [18]. Network operators could then act using our modular architecture to block flows from this switch, increase detection in other parts of the network and perhaps deploy further monitoring in the affected areas of the infrastructure to ensure normal behaviour is restored.

5.2   Results and Discussion

With typical operational data flowing in our simulated experiment, we introduced a flooding incident from H6 as seen in Fig. 4. This was performed using *iperf* in UDP mode for a prolonged 60 s burst at 5x operational traffic levels to all hosts on the network: H_1 to H_5. Our experiment parameters were set with

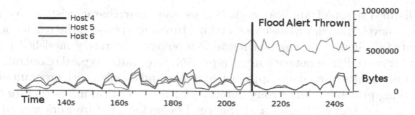

Fig. 4. Results of flooding and detection time plotted against normal operational traffic

MAX_NEW_ROUTES _THRESHOLD=2. As the UDP flows began, the controller added new routes from H_6 to H_2, H_4 and H_5 (routes to H_1 and H_3 are already present). This took place within a five second timer event. After the flood had initiated, the next time the timer event was triggered, a Flood Characteristic Alert was successfully thrown to the network monitoring at the controller. Considering the lengthy outages which have occurred through flooding events in the past, we believe that this prototype experiment and our architecture shows strong potential for better securing and increasing reliability of critical infrastructures in the future.

Other techniques to detect flooding incidents exist of course. Preventative approaches such as VLAN isolation or another means of blocking access between hosts could be implemented, e.g., firewalls. However, flooding is one challenge from many in the set we have identified. While other techniques exist, the implementation of these can involve manually distributed hard-coding of policies which can be overly restrictive and unresponsive. Our architecture places the network operators in greater direct, responsive control of their network since they have the ability to deploy distributed modules tailored to the scenarios they perceive unfolding. We argue, our approach allows for greater flexibility and security with faster results than typical monitoring provides. In our experience, many network operators rely upon Simple Network Monitoring Protocol (SNMP) based network monitoring applications which typically poll network devices once every 15 min. While there is always a trade-off amongst the frequency of monitoring, the traffic this monitoring produces and the desire not to interfere with operational traffic, we believe our architecture presents an optimal solution. If additional monitoring is temporarily desired, with more granular frequency or reviewing a wider set of parameters, this can be deployed and processed at distributed points throughout the infrastructure, on-demand. By exploiting the decoupled control plane approach we recognised a flooding event within a few seconds and presented an alert detailing the switch at the root cause. The operator then has detailed information and can act rapidly.

6   Conclusions and Future Work

In this paper, we presented the case for adopting the latest programmable network technologies, specifically SDN, for the control and management of CNI. We reviewed a series of incidents which affected Air Transportation systems and distilled a set of applicable challenges and their characteristics. We presented a novel, modular SDN-based architecture and discussed the results of our simulated challenge on a scaled network topology, accurately modelled on an EU radar surveillance network using representative traffic, typical of operational flows. Our results showed our approach is viable, and coupled with programmable networking principles, has strong potential for use in critical infrastructure data networks to detect challenges and abnormal behaviour. Future work will add to our simulated environment, creating a scaled version of our complete modular architecture and we will look at how to deploy security and monitoring components over the network on-demand. We intend to explore anomaly detection algorithms which we can distribute and tailor to exploit the characteristics of the challenges we present in this paper as well as attributes of critical infrastructures.

References

1. Dewaele, G., Fukuda, K., Borgnat, P., Abry, P., Cho, K.: Extracting hidden anomalies using sketch and non gaussian multiresolution statistical detection procedures. In: Workshop on Large Scale Attack Defense, pp. 145–152. ACM (2007)
2. Eurocontrol website: Rome Fiumicino Airport becomes the 10th A-CDM airport. https://www.eurocontrol.int/news/rome-fiumicino-cdm-implementation-gears-critical-mass-full-benefits. Accessed 27 April 2014
3. FAA FTI Review Panel: Report on November 19, 2009 Outage (2010)
4. Flavel, A., Roughan, M., Bean, N., Shaikh, A.: Where's Waldo? practical searches for stability in iBGP. In: ICNP, pp. 308–317. IEEE (2008)
5. IAA: Report of the IAA into the ATM System Malfunction, September 2008
6. Khurshid, A., Zhou, W., Caesar, M., Godfrey, P.: Veriflow : verifying network-wide invariants in real time. In: SIGCOMM, pp. 467–472. ACM (2012)
7. Kuniar, M., Pereni, P., Vasi, N., Canini, M., Kosti, D. Automatic failure recovery for software-defined networks. In: HotSDN, pp. 159–160. ACM (2013)
8. Los Angeles Times: LAX outage is blamed on 1 computer, August 2007
9. Mehdi, S.A., Khalid, J., Khayam, S.A.: Revisiting traffic anomaly detection using software defined networking. In: Balzarotti, D., Maier, G., Sommer, R. (eds.) RAID 2011. LNCS, vol. 6961, pp. 161–180. Springer, Heidelberg (2011)
10. Mirkovic, J., Reiher, P.: A taxonomy of DDoS attack and DDoS defense mechanisms. In: SIGCOMM, pp. 39–53. ACM (2004)
11. Open Networking Foundation: SDN: The New Norm for Networks, April 2012
12. Press of Atlantic City: Fire at Hughes Technical Center caused $2.2M in damage. http://www.highbeam.com/doc/1P3-2726195211.html. Accessed 27 April 2014
13. Rinaldi, S.M., Peerenboom, J.P., Kelly, T.K.: Identifying, understanding, and analyzing critical infrastructure interdependencies. In: IEEE Control Systems (2001)
14. Shalimov, A., Zuikov, D., Zimarina, D., Pashkov, V., Smeliansky, R.: Advanced study of SDN/OpenFlow controllers. In: CEE-SECR, p. 1. ACM (2013)
15. Sherwood, R., Gibb, G., Yap, K., Appenzeller, G., Casado, M., McKeown, N., Parulkar, G.: Flowvisor: a network virtualization layer. In: OpenFlowSwitch (2009)
16. Shin, S., Porras, P., Yegneswaran, V., Fong, M., Gu, G.: Fresco: modular composable security services for software-defined networks. In: Internet Society NDSS (2013)
17. Shirali-Shahreza, S., Ganjali, Y.: FleXam: flexible sampling extension for monitoring and security applications in openflow. In: HotSDN, pp. 167–168. ACM (2013)

18. White, K.J.S., Pezaros, D.P., Johnson, C.W.: Increasing resilience of ATM networks using traffic monitoring and automated anomaly analysis: In: ATACCS (2012)
19. White, K.J.S., Pezaros, D.P., Johnson, C.W.: Principles for increased resilience in critical networked infrastructures. In: Publication Pending, ICRAT (2014)
20. Zhang, Y.: An adaptive flow counting method for anomaly detection in SDN. In: Emerging Networking Experiments and Technologies, pp. 25–30. ACM (2013)

Security Stress: Evaluating ICT Robustness Through a Monte Carlo Method

Fabrizio Baiardi[1(✉)], Fabio Corò[1], Federico Tonelli[1], Alessandro Bertolini[1], Roberto Bertolotti[1], and Luca Guidi[2]

[1] Dipartimento di Informatica, Università di Pisa, Pisa, Italy
{baiardi,fcoro,tonelli}@di.unipi.it
[2] ENEL Ingegneria e Ricerca SpA, Pisa, Italy
luca.guidi@enel.com

Abstract. The security stress is a synthetic evaluation of how an ICT infrastructure resists to attacks. We define the security stress and show how it is approximated through the Haruspex suite. Then, we show how it supports the comparison of three versions of an industrial control system. Haruspex is a suite of tools that apply a Monte Carlo method and support a scenario-based assessment where in each scenario intelligent agents compose attacks to reach some predefined goals.

Keywords: Risk assessment · Intelligent agent · Robustness

1 Introduction

We consider the risk assessment of an ICT infrastructure under attack by intelligent agents that achieve some predefined goals through complex attacks, e.g. sequences of attacks. A complex attack escalates the privileges, e.g. access rights, of an agent till it owns all the privileges in one of its goals.

The *security stress* is a synthetic evaluation of how an infrastructure resists to the agents. This measure can assess an infrastructure or support the comparison of alternative infrastructures from a robustness perspective. Given an agent and a goal, the security stress plots, for each time t, the probability that the agent reaches the goal within t. We refer to the curve as a stress one because it shows how the infrastructure resists to the force due to an agent for increasing times. After discussing the security stress and its approximation through the Haruspex suite, we generalize it to any number of agents and of goals.

This paper is structured as follows. Section 2 briefly reviews the Haruspex suite and security metrics. Section 3 introduces the stress curve and shows how it supports the comparison of distinct systems. Section 4 use the stress to compare three versions of an industrial control system. Lastly, we draw some conclusions.

2 Related Works

We briefly recall the Haruspex suite and related works on metrics to evaluate the robustness of an infrastructure.

© Springer International Publishing Switzerland 2016
C.G. Panayiotou et al. (Eds.): CRITIS 2014, LNCS 8985, pp. 222–227, 2016.
DOI: 10.1007/978-3-319-31664-2_23

The tools in the Haruspex suite support the risk assessment of an ICT system by applying a Monte Carlo method to simulate a scenario where some intelligent, goal oriented agents attack the system. [1,2] outline the tools of the suite to build the models of interest and apply the Monte Carlo method. Three tools are the kernel of the suite: the *builder*, the *descriptor* and the *engine*. The first two tools build models of, respectively, the system and an agent. The *engine* uses these models to simulate the agent attacks. This tool builds a statistical sample to support an assessment by applying a Monte Carlo method and collecting a sample in each simulation.

The metrics in [3–5] evaluate the robustness of an ICT infrastructure under attack without integrating the proposed metrics with the simulation of the attacks. The metric in [6] is focused on the discovery of zero-day vulnerabilities. [7–9] review alternative security metrics. [12] is similar to security stress as it considers the amount of work to attack a system.

3 Security Stress of an ICT Infrastructure

The stress $Str^S_{ag,g}(t)$ at t of an infrastructure S is the cumulative probability distribution that the agent ag reaches g within t. Being a probability distribution, $Str^S_{ag,g}(t)$ is monotone non decreasing in t and $Str^S_{ag,g}(0) = 0$.

To justify the adopted definition, let us denote by t_0 the lowest time where $Str^S_{ag,g}(t)$ is larger than zero and by t_1 the time, if it exists, where it is equal to 1. If we consider ag as a force aiming to change the shape of S, then this force is ineffective till t_0. Then the shape of S changes due the attacks of ag and S cracks after t_1, because ag is always successful for larger times. $t_1 - t_0$ evaluates how long an infrastructure can, partially, resist to the attacks of ag before cracking.

We believe $Str^S_{ag,g}$ is a proper synthetic evaluation of the robustness of S because its shape is related to several attributes of S. t_0 depends upon both the time to execute an attack and the length of the shortest complex attacks to reach g. For each attack at in the sequences to achieve g, t_1 depends upon $succ(at)$ that determines the average number of executions of at. $t_1 - t_0$ depends upon both the standard deviation of the number of attacks to reach ag and their success probabilities. Because of these relations, $Str^S_{ag,g}(t)$ returns a more accurate evaluation of the robustness of S than metrics that consider just one value, such as the average time or the average number of attacks to reach g.

A lower bound on t_0 is the minimum of the set produced by mapping each complex attack ag can implement to reach g into the sum of the execution times of its attacks. This is the best case for ag where no attack fails. Computing this bound is not trivial because the size of the set increases exponentially in the number of the components of S [2].

To evaluate the robustness of S in a predefined time interval, we plot $Str^S_{ag,g}(t)$ in the considered interval. Obviously, $Str^S_{ag,g}(t)$ may be lower than 1 in the interval.

To generalize $Str^S_{ag,g}$ to a set of goal Sg, we assume that ag stops its attacks after reaching any goal in Sg. Under this assumption, $Str^S_{ag,Sg}(t)$ is the probability that ag is idle after t. To generalize to a set of agents Sag, we consider the most dangerous agent in Sag. This is the agent, if it exists, with the highest stress curve. As an alternative, $Str^S_{ag,g}(t)$ is the weighted sum of the stress due to each agent in Sag where the weigh of an agent evaluates its contribution to the overall impact. Further generalizations are possible but, in this paper, we focus on one agent aiming to achieve any goal in a predefined set.

$Str^S_{ag,g}$ is the inverse of a survival function [10] as it plots the probability of a success of ag instead than the one that S survives ag attacks.

We approximate $Perc^S_{ag,g}(t)$ as the percentage of samples collected in an *engine* experiment where ag reaches g before t. The experiment simulates ag for the time interval of interest.

3.1   Supporting a Comparison

To evaluate the relative fragility of two infrastructures, $S1$ and $S2$, with respect to an agent ag trying to achieve a goal we analyze $Str^{S1}_{ag,g1}(t)$ and $Str^{S2}_{ag,g2}(t)$. $g1$, the goal of ag in $S1$, may differ from $g2$, the goal in $S2$, because the same high level goal, e.g. read an information, may involve distinct rights in the two infrastructures.

The two stress curves show the time interval when an infrastructure better resists to the attack of ag, e.g. it has a lower stress. We say that $S1$ is more robust, or less fragile, than $S2$ if $Str^{S1}_{ag,g1}$ is always lower than or equal to $Str^{S2}_{ag,g2}(t)$, e.g. $Str^{S1}_{ag,g1}$ lies in the space bounded by $Str^{S2}_{ag,g2}$. This implies that, at any time, the amount of deformation in $S1$ is always lower than in $S2$. This condition is violated if $0 < Str^{S1}_{ag,g1}(t_x) = Str^{S2}_{ag,g2}(t_x) < 1$ for some t_x. However, even this comparison may return useful information. Suppose that, initially, $Str^{S1}_{ag,g1}$ is lower than $Str^{S2}_{ag,g2}$ but then two curves cross. In other words, initially, the deformation in $S1$ is lower than in $S2$ but, for values of t larger than t_x, the situation changes. This happens when ag can reach its goal in $S1$ only through complex attacks that require a long time either because they compose a large number of elementary attacks and/or because the time of to implement these elementary attacks is large. Hence, the lowest time to successfully attack $S1$ is larger than for $S2$ but, if all the success probabilities of the attacks against $S1$ are close to 1, the difference $t_1 - t_0$ will be small and $S1$ will quickly crack provided that ag has enough time available. The slower increase of $Str2$ may be due to the lower success probabilities of attacks against $S2$.

4   Comparing Distinct Version of an Infrastructure

This section applies the stress to compare three versions of a system to supervise and control power generation that is segmented into four types of subnets: Central, Power Context, Process and Control. Users of the intranet run the business processes of power generation through the nodes in a Central subnet. The plant operators interact with the SCADA servers through the nodes in a Power Context subnet. The SCADA servers and the systems to control power production

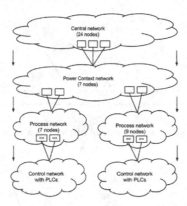

Fig. 1. First version of the infrastructure

belongs to a Process network. Finally, the PLCs in a Control subnet control the devices in the plant.

Figure 1 shows the first system version [11] with 49 nodes segmented into six subnet. The Central subnet includes 24 nodes, the Power Context includes 7 nodes. Then, Process subnet 1 and 2 include, respectively, 9 and 7 nodes. Each Process subnet is connected to a Control subnet with a PLC device. Three nodes of the Central subnet have a connection with the Power Context subnet. Two pairs of nodes in the Power Context network are connected to nodes in one Process subnet, Lastly, two nodes in each Process subnet are connected to the corresponding Control subnet.

We compare this version against two other ones. In the first one, we double the number of nodes by replicating each node without altering the number of connections between subnets. Also the third version includes 98 nodes as the second one, but the Central subnet is segmented into two subnets with 24 nodes each. Furthermore, all the nodes connected to the Power Context subnets belong to just one of the resulting subnets, as in Fig. 1. We consider four classes of agents and assume that any agent initially owns some rights on a node in the Central subnet and it aims to control the PLC devices. In particular, agent in the first class, $T1$, aim to control both devices and those in the second class, $T2$, aims to control any of the devices. Agents in the two last classes, $T3$ and $T4$, aim to control a distinct PLC device. Agents need to scan each node to discover its vulnerabilities. To cover alternative strategies to select the complex attack to a goal, each class includes seven agents. For each version, Figs. 2, 3, and 4 show the stress curves of the most dangerous agent in each class. The figures show that in the first version, the most dangerous agent in the $T2$ class reaches its goal in about twelve hours while an agent of another class reaches its goal in about fourteen hours, i.e. about two hours later. In the second version, the most dangerous agent belongs to the $T2$ class and it reaches its goal in about 21 h. Other agents take one more hour. Then, in the third version of the infrastructure, the time to reach the goal is a bit larger than in the second one. Indeed, the

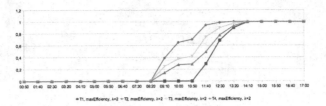

Fig. 2. First version: stress curve of the most dangerous agents

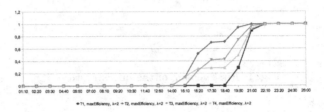

Fig. 3. Second version: stress curve of the most dangerous agents

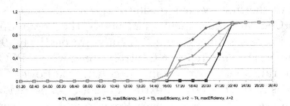

Fig. 4. Third version: stress curve of the most dangerous agents

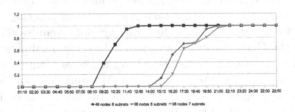

Fig. 5. Robustness of the three versions

class $T2$ agent reaches the goal only 20 min later than in the second version but the remaining agents reach their goal after more than two hours. Lastly, Fig. 5 compares the robustness of the three versions. Each curve refers to the most dangerous agent for the considered version. As expected, the first version is the most fragile one because its number of nodes reduces the number of attacks to reach a goal. The number of nodes in the second version confuses the agents and increases the time to reach their goal. Finally, the third version is the least fragile one because the larger numbers of nodes and of subnets increase the number of attacks and the time to reach a goal.

5   Conclusion

The stress curve is a synthetic evaluation of the robustness of an infrastructure with respect of complex attacks by intelligent agent. It simplifies the comparison of distinct infrastructures or of alternative versions of the same one and it is approximated through the Haruspex suite. We have applied this measure to compare three versions of an infrastructure and discussed how the stress curve changes according to the number of nodes or of subnets.

References

1. Baiardi, F., Sgandurra, D.: Assessing ict risk through a monte carlo method. Environ. Syst. Decisions **33**(4), 1–14 (2013)
2. Baiardi, F., Corò, F., Tonelli, F., Guidi, L.: Gvscan: Scanning networks for global vulnerabilities. In: First International Workshop on Emerging Cyberthreats and Countermeasures, Regensburg, Germany (2013)
3. Vaughn Jr., R.B., Henning, R., Siraj, A.: Information assurance measures and metrics - state of practice and proposed taxonomy. In: Proceedings of the 36th Annual Hawaii International Conference on System Sciences, 2003, p. 10 (2003)
4. Schudel, G., Wood, B.: Adversary work factor as a metric for information assurance. In: Proceedings of the 2000 Workshop on New Security Paradigms. NSPW 2000, pp. 23–30. ACM, New York (2000)
5. Langweg, H.: Framework for malware resistance metrics. In: 2nd ACM Workshop on Quality of Protection, pp. 39–44. ACM, New York (2006)
6. Wang, L., Jajodia, S., Singhal, A., Cheng, P., Noel, S.: k-zero day safety: A network security metric for measuring the risk of unknown vulnerabilities. IEEE Trans. Dependable Sec. Comput. **11**(1), 30–44 (2014)
7. Jaquith, A.: Security Metrics: Replacing Fear, Uncertainty, and Doubt. Addison-Wesley Professional (2007). ISBN:0321349989
8. Payne, S.C.: A guide to security metrics. SANS Institute (2006)
9. Swanson, M.: Security metrics guide for information technology systems. Technical report, NIST, US Department of Commerce (2003)
10. La Corte, A., Scatà, M.: Failure analysis and threats statistic to assess risk and security strategy in a communication system. In: ICSNC 2011, The Sixth International Conference on Systems and Networks Communications, pp. 149–154 (2011)
11. Nai Fovino, I., Masera, M., Guidi, L., Carpi, G.: An experimental platform for assessing scada vulnerabilities and countermeasures in power plants (2010)
12. Pamula, J., Jajodia, S., Ammann, P., Swarup, V.: A weakest-adversary security metric for network configuration security analysis. In: Proceedings of the 2nd ACM Workshop on Quality of Protection. QoP 2006, pp. 31–38. ACM, New York (2006)

Cyber Security

Model-Based Evaluation of the Resilience of Critical Infrastructures Under Cyber Attacks

Oleksandr Netkachov, Peter Popov$^{(\boxtimes)}$, and Kizito Salako

Centre for Software Reliability, City University London, London, UK
{Oleksandr.Netkachov.1,P.T.Popov,K.O.Salako}@city.ac.uk

Abstract. In this paper we report recent results on modelling the impact of cyber-attacks on the resilience of complex industrial systems. We use a hybrid model of the system under study, in which both accidental network failures and the malicious behaviour of an Adversary are modelled stochastically, while the consequences of failures and attacks are modelled in detail using deterministic models. This modelling approach is demonstrated on a complex case study - a reference power transmission network (NORDIC 32), enhanced with a detailed model of the computer and communication network used for monitoring, protection and control compliant with the international standard IEC 61850. We studied the resilience of the modelled system under different scenarios: (i) a baseline scenario in which the modelled system operates in the presence of accidental failures without cyber-attacks; (ii) several different scenarios of cyberattacks. We discuss the usefulness of the modelling approach, of the findings, and outline directions for further work.

Keywords: Critical infrastructures · Power transmission network · IEC 61850 · Stochastic modelling

1 Introduction

Security of industrial control systems (ICS) used to control critical infrastructures (CI) has attracted the attention of researchers and practitioners. The evidence is overwhelming that, the services offered by CI are somewhat robust with respect to single component failures of the underlying network. The reaction to multiple and cascade failures, however, is much more difficult to understand and to predict, especially when cyber attacks are taken into consideration. Dependencies and interdependencies between the elements of CIs are an important source of risk and risk uncertainty.

Although there are similarities between the ICS and the information and communication technology (ICT) systems, important differences between the two exist [1]. High availability and real-time response to events in industrial systems make some defenses against cyber-attacks, widely used in ICT (e.g. patching), inadequate for ICS. The literature rarely acknowledges *other differences* between the ICT and ICS, which make the detection of failures/cyber-attacks in the ICS

© Springer International Publishing Switzerland 2016
C.G. Panayiotou et al. (Eds.): CRITIS 2014, LNCS 8985, pp. 231–243, 2016.
DOI: 10.1007/978-3-319-31664-2_24

easier to achieve than in the ICT. The processes that an ICS controls are generally either *directly observable* or reliable methods for indirect measurement exist. For instance, whether a power generator is connected to the power grid or not, is either directly observable or can be established reliably using sophisticated software tools such as *state estimators*.

The paper is organized as follows: In Sect. 2 we state the problem of quantitative model-based risk assessment studied in the paper. In Sect. 3 we provide a description of the modeling approach we take to model cyber-attacks on ICS. A brief description of the case study used in the paper to illustrate the approach is also provided. Section 4 summarizes our findings, Sect. 5 - the related research. Finally, Sect. 6 concludes the paper and outlines directions for future research.

2 Problem Statement

In the past we developed a method for quantifying the impact of interdependencies between CI [2], which we called Preliminary Interdependency Analysis (PIA). PIA starts by a systematic search for CI interdependencies at a fairly *high level of abstraction*; interdependencies which might otherwise be overlooked. In a separate study [3] we demonstrated that, although using a high level of abstraction is useful, the risk assessment results are, in general, quite sensitive to the chosen level of abstraction. PIA allows the modeller to create hybrid models of the modelled infrastructures and choose the level of detail that suits the specific study. The software tools developed to support the PIA method allow the modeller to quickly build complex hybrid models which combine: (i) stochastic models of a system and its constituent elements, accounting for functional, spatial and other *stochastic dependencies* between these elements, and (ii) domain specific deterministic models, necessary in case a high fidelity analysis is sought, e.g. flow models that, typically, operate on a subset of modelled elements.

Cyber security of ICS has become a topic of active research (important contributions are summarised in the Related Research section). Its practical importance and the difficulties with these, have been widely recognised.

A common problem with cyber security research is that it concentrates on security incidents in the ICT/ICS, while the real impact of successful attacks is rarely quantified. As a result, quantitative risk assessment is difficult. While such an approach is, to some extent, justified in the ICT systems (for instance, how one assesses the impact of information theft is an open debate), with industrial systems the real impact of a cyber incident may be relatively easy to quantify. For instance, the impact of losing a generator in a power system as a result of a cyber-attack will vary between 0, in case other generators can compensate fully for the lost generator, to losses due to not supplying power to some consumers, in case the spare power generation capacity of the other generators in the network is insufficient to meet the current power demand. PIA models are well suited for quantitative risk assessment, as they model, stochastically, both the controlled plant and the ICS. Until recently, however, PIA had not been used to explicitly address cyber security concerns. In [6] we extended the PIA method by adding an Adversary model and building on the recent work by others in this direction, e.g. the ADVISE formalism [4]. The *focus of this paper* is to study the impact on network service of different attack strategies - where such strategies might be employed by naive or more sophisticated attackers - and to highlight the effectiveness of some precautionary measures that a network operator could undertake.

3 Solution

3.1 The System Under Study

We use a non trivial case study of a power transmission network to demonstrate the analysis one can undertake with the extended PIA and to evaluate how well the method scales to realistically complex industrial systems.

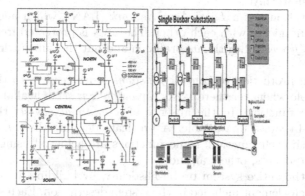

Fig. 1. NORDIC 32 power system topology.

The system model was developed by the FP7 EU project AFTER (http://www.after-project.eu/Layout/after/). It is based on a reference power transmission network, NORDIC 32, enhanced with an industrial distributed control system (IDCS) compliant with the international standard IEC 61850 "Communication networks and subsystems in sub-stations". Illustrations of NORDIC 32 and of the architecture of a sub-station are shown in Fig. 1. A detailed description of the case study is beyond the scope of this paper, but a short summary is provided below.

The transmission network (Fig. 1, diagram on the left) consists of a large number of transmission lines which connect 19 power generators and 19 loads. All connections of lines, generators and links are done in 32 sub-stations. Each sub-station is arranged in a number of bays. Each bay is responsible for connecting a single element - a line, a generator or a load - to the transmission network.

The sub-stations are assumed compliant with IEC 61850. Figure 1 (the diagram on the right) shows an example of a sub-station. The other sub-stations have similar architecture but may contain different numbers and types of bays. Some sub-stations may have generators and/or loads, and all sub-stations connect transmission lines.

The sub-stations are connected via a sophisticated ICT infrastructure (not shown for lack of space), which includes a number of control centres, communication channels and data centres.

Each bay is responsible for (dis)connecting one element from the transmission network. This is achieved by a set of elements - relays and electronic devices[1]. In this case study the electronic devices can be one of the following two types - either a protection device or a control device. The function of the protection devices is to disconnect power elements from the transmission network, e.g. as a result of overloading of a line or of a generator. The control devices, on the other hand, are used to connect or disconnect power elements from the network and are typically used by either the operators in the respective control centres or by "special purpose software" (SPS) designed to undertake some of the operators' functions automatically.

Each sub-station has a *Local Area Network* (LAN), which allows the local devices to communicate with each other. The LAN is protected from the rest of the world by a *firewall*. Legitimate traffic in and out the sub-station is allowed, of course.

Each of the protection or control *functions* (with respect to the individual bays) is available whenever there exists a *minimal cut set* of available equipment supporting the function. In the absence of a *minimal cut set* the respective function itself becomes unavailable. A predicate defining the *minimal cut sets* is provided with each function: some functions are achieved using functionally redundant components, others are not.

We model the entire system probabilistically, by building a *stochastic state machine* for each element included in the system description. Each state machine has three states - "OK", "Fail" and "Disconnected". Depending on the element type, its model, in addition to a state machine, may include specific additional non-stochastic properties. For instance, the model of a generator will have a property defining the maximum output power; the model of a load - an additional property defining the power consumed, etc. The interested reader may find further details in [2].

3.2   Modelling Cyber-Attacks

Now we describe an Adversary model, added to the model of the system.

For the system under study we assumed that each sub-station will have a dedicated firewall (indicated by the "brick wall" in Fig. 1) which isolates the sub-station from the rest of the world. We also assumed that an intrusion detection/prevention system (IDS/IPS) would monitor the traffic in the sub-station's

---

[1] IEC 61850 distinguishes between Intelligent Electronic Devices (IED), functions and nodes. Nodes are responsible for implementing a specific function (i.e. protection or control) and can involve several IED.

LAN. When the IDS/IPS detects illegitimate traffic it blocks the Adversary from accessing the assets located at the sub-station.

Our study is limited to the effect of a **single type of attack** on system behavior: a cyber-attack via the firewall of a sub-station. The Adversary model we developed is *adapted* from a recent publication [5]. The model is shown in Fig. 2 using the *Stochastic Activity Networks* (SAN) formalism.

This model assumes that the Adversary is initially idle (represented by the SAN *place labeled* "Idle").

With some regularity, defined by the *activity* Attack_interval, the Adversary launches a cyber-attack on the system by trying to penetrate the Firewall (modeled in Fig. 2 by the activity Firewall_attack) of *one* of the 32 sub-stations defined in NORDIC-32 model.

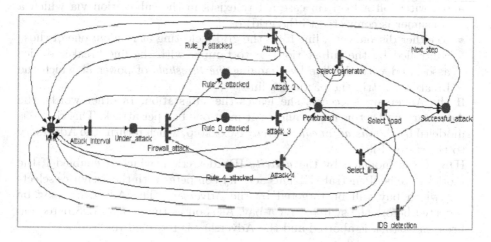

Fig. 2. Model of Adversary applied to NORDIC 32.

The selection of the sub-station to attack is driven by either a *uniform distribution*, defined over the 32 sub-stations ("Indiscriminate attacker profile") or by a *non-uniform distribution* defined in a way to capture the *preferences* of the Adversary. We discussed elsewhere [6] the difference between the cases of an indiscriminate Adversary and an Adversary with preferences. In this paper, we limit the study to an indiscriminate Adversary. Under the current model we also assume that the firewalls of all sub-stations are equally easy/difficult to penetrate. In fact, the SAN model in Fig. 2 is incomplete: it does not show how the Adversary chooses a sub-station. This model shows the steps that follow the Adversary's initial selection of a sub-station to attack:

– The Adversary may target each of the firewall *configuration rules*. The decision of which rule to attack is modeled by the *activity* Firewall_attack. In Fig. 2 we assume that there are 4 rules to choose between, which is just an example. The model assumes that the rules are equally likely to be chosen by an attacker - the probabilities associated with the outputs of the Firewall_attack activity are all set to 0.25.

- Once a rule is selected (modeled by the places Rule_1 - Rule_4), the Adversary spends time trying to break the selected rule, which is modeled by the *activities* Attack_1 - Attack_4, respectively. This effort may be successful or unsuccessful. In the case of a failed attempt, the Adversary returns to an idle state and may launch another attack later, likely to be on a different sub-station.
- In the case of a successful penetration through the firewall, the state "Penetrated" is entered, which has three alternative options for the Adversary to proceed[2]:
  - to switch off a generator (in case a bay exists in the sub-station, via which a generator is connected to the grid),
  - to switch off a load (in case a bay exists in the sub-station via which a consumer is connected to the grid) or
  - to either disconnect a line from the grid (selecting at random one of those controlled by the sub-station) or to tamper with the line breaker device associated with the line by changing *the threshold* of power at which the breaker will trip the particular line.
- If the Adversary succeeds, she leaves the sub-station. In other words, the Adversary under this model affects at most one bay per attack. This choice is modeled by the *instantaneous activity* Next_step, which returns the Adversary to the state "Idle".
- IDS/IPS is modeled by the *activity* IDS_detection, which is enabled if the model state is "Penetrated". This activity competes with the activities selecting which bay will be targeted by the Adversary. The Adversary may be detected before she switches off a bay. As soon as the *activity* IDS_detection fires, the attack is aborted and the Adversary is returned to "Idle".

A successful attack may trigger further *activities* in the system. For instance, any malicious switching-off of a bay may be "detected" when a new power flow calculations is run. If so, via the respective control function, an attempt is made to reconnect those bays which have been disconnected by the Adversary.

In the presented Adversary model we assume that all timed activities are *exponentially* distributed. We studied the effect of the rates of some of these distributions on the selected utility function (which is discussed next).

4   Findings

4.1   Rewards

We were interested in measuring the effect of cyber-attacks on the service provided by the system under study. We chose to compare the behavior of a *baseline model*, i.e. a model without cyber-attacks, with the behavior of the models

---

[2] The actions that an Adversary can undertake are not modeled in detail in Fig. 2. The specific logic of successful attacks, however, is implemented by the plug-ins to the PIA simulator.

in which cyberattacks are enabled ("system under attack"). The comparison is based on specific rewards (utility function). We selected, somewhat arbitrarily, the length of a simulation run to be the equivalent of 10 years of operation. We use different rewards all linked to the supplied power - supplied power, in particular, has been used in the analysis of power systems by others [5]. Clearly, for each simulation run, the supplied power varies over time to form a *continuous-time stochastic process*. We study the following three statistics of this process, each capturing a different aspect of interest:

- The average power supplied during a simulation run. This would be lower than the nominal power of 10,940 MW. The average will vary between simulated runs, and we look at the *distribution of this average* over a number of runs.
- Similarly, we compute the *standard deviations* per run and then look at the distribution of this statistic over the runs,
- We also estimate the distribution over the simulation runs of the minimum supplied power and use the percentiles of this distribution as an indication of how large the outage/blackout can be.

4.2 Studies

The studied system is non-trivial. It consists of more than 1500 state machines. With the chosen parameterization, based on input from domain experts, we observed a significant number ($\sim 4000 \ldots 40,000$) of events over a single simulation run. Many of these events require power flow calculations, which take considerable time to complete. Similarly, following overloads or generator failures, active "control" is required to find a new stable system state. Searching for a stable state is another time consuming algorithm. As a result, a single simulation run takes approximately 5 min to complete. Obtaining results with high confidence would require a large number of simulation runs. All our results are based on 200 simulation runs with each of the scenarios[3]. In a recent paper [6] we presented the results related to attacks targeted at switching off a single bay - a generator, load or a line - by an Adversary who selects the substations indiscriminately or who targets, with high probability, the important assets such as large generators large loads. In this paper, instead, we concentrate on attacks which do not lead to *immediate visible consequences*. An example of such attacks is changing the tripping threshold of a line breaker. More specifically, we assume that an Adversary can tamper with an intelligent protection device by setting the value of tripping the respective line to 110 % of the line load at the time of the attack. Clearly, a successful attack will have no immediate effect, but any subsequent accidental failures, which lead to power flow changes, may trigger a trip of the respective lines unnecessarily. A number of successful attacks over time may lead to multiple protection devices being tampered with, which in turn may lead to large cascades. In addition we introduce a model of *inspections* of

---

[3] We obtained *Relative Standard Errors (RSE)* for the statistics. The essential conclusions of the paper are based on statistically significant observations.

the modeled system. An inspection checks if the tripping values of the protection devices are set correctly. If a deviation from these is detected the respective thresholds are restored to correct values.

We completed several simulation campaigns which are summarized as follows:

- A *base-line scenario*. This represents the NORDIC 32 with only accidental failures of network components possible and no cyber-attacks.
- A *scenario of attacks with immediately visible effect*. The base line scenario is extended by adding cyber-attacks which, if successful, lead to a switch-off of a single bay (i.e. a transformer, or a load) in a substation. We model an *intelligent* adversary, who targets only the 5 largest loads and the 5 largest generators. The frequency of the attacks is varied: yearly, monthly, weekly and daily.
- *Scenarios of attacks with no immediately visible effects*. The base-line scenario is extended with attacks which, if successful, lead to a change of the tripping threshold of a *single line* in the bay selected by the Adversary. We distinguish between two groups of such scenarios:
  - A scenario without inspections. The tripping thresholds are never checked by the network operator and restored to their correct values.
  - Scenarios with periodic inspections. The intervals between inspections are assumed exponentially distributed, and the rate of inspections is varied: yearly, monthly, weekly and daily.

4.3   Results

Each of the scenarios described above for a particular parameterization (rates of attacks and inspections, if applicable) was simulated 200 times. We summarize our findings below.

Base Line vs. Attacks with an Immediately Visible Effect. Successful attacks of this type lead to switching off either a generator or a load. The empirical distributions characterizing the supplied power are shown in Fig. 3.

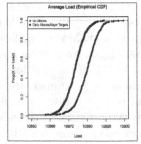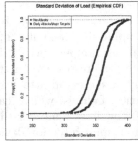

Fig. 3. Base line scenario vs. the scenario of attacks on the most important generators and loads: empirical distributions of Mean and Standard Deviations of the supplied power.

Attacks with no Immediately Visible Effect. In this study the attacks, if successful, lead to an alteration of the tripping levels of protection devices of a single line in a bay chosen by an Adversary. Figure 4 illustrates the impact of inspection frequency on the supplied power.

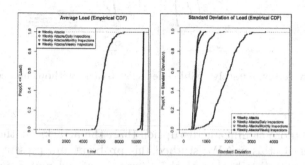

Fig. 4. The efficacy of inspection regimes for a system under weekly attacks: empirical distributions of the Mean and Standard Deviation of the supplied power.

The plot shows quite clearly that unless inspections are applied, very significant amounts of power will be lost - the average of the supplied power varies between 5000 and 8000 MW. The explanation is quite simple - unless the tripping thresholds are restored to their correct values, they will be gradually reduced by the successful attacks and many lines in the power network will operate with a significantly reduced capacity. Losing such a large amount of power is unlikely to remain unnoticed and some inspections, as a measure of protection against attacks of this kind, are likely to be put in place. Not surprisingly, inspections change the picture dramatically - the lost power is now significantly reduced to levels comparable with those shown in Fig. 3. Increasing the frequency of inspections results in ever greater average power supplied (i.e. the distributions are accumulating towards the right in Fig. 4) and reducing variability in power supplied (i.e. accumulating towards the left in Fig. 4).

Comparison of the Attacks. So far, we looked at the impact of different attacks on the supplied power, by varying the attack frequencies. Now, we compare the different attack scenarios.

The two attacks used are quite different in nature: one seeks an immediate effect by switching either a load or a generator, while the other only creates a potentiality for losses (i.e. hazards) which will manifest themselves only if a disruption of power flow occurs, e.g. by a failure of an element in the power system. They are also different in the way the Adversary chooses targets - with the immediately visible effects, the Adversary concentrates on major targets (the largest generators and loads). With the attacks with no visible effects, the Adversary selects targets at random. In these circumstances one is tempted to expect that the more intelligent Adversary (who targets the largest assets) is

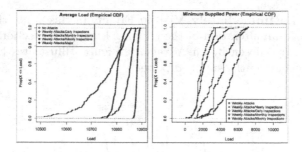

Fig. 5. Attacks with immediately visible effects vs. attacks without immediately visible effects.

likely to create more significant disruption than the attacks by the less sophisticated attacker. Is this so? We studied this problem and present our findings in Fig. 5, using the distribution of the average supplied power and the distribution of the minimum supplied power resulting from the attacks of the two types. The distributions obtained for the base line scenario are also included in the plot. In the plots of the "average supplied power" distributions, the base line and the scenario with attacks by an intelligent attacker are indistinguishable (both overlap on the far right of Fig. 5). Under the attacks of the second type, even with precautionary daily inspections carried out by the network operator, the average supplied power is lower. In other words, this type of attack, undertaken by a non-discriminating attacker, leads to more serious losses than the targeted attack with visible effects by an intelligent attacker. This ordering was not obvious before the study. The right hand half of Fig. 5 further corroborates this observation with another plot. The two right-hand-side curves, in this plot, represent the base line scenario and the scenario of intelligent attacks with visible effects, respectively. Quite clearly, the distributions of the minimum supplied power under the attacks with no immediately visible consequences are stochastically worse than under the targeted attacks with immediately visible effects. In other words, for any given value of power supply, the chances for, at most, this amount to be supplied by the system is greater under attacks with no immediately visible effects, compared with the chances under targeted attacks with visible effects.

5   Related Research

Different aspects of SCADA system security have been studied extensively.

Influential reports by both the Department of Homeland Security [7] and the National Institute of Standards and Technology (NIST) [1] provide a comprehensive discussion of SCADA architectures and best practice approaches for their security.

Stochastic models have been used in the past to address, specifically, the cyber security of industrial control systems. For instance, Ten et al. [5] offer a model based on stochastic Petri nets, adapted for cyber security on power transmission systems. The study is similar to ours, except that Ten et al. do not provide a base line study and primarily concentrate on cyber-attacks under a fixed model parameterisation. In our study we explore the space of plausible parameters (sensitivity analysis). Ten et al. also use an extreme model of consequences of a successful attack, assuming that all bays of a compromised sub-station will be disconnected.

The ADVISE formalism [4] offers an alternative approach to stochastic modelling of a *rational* Adversary. The utility function used by ADVISE is computed based on the preferences of an adversary and on the likelihood of an attack being detected. The modelling approach allows for non-determinism - in terms of an outcome of a particular step in an attack - but any decision that the adversary would need to take during the attack is driven by her preferences, defined in the model *statically*. As a result, the adversary would take the same decision even if she is presented with the same choice multiple times during an attack. The formalism allows one to study *one attacker and attack-strategy at a time*; comparison of the impact of multiple, different attackers and attack-strategies requires building separate models and studies. While the illustration of our approach dealt with a single attack too, there is no constraint in our approach which prevents us from combining simultaneous attacks by different adversaries. The utility function used in ADVISE is normalised and is defined in the range [0, 1], which may require some effort to link the model with the specific context of study in order to give domain experts - such as power engineers, as in the example we studied - a clear interpretation of the findings from the modelling. Our approach allows one the freedom to define the reward in a way that is most suitable for the stakeholders.

An interesting approach to modelling an adaptive adversary is developed by Martinelli et al. [8]. The key idea there is captured by a graph describing the steps that an adversary could take, including "stepping back" in case of unsuccessful attack.

Nash equilibrium has recently become popular in cyber security research, e.g. [9], the key idea being that under fairly broad assumptions, the existence of the *worst consequences* from cyber-attacks can be established without having to define, in detail, the attacks in specific contexts. Such studies, however, operate at a high level of abstraction and the findings from them may be difficult to interpret in practice.

6   Conclusions

We described an approach to stochastic modelling of industrial control systems in which both accidental failures and cyber-attacks are treated in a unified way:

- stochastic state machines are used to model the behaviour of the elements of the ICS which allow the modeller to capture the accidental failures;
- malicious behaviour of an Adversary (i.e. cyber-attacks) are modelled by stochastic state machines too, and these capture the behaviour of the Adversary

(their knowledge/preferences about the assets under attack and the particular
actions they would take once access to the assets is acquired);
- the dependencies between the behaviour of the modelled elements - including
  accidental failures and the effects of successful cyber-attacks - are captured
  explicitly via a set of additional models: either deterministic - such as power
  flows - or probabilistic - e.g. stochastic dependencies between the system
  elements.

We illustrated our approach on a non-trivial case study and report on the
initial findings from a useful sensitivity analysis of system resilience on the parameters of different threats and defenses. We also compare two types of attacks
using as a criterion how they affect the amount of supplied power.

We chose relatively simple attacks to illustrate the approach. Extending the
work to more sophisticated scenarios of attacks is straightforward. Every new
attack type would require a new model of the Adversary, which would define the
steps an Adversary should take in launching an attack, a relatively simple task.

We envisage extending the work in a number of ways. Expanding the work
on modeling the adversaries at the same level of abstraction, i.e. ignoring the
specifics of the communication protocols used in the ICS. A number of attack
scenarios are of immediate interest. An obvious extension of the adversary model
used in this paper is one in which the adversary may attack more than one sub-
station, e.g. until she eventually gets caught. Scenarios of simultaneous and/or
coordinated attacks by multiple Adversaries (SWARM attacks) are important
in practice, too. Modelling such attacks will require more complex models of an
Adversary.

An interesting question is whether the observed stochastic ordering between
the loss distributions due to different attacks is a consequence of our chosen
network topology. Will our discerning attacker become more disruptive than our
nondiscriminating attacker if, for example, the network topology is changed to
one with more elements and a few, highly connected nodes or "hubs"?

Last but not least, the recent work to re-engineer the tools supporting the
PIA method makes it suitable to "study the future", i.e. for studies, in which
the system under study *evolves*. The changes may concern the system topology
and the model parameters, as well as the impact of technological development
and various hypotheses about how cyber crime may evolve over time.

Acknowledgments. This work was partially supported by the European Commission, under FP7 AFTER project, grant agreement number 261788 and under the
Artemis JU project SESAMO, grant agreement number 295354.

References

1. Stouffer, K., Falco, J., Kent, K.: Guide to Supervisory Control and Data Acquisition (SCADA) and Industrial Control Systems Security. NIST, p. 164 (2006)
2. Bloomfield, R.E. et al.: Preliminary Interdependency Analysis (PIA): Method and tool support. Adelard LLP, p. 56 (2010)
3. Bloomfield, R.E. et al.: Stochastic modelling of the effects of dependencies between critical infrastructures. In: Critical Information Infrastructures Security: 4th International Workshop, CRITIS, 2010, Bonn. Springer, Germany (2009)
4. Ford, M.D., et al.: Implementing the ADVISE security modeling formalism in Mobius. In: The 43rd Annual IEEE/IFIP International Conference on Dependable Systems and Networks (DSN). Budapest, Hungary (2013)
5. Ten, C.-W., et al.: Vulnerability assessment of cybersecurity for SCADA systems. IEEE Trans. Power Syst. **23**(4), 1836–1846 (2008)
6. Netkachov, O., Popov, P., Salako, K.: Quantification of the impact of cyber attack in critical infrastructures. In: Bondavalli, A., Ceccarelli, A., Ortmeier, F. (eds.) SAFECOMP 2014. LNCS, vol. 8696, pp. 316–327. Springer, Heidelberg (2014)
7. US-CERT, Recommended Practice: Improving Industrial Control Systems Cybersecurity with Defense-In-Depth Strategies. US-CERT, p. 44 (2009)
8. Krautsevich, L., Martinelli, F., Yautsiukhin, A.: Towards modelling adaptive attacker's behaviour. In: Garcia-Alfaro, J., Cuppens, F., Cuppens-Boulahia, N., Miri, A., Tawbi, N. (eds.) FPS 2012. LNCS, vol. 7743, pp. 357–364. Springer, Heidelberg (2013)
9. Johnson, B. et al.: Are security experts useful? bayesian nash equilibria for network security games with limited information. In: 15th European Conference on Research in Computer Security. Springer, Athens (2010)

The Role of One-Class Classification in Detecting Cyberattacks in Critical Infrastructures

Patric Nader$^{(\boxtimes)}$, Paul Honeine, and Pierre Beauseroy

Institut Charles Delaunay (CNRS),
Université de Technologie de Troyes, Troyes, France
{patric.nader,paul.honeine,pierre.beauseroy}@utt.fr

Abstract. The security of critical infrastructures has gained a lot of attention in the past few years with the growth of cyberthreats and the diversity of cyberattacks. Although traditional IDS update frequently their databases of known attacks, new complex attacks are generated everyday to circumvent security systems and to make their detection nearly impossible. This paper outlines the importance of one-class classification algorithms in detecting malicious cyberattacks in critical infrastructures. The role of machine learning algorithms is complementary to IDS and firewalls, and the objective of this work is to detect intentional intrusions once they have already bypassed these security systems. Two approaches are investigated, Support Vector Data Description and Kernel Principal Component Analysis. The impact of the metric in kernels is investigated, and a heuristic for choosing the bandwidth parameter is proposed. Tests are conducted on real data with several types of cyberattacks.

Keywords: Critical infrastructures · Intrusion detection · One-class classification · SCADA systems

1 Introduction

Nowadays, the control of the majority of critical infrastructures is accomplished via Supervisory Control And Data Acquisition (SCADA) systems, which allow remote monitoring and control to physical systems such as electrical power grids, oil and natural gas pipelines, chemical processing plants, water distribution, wastewater collection systems and nuclear power plants [1]. The principal components of SCADA systems are: (a) The Human Machine Interface (HMI) allows operators to monitor the state of the process under control and modify its control settings, (b) the Master Terminal Unit (MTU) stores and processes the information from the field and transmits control signals, and (c) the Remote Terminal Units (RTU) receive commands from the MTU to control the local process, acquire data from the field and transmit it to the MTU. The common protocols (ModBus, Profibus, DNP3) used in the communication between these

© Springer International Publishing Switzerland 2016
C.G. Panayiotou et al. (Eds.): CRITIS 2014, LNCS 8985, pp. 244–255, 2016.
DOI: 10.1007/978-3-319-31664-2_25

components present many vulnerabilities [2]. These protocols do not perform any authentication mechanism between Master and Slave, do not check for the integrity of the command packets and do not apply any anti-repudiation or anti-replay mechanisms [3].

First generations of SCADA networks operate in isolated environments, with no connectivity to any system outside the network. Nowadays, SCADA systems use public network for system-to-system interconnection, which has introduced numerous vulnerabilities and has exposed the critical infrastructures to new sources of potential threats [4]. Many intentional cyberattacks against critical infrastructures relying on SCADA networks occured in the past few years. In 2000, an ex-employee of Maroochy Water Services in Australia released one million liters of untreated sewage into local parks and rivers [5]. In 2003, the Slammer worm penetrated Ohios Davis-Besse nuclear power plant and disabled a safety monitoring system for nearly five hours [6]. In 2006, a hacker penetrated a water filtering plant in Pennsylvania (USA) and installed malicious software capable of affecting the plants water treatment operations [7]. In 2009, cyberspies penetrated the U.S. electrical grid and left behind software programs that could be used to disrupt the system [8]. The most complex malware Stuxnet was discovered 2010. It installs malicious programs replacing the PLCs original file in a manner undetectable by the PLC operator [9]. The ultimate goal of Stuxnet was to sabotage nuclear centrifuges used for enriching uranium [10].

The vulnerabilities in the communication protocols between SCADA components and the intensive use of internet and communication technologies have increased the cyberthreats and opened new ways for carrying out cyberattacks against critical infrastructures relying on SCADA networks [11]. For these reasons, securing the critical infrastructures has become the ultimate priority of the researchers with the growth of cyberthreats and the diversity of aforementioned cyberattacks. Yang et al. proposed in [12] a signature-based approach that matches signatures of known attacks with the network traffic, and a model-based approach for detecting intrusions in SCADA systems. The first one cannot detect new attacks not existing in their databases, and the second one needs the existence of the exact system's model which is not the case for the majority of the critical infrastructures. A Bayesian network was implemented in [13] to reduce the false positive rate, but this statistical model relies on the conditional dependencies between the system's variables. A collaborative intrusion detection mechanism using a centralized server that dispatches activities coming from suspicious IP addresses was proposed in [14]. This approach do not provide any specific technique for identifying high level and complex cyberattacks. Carcano et al. presented in [15] a critical state-based IDS for a given industrial installation, which can only detect a particular type of cyberattacks against PLC systems. Morris et al. elaborated a SCADA testbed in [16,17], where false commands and responses were injected into the SCADA network to investigate the vulnerabilities of functional control systems. Cyberattacks studied in their testbed include command injection, response injection and denial of service (DOS) attacks. The complexity of the critical infrastructures and the diversity of cyberthreats restrict the use of model-based approaches, and emphasize the potential role of non-parametric methods in detecting intrusions.

Real world data analysis problems require, most of the time, nonlinear methods for detecting patterns and interdependencies within the data [18]. Machine learning techniques have become very popular in the past few years since they provide a powerful way for detecting nonlinear relations using linear algorithms in the feature space [19,20]. This paper outlines the complementary role of machine learning algorithms to traditional IDS in detecting intrusions in critical infrastructures. Two distinct approaches are investigated, the Support Vector Data Description (SVDD) [21] and the Kernel Principal Component Analysis (KPCA) [22]. This paper also studies the impact of varying the metric norm in the kernel functions, and proposes a heuristic for choosing the bandwidth parameter without any computational costs. The tests are conducted on real data from the gas pipeline testbed [16,17]. The remainder of this paper is organized as follows. Section 2 provides an overview on kernel methods for one-class classification, namely the SVDD and the KPCA. Section 3 discusses the metric variation and the heuristic for choosing the bandwidth parameter. Section 4 describes the gas pipeline testbed and the results on the real datasets. Section 5 provides conclusion and future works.

2   Kernel Methods for One-Class Classification

kernel methods have been widely used in the past few years to discover hidden regularities in large volumes of data [18]. They use positive definite kernel functions to map the data into a reproducing kernel Hilbert space (RKHS) via the mapping function $\phi(\cdot)$, and provide an elegant way to learn a nonlinear system without the need of an exact physical model [23]. In industrial systems, the majority of the available data designates the normal functional mode, and it is very difficult to acquire data related to malfunctioning or critical states [24]. For this reason, the role of one-class classification has been growing in detecting machine faults and intrusions, especially in critical infrastructures [25–27]. Each training sample x_i can represent measurements such as the gas pressure in a specific time, the temperature, the water level, the pressure for three consecutive instants, etc. One-class classification algorithms learn the normal behavior of the system through the relations between these components, and a decision function tests new samples to classify them as normal or outliers (suspicious behavior).

2.1   Support Vector Data Description

Support Vector Data Description (SVDD) estimates a spherically shaped decision boundary with minimum radius that encloses most of the training data $\phi(x_i)$ in the feature space $\mathcal{H}$ [21]. The hypersphere is characterized by its center a and its radius $R > 0$, and we minimize its volume by minimizing R^2. The presence of some outliers in the training set is allowed by introducing the slack variables $\xi_i \geq 0$. Samples that lay outside this description are considered outliers, and they should be rejected. This boils down to the following constrained optimization problem:

$$\min_{a,R,\xi_i} R^2 + \frac{1}{\nu N} \sum_{i=1}^{N} \xi_i \qquad (1)$$

subject to $\|\phi(\boldsymbol{x}_i) - \boldsymbol{a}\|_{\mathcal{H}}^2 \leq R^2 + \xi_i$ and $\xi_i \geq 0 \; \forall i = 1, ..., N$. The predefined parameter ν represents an upper bound on the fraction of outliers, and regulates the trade-off between the volume of the hypersphere and the number of outliers. Considering the Lagrangian of the above constrained optimization problem, and incorporating the relations from its partial derivatives with respect to R, $\boldsymbol{a}$ and ξ_i gives us the following objective functional to be maximized with respect to the Lagrangian multipliers α_i : $L = \sum_{i=1}^{N} \alpha_i k(\boldsymbol{x}_i, \boldsymbol{x}_i) - \sum_{i,j=1}^{N} \alpha_i \alpha_j k(\boldsymbol{x}_i, \boldsymbol{x}_j)$, subject to $\sum_{i=1}^{N} \alpha_i = 1$ and $0 \leq \alpha_i \leq 1/\nu N$. The solution of this quadratic programming problem is found using any off-the-shelf optimization technique, i.e., matlab's function quadprog.

In order to evaluate a new sample $\boldsymbol{z}$, we calculate the distance between the center of the sphere $\boldsymbol{a}$ and $\phi(\boldsymbol{z})$ in the feature space. If this distance is smaller than the radius, namely $\|\phi(\boldsymbol{z}) - \boldsymbol{a}\|_{\mathcal{H}}^2 \leq R^2$, $\boldsymbol{z}$ is accepted as a normal sample. Otherwise, $\boldsymbol{z}$ is considered as an outlier and an intrusion is detected. The radius of the optimal hypersphere is obtained with the distance in the feature space $\mathcal{H}$ from the center $\boldsymbol{a}$ to any sample $\phi(\boldsymbol{x}_k)$ on the boundary:

$$R^2 = k(\boldsymbol{x}_k, \boldsymbol{x}_k) - 2 \sum_{i=1}^{N} \alpha_i k(\boldsymbol{x}_k, \boldsymbol{x}_i) + \sum_{i,j=1}^{N} \alpha_i \alpha_j k(\boldsymbol{x}_i, \boldsymbol{x}_j).$$

2.2   Kernel Principal Component Analysis

Kernel Principal Component Analysis (KPCA) is a nonlinear application of PCA in a kernel-defined feature space, where using $k(\boldsymbol{x}, \boldsymbol{y}) = (\boldsymbol{x} \cdot \boldsymbol{y})$ is equivalent to performing the original PCA [22]. Hoffmann proposed in [26] the use the *reconstruction error* as a measure of novelty, since it takes into account the heterogeneous variance of the distribution of the data in the feature space. The first step in Hoffman's algorithm is to find eigenvalues λ and eigenvectors $\boldsymbol{v}$ of the covariance matrix $\widetilde{C}$ in the feature space $\mathcal{H}$, satisfying $\lambda \boldsymbol{v} = \widetilde{C} \boldsymbol{v}$. The second step is to project the data into the subspace spanned by the most relevant eigenvectors. Each $\boldsymbol{v}$ is a linear combination of the mapped data and takes the following form: $\boldsymbol{v} = \sum_{i=1}^{N} \alpha_i \phi(\boldsymbol{x}_i)$, and the coefficients α_i are given by solving the following eigen decomposition problem $N\lambda\alpha = \widetilde{K}\alpha$. The centered kernel matrix $\widetilde{K}$ is used in the optimization problem without the need to compute directly $\widetilde{C}$.

After projecting the data into the subspace spanned by the most relevant eigenvectors, the distance between each sample and its projection is computed. This distance is the reconstruction error, and it is used for novelty detection. Let $\mathcal{P}$ be the projection operator, the reconstruction error is computed as follows:

$$\|\widetilde{\phi}(\boldsymbol{z}) - \mathcal{P}\widetilde{\phi}(\boldsymbol{z})\|_{\mathcal{H}}^2 = \langle \widetilde{\phi}(\boldsymbol{z}), \widetilde{\phi}(\boldsymbol{z}) \rangle - 2\langle \widetilde{\phi}(\boldsymbol{z}), \mathcal{P}\widetilde{\phi}(\boldsymbol{z}) \rangle + \langle \mathcal{P}\widetilde{\phi}(\boldsymbol{z}), \mathcal{P}\widetilde{\phi}(\boldsymbol{z}) \rangle. \qquad (2)$$

Knowing in advance the number of outliers among the training dataset, an error threshold is fixed. If the reconstruction error of a new sample is smaller than this threshold, the corresponding sample is treated as a normal sample. Otherwise, it is considered as an outlier and an intrusion is detected.

3   Metric Variation and Parameter Optimization

The Gaussian kernel is adopted in our simulations, since it is the most common and suitable kernel for one-class classification problems [28]. The Gaussian kernel is given as follows: $k(\boldsymbol{x}_i, \boldsymbol{x}_j) = \exp(-\frac{\|\boldsymbol{x}_i - \boldsymbol{x}_j\|_2^2}{2\sigma^2})$, where $\boldsymbol{x}_i$ and $\boldsymbol{x}_j$ are input samples, $\|\cdot\|_2$ represents the l_2-norm in the input space, and σ is the bandwidth parameter of the kernel. The choice of the metric and σ has a great impact on the decision function of the classifier. The variation of the norm and the heuristic for choosing the bandwidth parameter are detailed in the next subsections.

3.1   Norm Variation

In order to understand the impact of l_p-norm on the classifier, the variation in the behavior of different norms in a 2-dimensional space is illustrated in Fig. 1. Each sample has two characteristics, feature 1 and feature 2, and p takes one of the values $\frac{3}{4}, 1, \frac{3}{2}, 2, 3, 4, 7$ and ∞. Each color represents equidistant contours with reference to the origin O. The following example clarifies the different behavior of several norms towards the same sample. The samples B and C are equidistant from the origin O with the l_2-norm, and D is much closer. However, for the l_1-norm, C and D are equidistant and much closer than B. Therefore, as p decreases, the norms are more sensitive on simultaneous variations of multiple features which become as important as large variation in a single one.

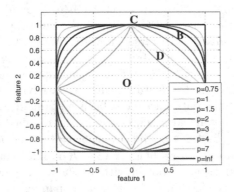

Fig. 1. The variation in the behavior of different norms ranging from $p = 0.75$ to $p = \infty$, where each color represents equidistant contours with reference to the origin O. The norms become more sensitive on simultaneous variation of multiple features as p decreases (Color figure online).

In critical infrastructures and industrial processes, the value of each variable is important to evaluate the state of the system, and to predict whether the process is leading to a critical state. The diversity of the studied physical processes requires more adapted kernels that depend on the behavior of the measured variables, i.e., the pressure inside a gas pipeline, the water level of a water distribution system, the temperature of a boiling water reactor, etc. For this reason, the choice of the norm in kernels affects the distribution of the data in the feature space, and has a great impact on the decision function of the classifier.

3.2   Choice of the Bandwidth Parameter

The performance of classification algorithms is highly related to the choice of the bandwidth parameter σ, as well as on the kernel's norm. σ plays a crucial role in defining the description boundary around the training data. With a large value of σ, the classifier underfits the data and we obtain a loose description boundary, where a small value of σ leads to overfitting. Several approaches were proposed in the literature for computing this parameter, but they are time consuming and do not always lead to an optimal choice [29–31].

The bandwidth parameter σ depends on multiple features, namely the spread of the training dataset, the number of input samples and the fraction of samples considered as outliers [32]. The estimation of σ should take into consideration all these factors. Therefore, we propose to use in the one-class classification algorithms the following expression for computing σ:

$$\sigma = \frac{d_{max}}{\sqrt{2M}},$$

where d_{max} refers to the maximal distance between any two samples in the input space, and M represents the upper bound on the number of outliers among the training dataset. The metric of the distance used in the kernel function is the same as the one in the expression of σ. The experiments showed that this proposed heuristic gives remarkable results without the need for the time consuming cross-validation step.

Fig. 2. Gas pipeline testbed

4   Results on the Gas Pipeline Testbed

In this paper, one-class classification algorithms are applied on real data from the gas pipeline testbed of the Mississippi State University SCADA Laboratory [16,17]. The gas pipeline illustrated in Fig. 2 is used to move natural gas or any other petroleum products to the market. Its control system contains an air pump that pumps air into the pipeline, a pressure sensor which allows pressure visibility at the pipeline and remotely on the HMI, a release valve and a solenoid release valve to loose air pressure from the pipeline. This testbed represents a typical SCADA system embracing a MTU, RTU and a HMI. Cyberattacks on the gas pipeline monitoring system can cause a loss of control of the physical process, and this may lead to huge financial and physical losses.

The pipeline operates in three principal modes; the first mode is characterized by a very low pressure maintained around 0.1 PSI, the second mode keeps it around 10 PSI (9 to 11 PSI), while the third mode should maintain the pressure around 20 PSI (18 to 22 PSI). The pressure greater than 22 PSI and the transitional states between different modes are considered as outliers. Several types of false commands and responses are injected into the normal behavior zone of the system to make its behavior abnormal. The *fast change response attack* returns measurements that change very fast opposed to the normal behavior of the pipeline. The *burst response injection attack* injects at high frequency a single value equals to 20 PSI while the system is running in several modes. The *wave response injection attack* injects pressure responses that vary in a wave form around 9 PSI which imitates exactly the second normal mode, while the real system is dealing with high pressures in the third mode. The primary objective of this paper is to detect these common and dangerous attacks that imitate the normal behavior of the system, and hide the real functioning status.

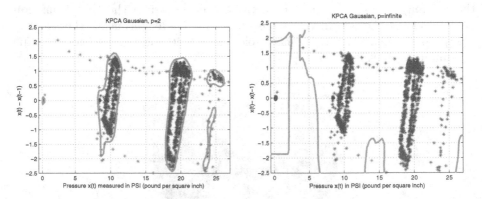

Fig. 3. Results on the gas pipeline real data with the KPCA approach. The decision boundaries are given by the green lines, the outliers correspond to the red samples and the normal samples are in blue. The l_2-norm (left) gives a good description while the infinite norm (right) underfits the data with a loose descriptions (Color figure online).

Table 1. Time computational cost of several approaches for computing the bandwidth parameter.

approach	5-fold CV	11-value range for σ	limited range (5 values)	proposed heuristic
SVDD	8 h 5 min	2 h 58 min	1 h 26 min	14.78 s
KPCA	3 h 47 min	1 h 32 min	34.6 min	14.78 s

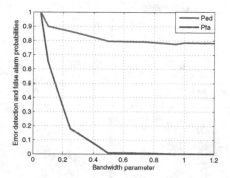

Fig. 4. The error detection and the false alarm probabilities as a function of the bandwidth parameter σ. The proposed heuristic leads to $\sigma = 0.9427$ with the highest error detection and the lowest false alarm rates.

Let $x(t)$ be the pressure in the pipeline at instant t. In normal functioning modes, the pressure measurements of two consecutive instants must be close to each other, and a gap between two consecutive instants may be a strong sign of a cyberattack. Therefore, the time series is folded into 2-dimensional input vectors composed of the pressure at instant t and the difference in the pressure between instants t and $t-1$, namely $x_t = [x(t) \quad x(t) - x(t-1)]$. The training phase is made on a train set of 2000 samples, and the tests are conducted on five different test sets containing several types of cyberattacks. The outliers in the test sets represent the simulated attacks that have to be detected by one-class classification algorithms. The different types of attacks are shown in Fig. 5.

The results on real data from the gas pipeline testbed for the KPCA approach are shown in Fig. 3. The decision boundary encloses the samples accepted as normal data, while the samples considered as outliers are rejected outside the boundary. The best results are obtained with the l_2-norm and the l_1-norm, having a tight decision boundary enclosing the normal behavioral modes. For small values of p, the norms become very sensitive to simultaneous variation of multiple features, and this leads to overfitting the data. On the other hand, the results for the values of p greater than $p = 2$ become worse as p increases, with a loose decision boundary that underfits the data. We have similar results with the SVDD approach. The prediction time for testing a new sample is 0.096 s with SVDD and 0.049 s with KPCA, which is very interesting in monitoring critical infrastructures. The error probabilities of the different types of cyberattacks are detailed in Table 2. The l_1-norm outperforms the l_2-norm in the wave and

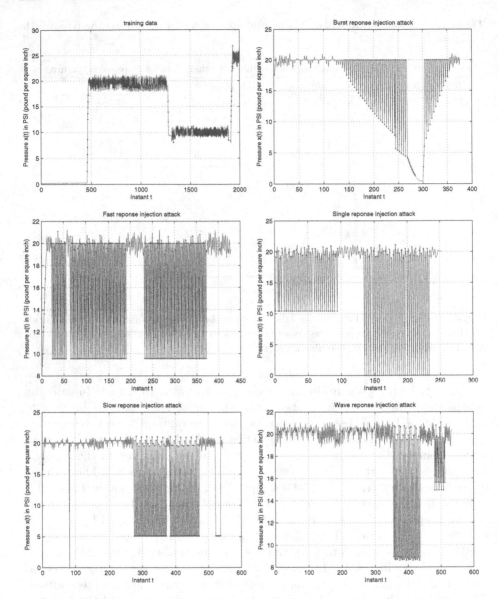

Fig. 5. Detection of outliers for several types of attacks with the SVDD approach using the l_1-norm. The blue samples refer to the data accepted as normal data while the red samples are considered as outliers (Color figure online).

the slow response injection attacks, where the data contain small simultaneous variation of its features. The best results are achieved with the slow and the single attacks having error detection probabilities around 99.52 %. We note that since these injections have already bypassed IDS and firewalls, the detection of the malicious attacks by operators comes mostly far too late after some severe

Table 2. The confusion matrix of several types of attacks with the KPCA approach.

		l_2-norm		l_1-norm	
		Normal	Outlier	Normal	Outlier
Slow injection	Normal	99.41	0.59	99.7	0.3
	Outlier	0.95	99.05	0.48	99.52
Fast injection	Normal	98.3	1.7	99.35	0.65
	Outlier	11.6	88.4	11.6	88.4
Burst injection	Normal	99.3	0.7	99.3	0.7
	Outlier	27.9	72.1	31.33	68.67
Single injection	Normal	98.37	1.63	99.2	0.8
	Outlier	0.78	99.22	0.78	99.22
Wave injection	Normal	98.8	1.2	98.09	1.91
	Outlier	35.1	64.9	34.21	65.79

consequences on the industry. This is where machine learning techniques play a crucial role to learn the industrial systems in order to detect all kinds of intrusions and avoid physical, financial and human lives losses.

The bandwidth parameter is computed as detailed in the previous section. We compared the time computational cost of the proposed heuristic with three other common methods existing in the literature as shown in Table 1. Our approach is clearly hundreds of times faster than the other methods, and it takes exactly the same time with SVDD and KPCA. In addition, the error detection and the false alarm probabilities for several values of σ are computed, and the results are illustrated in Fig. 4. The proposed heuristic leads to $\sigma = 0.9427$ having the highest error detection rates and the lowest false alarm rates, which confirms its relevance.

5   Conclusion

In this paper, we showed the importance of the complementary role of one-class classification algorithms in detection malicious cyberattacks in critical infrastructres relying on SCADA systems. The tests were conducted on real data containing several types of cyberattacks. We studied the impact of varying the norm in the kernels on the decision function of the classifier. We also proposed a simple heuristic for computing the bandwidth parameter of the Gaussian kernel, which led to the highest error detection and the lowest false alarm rates with minimum time computational cost. For future works, we are investigating a sparse one-class classification approach that should fasten the learning phase of the system. We are also working on increasing the performance of the algorithm by decreasing the time to test new samples. Finally, online one-class classification techniques should be integrated in the security systems critical infrastructures to improve the live detection of cyberattacks and reduce their consequences.

Acknowledgment. The authors would like to thank Thomas Morris and the Mississippi state university SCADA Laboratory for providing the real SCADA dataset.

References

1. Stouffer, K., Falco, J., Kent, K.: Guide to supervisory control and data acquisition (scada) and industrial control systems security. Technical report, National Institute of Standards and Technology (NIST) (2006)
2. Fovino, I., Masera, M., Guidi, L., Carpi, G.: An experimental platform for assessing SCADA vulnerabilities and countermeasures in power plants. In: 3rd Conference on Human System Interactions (HSI), pp. 679–686 (2010)
3. Fovino, I., Coletta, A., Carcano, A., Masera, M.: Critical state-based filtering system for securing SCADA network protocols. IEEE Trans. Ind. Electron. **59**, 3943–3950 (2012)
4. Ten, C.W., Hong, J., Liu, C.C.: Anomaly detection for cybersecurity of the substations. IEEE Trans. Smart Grid **2**, 865–873 (2011)
5. Slay, J., Miller, M.: Lessons learned from the maroochy water breach. In: Goetz, E., Shenoi, S. (eds.) Critical Infrastructure Protection, pp. 73–82. Springer, US (2007)
6. Christiansson, H., Luiijf, E.: Creating a European SCADA security testbed. In: Goetz, E., Shenoi, S. (eds.) Critical Infrastructure Protection. IFIP International Federation for Information Processing, vol. 253, pp. 237–247. Springer, US (2007)
7. Cárdenas, A.A., Amin, S., Lin, Z.S., Huang, Y.L., Huang, C.Y., Sastry, S.: Attacks against process control systems: risk assessment, detection, and response. In: Proceedings of the 6th ACM Symposium on Information, Computer and Communications Security, ASIACCS 2011, pp. 355–366. ACM, New York (2011)
8. Gorman, S.: Electricity grid in U.S. Penetrated by spies. Wall Street J. (2008)
9. Chen, T., Abu-Nimeh, S.: Lessons from stuxnet. Computer **44**, 91–93 (2011)
10. Langner, R.: Stuxnet: dissecting a cyberwarfare weapon. IEEE Secur. Priv. **9**, 49–51 (2011)
11. Urias, V., Van Leeuwen, B., Richardson, B.: Supervisory command and data acquisition (SCADA) system cyber security analysis using a live, virtual, and constructive (LVC) testbed. In: Military Communication Conference - MILCOM, pp. 1–8 (2012)
12. Yang, Y., McLaughlin, K., Littler, T., Sezer, S., Pranggono, B., Wang, H.: Intrusion detection system for IEC 60870-5-104 based SCADA networks. In: 2013 IEEE Power and Energy Society General Meeting (PES), pp. 1–5 (2013)
13. Bigham, J., Gamez, D., Lu, N.: Safeguarding SCADA systems with anomaly detection. In: Gorodetsky, V., Popyack, L.J., Skormin, V.A. (eds.) MMM-ACNS 2003. LNCS, vol. 2776, pp. 171–182. Springer, Heidelberg (2003)
14. Gross, P., Parekh, J., Kaiser, G.: Secure selecticast for collaborative intrusion detection systems. In: 3rd International Workshop on Distributed Event-Based Systems (DEBS 2004), Edinburgh, Scotland, UK (2004)
15. Carcano, A., Coletta, A., Guglielmi, M., Masera, M., Fovino, I., Trombetta, A.: A multidimensional critical state analysis for detecting intrusions in SCADA systems. IEEE Trans. Ind. Inf. **7**, 179–186 (2011)
16. Morris, T., Vaughn, R.B., Dandass, Y.S.: A testbed for SCADA control system cybersecurity research and pedagogy. In: CSIIRW, Oak Ridge, Tennessee (2011)

17. Morris, T., Srivastava, A., Reaves, B., Gao, W., Pavurapu, K., Reddi, R.: A control system testbed to validate critical infrastructure protection concepts. Int. J. Crit. Infrastruct. Prot. **4**, 88–103 (2011)
18. Hofmann, T., Schölkopf, B., Smola, A.J.: Kernel methods in machine learning. Ann. Stat. **36**, 1171–1220 (2008)
19. Shawe-Taylor, J., Cristianini, N.: Kernel Methods for Pattern Analysis. Cambridge University Press, New York (2004)
20. Chandola, V., Banerjee, A., Kumar, V.: Anomaly detection: a survey. ACM Comput. Surv. **41**, 15:1–15:58 (2009)
21. Tax, D.M.J., Duin, R.P.W.: Support vector data description. Mach. Learn. **54**, 45–66 (2004)
22. Schölkopf, B., Smola, A., Müller, K.R.: Nonlinear component analysis as a kernel eigenvalue problem. Neural Comput. **10**, 1299–1319 (1998)
23. Noumir, Z., Honeine, P., Richard, C.: Online one-class machines based on the coherence criterion. In: Proceedings of the 20th European Conference on Signal Processing, Bucharest, Romania (2012)
24. Khan, S.S., Madden, M.G.: A survey of recent trends in one class classification. In: Coyle, L., Freyne, J. (eds.) AICS 2009. LNCS, vol. 6206, pp. 188–197. Springer, Heidelberg (2010)
25. Mazhelis, O.: One-class classifiers : a review and analysis of suitability in the context of mobile-masquerader detection. S. Afr. Comput. J. **36**, 29–48 (2006)
26. Hoffmann, H.: Kernel PCA for novelty detection. Pattern Recogn. **40**, 863–874 (2007)
27. Nader, P., Honeine, P., Beauseroy, P.: Intrusion detection in SCADA systems using one-class classification. In: Proceedings of the 21th European Conference on Signal Processing, Marrakech, Morocco (2013)
28. Schölkopf, B., Platt, J.C., Shawe-Taylor, J.C., Smola, A.J., Williamson, R.C.: Estimating the support of a high-dimensional distribution. Neural Comput. **13**, 1443–1471 (2001)
29. Soares, C., Brazdil, P.B., Kuba, P.: A meta-learning method to select the kernel width in support vector regression. Mach. Learn. **54**, 195–209 (2004)
30. Cherkassky, V., Ma, Y.: Practical selection of SVM parameters and noise estimation for SVM regression. Neural Netw. **17**, 113–126 (2004)
31. Gurram, P, Kwon, H.: Support-vector-based hyperspectral anomaly detection using optimized kernel parameters. IEEE Geosci. Remote Sens. Lett. **8**, 1060–1064 (2011)
32. Haykin, S.: Neural Networks: A Comprehensive Foundation, 2nd edn. Prentice Hall, Upper Saddle River (1998)

Cyber Attacks in Power Grid ICT Systems Leading to Financial Disturbance

Yannis Soupionis[✉] and Thierry Benoist

European Commission, Joint Research Centre (JRC),
Institute for the Protection and Security of the Citizen (IPSC),
Security Technology Assessment Unit, Via E. Fermi, 2749, 21027 Ispra, Italy
{yannis.soupionis,thierry.benoist}@jrc.ec.europa.eu

Abstract. Decentralized Critical infrastructure management systems will play a key role in reducing costs and improving the quality of service of industrial processes, such as electricity production. In this paper, we focus on the security issues on the communication channel between the main entities of a smart grid, like generators, consumers and transmission/distribution operators and the energy market. We simulate the energy (spot) market auctions and the power grid network, but we emulate the ICT information part which is the focus of our work. We set in motion a well-known attack, Denial-of-Service (DoS), in Cyber-Physical systems and we are able to identify the consequences not only in power distribution network but also in financial area.

Keywords: Cyber physical · Cyber security · DoS attack · Energy market

1 Introduction

Information and Communication Technologies (ICT) is a key component of the current Critical Infrastructures (CI), since their operation is dependent on communication between the CI components. Moreover, ICT involvement in CI management is being promoted by most regulators, since it can lead to cost reduction, greater efficiency and interoperability between components. So the time that the CIs were isolated environments has passed and we have reached a state were most of them are interconnected and the lack of communication can lead to serious problems. Moreover, the isolation of the CIs has many functional limitations, e.g. higher installation, maintenance and operational costs coming from not infrastructure sharing. Therefore the reliance of CIs on distributed Networked Industrial Control Systems (NICS) brings a lot of positive attributes, but it makes them vulnerable to significant cyber-threats [1,2].

The CIs interdependency [3,4] uncertainty in the Cyber-Physical environmental and, as cyber attacks and errors in physical devices, make ensuring overall system robustness, security, and safety a critical challenge. A well-established cyber threat is the Distributed Denial of Service (DDoS) attacks, which is one of the most effective forms of attacks known today. By flooding a network element of the NCIS from many different sources, DDoS attacks can make part of the

© Springer International Publishing Switzerland 2016
C.G. Panayiotou et al. (Eds.): CRITIS 2014, LNCS 8985, pp. 256–267, 2016.
DOI: 10.1007/978-3-319-31664-2_26

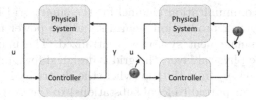

Fig. 1. DoS attack overview.

ICT infrastructure to be separated from important information for the operation of the CIs. This is depicted in Fig. 1, where either the control or the physical equipment is not able to communicate with the other infrastructure element.

Nowadays, CIs are very familiar with DDoS attacks. A McAfee report in November 2010 [15] shows energy providers are getting hit by some serious DDoS attacks. Across 200 industry executives over 14 countries revealed that 8 in 10 CIs had faced a significant DDoS attack in 2010. The full report have shown the sheer scale of attacks, with 29 per cent of critical infrastructure providers surveyed saying they were being hit by large scale DDoS attacks multiple times each month. Stuxnet [16] was listed as the most significant threat affecting CIs to date, which has been proven wrong about the possibilities of cyber attacks. Moreover, the last report [13] of the European Network and Information Security Agency (ENISA) shows clearly that a significant increase of Denial of Service attacks has been detected. The main reason is the DNS reflection attacks, which target poorly configured DNS servers. Additionally, there are tools which embrace DoS attack capabilities and can be obtained without any extreme cost [12]. The most destructive DDoS to date was not recorded against a CI but against the Spamhaus in 2013. Thanks to many misconfigured DNS servers (Open resolver) worldwide, the hosting service CyberBunker performed a DNS-amplified DDoS on Spamhaus with bursts of up to 300 Gbps.

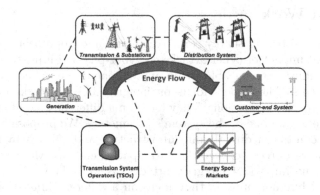

Fig. 2. Information and energy flow in smart grid infrastructure.

An important communication channel for the smart grid is the exchanging data between the power production elements and the power market, especially when the power management system is centralized. The main feature of this model is that at the physical layer, the grid is designed for a one-way flow of the electricity. More precisely from the top (where the electricity is generated in large power plants and transported to local substations) to the bottom (final stage in the delivery of electricity to end users). An abstract view of the communication between the main elements of the power grid is illustrated in Fig. 2 and it is obvious that any communication interruption can lead to unexpected results.

In this paper we present the development of an infrastructure which is composed of an IEEE simulated power grid, a simulated power market and the emulated network connecting those elements. We experimentally show that there are serious consequences on the power grid stability and on the market, by attacking solely on the provided communication data between the SCADA systems, the local Programmable Logic Controllers (PLCs) of the power grid nodes and the market. This research work provides a preliminary effort to (a) integrate those three smart grid elements (power, ICT infrastructure and power market) in a real-time experimental platform and (b) indicate the lack of models/approaches to reproduce the state of the network in extreme conditions such as DDoS attacks

Nevertheless, simple topology changes can have a significant impact on the network's resilience which is going to be presented in experimental section. Such solutions can already be deployed using existing routing hardware and software which can render DDoS attacks ineffective even with default configurations.

The paper is organized as follows: Sect. 2 describes the related work while in Sect. 3 we present the main elements of our research work. In Sect. 4 we explain the proposed the created experimental framework, which includes the emulated and simulated elements of the infrastructure. Section 5 illustrates the impact of the DDoS attacks onto a power grid and describes the experimental results. Finally, Sect. 6 concludes this work and identifies some open subjects for future work.

2   Related Work

In this section, we briefly survey some techniques and approaches, which focus on the financial impact of cyber attacks on cyber-physical infrastructures.

Article [8] illustrates an able to be approximated the cyber-attack impact in financial terms. The papers focus on integrity cyber attacks occurring on electric power market operations. They focus on a different kind of attack which is based on the knowledge of the system's parameters. We propose a brute force attack, which can target directly our infrastructure and affect it by limiting the communication resources between the participating entities. Moreover, in [9] the authors show the impact of integrity attacks, as well. The attack's impact is well illustrated but not only do they focus on a different kind of attack, they concentrate mainly on attack detection and identification procedures.

The financial impact is studied via a game theoretical approach in [10]. The effect of compromising measurements on the price of electricity is expressed as a zero-sum game between the attacker and the defender. The game identifies the effectiveness as well as the properties of the participants' strategy, justifies them through a detailed simulation, but fails to reach an equilibrium that is the best point for the operator/defender for designing a proper detection method. This work is a nice approach for the operators in order to draw their financial strategy but does not take into account any specific security issues.

3   ICT Infrastructure and Power/Spot Market

The main two elements for our implementation is the ICT infrastructure serving the communication channel and the power market which is based on auction algorithms for serving the optimal energy bids and offers equilibrium.

3.1   Networked Industrial Control Systems

In this section we provide a brief description of the NICS architecture used in this work. We present the standardized architecture and subsequently our implementation of the simulation/emulation framework.

The ICT infrastructure of a power grid system is consisted mainly by the automation control. It includes of control centers, which supervise the operation of the substations. The layers of the power grid controlling system are depicted in Fig. 3 and they perform all the controlling procedures and data collection.

The physical layer is composed of field devices, like sensors, meters, phase measuring units, which send raw information to the first layer. There we have Remote Terminal Unit (also called a SCADA slave), Programmable Logical Controllers (PLCs) and lower-level distributed controls. The higher layers contain more advanced controlling processes as Supervisory Control and Data Acquisition (SCADA) server.

Moreover, in order to deliver electrical power from producers to consumers in a cost-effective way, the central power grid operators have to exchange information with various organization and devices, as Independent System Operators

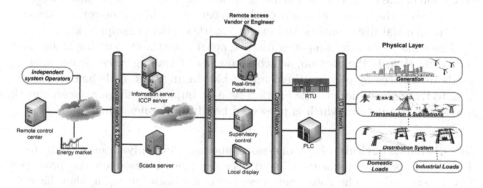

Fig. 3. The layers of the ICT power grid controlling system.

and Energy market. This data is collected at corporate and control center level (remote control center). Even though the communication at an operation center level is generally based on dedicated lines using ICCP (Inter Control Center Protocol), the link that is deployed between operation center and corporate/control relies on IP-based (Internet Protocol) protocols.

Traditionally, power grid automation systems have been physically isolated from the corporate network, often using proprietary protocols and legacy hardware and software. However, this has been changing to public infrastructures so as to reduce the operational cost [11]. From the financial point of view, it seems like a reasonable choice, however one should be aware of the fact that it definitely increases the vulnerability of power grids to cyber attacks and the associated implications.

3.2 Power Market

Electricity is an essential good in our society. Since more than one decade, a political change of mind has led to the liberalization of the power markets. Its goal: the creation of an internal European market which achieves security of supply and competitive prices and services for the customers. In this market, a growing variety of enterprises organizes the production, the trading, the marketing, the transmission and the supply of electricity, respecting appropriate regulation. Producers compete to sell energy at the best possible price. The suppliers which deliver electricity to the final consumers buy the energy on the wholesale market from the producers or the trading companies.

Power markets or spot markets offer trading platforms [18–20] to exchange members submitting bids for buying and selling power. They organize markets that are optional, anonymous and accessible to all participants satisfying admission requirements. The main objective of power exchanges is to ensure a transparent and reliable wholesale price formation mechanism on the power market by matching supply and demand at a fair price and ensure that the trades done at the exchange are finally delivered and paid. Summarizing, for the cyber security point of view the power market processes should guarantee fair and orderly execution of the orders of the exchange members. Therefore a possible interruption between the communication of the power grid and the power market can lead to financial disturbances and even to market/prices manipulation.

The main procedure of a power market, apart from the exchanging money and anonymization, is the auction, which is any set of trading rules for exchanging goods or services by offering them up for bid, taking bids, and then selling the item to the highest bidder. The auction type we implement for our research work is a one-sided auction, which is presented briefly in the next subsection.

One-Sided Auctions. In a one-sided auction bids only inserted only from the producers, and are sorted in an ascending order based on the price per KW (power grid). The consumers demand is unelastic, meaning they have to absorb/consume the requested power. Offers are accepted beginning with the least expensive and continuing until the demand is satisfied. The uniform price is then set equal to either the last accepted offer. The offers by the producers are arranged by blocks which contain a certain amount of KW. Usually the last block is partially accepted, except for the special case where the quantity clears all the offed block. This block is taken as the last accepted block and its price corresponds to the incremental cost of additional demand. Moreover, the distance between the power grid buses (Sect. 4.2) are included in the prices adjustment, which represents the cost of transmission between locations. Generalizing to a network with possible losses and congestion results in nodal prices λ^p which vary according to location. These λ^p values can be used to normalize all bids and offers to a reference location by multiplying by a locational scale factor. For bids and offers at bus i, this scale factor is $\lambda_{ref}^p/\lambda_i^p$, where ref is the nodal price at the reference bus. The desired uniform pricing rule can then be applied to the adjusted offers and bids to get the appropriate uniform price at the reference bus. For example, if the normalized uniform price at bus ref is u_{ref}^p, then the uniform price at each bus k is

$$u_k^p = \left(\frac{u_{ref}^p}{\lambda_{ref}^p} \right) \lambda_k^p$$

A simple example for clarity reasons: Potential buyers submit the quantity desired and a price per unit in sealed bids. When all bids are collected, the seller gives the desired quantity to the bidder who offered the highest price, then the second highest, and so forth, until all available units are sold. All buyers pay the price per unit of the lowest bid that was awarded units. More specifically, suppose there are 1000 available units (KW) and three bidders. Bidder A offers 20 euros per unit and wants 600 units; Bidder B wants 400 units at 30 euros per unit. Finally, Bidder C wants 300 units at 35 euros per unit. Under this scenario, Bidders A and B both receive their desired units and they both pay 20 euros per unit. The proposed offered prices include the distance cost between buses.

Therefore by affecting the communication of (a) a market's seller the available units may be affected, and (b) a bidder can manipulate the final uniform price.

4   Experimental Setup

In this section we briefly present the framework that was used for (a) simulating the physical components of a smart grid and the power market, and (b) emulating the cyber elements. An overview of the experimental setup is illustrated on Fig. 4.

4.1   Network Emulation

In our laboratory we have installed an infrastructure using the Emulab [17] architecture and software, called EPIC [14]. The testbed of the NICS cyber part (SCADA servers, corporate network etc.) facilitating the emulation of the ICT

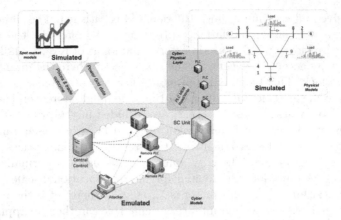

Fig. 4. The overall architecture of the simulation & emulation framework used in this work.

infrastructure is based on Emulab. We can automatically and dynamically map physical components, e.g., servers and switches, to a virtual topology and the communication channels between them. In other words, the Emulab software configures the physical topology in a way that it emulates the virtual topology as transparently as possible. This way we gain significant advantages in terms of repeatability, scalability and controllability of our experiments. Furthermore, the software configures network switches in order to recreate the virtual topology by connecting experimental nodes using multiple VLANs. Within the ICT network we used the Open Shortest Path First (OSPF) for traffic routing purposes.

A summary of experimental resources employed for the present study are:

- 3 Routers (Cisco 6503), which have four Gigabit experimental interfaces and one control interface (emulation).
- 14 virtual PCs (HP Proliant GL380p), which have Xeon(R) 4 CPUs @ 2.40 GHz, 3 GB RAM, two Gigabit experimental interfaces and one control interface. They were are used as experimental nodes (attackers and simulated elements) and their operating system is FreeBSD8.2.
- 3 Switches(Cisco 3750G), which have 48 ports each. They were used for the communication network (emulation).

Finally, a network measurement reveals an average Round Trip Time (RTT) below 3 ms. This means that the implementation exhibits the operational behavior of real communications systems where the delivery of high-speed messages must be below the maximum limit of 10 ms, as stated by the IEEE 1646-2004 standard [21] on communications delays in substation automation.

4.2   Simulation Elements

The simulation elements constructed for our experimental environment are two: the physical systems (power grid) and the power/smart market system.

The main role of the simulation element (Sim) is to run the physical process model in real-time. This is done by coupling the model time to the system time in such a way to minimize the difference between the two. Models are constructed in Matlab Simulink from where the corresponding C code is generated using Matlab Real Time Workshop. These are then integrated using an XML configuration file that is flexible enough so that researchers do not need to modify the code. The generated code is then executed in real time and interacts with the real components of our emulation testbed. From a technical point of view, real-time simulation of IEEE grid models is implemented in AMICI [6], which is based on Matlab open-source libraries, i.e. MatPower [5] and MatDyn [7]. The IEEE model used for our experiments is the IEEE 9 buses, where 3 buses are the generators, 3 buses serve as connecting ones and the last three are the consumers.

The power market element is developed in Matlab simulink, as well, and is based on the principles presented in Sect. 3.2. The communication channel with the power grid is presented in Fig. 4 and it interacts real time based on newly entered power demands from the consumers. Interaction with other simulation elements is enabled by implementing not only RPC (Remote Procedure Call) server-side operations but client-side calls as well. By using only the XML configuration file, the simulation element can be configured to read/write inputs/outputs of models run by remote ones. In our testbed, the two communicating elements via the cyber-emulated topology, are power market and power grid. Finally, the controller is based on the Matpower implemented functions.

4.3 DoS Attack Implementation

The DDoS attacks were implemented in the presence of an upto 100 Mbit/s UDP-based background traffic, generated by either PathTest[1] or Iperf[2]. We have installed those tools in all the attacker nodes.

We are going to implement two kind of DDoS attacks:

- the first one is going to be against specific equipment, meaning PLC or router. This is going to be implemented by bots sending large amount of network traffic (flood) to a specific IP or network interface.
- the second one is going to aim to minimize the network bandwidth between the physical equipment and the power market. Therefore there may be partial loss of communication between those entities.

The impact of the DDoS attacks is going to be expressed by measuring the Round Trip-Time (RTT). The RTT of a TCP segment is defined as the time it takes for the segment to reach the receiver and for a segment carrying the generated acknowledgment to return to the sender [22]. This technique expresses the latency of TCP communications.

To summarize this section, the important characteristics of the proposed framework are the following:

---

[1] PathTest, Free Network Capacity Test tool, 2014.
[2] Iperf: The TCP/UDP Bandwidth Measurement Tool, 2014.

- The Matlab Simulink facilitates the integration of physical infrastruc-
  tures/plants based on the a-priori known system's analytical equations.
- The communication between the remote PLCs and the controlling units is
  based on the Modbus over TCP protocol. However, another protocol can be
  easily integrated due to the modularity provided by our implementation.
- There is a synchronization algorithm between the models execution time and
  the system clocks ensuring reliable exchange of data.
- The tools used for the DDoS attacks are well-established for this kind of
  experimentation.

5   Experimental Results

In this section we evaluate the various network setups against DDoS attacks. The
main scenario is that *there is an emergent need for energy from the customers.
The producers (generators) place their bids and the consumers accept the offer
according to the power market rules* Sect. 3.2. In all scenarios the consumers
need a fixed amount of energy load, which have been already auctioned through
power market (previous-day auction), but there is a sudden need for 10, 20 and
30 Mwh for each of three customers (1, 2 and 3 respectively) and the bidders (3
generators) offer 30, 40 and 50 €/MWh from generators 1, 2 and 3 respectively
(Fig. 5). We attacked always bus 1, because this provides the maximum financial
disturbance since generator 1 has the lowest price.

Moreover, the response strategy for the controller during a DDoS attack is
the last received data/signal as a current command:

$$c(t) = \begin{cases} c^{past}(t) \in T_{DoS} \\ c^{real}(t) \notin T_{DoS}, \end{cases}$$

where c(t) is the values provided to the controller, T_{DoS} is the time period of
the DDoS attack, $c^{past}(t)$ is the last received value of the PLC (stack-at fault),

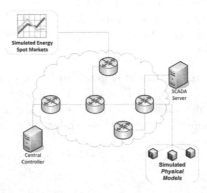

Fig. 5. The Emulab laboratory architecture for the experimental phase.

Table 1. Topology and results against a DDoS attack

Topology	Outcome description	Loss (€)	RTT (msec)
Public PLC	No data reached the market	10.43/MWh	1.2×10^6
Public Dedicated Router	Data reached the controller, but critical situations existed. The market did not received adequate information	10.43/MWh	$max(1.22 \times 10^4)$
Non-Public Dedicated Router - Priority policy	Data reached the controller without issue. Data not always reached the market during repeatable experiments	10.43/MWh	$max(3.45 \times 10^2)$

till a new value is received by the controller, and $c^{real}(t)$ is the real time values provided to the controller.

The proposed ICT network topologies and the outcomes are depicted briefly in Table 1. We sorted our results based on the network position of the PLC:

1. Public PLC: In this scenario we have a generator's PLC to be reachable through Internet. This mean that a DoS attack can aim directly to a PLC's port/interface. The attack duration was 20 min and the PLC was not able to provide any data through this period. Having implemented an exact replica of a PLC (memory-wise), we identified that the PLC crashed after only 2 min because its computational resources were exhausted. The outcome was that the market and the controller were unable to receive information. So when an urgent demand for additional energy was introduced, the specific generator was not able to verify its bid. Therefore there was a loss of 10.43 €/MWh and a large increase to the voltage, where the connecting bus 2 reached its limit.

2. Public Dedicated Router: In this scenario we have a dedicated router connecting the main elements to be reachable through Internet. This means that a DDoS attack can aim directly to the router. The attack duration was 20 min. The outcome was that the controller received partially some data, but the market was unable to retrieve the appropriate data from the generator. So when an urgent demand for additional energy was introduced, the specific generator was not able to verify its bid. Therefore, the requested power was bought from another generator at a higher price and there was a loss of 10.43 €/MWh. Moreover, a large increase to the voltage of the connecting bus 4 occurred (Fig. 6).

3. Non-Public Dedicated Router: In this scenario we have a dedicated router connecting the main elements, which is not reachable through Internet, but is used to pass communication for other services, as webservices, etc. This means that a DDoS attack cannot aim directly to the router, but by attacking a specific other service the network bandwidth is going to be limited. The attack duration was 20 min. The outcome was that the controller received partially some data,

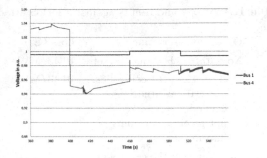

Fig. 6. The voltages (in p.u.) of buses 1 and 4, where bus 1 is under DDoS attack.

meaning that there were a few voltage sudden increases but there was not a extreme situation for the specific time period. The market was unable to retrieve the appropriate data from the generator, unless there is a special router policy giving priority to specific IP ranges. So when an urgent demand for additional energy was introduced, the specific generator was not always able to verify its bid. Therefore the loss was from 0 to 10.43 €/MWh.

6 Conclusions and Further Research

In this paper we presented the financial disturbance and the affect on the voltage of a power grid due to a DDoS attack against the ICT communication system. For all the intents and purposes, we used a well-defined testbed in order to validate the outcome of these cyber attacks. We show that there are issues for the control schemes, which use public infrastructure due to operational costs without taking into consideration possible malicious implications. Even though this architecture is advantageous, the stakeholders should think thoroughly how to setup their interface and use the public infrastructure.

As future work we intend to perform a more detailed analysis of the behavior of real networking devices under other attacks, as integrity attacks, and introduce additional monitoring attributes, as frequency. We intend to develop a novel approach by integrating real physical infrastructure like PLCs and energy generators equipments (windmill and solar systems).

References

1. Sridhar, S., Hahn, A., Govindarasu, M.: Cyber - physical system security for the electric power grid. Proc. IEEE **100**(1), 210–224 (2012)
2. Mo, Y., Kim, T.-H., Brancik, K., Dickinson, D., Lee, H., Perrig, A., Sinopoli, B.: Cyber - physical security of a smart grid infrastructure. Proc. IEEE **100**(1), 195–209 (2012)
3. Kotzanikolaou, P., Theoharidou, M., Gritzalis, D.: Accessing n-order dependencies between critical infrastructures. Int. J. Crit. Infrastruct. **9**(1–2), 93–110 (2013)

4. Theoharidou, M., Kotzanikolaou, P., Gritzalis, D.: A multi-layer criticality assessment methodology based on interdependencies. Comput. Secur. **29**(6), 643–658 (2010)
5. Zimmerman, R., Murillo-Sanchez, C., Thomas, R.: Matpower: steady-state operations, planning, and analysis tools for power systems research and education. IEEE Trans. Power Syst. **26**(1), 12–19 (2011)
6. Genge, B., Siaterlis, C., Hohenadel, M.: AMICI: an assessment platform for multi-domain security experimentation on critical infrastructures. In: Hämmerli, B.M., Kalstad Svendsen, N., Lopez, J. (eds.) CRITIS 2012. LNCS, vol. 7722, pp. 228–239. Springer, Heidelberg (2013)
7. Cole, S., Belmans, R.: Matdyn, a new matlab-based toolbox for power system dynamic simulation. IEEE Trans. Power Syst. **26**(3), 1129–1136 (2011)
8. Pasqualetti, F., Dorfler, F., Bullo, F.: Cyber-physical attacks in power networks: models, fundamental limitations and monitor design. In: 2011 50th IEEE Conference on Decision and Control and European Control Conference (CDC-ECC), pp. 2195–2201, December 2011
9. Xie, L., Mo, Y., Sinopoli, B.: Integrity data attacks in power market operations. IEEE Trans. Smart Grid **2**(4), 659–666 (2011)
10. Esmalifalak, M., Shi, G., Han, Z., Song, L.: Bad data injection attack and defense in electricity market using game theory study. IEEE Trans. Smart Grid **4**(1), 160–169 (2013)
11. Yan, Y., Qian, Y., Sharif, H., Tipper, D.: A survey on smart grid communication infrastructures: motivations, requirements and challenges. IEEE Comm. Surv. Tutorials **15**(1), 5–20 (2013). First
12. Thompson, J., McKeay, M., Brenner, B., Mller, R., Sintorn, M., Huston, G.: Akamai's state of the internet. Q4 2013 Report, vol. 6, Nm. 4, Prolexic Quarterly Global DDoS Attack Report
13. Marinos, L.: ENISA Threat Landscape Report 2013. European Union Agency for Network and Information Security, December 2014. Accessed April 2014
14. Siaterlis, C., Garcia, A., Genge, B.: On the use of Emulab testbeds for scientifically rigorous experiments. IEEE Commun. Surv. Tutorials **15**(2), 1–14 (2012)
15. Baker, S., Filipiak, N., Timlin, K.: In the Dark Crucial Industries Confront Cyber attacks mcaffee. McAfee second annual critical infrastructure protection report (2010) Accessed April 2014
16. Langner, R.: Stuxnet: dissecting a cyberwarfare weapon. IEEE Secur. Priv. **9**(3), 49–51 (2011)
17. White, B., Lepreau, J., Stoller, L., Ricci, R., Guruprasad, S., Newbold, M., Hibler, M., Barb, C., Joglekar, A.: An integrated experimental environment for distributed systems and networks. In: OSDI02, pp. 255–270, December 2002
18. European Energy Exchange AG. http://www.eex.com/en/market-data/natural-gas/spot-market. Accessed May 2014
19. Epex Spot. http://www.epexspot.com/en/. Accessed May 2014
20. APX Power spot exchange. http://www.apxgroup.com/. Accessed May 2014
21. Institute of Electrical and Electronics Engineers, IEEE, 1646-2004 standard: communication delivery time performance requirements for electric power substation automation (2004)
22. Aikat, J., Kaur, J., Smith, F.D., Jeffay, K.: Variability in TCP round-trip times. In: Proceedings of the 3rd ACM SIGCOMM on Internet Measurement Conference, pp. 279–284 (2003)

Obfuscation of Critical Infrastructure Network Traffic Using Fake Communication

Sungho Jeon, Jeong-Han Yun[✉], and Woo-Nyon Kim

The Attached Institute of ETRI, Daejeon, South Korea
{sdeva,dolgam,wnkim}@ensec.re.kr

Abstract. The tendency in cyber attacks has evolved from ones immediately causing abnormal operations to advanced attacks after information extraction by traffic sniffing. In particular, the unchanging characteristics of CIS networks are more susceptible to advanced attacks through information extraction. In this paper, we suggest the concept of an obfuscation method for CIS network traffic to interfere with information extraction. We investigated the characteristics of CIS traffic as found from real data. Based on our observations, we propose a method of creating fake communication to make the best use of surplus network bandwidth. We show that our method can vary the characteristics of a CIS network to prevent information extraction by sniffing.

Keywords: Critical infrastructure network traffic protection · Fake communication

1 Introduction

Motivation. The trend of cyber-attacks have evolved from ones immediately causing abnormal operations to advanced attacks after extracting information through traffic sniffing. Extracting information itself may not seem dangerous, but it can be the beginning of a tremendous conspiracy. The A-IDS [1] used in SCADA [2] cannot prevent the extraction of information through traffic sniffing; rather, both can be rendered useless through the extracted information. To the best of our knowledge, although there have not yet been any official reports of Critical Infrastructure Systems (CISs) being defeated by extracting information from SCADA traffic, the aim of this research is to preempt such attacks.

Challenge. The current SCADA system was designed several decades ago when cyber-attacks were not fully considered. Hence, SCADA network traffic is not encrypted, but in plaintext. Unfortunately, sometimes, this situation is overlooked and thought to be safe through the belief that a few security devices will provide sufficient protection. Even if SCADA network traffic is encrypted in the next generation SCADA, there is still room for information extraction.

A previous version of the manuscript is published in Proc. of the 2013 the 29th Annual Computer Security Applications Conference (ACSAC) as a poster paper.

© Springer International Publishing Switzerland 2016
C.G. Panayiotou et al. (Eds.): CRITIS 2014, LNCS 8985, pp. 268–274, 2016.
DOI: 10.1007/978-3-319-31664-2_27

- Communication relationships, which represent who communicates with others, are easily identified by a few days worth of sniffing. The identification means that the ACL is revealed to attackers, thereby it renders firewalls based on the ACL useless.
- The periodic characteristics are distinct characteristics of the SCADA network. For example, solicited messages in the DNP3 protocol [3] are sent out periodically to perform remote commands and monitor tasks. These characteristics can be a useful feature on A-IDS, but they are easily identified through sniffing.
- Only a few types of commands are actually used to manage devices operating using the SCADA network protocol, and these commands have different templates for communication. Therefore, an attacker can infer a type of command just through a communication template. This information can not only be a useful feature on A-IDS, but it can also give clues to the regular reset time of SCADA or the status that SCADA is under renovation.

Therefore, even if encryption is applied to SCADA traffic, important information can be leaked from the traffic itself. To our knowledge, there have been no studies on protection against information extraction on SCADA.

Threat Model. In our model, we assumed that the attacker has already invaded the SCADA, but could not perform malicious activity because it had an A-IDS, a firewall based on ACL. However, if an attacker has prior knowledge of A-IDS on SCADA, then the attacker would know how the normal profile of A-IDS was created and what features were used to detect an attack. Therefore, the attacker could first try to reveal the normal profile of A-IDS. After getting an artificial profile similar to the normal one, the attacker could bypass A-IDS on SCADA.

Contribution. We do not propose a completely implemented solution. We investigated the characteristics of SCADA traffic using real data. This provided us with clues regarding the possibility of complex attacks using information extraction on SCADA even when encryption is applied. For this problem, we suggest the concept of an obfuscation method for SCADA network traffic to interfere with information extraction.

Our idea is to blend real SCADA traffic with fake communication. The system in SCADA rarely changes; on the other hand, an advanced Ethernet device upgrades the network environment continuously, replacing an outdated device, so as not to cause a network problem. For this reason, the actual network bandwidth used in SCADA is much smaller than the maximum value. Thus, our approach is based on the idea of fully exploiting the surplus network bandwidth. Instead of the additional overhead of system resources, we create fake communications similar to the normal ones so that the attacker cannot identify them. Also, we consider creating fake communication at the transaction level, which include responses to requests and acknowledgements beyond the packet level, so as not to be identified by the attacker. In summary, we propose the concept of this framework to generate and filter fake communications.

We evaluated our method by the implementing a fake generator simulator. The fake generator simulator added fake communication to the original packet file. We proved the effectiveness of our method by varying the "periodicity of the Read function code", "frequency distribution of the function code", and "frequency distribution of the DNP3 object on each master-outstation connection" to interfere with the information extraction.

2   Real Data Investigation

2.1   Data Description

We manually collected network traffic data on national critical infrastructures – whose names and sites cannot be revealed for security reasons – using Wireshark, a well-known packet capture program. We collected data for two weeks on two different sites. We collected 995 GB on site A and 330 GB on site B; the network bandwidth of these two sites is 100 Mbps. This means that the actual usage of network bandwidth on the sites was just 3.8 Mbps and 1.2 Mbps, respectively, so there was excess network bandwidth available on both sites. Next, we extracted only DNP3 traffic from the original traffic data. The reason that the amount of DNP3 traffic was so small compared to the total traffic was that only a small portion of the connections used DNP3 on the entire network. There were 24 types of DNP3 function codes.

2.2   Well-Known Facts About SCADA Protocol

There were two major prior well-known facts to consider. First, the fact that most communication in the SCADA network is related to "Read" and "Response" function codes, which play the role of monitoring data reported from the RTU device. In our observation, about 99.4 % of the DNP3 communication was related to the "Read" and "Response" function codes. Second, "Read" function code communication was raised periodically. In our data, there were notable periodic characteristics in the "Read" function code communication depending on the DNP3 object in the solicited response data, unlike in the unsolicited responses (Tables 1)[1].

2.3   Different Distribution of Object Type by Connection

Next, we investigated not only the distribution of the object types on the entire network and based on each function code but also on each outstation-master pair. Unlike the DNP3 function code, the distribution of the object type varied by host. This means that each connection played a different role in SCADA, and this information was easily identified based on the sniffing object ratio.

---

[1] Object name is an alias for security reasons.

Table 1. Mean and variance of inter-arrival time of "Read" Function Code, "Unsolicited Response" for top 3 object and frequency distribution ratio

Function code	Object name(alias)	Mean(sec)	Var(sec)	Ratio(%)
Read	Object1	8.75	1.48	77.74
	Object2	0.05	0.06	10.74
	Object3	58.22	8.62	7.02
Unsolicited response	Object1	1838.01	8240.12	84.29
	Object2	1390.41	6342.08	10.78
	Object3	227.88	1073.86	2.44

2.4   DNP3 Communication Template

One of the reasons why information can be leaked even when encryption is applied is that we can guess the function code just by sniffing the communication template. To validate this idea, we investigated the actual communication template when each of the DNP3 function codes arrived. There were five types of template. For example, when the "Read" function code arrived, acknowledgement occurred and the "Response" with the object was outputted; finally, an acknowledgement of the "Response" was sent. Usually, a fragmentation (Frag) packet was used in this case. Some function codes did not need a DNP3 object, such as "Confirm", "Warm Restart", and "Authenticate Request". These communications of the DNP3 function code were simply used without an object. Even with the same function code, the template changed to a DNP3 object. For example, there was at least one fragmentation packet in the "Read" function code with object 1, but this was not true in the "Read" function code with object 2. In summary, few function codes or distinct templates with object types that offered clues to identifying communication by sniffing were actually used, even when the information was encrypted.

3   Fake Communication Generation

Inspired by our observation, we propose a method of interfering with the information extraction process using fake communication to fully exploit the surplus network bandwidth. In this section, we explain when we create and how we control the amount of fake traffic, and then introduce the process of creating fake communication.

3.1   Fake Communication Algorithm

There are four steps employed to create fake communication in each master-outstation connection: "Select fake function code," "Select fake object," "Make fake template," and "Notify fake communication".

First, we select a fake function code, followed by an object with a function code selected at the previous step. After selecting the fake function code and object, we create a fake transaction template which was obtained from our manual study. An attacker who knows how to conduct packet sniffing could easily identify the creation of a fake packet, so we have to create fake communication not at the packet level, but at the transaction level, which includes an acknowledgement and response.

3.2   Timing and Fake Traffic Control

When designing our method, we considered two important properties. First, our approach has to be a probabilistic method to avoid generating a distinguishable pattern. Also, generating fake communications at the first or last periodic time is not effective in concealing the periodic time, because it could still provide a clue which would enable this information to be approximated. Our intention was to assign a high fake generation probability when the time was not near the first and last periodic times and a low probability near the first and last periodic times. To achieve our goal, we decided to assign fake generation probability using the "Probability density function of a Normal distribution" with a mean value of the periodic time divided by 2, then multiplied by 2 again, to increase the probability.

The second important property of our method is that it was able to control fake communication traffic. To accomplish this, we introduced a generating decision parameter (gd) that indicates whether fake traffic to be generated or not. For example, if gd is 1 s, we consider generating fake traffic every second. Note that, if gd is assigned a value that satisfies the periodic time modulo $gd = 0$, then the fake generation probability is 0. Thus, gd is selected in comparison with the periodic time whose value is obtained from the pre-processing stage. By adjusting this parameter, we can control the fake communication traffic, as well as the degree of protection. Additionally, the variance of the normal distribution used in the fake generation probability plays the role of controlling the fake traffic. In summary, for every gd time, our method considers generating fake communication with a certain generation probability.

4   Evaluation

To verify the effectiveness of our method, we built a fake generator simulation in Java. We changed the characteristics of the SCADA traffic, such as the "periodic time of the Read function code", "DNP3 function code frequency distribution", and "DNP3 object frequency distribution". However, only result of "periodic time of the Read function code" is explained in this section, because of length problem. To create the fake communication, our fake generator required a few pieces of information. We identified this necessary information in the preprocessing stage; it only needs to be identified once, except in the case where there is a system or network change in the SCADA network.

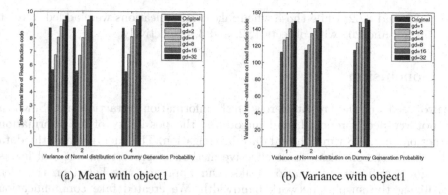

(a) Mean with object1   (b) Variance with object1

Fig. 1. Inter-arrival time evaluation on site A: mean and variance with objects 1

We measured the inter-arrival time between the read function code with the top three objects described in Table 1. Through experiments, we verified that our method could destroy the periodic time characteristics of the read function code communication. We report the inter-arrival time as a function of two parameters: gd, which refers to the decision parameter introduced in Sect. 3.2, and $vndgp$ which means the variance of the normal distribution of the fake generation probability. We conducted the experiments with gd 1 to 32 and $vndgp$ 1 to 8 as increased by two times with the top 3 DNP3 objects of the Read function code (Fig. 1).

Changing gd influenced the mean of the inter-arrival time of the Read function code (Fig. (1a)) When gd was small, the mean of the inter-arrival time was small because it offered more opportunities to create fake communication. For this reason, the variance of the inter-arrival time was small when gd was small (Fig. (1b)). $vndgp$ hardly affected the mean value, but the same cannot be said for the variance of the inter-arrival time. When $vndgp$ was high, fake communications were generated uniformly; hence, the variance was higher than that with low $vndgp$. We noted that this effect seemed weak in our result graph, because a large number of generated fake communications weakened this effect, especially on site A. In this evaluation, the most important finding was that the fake communications broke down the periodic characteristics. The variances of the original inter-arrival time were 1.48, 0.06, and 8.62 with objects 1, 2, and 3, respectively; in contrast, the variances of the inter-arrival time with the fake communications added were at least 112, 491, and 2187 with objects 1, 2, and 3, respectively.

To validate the generality of our method, we evaluated the mean and variance of the inter-arrival time on the site B dataset. Unlike site A, the periodic time of the Read function code was about 32 s, with a different DNP object distribution. Likewise, in the evaluation of the site A dataset, the addition of the fake communication yielded a different variance and mean of the inter-arrival time compared with the original value. Variance of the original inter-arrival time were

1.48, 0.06, and 8.62, while those when fake communications were added were at least 59, 23, and 201 with objects 1, 2, and 3, respectively.

5   Conclusion

We proposed a method to interfere with the information extraction on CIS, which has not yet been proposed, and introduced the possibility of for information extraction on a CIS through real data investigation. The encryption of the data seems to be the simplest, most effective method of protection, but still leaves room for significant information leaks. Our approach was based on the idea of utilizing the surplus network bandwidth. We created fake communication that was similar to the real communication, which could not be detected by the attacker. In the simulation, our method changed the characteristics of the SCADA network. We expect our study to be one of the starting points for research into preventing information leakages through sniffing on a CIS.

References

1. Düssel, P., Gehl, C., Laskov, P., Bußer, J.-U., Störmann, C., Kästner, J.: Cyber-critical infrastructure protection using real-time payload-based anomaly detection. In: Rome, E., Bloomfield, R. (eds.) CRITIS 2009. LNCS, vol. 6027, pp. 85–97. Springer, Heidelberg (2010)
2. Karnouskos, S., Colombo, A.W.: Architecting the next generation of service-based scada/dcs system of systems. In: IECON 2011–37th Annual Conference on IEEE Industrial Electronics Society, pp. 359–364. IEEE (2011)
3. MicroWorks, T.: Dnp3 overview. Raleigh, North Carolina (2002). www.trianglemicroworks.com/documents/DNP3Overview.pdf

CyNetPhy: Towards Pervasive Defense-in-Depth for Smart Grid Security

Mohamed Azab[1]($\boxtimes$), Bassem Mokhtar[2], and Mohammed M. Farag[2]

[1] The City of Scientific Research and Technological Applications,
Alexandria, Egypt
Mohamed.m.azab@gmail.com, mazab@vt.edu
[2] Electrical Engineering Department, Alexandria University, Alexandria, Egypt
{bmokhtar,mmorsy}@alexu.edu.eg

Abstract. Security is a major concern in the smart grid technology extensively relying on Information and Communication Technologies (ICT). New emerging attacks show the inadequacy of the conventional defense tools that provision isolated uncooperative services to individual grid components ignoring their real-time dependency and interaction. In this article, we present a smart grid layering model and a matching multi-layer security framework, CyNetPhy, towards enabling cross-layer security of the grid.CyNetPhy tightly integrates and coordinates between a set of interrelated, and highly cooperative real-time defense solutions designed to address the grid security concerns. We advance a high-level overview of CyNetPhy and present an attack scenario against the smart grid supported by a qualitative analysis of the resolution motivating the need to a cross-layer security framework such as CyNetPhy.

Keywords: Smart grid · Smart grid security · Pervasive monitoring and analysis · Autonomic management · Elastic computing · Privacy-preserving

1 Introduction

The smart grid is a cyber-physical system that tightly integrates control, computation, and communication technologies into the electrical power infrastructure. Smart grid has emerged as the next generation power grid aiming at enhancing the efficiency, reliability, and resilience of legacy power systems by employing information and communication technologies (ICT) [7]. To establish the smart grid global vision, widespread sensing and communication between all grid components are established via communication networks and managed by cyber systems. Extensive deployment of and reliance on ICT inevitably exposes the smart grid to cyber security threats increasing the risk of compromising reliability and security of the electrical power infrastructure [6]. Scale and complexity of the smart grid network create several vulnerabilities providing numerous attack entry points. Inadvertent infiltration through infected devices, network-based intrusion, and a compromised supply chain are examples of such attacks.

© Springer International Publishing Switzerland 2016
C.G. Panayiotou et al. (Eds.): CRITIS 2014, LNCS 8985, pp. 275–282, 2016.
DOI: 10.1007/978-3-319-31664-2_28

Liu *et al.* presented a detailed overview of relevant cyber security and privacy issues in smart grids [5]. Authors showed that every aspect related to cyber technology in the smart grid has potential vulnerabilities due to inherent security risks in the classical cyber environment.

The proliferation of increasingly sophisticated cyber threats with massive destructive effects, necessitates that smart grid security systems must systematically evolve their detection, understanding, attribution, and mitigation capabilities. Unfortunately, most of the current security systems fall short to adequately provision security services while maintaining operational continuity and stability of the targeted applications especially in presence of advanced persistent attacks. Most of these security systems use uncoordinated combinations of disparate tools to provision security services for the cyber and physical domains. Such isolation and lack of awareness of and cooperation between security tools may lead to massive resource waste due to unnecessary redundancy, and potential conflicts that can be utilized by a resourceful attacker to penetrate the system. Recent attacks against the power infrastructures such as Stuxnet have highlighted vulnerabilities and inadequacy of existing security systems. The Stuxnet worm infects the cyber domain (computers and workstations), spreads via networks and removable storage devices, and exploits four zero-day attacks to manipulate the physical equipment. The primary target is believed to be an Iranian nuclear power plant, and likely caused a 15 % drop in production of highly enriched uranium [3]. Defense against complex cyber threats such as Stuxnet, requires coordination between various security domains to address strict security concerns.

Figure 1 depicts a hierarchical model of the smart grid as a set of correlated interacting layers where each layer has a complete hierarchical layering model. At the top of the model is the grid users and system operators with direct access to the physical domain of the grid. The next layer represents the physical systems and components participating in the generation, transmission, distribution, and consumption sectors. The physical domain is managed and controlled by a cyber-base that provides the needed computation and communication services facilitating local control and processing operations and inter- and intra-communication between the physical and the cyber domains. The physical domain is tightly coupled to the cyber domain via a cyber-network represented by a network layer encapsulating both data and control traffics.

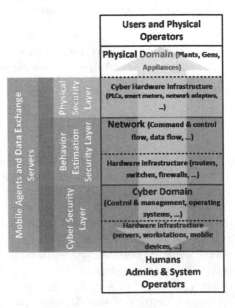

Fig. 1. Smart grid hierarchical model and layers interaction with CyNetPhy

The cyber domain is represented by two sub-layers, the cyber or the application sub-layer where the management and control logic resides, and the hardware sub-layer hosting such logic and providing the needed interfaces for data exchange. The high-level system management resides in the upper two layers, the Cyber layer where the management and control application and software are running on top of a hardware layer and operated by a set of operators and administrators.

Each layer in the presented model denotes a broad hierarchical model encapsulating interrelated sub-layers. For example the network layer in the smart grid model is a representation of the hierarchical OSI model. Most security systems addresses security of a single layer or sub-layer neglecting security concerns of other layers and interaction between interrelated layers. The smart grid with its large scale, complexity, and importance is an easy target for such at-tacks exploiting the lack of collaboration between security tools at different layers.

We advance an integrated security framework, termed CyNetPhy, supported by three main pillars namely, the Cyber Security Layer (CSL), the Behavior Estimation Layer (BEL), and the Physical Security Layer (PSL) collaborating towards enhanced smart grid security. Figure 2 illustrates The CyNetPhy multi-layer architecture.

In this article, we present a high-level description of the CyNetPhy security framework and introduce an attack scenario supported by a qualitative analysis showing the need to the CyNetPhy cross-layer security framework. For further details about the CSL,BEL, and PSL please refer to [1,2,4,8]. The remaining of this paper is organized as follows: Sect. 2 provides a brief overview of the CyNet-Phy framework. An attack scenario and a qualitative analysis of the resolution is introduced in Sect. 3. Conclusions and future work are portrayed in Sect. 4.

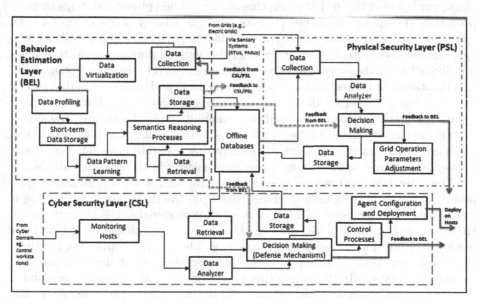

Fig. 2. The CyNetPhy architecture

2   CyNetPhy Framework Overview

The BEL monitors, analyzes and learns patterns of grid data and control flows independently extracting semantic feedback about the behavior of each grid component. The independent feedback by the BEL relies on deploying distributed dynamic reasoning models in order to fine-granulate semantics extraction processes to build efficient dynamic behavior models regarding normal/abnormal behavior of various grid components. Data profiling and dimensionality reduction techniques are used to enable efficient data storage and pattern learning. Analyzing the data flow independently from the control flow enables the BEL to spot accidental/deliberate human errors. The BEL is the intelligent part of CyNetPhy with the ability to read between the lines and initiate proactive measures to counter potential cyber threats in collaboration with the PSL and CSL.

The CSL is responsible for monitoring the cyber layer using a set of smart distributed mobile agents, pervasively crawling the systems cyber and physical domains searching for possible attack indications. In addition to the smart utilization of the agents in provisioning on-demand conventional defense services to the cyber hosts, the CSL collects host-oriented real-time feedback from its agents investigating various aspects that might to be an indication for a malicious behavior not detectable by regular techniques. The CSL is a responsible for information sharing between the three CyNetPhy security layers.

The PSL is responsible for monitoring and securing individual cyber systems with direct access to the physical domain. The cyber layer comprises a set of application-specific embedded systems and devices with clearly defined functionality and objectives. Usually cyber-attacks against this layer aim at misleading the upper layers of the grid or disrupting the underlying physical systems by compromising the operation of the cyber components. Clarity of objectives for both cyber systems and associated threats facilitates deriving security policies and specifications to protect cyber systems in the physical domain. Security policies are derived from the system physical characteristics and component operational specifications, and translated into security monitors and components that can be implemented in either hardware- or software-based platforms. Hardware-based security is preferred due to the hardware immunity against software attacks and high-performance offered by hardware [4]. The PSL collaborates with the BEL and CSL by exchanging relevant data, delivering accurate measurements about particular systems, and applying adequate measures in the physical domain.

The inter layer interaction is established through a set of circulating CSL mobile agents collecting high-level feedback from the three layers and feeding it to the data exchange servers. These servers are considered as the memory for the BEL. Patterns of maintained data in those servers are learned by the BEL for behavior estimation and semantics extraction. The security framework has three phases of operation: real-time monitoring, anomalous event investigation, and proactive actuation. In the monitoring phase the three security systems monitor and analyze real-time data and operation of the under-lying protected layers and pass abstract reports to the BEL to be analyzed at a higher abstraction level. Upon detecting anomalous or malicious behavior, the concerned layer initiates the investigation phase where the three security layers exchange relevant data to ascertain about the event and initiate the resolution procedures. In the actuation phase the concerned layer applies a set of actions and measures to resolve detected attacks. Countermeasures include raising alarms to system operators and isolating and finding suitable alternatives for infected systems.

3 Attack Scenario

To further motivate our research and to illustrate the effectiveness of CyNet-Phy in achieving its mission we utilize the following working scenario depicting a hypothetical Smart Grid attack named the BlackWidow (BW) attack. The main players are a resourceful malicious organization XYZ trying to sabotage infrastructure assets for a neighbor country. The victim in this attack is the country's smart grid, namely the power distribution section. The BW is designed to split into a set of code parts and spread in different directions and locations to decrease the probability of detection. The distribution of parts and the interconnection between them in different hosts weave a large web. This web is bi-directionally traversed to send any harvested data from the attacked target and to update the malware with new tools and missions. The BW is designed to be as generic as possible; it is not oriented to any specific application. By constructing the BW web the attacker can start to task the BW towards its designated mission based on the attackers target. BW tasks might be remotely assigned through internet or preprogrammed in internet-inaccessible locations.

The attack is designed to be stealthy by hiding from the security system sensors searching for attack signatures. The attack will target an intermediate host machine that shall host the BW command and control channel communications. In order to do so, the BW is designed to not harm the host or change any of its settings that might raise the anti-malware alerts. The malware will use minimal resources and will work in a very slow fashion not to alert the security systems of its existence. The BW uses stolen digital certificates to authenticate its existence in the host machine in the form of drivers. The only way to detect this malware is through deep analysis and investigation for the entire system component behavior, this includes both Cyber and physical components. Current oblivious defense tools that shares the same host resources with its targets cannot realize such level of awareness. Additionally, most of the physical components are always assumed to be secured by perimeter defenses with no/limited consideration to the other security measures. The attacker utilizes these limitations to his advantage as illustrated later. The malware is intended to be targeted, but due to the intentionally random deployment method, the code works in two modes as follows: (1) Benign mode where the malware infects other machines that do not belong to the target space. Those machines might be used later in case of target change, or as a base for future attacks; and (2) Malicious mode, where the BW works only on the target host systems.

3.1 Attacker Assumptions

1. The security and management system shares the same network or host with the target of attack/security system. [Note: security system might be exposed to attack by compromising the Target of Security (ToS). Additionally, stolen passwords can simply be used to modify rules of IDS, routers,firewalls, proxies, etc].
2. The ToS or major parts of it uses COTS and signature based security products.
3. The system is computationally incapable of being fully situation aware of all its components in a massive-scale network, in real-time.
4. Cyber security is oblivious of and is not coordinated with physical security to protect the target cyber- physical system.

3.2 Attack Procedures (in Air-Gapped Target)

The attacker uses phishing attack or an insider to inject the malware seed into the grid computers. The BW is programmed to search the network for connected computers then it starts using one of the zero days exploits to clone itself into these computers. The attack victims will receive parts of the malware. Each of these parts will contain a fraction of the designated mission and a simple communication module. The communications module will be used to open a direct channel with the attacker and to search and establish communication with other parts. Directions to other parts locations might be sent by the attacker to minimize the search time.

The attacker uses malware fractions to construct logical executable entities in the form of mobile software agents targeting different objectives. The first objective will be to search and infiltrate the network for data stores. The malware will sniff the network traffic searching for predetermined signatures for such locations. The second objective will be to attack such data stores using the zero day exploits and the stolen certificates to locate the power distribution planer and the RTU command and configuration credentials. The malware will frequently update the attacker of its findings based on a predetermined update methodology. After successful reception of this data, the attacker will use it to transfer the BW to the grid Command and Control Center (CCC) using a compromised RTU hocked on the grid. The CCC controls the entire grid by real-time configuration of the distributed RTUs managing the operation of the distribution centers.

The drastic effect of the attack begins when the BW use the stolen configuration credentials to reprogram the RTUs to include a set of programmed blackouts across the nation among a series set of power overloads on the transmition lines causing them to breakdown. The attacker can launch data injection attacks that propagates through the network and send fake power shortage and network overload indications. Such attacks cause imbalance between the generation and demand power which can directly result in a major financial lose.

4   Conclusions

We have presented a multi-layer model of the smart grid and a matching cross-layer remote defense and management framework, termed CyNetPhy. CyNetPhy integrates and coordinates between three interrelated and highly cooperative real-time defense systems crossing section various layers of the smart grid cyber and physical domains. We presented a complex synthetic attack scenario to illustrate the limitations and challenges of the current SG defenses. In this section, we shall discuss how CyNetPhy invalidates the attacker assumptions, the pillars that supports that attack. The first two assumptions assumed that the defense platform shares the same host with the ToS and uses a signature based COTS defense products giving the attacker the chance of disabling or even tricking the defense system. CyNetPhy presents a smart isolation of defense and control concerns into a set of stacked self-managed interconnected layers of hierarchical distributed management. CyNetPhy operates from a remote secure cloud-like platform isolating the computational needs of the defense platform from the resource constrained grid hosts. CyNetPhy delivers its monitoring and defense services through a circulating mobile agents hiding the platform heterogeneity from the defense and control. It delivers tailored defense services to each host when needed and where needed. These features invalidates the first two assumptions. CyNetPhy Layers are highly cooperative, each layer exchange its defense related feedback with the other layers through CyNetPhy brain that process such feedback and provide directed guidelines to each layer taking into consideration the current state to the other layers. Such level of global awareness invalidates the last two assumptions and the entire attack. Our future work includes building network and security threat models for CyNetPhy. These models can be used to construct a complex large-scale simulation scenario for various smart grid cyber and cyber-physical attacks, showing the effectiveness of the comprehensive CyNetPhy's subsystems in detecting and mitigating such attacks.

Acknowledgment. This work is supported by the SmartCI Research Center, Alex., Egypt.

References

1. Azab, M., Eltoweissy, M.: Defense as a service cloud for cyber-physical systems. In: 2011 7th International Conference on Collaborative Computing: Networking, Applications and Worksharing (CollaborateCom), pp. 392–401. IEEE (2011)
2. Azab, M., Eltoweissy, M.: Bio-inspired evolutionary sensory system for cyber-physical system security. In: Hassanien, A.E., Kim, T.-H., Kacprzyk, J., Awad, A.L. (eds.) Bio-inspiring Cyber Security and Cloud Services: Trends and Innovations. ISRS, vol. 70, pp. 39–69. Springer, Heidelberg (2014)
3. Chen, T.M., Abu-Nimeh, S.: Lessons from stuxnet. Computer **44**(4), 91–93 (2011)
4. Farag, M.M.: Architectural Enhancements to Increase Trust in Cyber-Physical Systems Containing Untrusted Software and Hardware. Ph.D. thesis, Virginia Polytechnic Institute and State University (2012)

5. Huang, Y.F., Werner, S., Huang, J., Kashyap, N., Gupta, V.: State estimation in electric power grids: Meeting new challenges presented by the requirements of the future grid. Signal Process. Mag. IEEE **29**(5), 33–43 (2012)
6. Kopetz, H.: Real-time systems: design principles for distributed embedded applications. Springer, Heidelberg (2011)
7. Liu, Y., Ning, P., Reiter, M.K.: False data injection attacks against state estimation in electric power grids. ACM Trans. Inf. Syst. Secur. (TISSEC) **14**(1), 13 (2011)
8. Mokhtar, B., Eltoweissy, M.: Hybrid intelligence for semantics-enhanced networking operations. In: The Twenty-Seventh International Flairs Conference (2014)

Faults and Cyber Attacks Detection in Critical Infrastructures

Yannis Soupionis[✉], Stavros Ntalampiras, and Georgios Giannopoulos

Security Technology Assessment Unit, European Commission,
Joint Research Centre (JRC), Institute for the Protection and
Security of the Citizen (IPSC), Via E. Fermi 2749, 21027 Ispra, VA, Italy
{yannis.soupionis,stavros.ntalampiras,
georgios.giannopoulos}@jrc.ec.europa.eu

Abstract. In this paper we study the case of Critical Infrastructures (CIs), and especially power grid systems, which nowadays rely on computers and the Internet for their operation. We propose a combinatorial method for automatic detection and classification of faults and cyber-attacks, when there is limited data from the power grid nodes due to cyber implications. We design an experimental platform consisting of a power grid simulator and a cyber network emulator in order to demonstrate the efficiency of the proposed method.

Keywords: Critical infrastructures · Cyber security · Fault diagnosis · LTI modeling

1 Introduction

Nowadays, CIs and more specifically Distributed Control Systems (DCS) are exposed to significant cyber-threats, a fact that has been highlighted by many studies [1]. In this paper we propose a method able to automatically detect and classify faults and/or cyber-attacks based solely on the provided communication data between the SCADA systems and the local Programmable Logic Controllers (PLCs) of *power grid* CIs. This article comprises a preliminary effort towards identifying failures in interdependent CIs [2,3].

Cyber attacks or faults occurring on the cyber layer comprise the main implication of an interdependent cyber-physical system. In [4,5] is clearly illustrated that the existing techniques are not adequate to address the series of new security challenges posed by highly complex environments. Even though, they present the significance of the cyber infrastructure security, they do not propose a detection or mitigation process. *Fault detection* systems usually operate on data coming from sensor networks. Approaches using multiple sensors detect faults by exploiting potential redundancies and/or correlations existing within the data. Here we find two lines of thought: (a) the first one exploits physical redundancy, i.e. redundant sensors [6], and (b) the second one takes advantage of analytical redundancy based on the functional relationships existing among different, but correlated, quantities [7].

© Springer International Publishing Switzerland 2016
C.G. Panayiotou et al. (Eds.): CRITIS 2014, LNCS 8985, pp. 283–289, 2016.
DOI: 10.1007/978-3-319-31664-2_29

The paper is organized as follows: Sect. 2 we explain the proposed detection and classification method. Section 3 illustrates the main elements of our implementation framework, our method's application onto a power grid, presents the examined cyber-physical implications and describes the experimental results. Finally, Sect. 4 concludes this work and identifies further research subjects.

2 The Fault Detection Method

The fault detection method is comprised of two algorithms running concurrently. It detects a fault only when both methods detect one for specific data (Fig. 1).

Let us consider an energy monitoring framework comprised of N buses and K generators each of which provides a time-series datastream. Denote by X_i : $\mathbb{N} \rightarrow \mathbb{R}$ the stream of data acquired by the i-th bus and $X_j : \mathbb{K} \rightarrow \mathbb{R}$ the stream of data acquired by the j-th generator. Let $O_{i,T_0} = \{X_i(t), t = 1, \ldots, T_0\}$ and $O_{j,T_0} = \{X_j(t), t = 1, \ldots, T_0\}$ be the data sequence of the i-th bus and the j-th generator respectively. Finally, let us assume that at an unknown time instant $T^* > T_0$ a fault occurs in the datastreams while no assumption is made about its magnitude or time profile. Specifically for the IEEE network model X_i corresponds to the V_t output per bus and X_j to the real power demand.

We designed two methods trying to detect a fault appearing the data sequence:

Limit Checking: This method checks whether the datastream of interest is withing a bandwidth specified by a maximum and a minimum value: $[U_{bound}, L_{bound}]$. In case an incoming datum $O_t, t > T_0$ is out of the bandwidth determined during the training phase, it is marked as faulty (explained in Algorithm 1).

LTI Modeling: This method models the relationships between the datastreams belonging to physical variables of the CI under study. The underlying assumption here is that the pattern of the relationship remains consistent when the system operates in a certain state (nominal, faulty, etc.). The proposed fault detection technique assumes that the relationship between two generic correlated datastreams i and j, j used to infer i, can be described through an input-output dynamic model of the form $X_i(k) = f_\theta\big(X_i(k-1), X_i(k-2), \ldots, X_i(k-k_i), X_j(k), X_j(k-1), \ldots, X_j(k-k_j)\big)$, where f is a linear function of autoregressive model with exogenous input (ARX) type in its parameters θ and k_i and k_j

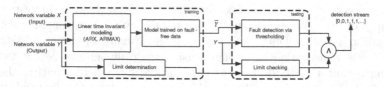

Fig. 1. The block diagram of the proposed fault detection method. The algorithm detects faulty data coming from variable Y (1 stands for detection and 0 for nominal data). Y corresponds to the V_t output per bus and X to the real power demand.

are the orders of the model. The model with the lowest reconstruction error is chosen. This process is given in Algorithm 2.

1. Identify the maximum and lower values of the training sequence $O_{i,T_0} = \{X_j(t), t = 1, \ldots, T_0\}$ as $U_{bound} = max(O_{i,1\ldots T_0}), L_{bound} = min(O_{i,1\ldots T_0})$;

repeat

    2. t=1;

    3. **if** $O_{(j,t)} > U_{bound} \vee O_{(j,t)} < L_{bound}$ **then**

        $O_{(j,t)}$ contains data associated with a fault;

    else

        $O_{(j,t)}$ contains data coming from the normally operating network;

    end

    4. $t = t + 1$;

until (1);

Algorithm 1. The limit checking fault detection algorithm.

1. Find the model $\mathbb{M}$ explaining the relationship between $X_i(k)$ and $X_j(k)$ with the lowest reconstruction error ;

2. Apply $\mathbb{M}$ on $O_{i,T_0} = \{X_i(t), t = 1, \ldots, T_0\}$ and compute the estimated data values $\bar{O}_{j,T_0} = \{\bar{X}_i(t), t = 1, \ldots, T_0\}$;

3. $T_h = max(|\bar{O}_{j,T_0} - O_{j,T_0}|)$;

repeat

    2. t=1;

    3. **if** $|\bar{O}_{j,T_0} - O_{j,T_0}| > T_h$ **then**

        $O_{(j,t)}$ contains data associated with a fault;

    else

        $O_{(j,t)}$ contains data coming from the normally operating network;

    end

    4. $t = t + 1$;

until (1);

Algorithm 2. The model based fault detection algorithm.

With respect to isolation and classification of a detection into fault, integrity attack or DDoS we rely on a distance matrix D including all the discrepancies which are observed between the actual data and the values predicted from the ARX model. More precisely, for each state we produce a distance matrix D, where $d_{ij} = |\bar{O}_{j,T_0} - O_{j,T_0}|$ given a fault on BUS i. Each line is associated with a fault occurring on a BUS, e.g. element d_{21} includes the discrepancy observed on the Voltage of BUS 1 when a fault on BUS 2 has occurred. The buses presenting faults comprise the column elements.

3   Experimental Setup and Results

Firstly, in this section we provide a brief description of the DCS architecture (simulation/emulation framework) used in this work. The used implementation framework (a) simulates the physical components of a power grid and (b) emulates the cyber elements. The real-time simulation of IEEE grid models is implemented in the Assessment platform for Multiple Interdependent Critical Infrastructures (AMICI) [8], which is based on Matlab open-source libraries,

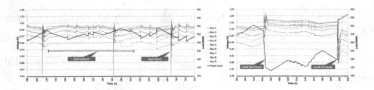

Fig. 2. Training session data graph (DoS attack on bus 9, fault on Bus 8 & load increase-decrease)

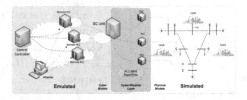

Fig. 3. The overall architecture of the simulation & emulation framework.

i.e. MatPower and MatDyn. The power grid employed in this experiment is the well-known IEEE 9-bus model (Fig. 3). Finally, the sampling rate of the simulated model is 20ms which it the time to calculate its parameters including the interaction with the emulated environment. The testbed of the *DCS cyber part* facilitating the emulation of the ICT infrastructure is based on Emulab, which is a well-established network emulator, and developed in our laboratory [9].

Our evaluation procedures follows three distinct steps. First we create a detailed case study of the virtual network topology and physical simulated power grid as described above. We should state that the simulation step is 20 ms. Secondly, the experiments are then initiated in order to collect data and train the detector. Finally, experimental scenarios are executed in order to evaluate our system's performance.

The cyber physical infrastructures implications we took into consideration are: (a) *Distributed Denial of Service Attacks:* During a DDoS attack only sparse data reach the controller, which keeps the last received value till a new one arrives. More specifically, $V_i(t) = V_i(t_0), t_0 < t < t_1$, where t_0 is the time that the last datum was received and t_1 is the time that the new datum may arrive (Fig. 2), (b) *Integrity & replay attacks:* These can be implemented either by affecting the power grid component/equipments, which are responsible for distribution systems, or by manipulating the exchanging protocol messages in order for the attacker to send malicious data to the field device or the control center operator, and (c) *Fault:* We take into account sudden losses of connectivity affecting one bus for a short period of time (fault supported by MatPower software).

During the training process a set of scenarios on the aforementioned experimental environment were simulated. The produced dataset was provided to the detection mechanism for creating a schema of the possible experimental environment states. The experimental scenarios executed for the training are (Table 1).

Table 1. Training scenarios

Scenarios	Values (V in p.u.)	Description
Normal conditions	$0.9 <= V_{busi} <= 1.1$	The power grid operates smoothly
Sudden load increase and decrease	$Load_{alteration} > 250\,\text{MW}$	The power grid reaches marginal state
Bus fault to i node	$V_{busi} \simeq 0$	Bus is down for 0.2 s
DDoS attack to i node	$V_{busi} \simeq V_{busi_{Lastreceived}}$	Bus data partially reaches central control
DDoS attack & bus fault to i node	$V_{busi} \simeq V_{busi_{Lastreceived}}$	Fault during a DDoS attack

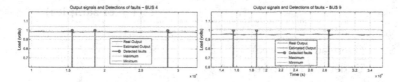

Fig. 4. DDoS attack on Bus 1: Bus 1 stops providing data and afterwards a fault occurs to it. We detect a fault on Bus 1, by consulting the distance matrix D on neighbor Buses 4 and 9.

Moreover, in Fig. 2 three specific scenario outcomes, in terms of bus voltages, are illustrated: (a) a scenario where either excessive additional consumed load is needed or a sudden consumed load drop occurs, (b) a scenario about physical faults, and (c) a scenario where a DDoS attack against a node's PLC for a limited period of time occurs.

3.1   Detection Results

The detection framework is trained on data coming from the normal modality of total length of 10000 samples. The limit checking method uses the entire length for bound estimation $[U_{bound}, L_{bound}]$. The model-based method uses the scenarios in Sect. 3 for training. The input is the exchanging data and the current state of the smart grid. The needed samples for the model training for each state are less 8000, meaning less than 2.5 min of sampling data. The model order is determined by minimizing a robustified quadratic prediction error criterion which serves the computation of the ARX parameters. Finally, the model which provided the best performances was the following ARX(2,2): $X_i(t) = a_1 X_i(t-1) + a_2 X_i(t-2) + b_1 X_j(t-1) + b_2 X_j(t-2)$, where $a_1 = 0.5$, $a_2 = 0.2$, $b_1 = 0.1$, $b_2 = 0.3$. The figures of merit are computed both on data coming from the nominal and faulty states. They are tabulated in Table 2.

The first experiment was a two events scenario: we initiated a DDoS against a node and in a few seconds we injected a fault to the same node. Even though

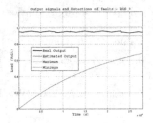

Fig. 5. Integrity attack on Bus 9: The method detects the attack since the data coming from Bus 9 is not consistent with the data provided by the rest of the buses.

Table 2. The detection results of the proposed method.

Test data type	FP (%)	FN (%)	Detection Delay (# of samples)
Nominal	0	-	-
Overload (fault-free)	0.2	-	-
Underload (fault-free)	0.5	-	-
Fault	6.1	2.7	12
DDoS	7.1	1	4.2
Integrity	10.1	2.3	5.75

the information is extremely limited from the faulty node, we have to find a way to identify that the fault was initiated from the specific node. In Fig. 4 we illustrate the method to identify the fault to one node by analyzing the input from its neighbor ones. The second scenario was an integrity attack against a single node. The integrity attack compromised the node's PLC and force the sending of false logical data to the central control. For example, the attacker has previously implemented a Man-in-the-Middle attack, copied the transmitted data and now is able to replicate it. In Fig. 5 we demonstrate the operation of the proposed fault diagnosis system when an integrity attack takes place.

We conducted experiments with most of the nodes and we claim that our method is able to predict the malicious state close to 98 % (Table 2). In addition Table 2 provides the FPs, FNs and delays with respect to every faulty/attack situation.

4   Conclusions and Further Research

In this paper, we provided an automatic method for detecting and classifying cyber implications and physical faults affecting a power grid infrastructure for enhancing the overall resilience. The method is able to identify the power grid node state even when the node is unreachable or off-line or exchanging data is malformed. The method was evaluated not only on theoretical level but also in practice, by combining a simulated power grid and an emulated ICT network. Further research includes: (a) evaluate the method on real-world datasets, and (b) identify the state of larger networks based on narrow incoming information.

References

1. Ten, C.W., Liu, C.C., Manimaran, G.: Vulnerability assessment of cybersecurity for scada systems. Power Syst. IEEE Trans. **23**(4), 1836–1846 (2008)
2. Zio, E., Sansavini, G.: Modeling interdependent network systems for identifying cascade-safe operating margins. Reliab. IEEE Trans. **60**(1), 94–101 (2011)
3. Kotzanikolaou, P., Theoharidou, M., Gritzalis, D.: Accessing n-order dependencies between critical infrastructures. Int. J. Crit. Infrastruct. **9**(1–2), 93–110 (2013)
4. Mo, Y., Kim, T.-H., Brancik, K., Dickinson, D., Lee, H., Perrig, A., Sinopoli, B.: Cyber - physical security of a smart grid infrastructure. In: Proceedings of the IEEE, vol. 100, no. 1, pp. 195–209, January 2012
5. Sridhar, S., Hahn, A., Govindarasu, M.: Cyber - physical system security for the electric power grid. Proc. IEEE **100**(1), 210–224 (2012)
6. Goebel, K., Yan, W.: Correcting sensor drift and intermittency faults with data fusion and automated learning. IEEE Syst. **2**(2), 189–197 (2008)
7. Napolitano, M.R., Windon, D.A., Casanova, J.L., Innocenti, M., Silvestri, G.: Kalman filters and neural network schemes for sensor validation in flight control systems. IEEE Trans. Control Syst. Technol. **6**(5), 596–611 (1998)
8. Genge, B., Siaterlis, C., Hohenadel, M.: AMICI: An assessment platform for multi-domain security experimentation on critical infrastructures. In: Hämmerli, B.M., Kalstad Svendsen, N., Lopez, J. (eds.) CRITIS 2012. LNCS, vol. 7722, pp. 228–239. Springer, Heidelberg (2013)
9. Siaterlis, C., Garcia, A., Genge, B.: On the use of Emulab testbeds for scientifically rigorous experiments. IEEE Commun. Surveys Tuts. **15**(2), 929–942 (2012)

Security Tools and Protocols

Recovering Structural Controllability on Erdős-Rényi Graphs via Partial Control Structure Re-Use

Bader Alwasel[1] and Stephen D. Wolthusen[1,2(✉)]

[1] School of Mathematics and Information Security, Royal Holloway,
University of London, Egham TW20 0EX, UK
Bader.Alwasel.2012@live.rhul.ac.uk
[2] Norwegian Information Security Laboratory, Faculty of Computer Science,
Gjøvik University College, Gjøvik, Norway
stephen.wolthusen@rhul.ac.uk

Abstract. Large-scale distributed control systems such as those encountered in electric power networks or industrial control systems must be assumed to be vulnerable to attacks in which adversaries can take over control over at least part of the control network by compromising a subset of nodes. In this paper we study *structural controllability* properties of the control graph in LTI systems, addressing the question of how to efficiently re-construct a control graph as far as possible in the presence of such compromised nodes.

We study the case of sparse Erdős-Rényi Graphs with directed control edges and seek to provide an approximation of an efficient reconstructed control graph by minimising control graph diameter. As the underlying POWER DOMINATING SET problem does not permit efficient re-computation, we propose to reduce the average-case complexity of the recovery algorithm by re-using remaining fragments of the original, efficient control graph where possible and identifying previously un-used edges to re-join these fragments to a complete control graph, validating that all constraints are satisfied in the process. Whilst the worst-case complexity is not improved, we obtain an enhanced average-case complexity that offers a substantial improvement where sufficiently many fragments of the original control graph remain, as would be the case where an adversary can only take over regions of the network and thereby control graph.

Keywords: Structural controllability · Control systems resilience · POWER DOMINATING SET

1 Introduction

Controllability and observability form core concepts in the study of control systems and networks, as it determines the ability to monitor or force the state of a system. As the computational complexity of determining Kalman controllability

© Springer International Publishing Switzerland 2016
C.G. Panayiotou et al. (Eds.): CRITIS 2014, LNCS 8985, pp. 293–307, 2016.
DOI: 10.1007/978-3-319-31664-2_30

makes this problematic for time-critical large networks such as electric power networks, more general properties are of particular interest. The problem of structural controllability originally defined by Lin [1] offers such a graph-theoretical interpretation of controllability, which is particularly suitable for studying sets of nodes able to control an entire system as represented by a control graph (the reader is referred to [1–3]); the identification of minimum Driver Nodes (*DN*) via maximum matchings was proposed by Liu *et al.* [2] as a powerful mechanism, but also offering full control over the network for possible attackers seeking to take over or disrupt these relations. Both attackers and defenders can hence identify nodes of particular interest, thereby strongly motivating the development of algorithms for identifying such sets of *DN*, particularly after an attack or reconfiguration of the underlying network. This offers a strong motivation to study the ability of such systems to recover from deliberate attacks. Informally, controllability requires that a desired configuration can be forced from an arbitrary configuration in a finite number of steps; for a time-dependent linear dynamical system:

$$\dot{x}(t) = \mathbf{A}x(t) + \mathbf{B}u(t), \qquad x(t_0) = x_0 \tag{1}$$

with $x(t) = (x_1(t), \ldots, x_n(t))^T$ the current state of a system with n nodes at time t, a $n \times n$ adjacency matrix $\mathbf{A}$ representing the network topology of interactions among nodes, and $\mathbf{B}$ the $n \times m$ *input* matrix ($m \leq n$), identifying the set of nodes controlled by a time-dependent *input vector* $u(t) = (u_1(t), \ldots, u_m(t))$ which forces the desired state. The system in Eq. 1 is *controllable* if and only if rank$[\mathbf{B}, \mathbf{AB}, \mathbf{A}^2\mathbf{B}, \ldots, \mathbf{A}^{n-1}\mathbf{B}] = n$ (*Kalman rank criterion*), giving the mathematical condition for controllability, where the rank of the controllability matrix provides the dimension of the controllable subspace of the system (A, B). As verifying the criterion is prohibitively expensive [2,3], efficient ways to achieve structural controllability of LTI systems has been extensively studied in recent years, also regarding robustness [4–6].

We study structural controllability via the POWER DOMINATING SET (PDS) problem introduced by Haynes [7], for more details we refer the reader to [8–10], and in this paper propose an algorthim for solving PDS in directed Erdős-Rényi graphs. For this we assume that parts of an existing PDS for the original graph, such as after an attack, and rely on a Depth-First Search and articulation points (cut-vertices), allowing faster re-construction of PDS, and ultimately the regaining of control for operators of control systems.

2   Preliminary Definitions and Notation

Let $G = (V, E)$ be a directed graph. A vertex u is called an out-neighbour of a vertex v if there is a directed edge from v to u in G. Similarly, u is called an in-neighbour of v if the directed edge (u, v) is present. The neighbourhood of a vertex v in the graph G, denoted $N_G(v)$, is the set $N_G(v) = u \in V : uv \in E$. The members of $N_G(v)$ are called the open neighbours of v. The closed neighbourhood of a vertex v, denoted $N_G[v]$, is the set $N_G[v] = N_G(v) \cup v$. The degree of a vertex

v is denoted by $d_G(v)$. The number of out-neighbours of v is called the out-degree of v and is denoted by $d_G^+(v)$, the in-degree $d_G^-(v)$ is defined as the number in-degree of v. Let T_v denote the subtree of T rooted at T-node v. A path in G from a vertex u to a vertex v is a sequence of distinct vertices $u = v_0, v_1, \ldots, v_t = v$ so that (v_i, v_{i+1}), $i = 0, \ldots, t-1$, are in $E(G)$. A path from u to v together with the edge (vu) is called a cycle. We denote $\{E^t, E^f, E^c, E^b\}$ tree, forward, cross and back edges respectively.

3   Related Work

Non-trivial control systems and controlled networks are necessarily sparse, and direct control of all nodes in such a network is not feasible as direct edges to these would typically result in too high costs as well as an out-degree of the controller node that would be difficult to realise in larger networks. Instead, the general case to be considered is for control to be indirect. However, as control systems will seek to minimise parameters such as latency, the formulation of PDS by Haynes *et al.* [7] extended the classic DOMINATING SET (DS) problem to seek a minimal POWER DOMINATING SET where the covering rule is the same as in DS with a propagation rule. Here we consider a straightforward extension to directed graphs in Definition 1.

Definition 1 (Directed PDS). *Let G be a directed graph. Given a set of vertices $S \subseteq V(G)$, the set of vertices power-dominated by S, denoted by $P(S)$, is obtained as:*

D1 *If a vertex v is in S, then v and all of its out-neighbors are in $P(S)$;*
D2 *(Propagation) if a vertex v is in $P(S)$, one of its out-neighbors denoted by w is not in $P(S)$, and all other out-neighbors of v are in $P(S)$, then w is inserted into $P(S)$.*

One problem immediately arising from vertex removal from a minimal power dominating set is the *reconstruction* and recovery of control. However, even the basic minimal DS problem is known to be **NP**-complete with a polynomial-time approximation factor of $\Theta(\log n)$ as shown by Feige [11]. The approach by Feige gives a polynomial-time solution for graphs with maximum out-degree 2, otherwise the best currently known approach gives exponential time in **PSPACE**, as shown recently for cubic graphs by Binkele-Raible and Fernau [12], requiring a trade-off in the complexity against the achievable approximation factor. Guo *et al.* [10] proposed a linear dynamic programming (DP) algorithm based on valid orientations for optimally solving PDS on graphs of bounded tree-width, introducing the notion of valid orientations for a new formulation of PDS (over undirected graphs). Computational complexity is dominated by determination of the mapping A_i for a join node, where for each bag state s we need to consider all pairs of compatible bag states of its two children, yielding $O(nc^{k^2})$ complexity with n the tree node set size. Subsequently, Aazami and Stilp [13] reformulated *Directed PDS* (DPDS) as valid colourings of edges and proposed a DP algorithm for DPDS where the underlying undirected graph has bounded tree-width.

In earlier work, we proposed a reconstruction algorithm for the partition elements of (directed) control graphs of bounded tree width embedded in Erdős-Rényi random graphs arising after attacks [14] yielding a best-case complexity (where uncovered vertices W of H_i are not **join** nodes) is $\mathcal{O}(nc^k)$, a worst-case complexity of $\mathcal{O}(nc^{k^2})$, and an average complexity of $\mathcal{O}(\log nc^{k^2})$.

3.1   The Physical Concept of a Graph-Theoretical Interpretation for Electrical Power Networks

We motivate our study by the real-time monitoring and control of electrical power networks as defined by a set of state variables. The PDS problem allows us to minimise the number of sensors such as phasor measurement units (PMU) and hence cost whilst still maintaining observability and controllability. Roughly, a system is said to be *observable* if all state variables can be determined from a given set of variables.

Let G = (V,E) be a graph representing a power network, where vertices represent nodes (a *bus* where transmission lines, loads, and generators are connected) and an edge represents a transmission line joining nodes. The problem of locating a smallest set of sensors to monitor the entire system is a graph theory problem introduced by Haynes et al. as a model for studying electric power networks and their efficient monitoring as an extension to the well-known DOMINATING SET (DS) problem; one of the classic decision problems [7–9].

4   Problem and Approach

We seek to reduce the average-case complexity through partial re-use of PDS fragments retaining after a graph has been modified e.g. by and attack on a control system, and apply the valid colouring proposed in [13]. This re-use allows the reduction of average-case computational complexity through

1. Finding articulation points (cut-vertices) of degree ≥ 2, as the sub-tree T_v of a cut-vertex v are connected by tree edges (no back, forward, and cross edges are incident to vertices in T_v) and downstream of v, then v power-dominates vertices in T_v,
2. The algorithm only computes the red edges forming flow of control and does not need to consider other edge colours as originally proposed by Aazami and Stilp [13],
3. Minimising checks for dependency cycles as the DFS approach does not require colouring of back edges,
4. Minimising a PDS by using forward and cross edges, where there are at most $2^{N(v)}$ states of colouring the neighbours of $v \in PDS$, and
5. Relying on existing PDS and a DFS allows to consider only *uncovered* vertices $H_i(V_i^{un})$, where the total time is $O(|V_i^{un} + \left\{ E_i^t \cup E_i^f [N(v)] \cup E_i^c [N(v)] \right\} \setminus E_i^b|)$ time, where $v \in PDS$, with $2^{N(v)}$ states of colouring the neighbours of $v \in PDS$. However, the worst-case complexity of the algorithm is

$O(|V_i + \left\{ E_i^t \cup E_i^f \left[N(v) \right] \cup E_i^c \left[N(v) \right] \right\} \setminus E_i^b|)$ through computing the all vertices in the partition elements.

4.1 Assumptions

We rely on a number of assumptions:

1. Given a directed graph $G = (V, E)$, constructed as $ER(n, p)$. Any ordered pair of vertices $u, v \in V(G)$ is connected with the edge probability p by a directed edge, such that there is a directed edge $e = \{u, v\} \in E(G)$ from u to v. For the resulting instances of G, we consider the directed graphs where the underlying undirected graph has bounded tree-width and have no self-loops nor parallel edges, but may have two edges with different directions on the same two end vertices (called antiparallel edges) and may have directed cycles. We assume that an instance of PDS for G is given, and is generated by our algorithm in [14] in terms of the valid colouring, where a set of vertices $S \subseteq V(G)$, denoted by $P(S)$, power dominates G if $P(S) = V(G)$.
2. The resulting graph G is partitioned into k subgraphs $H_1, H_2, \ldots H_k$, where $1 \leq i \leq k$, such that the partition of G satisfies:
   - $\forall H_i : V_i \neq \emptyset$
   - $\forall (i, j) \in \{1, \ldots k\}, i \neq j, V_i \cap V_j = \emptyset$
   - The union of V_i is equal to $V(G)$, where $\bigcup_{1 \leq i \leq k} V_i = V(G)$

   Each subgraph $H_i = (V_i, E_i)$ is weakly connected (i.e., the underlying undirected subgraph is connected). All subgraphs H_i are assumed to contain a tree-embedding,
3. For a set of subgraphs of G, there exists a set of vertices $u, v \in V_i, V_j$, respectively, where $1 \leq i, j \leq k$, such that $\forall i, j: \exists u \in V_i, v \in V_j$: $((u, v) \in E(G)) \wedge ((u, v) \notin E_i) \wedge ((v, u) \notin E_j)$.
4. Given arbitrary partition elements $H_i = (V_i, E_i)$ of a directed graph G, where a PDS of the partition elements may be different of the remaining of G's PDS. This requires (re-)construction of PDS for partition elements H_i.

5   Reconstructing DPDS via DFS

Depth-first search (DFS) can be used to seek edges of the partition elements of H_i, identifying *articulation points* and constructing the H_i as a tree-like structure, which gives equivalent characterisations of trees. DFS separates edges into groups revealing information on partition elements, and articulation points (cut-vertices) giving an equivalent formulation for identifying PDS in undirected graphs as shown by [8] for block graphs. An articulation point is a vertex whose removal (together with the removal of any incident edges) results in a disconnected graph. There are several well-known efficient algorithms; for a construction relying on DFS, this is $O(V + E)$. Based on this we identify articulation points on DPDS:

Definition 2 *(Observations on Articulation Point and PDS).* *Given the partition elements $H_i = (V_i, E_i)$ of a digraph G constructed by DFS, an articulation point u is said to be $u \in PDS$ if it satisfies*

1. *The root r of the DFS tree is an articulation if $d^+(r) \geq 2$ is connected by a tree edge, and no cross edges between the subtrees of the root,*
2. *Any other internal vertex v in the DFS tree (other than the root), if it has a subtrees rooted at a child of v such that there is no back edge from any vertex in this subtrees connected to a higher level vertex than v and $d^+(v) \geq 2$, is an articulation point,*
3. *A vertex v is $\in PDS$ if $d^+(v) \geq 2$ connected by a tree edge, and there exists a cross edge that is incident from the subtrees of v to neither an ancestor or descendant of v (or inversely), or a back edge connected to a higher level vertex than v, .*
4. *If a vertex v has only one child (i.e., $d^+(v) \geq 1$ and $d^-(v) = 0$), then $v \in PDS$,*
5. *A leaf vertex is not an articulation point as its removal from a tree does not affect the rest of the tree, thus the tree remains connected.*

We now can define four edge types produced by DFS on the partition elements of a digraph $H_i = (V_i, E_i)$:

Definition 3 *(DFS Edge Classification).* *During executing DFS on graph G, edges can be classified by type:*

- *If v is visited for the first time as we traverse the edge (u, v), then the edge is **a tree edge**. A tree edge always describes a relation between a vertex and one of its direct descendants*
- *If v has already been visited:*
  1. *If v is an ancestor of u, then edge (u, v) is a* back edge *(i.e. connecting a vertex u to an ancestor v in DFS tree (self-loop), which may occur in directed graphs)*
  2. *If v is a descendant of u, then edge (u, v) is a forward edge (i.e., non-tree edges (u, v) connecting a vertex u to a descendant v in DFS tree)*
  3. *If v is neither an ancestor or descendant of u, then edge (u, v) is a cross edge*

When drawing diagrams, we represent edges by line types $\{t, b, f, c\}$, where a solid line (t) represents a tree edge _____, a dotted line (b) a back edge ...., a dashed line (f) a forward edge _ _ _ _ _, and a dash-dotted line (c) a cross edge _._._._., respectively.

Theorem 1. *Given the partition elements $H_i = (V_i, E_i)$ of a directed graph G, $v \in PDS$ is said to be an articulation point (cut-vertex) if it satisfies*

1. *v has more than one child connected through a tree edge where $d^+_{E_i^t}(v) \geq 2$,*
2. *there is no back edge that is incident from any child x in the subtrees of v such that x is connected to a higher level vertex than v (Fig. 1a),*

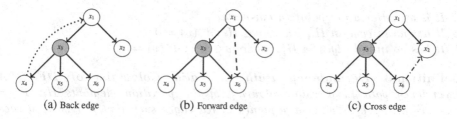

(a) Back edge   (b) Forward edge   (c) Cross edge

Fig. 1. Articulation points with different edge types

3. there is no forward edge that is incident from an ancestor of v to any child in the subtrees of v (Fig. 1b), and
4. there is no cross edge that is incident from the subtrees of v to neither an ancestor or descendant of v (or vice versa), (Fig. 1c).

Proof. Assume that DFS contains $\{x_1, x_2, \ldots, x_n\}$ rooted at x_1, and suppose that there exists a vertex x_3 with more than one child, where $d^+(x_3) \geq 2$, and one of its children is connected to the ancestor of x_3 by a back edge (x_4, x_1) (Fig. 1a). Proof is by contradiction in three cases (using Fig. 1 to demonstrate the construction):

1. If one of the subtrees (here: x_4) of x_3 are connected to an ancestor of x_3 by a back edge (Fig. 1a), then a vertex x_4 is still connected to an ancestor of x_3 by a back edge after omitting x_3. Therefore, x_3 is not an articulation point.
2. If there exists a vertex x_6 of the subtrees of x_3 connected to the ancestor of x_3 by a forward edge (Fig. 1b), then x_6 is still connected to G after omitting x_3, thus x_3 is not an articulation point.
3. If there exists a vertex x_6 of the subtrees of x_3 connected to neither an ancestor or descendant of x_3 by a cross edge (Fig. 1c), then after removing x_3, x_6 will be connected to G, thus x_3 is not an articulation point.

We can now reformulate PDS of the partition elements of directed graph in terms of valid colourings of (similar to the formulation by [10], where blue and red edges play the same role as unoriented and oriented edges, respectively) to obtain DPDS. Our approach applies to the partition elements of a directed graph such partition elements are structured by DFS:

Definition 4 (Colouring of the Partition Elements of a Directed Graph). *A colouring of the partition elements $H_i = (V_i, E_i)$ of a directed graph G is colouring the edges in H_i in red. We denote the colouring by $C = (V_i, E_i^r)$ where E_i^r is the set of red edges.*

Definition 5 (Origin of Valid Colouring). *We refer to a vertex as an origin of the colouring of the partition elements $H_i = (V_i, E_i)$ of a directed graph G if it satisfies one of:*

1. *It is an articulation point (a cut-vertex).*
2. *It has no in-edge in H_i, where $v \in H_i : d^-(v) = 0$*
3. *It has no in-red edges in H_i^r, where $v \in H_i^r : d^-(v) = 0$.*

Definition 6 (Dependency Path in Valid Colouring of DFS). *A dependency path in a valid colouring of the partition elements H_i, $P = v_1, e_1, v_2, e_2, \ldots, e_{i-1}, v_i$ is a sequence of red edges such that P has no a back edge coloured red (i.e. all red edges are directed away from the start vertex (v_1) of P and ends in a vertex (v_i)). The length of a dependency path is defined as the number of red edges in the path. A dependency cycle in a directed graph is a sequence of directed edges whose underlying undirected graph forms a cycle such that all the red edges are in one direction, and a red back edge in the other direction.*

Definition 7 (Valid Colouring of Partition Elements). *A valid colouring of edges of the partition elements $H_i = (V_i, E_i)$ of a directed graph G is a colouring of H_i satisfying*

1. *An origin of the colouring of the partition elements in $H_i^r = (V_i, E_i^r)$ satisfies:*
    (a) *The root of DFS may exist a cut-vertex, denoted by ($v_{R_{ct}}$), with out-degree at least 2 and no in-edge incident to ($v_{R_{ct}}$) with no cross edge between the subtrees of ($v_{R_{ct}}$), **has** at least 2 out-red edges:*

    $$\exists v \in V(H_i) : \Big(\big(d_{H_i}^-(v_{R_{ct}}) = 0 \big) \wedge \big(d_{H_i}^+(v_{R_{ct}}) \geq 2 \big) \wedge \big(\forall \text{ child } x \text{ of } (v_{R_{ct}}) :$$
    $$E_i^c(x) = \emptyset \big) \Big) \Longrightarrow d_{H_i^r}^+(v_{R_{ct}}) \geq 2$$

    (b) *The root of DFS, denoted by v_R, with out-degree at least 2 and no in-edge incident to v_R and there is at least one cross edge between the subtrees of v_R, **has** at least 2 out-red edges (i.e., v_R is not cut-vertex):*

    $$\exists v \in V(H_i) : \Big(\big(d_{H_i}^-(v_R) = 0 \big) \wedge \big(d_{H_i}^+(v_R) \geq 2 \big) \wedge \big(\exists \text{ child } x \text{ of } v_R :$$
    $$E_i^c(x) \geq 1 \big) \Big) \Longrightarrow d_{H_i^r}^+(v_R) \geq 2$$

    (c) *There may exist a cut-vertex, denoted by v_{ct}, with out-degree at least 2 and no in-red edge incident to $E_{H_i^r}(v_{ct})$ and no cross edges between the subtrees of v_{ct} and no back edge incident to an ancestor of v_{ct}, **has** at least 2 out-red edges:*

    $$\exists v \in V(H_i) : \Big(\big(d_{H_i^r}^-(v_{ct}) = 0 \big) \wedge \big(d_{H_i}^+(v_{ct}) \geq 2 \big) \wedge \big(\forall \text{ child } x \text{ of } v_{ct} :$$
    $$E_i^c(x) = \emptyset \wedge E_i^b(x) = 0 \big) \Big) \Longrightarrow d_{H_i^r}^+(v_{ct}) \geq 2$$

(d) *There may exist a domination vertex, denoted by v_D, with out-degree at least 2 and no in-red edge incident to $E_{H_i^r}(v_D)$ and there is at least one cross edge between the subtrees of v_D or back edge incident to an ancestor of v_D, **has** at least 2 out-red edges (i.e. V_D is no cut-vertex):*

$$\exists v \in V(H_i) : \Big((d_{\overline{H_i^r}}(v_D) = 0) \wedge (d_{H_i}^+(v_D) \geq 2) \wedge (\exists \ child \ x \in v_D :$$

$$E_i^c(x) \geq 1 \vee E_i^b(x) geq 1) \Big) \Longrightarrow d_{H_i^r}^+(v_D) \geq 2$$

(e) *There may exist a simple vertex, denoted by v_S, with no in-degree and at least out-degree of exactly one, **has** at least one out-red edge:*

$$\exists v \in V(H_i) : \Big((d_{\overline{H_i}}(v_S) = 0) \wedge (d_{H_i}^+(v_S) \geq 1) \Big) \Longrightarrow d_{H_i^r}^+(v_S) \geq 1$$

2. *The remaining vertices in $\{H_i \setminus (v_{R_{ct}} \cup v_R \cup v_{ct} \cup v_D \cup v_S)\}$ covered by the red edges in $H_i^r = (V_i, E_i^r)$ have the following properties:*
   (a) $\forall v \in H_i : d_{\overline{H_i^r}}(v) \leq 1$, *and*
   (b) $\forall v \in H_i : d_{\overline{H_i^r}}(v) = 1 \Longrightarrow d_{H_i^r}^+(v) \leq 1$.
3. H_i *has no dependency cycle.*

Note that a vertex with $d_{\overline{H_i^r}}(v) = 0$ in $H_i^r = (V_i, E_i^r)$ is an origin, denoted by Φ, of C.

We can now define the colouring of neighbours of PDS vertices:

Definition 8 (*Colouring of a PDS Vertex' Neighbours*). *In order to obtain an optimal PDS in H_i, we define two colours for $N(v)$ where $v \in PDS$ depending on forward and cross edges which are incident from $u \in PDS$ to $N(v)$, such that a colouring of the neighbours of PDS in $H_i = (V_i, E_i)$ of a digraph G is a colouring of $N(v)$ satisfying:*

- *A gray colour is assigned to each neighbour $V_{H_i}(w)$ of $v \in PDS$ that has a forward edge incident from v to $w \in N(u)$ where $u \in PDS$, (Fig. 2a):*

$$\exists v, u \in PDS : \Big(\exists w \in N(u) : E_i^f(v, w) \Big)$$

- *An orange colour is assigned to each neighbour $V_{H_i}(w)$ of $v \in PDS$ with a cross edge satisfying:*
  1. *there exists a cross edge (v, w) that is incident from $v \in PDS$ to $w \in N(u)$ where $u \in PDS$, (Fig. 2b):*

$$\exists (v, w) \in E_c : \Big((v, u \in PDS) \wedge (w \in N(u)) \Big)$$

  2. *there exists a cross edge (u, w) between the subtrees of an ancestor $v \in PDS$ incident from $u \in N(v)$ to $w \in N(v)$ and the vertex u is a leaf or has no out-red edge (Fig. 2c):*

$$\exists (u, w) \in E_i^c : \Big((v \in PDS) \wedge (u, w \in N(v)) \wedge (d_{E_i}^+(u) = 0 \vee d_{E_i^r}^+(u) = 0) \Big)$$

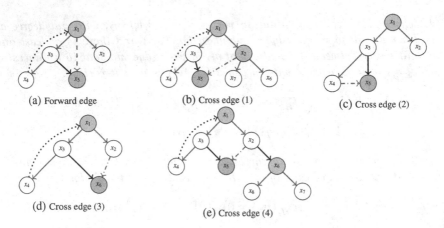

(a) Forward edge   (b) Cross edge (1)   (c) Cross edge (2)

(d) Cross edge (3)   (e) Cross edge (4)

Fig. 2. Case enumeration for colouring PDS vertex neighbours

3. *there exists a cross edge* (v,w) *incident from a leaf vertex* v *such that* $E_t^+(v) = 0$ *to* $w \in N(u)$ *where* $u \in PDS$, *(Fig. 2d):*

$$\exists(v,w) \in E_c : \Big((u \in PDS) \wedge (w \in N(u)) \wedge (E_t^+(v) = 0)\Big)$$

4. *there exists a cross edge* (v,w) *incident from a vertex* v *with no out-red edge such that* $d_{H_i^r}^+(v) = 0$ *to a vertex* $w \in N(u)$ *where* $u \in PDS$, *(Fig. 2e):*

$$\exists(v,w) \in E_c : \Big((u \in PDS) \wedge (d_{H_i^r}^+(v) = 0) \wedge (w \in N(u))\Big).$$

We observe that we have at most $2^{N(v)}$ colouring states for the neighbours of the $v \in PDS$. We therefore seek to employ the valid coloring of $N(v)$ to reduce the state space by utilising forward and cross edges drawing on the following lemma due to Guo [10]:

Lemma 1 *(Guo et al. [10]).* *Let* $C = (V_i, E_i^r)$ *denote a valid colouring of a directed graph* G *with origin* $\Phi \subseteq V_i$:

1. *For each* $v \in V_i \setminus \Phi$, *there is exactly one directed path from the vertices in* Φ *to* v.
2. *Two directed paths from* Φ *to distinc vertices in* $V_i \setminus \Phi$ *are vertex-disjoint with the possible exception of their tail endpoints in* Φ.

Together with Lemma 1, we prove the next lemma:

Lemma 2. *Given power dominating set* $S \subseteq V_i$ *in* $H_i(V_i)$, *the number of dependency paths of* $v \in S$ *is equal to the number of neighbours of* v.

Proof. Assume that $v \in S$, by applying rule D1 for PDS, all v's neighbours are power dominated such that for each vertex $u \in N(v)$, there is exactly one directed edge from the vertex v to u. For instance, if $v \in S$ has the out-degree of 3 (i.e., $d^+(v) = 3$), then the number of dependency paths that are incident from v is also 3.

Let assume that there exists $w \in N(v)$ that is not covered yet. In the case, w should be covered in two ways:

1. there exists en edge (z, w) that is incident from $z \in S$ to w. Since there is no another edge that is incident to w excpet the one coming from v, w is still not covered, or
2. there exists a vertex $x \in V_i \setminus S$, where x is already covered, that has an edge $(e = xw)$ to w, and that would imply $d^+(x) > 1$ which is not allowed by Definition 7.

Thus, all the neighbours of v should be power dominated by v, meaning the number of directed paths that are incident from v is the same as the number of v's neighbours. As a result, the minimisation of the covered neighbours by v results in the reduction of dependency paths and, therefore, leads to reduce PDS in H_i.

Definition 9. *(Minimising PDS by Colouring Forward and Cross Edges). Edges (u, w) are coloured red if and only if:*

1. *It is a forward edge (u, w) incident from $u \in PDS$ to $w \in N(v)$ where $v \in PDS$, (Fig. 2a):*

$$\exists e = (u, w) \in E_i^f : \Big((u, v \in PDS) \wedge (w \in N(v)) \Big)$$

2. *It is a cross edge (u, w) incident from $u \in PDS$ to $w \in N(v)$ where $v \in PDS$, (Fig. 2b):*

$$\exists e = (u, w) \in E_i^c : \Big((u, v \in PDS) \wedge (w \in N(v)) \Big)$$

3. *It is a cross edge (u, w) between the subtrees of an ancestor $v \in PDS$ incident from $u \in N(v)$ to $w \in N(v)$, and the vertex u is a leaf or has no out-red edge (Fig. 2c):*

$$\exists (u, w) \in E_i^c : \Big((v \in PDS) \wedge (u, w \in N(v)) \wedge (d_{E_i}^+(u) = 0 \vee d_{E_i^r}^+(u) = 0) \Big)$$

4. *It is a cross edge (u, w) incident from a leaf vertex $(E_t^+(u) = 0)$ to $w \in N(v)$, where $v \in PDS$, (Fig. 2d):*

$$\exists e = (u, w) \in E_i^c : \Big((E_t^+(u) = 0) \wedge (v \in PDS) \wedge (w \in N(v)) \Big)$$

5. *There exists a cross edge (u, w) incident from a vertex u with no out-red edge such that $d^+_{H^r_i}(u) = 0$ to a vertex $w \in N(v)$ where $v \in PDS$, (Fig. 2e):*

$$\exists (u, w) \in E^c_i : \Big((v \in PDS) \wedge (d^+_{H^r_i}(u) = 0) \wedge (w \in N(v)) \Big).$$

We can now formulate the relationship between the DFS tree and PDS:

Theorem 2. *Given a digraph G structured by DFS, colouring the neighbours of $v \in PDS$ depending on the forward and cross edges will give a PDS in G.*

Proof. Suppose that given digraph G matching the Fig. 2a, by applying the rules of PDS, regardless of forward and cross edges, then $\{x_1, x_3\}$ are PDS in G. Since there is a forward edge that is incident from $x_1 \in PDS$ to a neighbour x_6 of x_3, then one can take an advantage of the edge to minimise the number of PDS to become one. Thus, x_6 should be coloured to achieve a minimum PDS in G. Now, let assume that there exists a cross edge in G. According to Definition 9, there are four cases of colouring a cross edge. Consider only the first case matching Fig. 2b, by applying the same argument above, the number of PDS in G can be $\{x_1, x_2, x_3\}$. Becuase of the cross edge (x_2, x_5), the vertices in PDS are reduced to two $\{x_1, x_2\}$, hence in the case, a vertex x_5 that a cross edge is incident to it should be coloured. We observe that a directed graph has a cycle if and only if DFS finds a back edge, as a result, it can form a dependency cycle in the partition elements of G. Thus, a back edge is not considered in valid colourings of H_i (consider Fig. 2a, colouring the back edge (x_4, x_1) can lead to a dependency cycle in H_i). A valid colouring of partition elements hence has no dependency cycle (Definition 7).

We may now formulate a bottom-up DP algorithm generating PDS for partition elements H_i based on earlier results [10,13,14] and the following theorem:

Theorem 3. (Partition Colouring). *Given the partition elements $H_i = (V_i, E_i)$ of a digraph G constructed by DFS and $S \subseteq V(H_i)$, S power dominates H_i if and only if there is a valid colouring of H_i with S as the set of origins.*

Proof. Assume $S \in V(H_i)$ is a PDS of partition elements H_i; thus, $P(S) = V(H_i)$. We apply a valid colouring C with S as the set of sources by colouring the edges in H_i according to the degree constraints in Definition 7. We colour an edge (u, v) red from u toward v if either u is a domination vertex and v is covered by applying **D1** on u, or vertex v is covered by applying the propagation rule **D2** on u. Note that all possible domination and the propagation rules to S should be in order. Moreover, we do not apply **D1** or **D2** to cover previously covered vertices. It is easy to check that with this colouring the degree constraints of Definition 7 are satisfied. We can now show by contradiction that there is no dependency cycle in the valid colouring. Let $u \rightarrow v$ denote a vertex v power dominated by a vertex u, assume further that $C = u_1, u_2, \ldots, u_m$ is a dependency cycle and all red edges in C are in the same (i.e. forward) direction. Red edges (u_i, u_{i+1}) imply

---

Algorithm 1. Generation of DPDS

Input: Given partition elements $H_i = (V_i, E_i)$ of a digraph G constructed by
      DFS, with DFS traversal resulting in tree T based on tree edges
Output: An minimum PDS of H_i

1   Let the inner vertices of T be sorted as L based on tree edges in post-order
    traversal of T, where r is a root of T and bottom-up DP from leaves to root.
2   Let $P \leftarrow \emptyset$
3   **while** $L \neq r$ **do**
4 | $v \leftarrow$ the first vertex in L;
5 | $L \leftarrow L \setminus \{v\}$
6 | **if** $d^+(v) \geq 2$ *are uncovered children* **then**
7 | | **if** (v) *is a cut-vertex* **then**
8 | | | $P \leftarrow P \cup \{v_{ct}\}$;
9 | | | Apply valid colouring for all vertices downstream of v;
10 | | **else**
11 | | | $P \leftarrow P \cup \{v\}$;
12 | | | Apply valid colouring;

13 | **forall the** $v \in PDS$ **do**
14 | | **if** $w \in N(v)$ **then**
15 | | | Minimising P by colouring w and its forward and cross edges;

16   **if** r *is uncovered* **then**
17 | **while** r has $e \in E_i^f$ or $e \in E_i^c$ *that is incident to* $N(P)$ **do**
18 | | Applying the valid colouring and the degree constraints
19 | | Minimising P;
20 | $P \leftarrow P \cup \{r\}$;
21 **return** P

---

that $u_i \to u_{i+1}$ for all $i = 1, 2, \ldots, m - 1$; then we obtain $u_1 \to u_2 \to \cdots \to u_m$, but this is a contradiction since the last red edge from u_m back to u_1 implies that $u_m \to u_1$. Moreover, back edges are not considered in the valid colouring of DFS, therefore, those edge are not coloured red. Hence, there is no dependency cycle with all edges coloured red. The final result is that elements H_i of a graph G have a valid colouring $C = (V_i, E_i^r)$ with $S \subseteq V(H_i)$ as the set of origins.

Together with Theorem 3, we immediately obtain our main result:

Lemma 3. *Given the partition elements H_i of a digraph G constructed by DFS, one can solve PDS in $O(|V_i + \left\{ E_i^t \cup E_i^f \left[N(v)\right] \cup E_i^c \left[N(v)\right] \right\} \setminus E_i^b|)$ time, where $v \in PDS$.*

We give this result also in constructive form in Algorithm 1.

6   Conclusions

The timely recovery of control as represented by structural controllability (for LTI systems) after a control graph has been damaged such as following an attack is an important problem in control systems. If control can be recovered entirely or to the largest extent possible, the potential service degradation or damage caused by an attacker can be reduced substantially, or attackers can be kept from taking over a network and control over it entirely. This, however, requires the ability to recover controllability as fast as possible since adversaries may — particularly where such attacks occur after a substantial period of intelligence-gathering — repeatedly attack even while recovery operations are still in progress. In this paper we have therefore proposed a novel algorithm based on re-using as much as possible of a remaining PDS structure offering controllability after an event or attack leading to the partitioning of the original control network. This DFS-based approach yields improved average-case complexity over previous [14] and related work.

Future work will seek to improve the approximation of the resulting PDS of a number of network topologies over a wholly re-computed PDS for the graph after attack, and to study the approximation characteristics of resulting PDS graphs after subgraph removal in particular.

References

1. Lin, C.T.: Structual controllability. IEEE Trans. Autom. Control **19**(3), 201–208 (1974)
2. Liu, Y.Y., Slotine, J.J., Barabási, A.L.: Controllability of complex networks. Nature **473**, 167–173 (2011)
3. Wang, W.X., Ni, X., Lai, Y.C., Grebogi, C.: Optimizing controllability of complex networks by minimum structural perturbations. Phys. Rev. E **85**(2), 026–115 (2012)
4. Pu, C.L., Pei, W.J., Michaelson, A.: Robustness analysis of network controllability. Phys. A **391**(18), 4420–4425 (2012)
5. Pósfai, M., Liu, Y.Y., Slotine, J.J., Barabási, A.L.: Effect of correlations on network controllability. Nat. Sci. Rep. **3**(1067), 1–7 (2013)
6. Nacher, J.C., Akutsu, T.: Structural controllability of unidirectional bipartite networks. Nat. Sci. Rep. **3**(1647), 1–7 (2013)
7. Haynes, T.W., Hedetniemi, S.M., Hedetniemi, S.T., Henning, M.A.: Domination in graphs applied to electric power networks. SIAM J. Discrete Math. **15**(4), 519–529 (2002)
8. Xu, G., Kang, L., Shan, E., Zhao, M.: Power domination in block graphs. Theoret. Comput. Sci. **359**(1–3), 299–305 (2006)
9. Kneis, J., Mölle, D., Richter, S., Rossmanith, P.: Parameterized power domination complexity. Inf. Process. Lett. **98**(4), 145–149 (2006)
10. Guo, J., Niedermeier, R., Raible, D.: Improved algorithms and complexity results for power domination in graphs. Algorithmica **52**(2), 177–202 (2008)
11. Feige, U.: A threshold of ln n for approximating set cover. J. ACM **45**(4), 634–652 (1998)

12. Binkele-Raible, D., Fernau, H.: An exact exponential time algorithm for power dominating set. Algorithmica **63**(1–2), 323–346 (2012)
13. Aazami, A., Stilp, K.: Approximation algorithms and hardness for domination with propagation. SIAM J. Discrete Math. **23**(3), 1382–1399 (2009)
14. Alwasel, B., Wolthusen, S.: Reconstruction of structural controllability over Erdős-Rényi graphs via power dominating sets. In: Proceedings of the 9th Cyber and Information Security Research Conference (CSIRC 2014), Oak Ridge, TN, USA, pp. 57–60. ACM Press, April 2014

Self-Healing Protocols for Infrastructural Networks

Antonio Scala[1,2,3]($\boxtimes$), Walter Quattrociocchi[2,3], Giuliano Andrea Pagani[4], and Marco Aiello[4]

[1] ISC-CNR Physics Department, University "La Sapienza", Piazzale Moro 5, 00185 Roma, Italy
antonio.scala@cnr.it
[2] IMT Alti Studi Lucca, piazza S. Ponziano 6, 55100 Lucca, Italy
[3] London Institute of Mathematical Sciences, 22 South Audley Street Mayfair, London W1K 2NY, UK
[4] Distributed Systems Group, Johann Bernoulli Institute for Mathematics and Computer Science, University of Groningen, Groningen, The Netherlands

Abstract. A crucial feature in implementing the next generation of smart grids is how to introduce self-healing capabilities allowing to ensure a high quality of service to the users. We show how distributed communication protocols can enrich complex networks with self-healing capabilities; an obvious field of applications are infrastructural networks. In particular, we consider the case where the presence of redundant links allows to recover the connectivity of the system. We then analyse the interplay between redundancies and topology in improving the resilience of networked infrastructures to multiple failures; in particular, we measure the fraction of nodes still served for increasing levels of network damages. Hence, we consider healing performances respect to different network topologies (planar, small-world, scale-free) corresponding to various degree of realism. We find that the most balanced strategy to enhances networks' resilience to multiple failures while avoiding large economic expenses is to introduce a finite fraction of long-range connections.

Keywords: Critical infrastructures · Distributed protocols · Complex networks · Self-healing

1 Introduction

Nowadays, one of the most pressing and interesting scientific challenges deals with the analysis and the understanding of processes occurring on complex networks; one of the most important target for applying the results of such a field are real infrastructural networks. Our society critically depends on the continuity of functioning of Physical Networked Infrastructures ($PNIs$) like power, gas or water distribution; securing such critical infrastructures against accidental or intentional malfunctioning is a key issue both in Europe and in the US.

© Springer International Publishing Switzerland 2016
C.G. Panayiotou et al. (Eds.): CRITIS 2014, LNCS 8985, pp. 308–313, 2016.
DOI: 10.1007/978-3-319-31664-2_31

While most studies have been focused on how to improve the *robustness* (i.e. the capability of surviving intentional and/or random failures) of existing networks, much less has been done regarding the *resilience* (i.e. the capability of recovering failures). In fact, the implementation of smart (as well as economic) strategies aimed at maintaining high level of performances is a crucial issue yet to be solved.

Self-healing can be introduced as a constrained mechanism in which only a limited amount of resources is available; such strategy is alternative to the standard approach of ensuring of the continuity of a system by introducing redundancy in the interconnectivity of its components.

2 Methods

Model. In this paper we introduce a model targeted to study and analyse abstract, general cases; going to more concrete case studies will require considering non-random trees, performance metrics and realistic network topologies.

In our scenario we consider network systems distributing some utility; for sake of simplicity, we will consider a single node to be the source of the quantity to be distributed on the network. Examples of such network utilities are water, power, gas or oil pipelines or electric power distribution. At each instant of time, the topology of the network distributing the utility (the *active tree*) is assumed to be a tree; this assumption is partially verified in the above mentioned system; in particular, it is mostly verified in the case of electric power distribution [6]. In fact, such a structure meets the infrastructures' managers needs – i.e., to measure (for billing purposes) in an easy and precise way how much of a given quantity is served to any single node of the network. Finally, as a further simplification we will not take into account the magnitudes of flows – i.e., all links and sources are assumed to have infinite capacity – but we will focus on maximizing the connectedness of the system in order to serve as many nodes as possible.

In order to implement our strategy and its self-healing capabilities, we consider the presence of *dormant* backup links – i.e., a set of links that can be switched on. Nodes are assumed to be able to communicate with their neighbours by means of a suitable distributed interaction protocol with a limited amount of knowledge: the set of neighbouring nodes connected either via active or via dormant links. Then, when either a node or a link failure occurs, all the nodes below the failure will disconnect from the active tree and become unserved. Such unserved nodes can now try to reconnect the active tree by waking up through the protocol some dormant backup links. Such a process will reconstruct a new active-tree that can restore totally or partially the flow, i.e. heal the system.

In order to identify the system's properties that are able to maximize the fraction of service (FoS) – i.e., the fraction of served nodes – we study the effects of the backup links (redundancy) disposed according to different connectivity patterns – i.e., different underlying networks on top of which the active tree is build – with respect to multiple random failures. We start our investigation by focusing on the case which best resembles the actual situation of $PNIs$ – i.e. nodes disposed over a grid. Then, we stress the role of the networks' connectivity patterns by using small-world and scale free networks as underlying topology. A more formal description of the model is provided in [7].

Network Topologies. In general, when dealing with technological networks one should consider distance-dependent constraints [2] or even more sophisticated ones like the spectrum of the adjacency matrix of the network [10]. For the sake of this study, we will instead consider more abstract classes of network structures that allow to concentrate on particular structural properties. In particular, we generate three different classes of graphs generated by using the IGRAPH library [4]: planar square grids (SQ), Barabasi-Albert scale-free (SF) networks [1] and Watts-Strogatz small world (SW) networks [11]. We then apply Wilson's algorithm [12] to generate a random spanning trees associated with a network: such spanning trees are our model for the initial distribution networks in absence of redundant links. The source node is chosen at random within all the nodes of the underlying network for SQ and SW topologies. In the case of the SF topologies we use the natural choice of having the node with the highest number of neighbours (the central hub) as the source. The set of all possible backup links is given by the links of the network not belonging to the initial spanning tree. We parametrise with r the fraction of *dormant* links that can be used to heal the system; such links are chosen at random among all the possible backup links.

Random Failures and Self-Healing. We consider uncorrelated multiple link failures; notice a node failure is equivalent to the simultaneous failure of all the links insisting on that nodes. To simulate the occurrence of such failures, we delete at random a fraction f of links in the initial spanning tree. We then apply the routing protocol of [7] to implement self-healing, i.e. to reconstruct the maximum tree connected to the source after the occurrence of the failure; to achieve such a scope, we use both the survived links of the initial tree and the dormant links. We then parametrise the effectiveness of the recovery by FoS, the fraction of nodes connected to the source after the recovery.

2.1 Self-Healing Protocol

The self healing protocol of [7] starts from a configuration of a grid after a failure. In such configuration there is a single non-spanning tree of active links containing the source; all the nodes in such a tree are in the served state S, while all the other nodes in the unserved state. At this point, any routing protocol reconstructing a spanning tree could be used [8]. For simplicity, we will employ the following synchronous algorithm: all served nodes broadcast their state to their neighbours; when an unserved node receives a message of a served node through a link, it activates such link, switches in the served state and start broadcasting. If a node has more than one possibility of activating a link, it just chooses one at random. Such algorithm re-links all the nodes reachable from the source in a number of steps at most equal to the number of nodes. Notice that to implement such procedure, nodes must have a backup power source that allows their functioning for the finite time necessary to rewire the network.

3   Results

Effects of Redundancy. We start our study by addressing planar square grid (SQ) networks since, among our synthetic topologiess, they are the most similar to the real physical networked infrastructures. We then analyse small-world (SW) networks [11]. Small world networks are important since they can show the effects of introducing long-range links in the planar topologies common to many technological networks. We start from an initial planar square grid and rewire a fraction p of links with randomly selected nodes; thus, we can interpolate from the case of SQ networks ($p = 0$) to the case of a random graph ($p = 1$).

In both cases, we generate spanning trees on a square grids and study the variation of the FoS restored by our self-healing algorithm respect to the fraction f of failures at different redundancies rs. In the case of square grids, we do not observe any relevance of the redundancy on the FoS; this means that a very small fraction backup links already suffices to attain the maximum resilience; on the other hand, for SW networks increasing the number of redundant links increases the robustness.

Such behaviour is due to the local nature of back-up links in planar networks: in fact, imagine isolating a region of size N on the plane by random link failures. The number of possible dormant links among nodes in this region scales as the area ($\sim N$) of such region, while the number of possible dormant links connecting this region to the remaining part of the system scales as the perimeter ($\sim \sqrt{N}$) of such region. Hence, he probability that a dormant link allows to re-connect such region with the remaining of the system is proportional to the ratio among the perimeter and the area of the region, i.e. to $1/\sqrt{N}$ independently from the fraction r of backup links. On the other hand, for SW topologies the probability that a backup link connects an isolated region with the remaining of the system is proportional to p and hence the probability that a region can reconnect with the system is proportional to the product $r * p$. We show in Fig. 1 that such is the case.

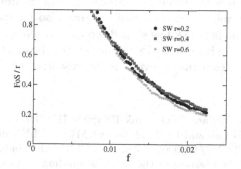

Fig. 1. Simple scaling arguments predict that for SW networks the FoS restored by the self-healing algorithm is proportional to the fraction r of backup links. We show that such behaviour is verified in the case of $p = 0.1$ SW networks.

4 Discussion

In this paper we have discussed the resilience of networks upon a minimal self-healing procedure that exploits the presence of redundant edges to recover the connectivity of the system. Our scenario is inspired by real-world distribution networks that are, often for economic reasons, tree-like and are also often provided with alternative backup links that can be activated in case of malfunctioning; as an example, this is the case for low-voltage distribution networks.

Our model, albeit schematic, is realistic in the sense that it could be readily and easily implemented with the current technologies. In fact, routing protocols represent a vast available source of distributed algorithms able to maintain the connectivity of a system. Therefore, our scheme could be implemented using an ICT network to augment current infrastructures with the needed distributed capabilities of communicating and self-reconfiguring according to the routing protocol. Our case is an example in which interdependencies can enhance the resilience instead of introducing catastrophic breakdowns [3].

We have studied the performances of our self-healing protocol varying the redundancy on different network substrates – i.e., planar square grid, scale-free and small-world networks. Within our model, we find that distribution networks akin to real world ones - i.e., based on SQ topologies - are the less resilient to multiple random failures. In fact, as expected the most robust networks are based on the SF topology that is unrealistic for technological networks. A further direction of study would be to consider the effects of more detailed structural characteristics on the dynamics of the system [5].

Our results on SW topologies hint that a very effective strategy to strengthen planar networks is to add long range links. The feasibility of such a strategy depends on cost-benefit analysis about the implementation of physical long-range links in $PNIs$.

While our minimal model considers only the connectivity of the system, it can be easily expanded to take account of the magnitude of the flows: in fact, routing algorithms can both account for the capacity of the links and dynamically swap re-routing of flows. Our model easily allows also for *cold starts* – i.e., for situations in which the network has shut down due to some major events (like a black-out) [9]. This is an important issue since one of the most time (and money) consuming activity after a major event is the restoring of the functionality of the network.

Acknowledgements. AS and WQ thank US grant HDTRA1-11-1-0048, CNR-PNR National Project Crisis-Lab and EU FET project MULTIPLEX nr.317532. AS thanks EU HOME/2013/CIPS/AG/4000005013 project CI2C. The contents of the paper do not necessarily reflect the position or the policy of funding parties. AS thanks Claudio Mazzariello for very useful discussions on routing algorithms and Michele Festuccia for pointing out the technological feasibility of our approach.

References

1. Barabási, A.L., Albert, R.: Emergence of scaling in random networks. Science **286**(5439), 509–512 (1999). http://dx.org/10.1126/science.286.5439.509
2. Barthelemy, M.: Spatial networks. Phy. Rep. **499**(1–3), 1–101 (2011)
3. Buldyrev, S.V., Parshani, R., Paul, G., Stanley, H.E., Havlin, S.: Catastrophic cascade of failures in interdependent networks. Nature **464**(7291), 1025–1028 (2010). http://dx.org/10.1038/nature08932
4. Csardi, G., Nepusz, T.: The igraph software package for complex network research. Inter. J. Complex Syst. **1695** (2006). http://igraph.sf.net
5. D'Agostino, G., Scala, A., Zlatić, V., Caldarelli, G.: Robustness and assortativity for diffusion-like processes in scale-free networks. EpPL **97**(6), 68006 (2012). http://dx.org/10.1209/0295-5075/97/68006
6. Pagani, G.A., Aiello, M.: Towards decentralization: a topological investigation of the medium and low voltage grids. IEEE Trans. Smart Grid **2**(3), 538–547 (2011)
7. Quattrociocchi, W., Caldarelli, G., Scala, A.: Self-healing networks: Redundancy and structure. PLoS ONE **9**(2), e87986 (2014). http://dx.doi.org/10.1371%2Fjournal.pone.0087986
8. Santoro, N.: Design and Analysis of Distributed Algorithms. Wiley Series on Parallel and Distributed Computing. Wiley-Interscience, Hoboken (2006)
9. Sudhakar, T.D., Srinivas, K.N.: Restoration of power network–a bibliographic survey. Eur. Trans. Electr. Power **21**(1), 635–655 (2011). http://dx.org/10.1002/etep.467
10. Wang, Z., Scaglione, A., Thomas, R.: Generating statistically correct random topologies for testing smart grid communication and control networks. IEEE Trans. Smart Grid **1**(1), 28–39 (2010)
11. Watts, D.J., Strogatz, S.H.: Collective dynamics of /'small-world/' networks. Nature **393**(6684), 440–442 (1998). http://dx.org/10.1038/30918
12. Wilson, D.B.: Generating random spanning trees more quickly than the cover time. In: Proceedings of the 28th annuan ACM Symposium on the Theory of Computing, pp. 296–303. ACM (1996)

PRoCeeD: Process State Prediction for CRITIS Using Process Inherent Causal Data and Discrete Event Models

Christian Horn[✉] and Jörg Krüger

Department of Industrial Automation Technology,
Technische Universität Berlin, Berlin, Germany
christian.horn@iat.tu-berlin.de, joerg.krueger@iwf.tu-berlin.de

Abstract. It is getting harder for operators to secure their Critical Infrastructures (CRITIS). The reasons are a higher complexity and vulnerability of infrastructures in combination with the pressure of being cost-effective, as well as the availability of more evolving attack techniques. New and sophisticated Advanced Persistent Threats cannot be detected using common security measures like signature-based detection. New techniques for detection in CRITIS are necessary. As one part of a comprehensive detection framework for CRITIS we introduce PRoCeeD – Process secuRity by using Causal Data. Our approach combines methodologies from control theory, distributed computing and automata theory. The goal is to create a mathematical model of the nodes, i.e. Programmable Logic Controller or other control systems. Furthermore this is done in an automated fashion using existing information like the Source Code, input and output values like network traffic and process variables and data models. The generated model can be simulated in conjunction with on-line data of a running process to predict probable process states. A combination of this prediction with an anomaly detection framework can reveal attacks, misuses or errors that cannot be detected using common security measures.

Keywords: Cyber security in CRITIS · Anomaly detection (attacks, misuse, errors) in CRITIS · Industrial process security · Automation security

1 Introduction

The vision of secure information and automation infrastructures cannot be achieved only by securing single parts, like a Programmable Logic Controller (PLC) or Personal Computer, without looking at the interplay of components. In Critical Infrastructures, such as water supply and gas or electricity distribution, industrial information and automation technology forms a second infrastructure within these. The supply networks have become critically dependent to this second infrastructure. The rise of industrial information and automation technology in the last decades offers great potential for optimization of efficiency and

© Springer International Publishing Switzerland 2016
C.G. Panayiotou et al. (Eds.): CRITIS 2014, LNCS 8985, pp. 314–325, 2016.
DOI: 10.1007/978-3-319-31664-2_32

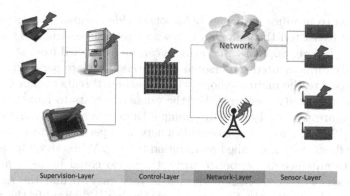

Fig. 1. Sample IT-atack-vctors towards an automation infrastructure

expenses. For example several facilities can be supervised by a few people using automation and fast networking technology. These cost-effective structures have been implemented in most of the Critical Infrastructures, assuming these technologies are secure. But unfortunately industrial information and automation technologies were not developed with security in mind [1–3]. The advancing connection of these technologies to public networks makes the protection even more difficult. Figure 1 shows an example automation and information infrastructure containing the four common layers: supervision-, control-, network- and sensor-layer. Each one contains its specific technologies that are connected using different networks, rendering the infrastructure very heterogeneous. As shown in Fig. 1 we assume that it is possible to attack every single technology in the infrastructure.

The protection of infrastructures, especially in critical areas, is one of the major challenges for the operating companies. Since the discovery of the computer worm STUXNET [4] and later observed so called "Advanced Persistent Threats" like FLAME and DUQU [5,6], awareness has been risen. These security flaws also made clear, that the software used to launch the attacks gets more complex and evolved. Further effort has to be done to secure the automated systems in critical areas especially in interaction with other systems, which is common in automated infrastructures. Operating companies mostly have to secure their technology infrastructures without the support of additional resources. Extensive studies like [8] by the European Union Agency for Network and Information Security (ENISA) have been published along with guidelines like [7] by the US National Institute of Standards and Technology (NIST) to enhance security in these kind of infrastructures. These publications mainly focus on organizational topics or the technological implementation of existing technologies like firewalls, demilitarized zones, keeping the systems up-to-date or the use of antivirus software as well as rising awareness among managers and operators of these infrastructures.

Nowadays we face completely new kinds of attacks like return-oriented-programming [9], where the attacker uses the code of the software installed on the machine itself to produce malicious behavior, or side-channel attacks [10], where data can get extracted through channels whose interdependence to the systems was not clear before. Sophisticated attacks can be unleashed from stealthy platforms already implemented in personal computers, that are persistent and have complete access to the main-memory [11]. These new threats cannot be detected using common security measures. For the worse the costs to launch a sophisticated attack are getting lower. For example there are already frameworks like metasploit [12] freely available to enable a network operator to test his networks for security flaws, which is called penetration testing. While those tools are very important to enhance the cyber-security, they also could be used maliciously by an attacker. Furthermore nowadays it is very easy to find the right target for an attack. Tools like the Shodan Search Engine [13] simplify the task. The combination of [12,13] could lead to sophisticated attacks by non-sophisticated attackers, so called script-kiddies.

Given a higher complexity and vulnerability of the infrastructures in combination with the pressure of being cost-effective for the operating companies, as well as the availability of more evolving attack techniques it is getting harder for the operators to secure their infrastructures or furthermore to determine the origin of a systems misbehavior, if even detectable. The first step towards resilience in a technological way is to focus on detection of sophisticated attacks.

This leads to the research question: How can a sophisticated attack in the given automation and information infrastructures be detected?

2   Related Work

The boundaries of the classic automation hierarchy between the supervision-, control, and sensor-level should not limit a well designed monitoring system in the detection of malfunctions, misuses or attacks. Usually monitoring systems take only one specific part of a complex infrastructure into account. For example most detection systems, like host-based or network-based intrusion detection systems, rely only on the data of a specific part of the whole infrastructure. Interdependencies inside the infrastructure are mostly not taken into account. It is also important to mention that conventional approaches usually rely on signatures or other known patterns to detect misuse. Systems that are able to detect anomalies unknown to the system at the time of integration into the process were introduced more recently.

A comprehensive overview about anomaly detection methods and algorithms can be found in [14,15]. It is very common to combine machine learning approaches with statistical methods to detect anomalies in network traffic (refer to [17,18]). To use these methods and algorithms effectively it is very important to transform the data into the appropriate feature space. This step is usually seen as the research innovation itself, since the methods and algorithms for statistic analysis and machine learning are often just used or adopted in the specific domains of research.

The formal specification of a systems behavior requires to capture the behavior of the software in an adequate semantic model. The creation, simulation and evaluation of formal models for different systems is commonly used in the domains of fault diagnosis [19], software engineering [20] or software quality assurance [21]. The success of Petri nets in those domains is based in its simple and intuitive, but also at the same time formal and expressive nature. A broad variety of systems can be modeled by Petri nets. Numerous computer-based tools are available to support the development, validation and verification of Petri net models.

3 Concept and Methodology

To detect abnormal behavior in the daily routine of CRITIS we have to apply dynamically adopting methods and algorithms. This is because the whole systems behavior is changing according to different reasons that are mostly unknown to the system itself. For example if we look at an event like a football game, during the break we can observe a significant increase in sewage water at the stadium. The same applies to heavy rain showers in parts of a big city. For both examples an automated anomaly detection mechanism could produce a false alarm, forcing the operators to react. If the operators get used to these false positives of the detection mechanism, they would naturally lose trust in the detection mechanism, rendering it unnecessarily.

The analysis of three different crucial infrastructures of a capital city, i.e. electric power distribution, water distribution and natural gas transport preceded our development. Real data as well as technological parameters were captured and evaluated. This analysis inspired the development of our concept and methodology.

Figure 2 displays the basic idea of Process Security. On-Line Data is captured in different parts of the Automation Pyramid. This includes the field network, control nodes (PLCs), control network and supervision- (process servers and databases) and monitoring machines (operator machines). This data is used in two different methods, anomaly detection and process state prediction. The results are transformed into a normalized feature space, where a classification concerning process states can be done.

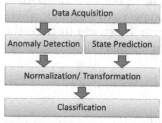

(a) Methodological Concept

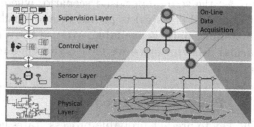

(b) Online Data Acquisition Spots

Fig. 2. Overview of process security

3.1   Causal Data

The achievement of the desired objectives is coupled to the identification of features and causations of each process in every use case, forming a significant pattern – a process-fingerprint– that can be monitored. The challenge is the complexity of processes in CRITIS where deviations of normal process behavior have to be dynamically adopted without generating a false alarm. The most important toehold is the analysis of causal chains, which are already defined in the different layers of the automation pyramid in terms of software.

$$\forall\, t \leq \tau\ u_1(t) = u_2(t) \ \Rightarrow\ \forall\, t \leq \tau\ T(u_1(t)) = T(u_2(t))$$
$$T(u) = T_1(u) + T_2(u) \tag{1}$$

Formula 1 shows the aforementioned causality as an example. If a signal u_1 is equal to a signal u_2, then the response of the system $T(u_1)$ is also equal to the response to $T(u_2)$. This statement is valid, even if the system $T(u)$ is itself an aggregation of different sub-systems. Given that we define an anomaly in this scenario as an interruption of this cause-and-effect chain, which is caused either by a technical malfunction or manipulation, e.g. a cyber attack. Suitable techniques in the research areas of pattern recognition and machine learning are applied to detect a disturbance in this cause-and-effect chain.

3.2   Anomaly Detection

Our approach rests upon the availability of sensors data as well as a model of automation technology, which is periodic and predictable regarding systems behavior. The health state of the computer systems on the control and supervision level (refer to Fig. 2), as well as the networks conditions is monitored and reported to our process monitoring system. This is a model of the aggregated systems $T(u)$ in Formula 1.

For the model of the whole infrastructure we can define the normal behavior by capturing data in different parts of the whole process to create a daily routine. [16] introduces three scenarios for outlier detection, as used in anomaly detection: the supervised scenario, where training data with normal and abnormal data objects are provided and this may result in multiple normal and/or abnormal classes; the semi-supervised scenario, where only training data for the normal or abnormal class(es) is provided; and finally the unsupervised scenario, where no training data is available. We use the semi-supervised scenario to train the normal behavior since we have a two-class problem in anomaly detection as we define it here.

3.3   Process State Prediction

The key to predict probable process states lies in building the sufficient detailed and exact model of the infrastructures computing nodes. These are the individual systems $T_x(u)$ in Formula 1. To get a mathematical model of a node in the infrastructure there are three different categories of approaches state of thetechnology:

- Using Machine Learning
- Using System Identification
- Manually transfer it into a numerical description.

The first approach, using machine learning, is somehow equivalent to a brute-force approach to solve a specific problem. The calculated result might work well, but if the system was parametrized without keeping all possible start- and boundary conditions in mind the possibility of getting a correct solution is very low. It depends highly on the training dataset. The second approach might work too, but much a-priori knowledge of the system is necessary. Additionally this approach is very hard to automate. The third approach is common to simulate relatively static systems using differential equations. Here dynamic behavior is modeled as error or disturbance functions. None of those approaches is applicable in a complex infrastructure to create models of the different nodes in an automated fashion. All of them are too complex to handle for the operators, need too much time to create usable results or creates improper models. Therefore we created our own automated method to generate a mathematical model of a computational system like a PLC.

A PLC is running in a cyclic and predictable manner. This is the foundation of all automated systems and desired behavior. For that reason we can model a Critical Infrastructure by modeling its individual systems behavior. This can be done using formal methods to model systems and processes. The Petri net is a model for the description and analysis of systems with concurrent and non-deterministic processes. They are suitable for the description of dynamic systems that have a fixed base structure such as computer systems, operating systems or organizational processes. Sequential as well as concurrent processes can be represented. The extension to Colored Petri Nets (CPNs) allows us to model the tokens to have a data value attached to them, which is referred to as the color. This is necessary for modeling a variables type and value inside a Petri net.

Our approach uses the already existent model of the node's behavior, the software running on the node in conjunction with on-line parameters. The Transformation of PLC Source Code into a CPN (refer to [22,23]) forms the basis of our development. As shown in Fig. 3 we implemented a tool to convert PLC Source

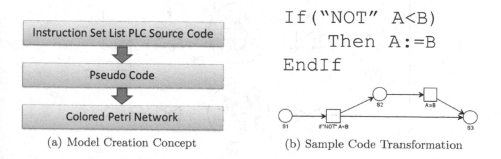

(a) Model Creation Concept   (b) Sample Code Transformation

Fig. 3. Colored Petri Network from PLC source code

Code in the form of Instruction Set List (ILC) to Pseudo Code, which is parsed and transformed into a colored Petri Network (see Fig. 3(b)). It is based on the freely available CPN-Tools [24]. This software enables a simulation of the created CPN using real parameters (data models) from live running process control nodes. Given that we are able to predict probable process states by calculating the next probable steps of the individual nodes.

4   Results

To demonstrate the functionality of the CPNs created by our software in an automated fashion we implemented an experimental hard- and software setup. The idea is to generate some in- and output data using a real PLC and compare that to the data generated by the simulation of the same system. The experimental setup is shown in Fig. 4. Here a possible waterworks system is indicated. It contains two PLC'c, a pump, two feeder gates and a water tank. The water tank is simulated, while the PLC's and the engine are existent in reality. The limit switches of the feeder gates are approximated using hardware buttons and LED's. The SUB-PLC controls the pump-engine and the feeder gates, while getting the desired pump revolutions and the current water level as input. The safety mechanism requires the pump to be shut down if the water level in the tank is very low. The Master-PLC controls the total water flow output of the facility by setting desired pump revolutions to specific SUB-PLC'c. It has to regulate the output to be relatively constant which is influenced in reality

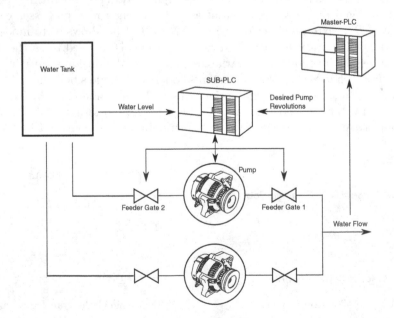

Fig. 4. Experimental setup

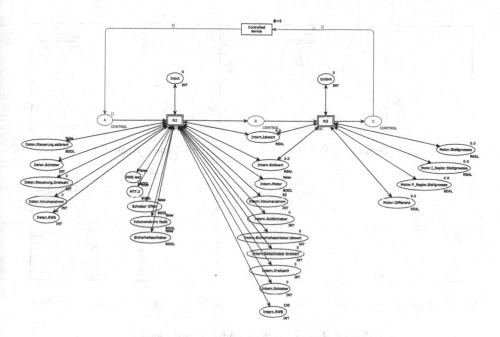

Fig. 5. Resulting Colored Petri Network

by the need and extraction of water in the supply area of the facility. A second line containing another pump and the corresponding PLC is implied in Fig. 4. The software for this experimental setup was developed from scratch. The code running on the SUB-PLC is the one to be evaluated. It was transferred into a CPN using our toolkit. This CPN was simulated using the same input data that was captured from the live running PLC. For this experimental setup we use two different test cases to evaluate the resulting CPN. The main block of the resulting CPN is shown in Fig. 5.

Test Case 1 simulates a connection failure between the SUB-PLC and the Master-PLC. The SUB-PLC calculates the output variables only depending on the water level in the tank and the built-in logical functions and thresholds. The input variables itself are modeled as ramp-functions.

Test Case 2 defines regular behavior, where the Master-PLC dictates the revolution speed of the pump to the SUB-PLC. The input variables are also modeled as ramp-functions.

The input for these test cases and the system response for the SUB-PLC in the experimental setup can be found in Fig. 6(a) to (d). The Fig. 6(a) and (b) show the input variables (refer to Fig. 4) and the Fig. 6(c) and (d) show the system responses. As can easily be seen, the engine follows the given reference speed. The safety shutdown works for a water-level below 10 % in the water tank. The feeder gates also react accordingly. The oscillation of the pump revolutions is usual behavior and common to the implemented proportional-integral-derivative

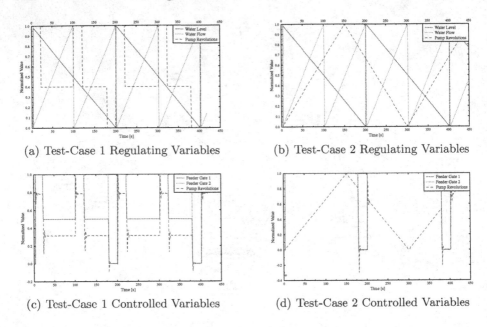

(a) Test-Case 1 Regulating Variables   (b) Test-Case 2 Regulating Variables

(c) Test-Case 1 Controlled Variables   (d) Test-Case 2 Controlled Variables

Fig. 6. Real system response to test cases

control for the engine. In comparison to the results of the real system the simulation results can be found in Fig. 7(a) to (d). Please note that the system response of the proportional-integral-derivative control does not oscillate here, because the mathematical model of the engine is only a rough approximation. Using proper system identification to generate a better model could significantly increase the results.

5   Discussion and Perspective

The results in the previous section imply the successful operation of our approach to automatically generate a formal description from real source code found on a PLC under the tested circumstances. This model represents the softwares functionality and can be simulated using on-line conditions and parameters. The simulation generates close-to-reality system responses, which can be used in different domains.

An application of our work is the prediction of probable process states. Based on the trend of the actual input parameters of a system different sets of input parameters could be assumed. These different parameter sets could then be used for the simulation generating system responses for each parameter set. Depending on the probability of occurrence for the system responses a prediction for the process state can be done. Another application domain is the on-line validity test of process values from a PLC. If a worm like STUXNET alters process values in an unnoticed fashion, this approach is able to detect that.

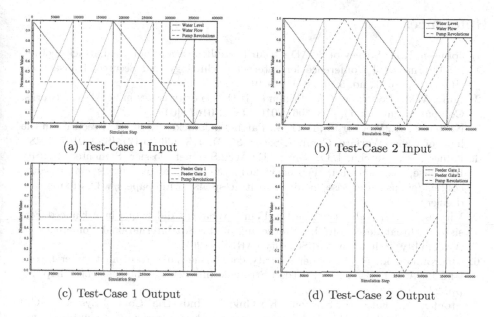

(a) Test-Case 1 Input

(b) Test-Case 2 Input

(c) Test-Case 1 Output

(d) Test-Case 2 Output

Fig. 7. Simulation system response to test cases

The input values of the PLC in question are put into the simulation of the according CPN. This way we are able to detect deviations of the process values that are triggered inside the PLC.

The approach will be used in the demonstration platform of our research project [25]. Here real data from different Critical Infrastructures is combined to form a cross-domain scenario with electric power distribution, water distribution and natural gas. Real hardware and simulation platforms form the basis of our demonstration platform where the algorithms and methods can be evaluated. Given that we are able to show that it is possible to detect a sophisticated attack in the given automation and information infrastructures using our method.

Acknowledgment. The authors would like to acknowledge the funding of the research project STEUERUNG by the senate of the state Berlin and the European Regional Development Fund. Furthermore we would like to thank our students Stefanie Teinz, Miklòs Tolnai, Max Klein and Marco Schwabe for their contribution to our research.

The Authors

The authors are working at the department of Industrial Automation Technology, which is an integral part of the Institute for Machine Tools and Factory Management at the School of Mechanical Engineering and Transport Systems of the Technische Universität Berlin.

References

1. Johnson, R.E.: Survey of SCADA security challenges and potential attack vectors. In: International Conference for Internet Technology and Secured Transactions (ICITST), vol. 1, no. 5, pp. 8–11 (2010)
2. Igure, V.M., Laughter, S.A., Williams, R.D.: Security issues in SCADA networks. Comput. Secur. **25**(7), 498–506 (2010). ISSN 0167–4048
3. Nicholson, A., Webber, S., Dyer, S., Patel, T., Janicke, H.: SCADA security in the light of Cyber-Warfare. Comput. Secur. **31**(4), 418–436 (2012). ISSN 0167–4048
4. Falliere, N., Murchu, L.O., Chien, E.: W32.Stuxnet Dossier. Symantec Security Response, Version 1.4, February 2011. Online: http://www.symantec.com/content/en/us/enterprise/media/security_response/whitepapers/w32_stuxnet_dossier.pdf
5. Virvilis, N., Gritzalis, D.: The Big Four - What we did wrong in Advanced Persistent Threat detection? In: Proceeding of the 8th International Conference on Availability, Reliability and Security (ARES-) (2013)
6. MacKinnon, L., et al.: Cyber security countermeasures to combat cyber terrorism. In: Akhar, B., Yates, S. (eds.) Strategic Intelligence Management, Chap. 20, pp. 234–261 (2013)
7. Stouffer, K., Falco, J., Scarfone, K.: Guide to Industrial Control Systems (ICS) Security. NIST Special Publication 800–82. http://csrc.nist.gov/publications/nistpubs/800-82/SP800-82-final.pdf
8. European Union Agency for Network and Information Security (ENISA). Protecting Industrial Control Systems - Recommendations for Europe and Member States. Deliverable 09 December 2011. http://www.enisa.europa.eu/activities/Resilience-and-CIIP/critical-infrastructure-and-services/scada-industrial-control-systems
9. Buchanan, E., Roemer, R., Shacham, H., Savage, S.: When good instructions go bad: generalizing return-oriented programming to RISC. In: Proceedings of CCS 2008. ACM Press, October 2008
10. Chen, S., Wang, R., Wang, X., Zhang, K.: . Side-channel leaks in web applications: a reality today, a challenge tomorrow. In: IEEE Symposium on Security & Privacy 2010, May 2010
11. Stewin, P., Seifert, J.-P.: In God we trust all others we monitor. In: Proceedings of the 17th ACM Conference on Computer and Communications Security (2010)
12. The Metasploit Framework. http://www.metasploit.com
13. The Shodan Computer Search Engine. http://www.shodanhq.com/
14. Chandola, V., Banerjee, A., Kumar, V.: Anomaly detection: a survey. ACM Comput. Surv. (CSUR) **41**(3), 15 (2009)
15. Chandola, V., et al.: Anomaly detection for discrete sequences: a survey. IEEE Trans. Knowl. Data Eng. **24**(5), 823–839 (2012)
16. Kriegel, H.-P., Kröger, P., Zimek, A.: Outlier detection techniques. In: Proceedings of the Thirteenth Pacific-Asia Conference on Knowledge Discovery and Data Mining (2009)
17. Marnerides, A.K., et al.: Multi-level network resilience: traffic analysis. anomaly detection & simulation. ICTACT J. **2**(2) (2011). Special Issue on Next Generation Wireless Networks and Applications
18. Genge, B., Rusu, D.A., Haller, P.: A connection pattern-based approach to detect network traffic anomalies in critical infrastructures. In: ACM European Workshop on System Security (EuroSec), Amsterdam, The Netherlands. pp. 1–6 (2014)

19. Ashouri, A., Jalilvand, A., Noroozian, R., Bagheri, A.: A new approach for fault detection in digital relays-based power system using Petri nets. In: Joint International Conference on Power Electronics, Drives and Energy Systems (PEDES), pp. 1–8 (2010)
20. He, X.: A comprehensive survey of Petri net modeling. In: Software Engineering, International Journal of Software Engineering and Knowledge Engineering, pp. 589–625 (2013)
21. Liao, H., et al.: Concurrency bugs in multithreaded software: modeling and analysis using Petri nets. Discrete Event Dyn. Syst. **23**(2), 157–195 (2013)
22. Hanisch, H.-M., Thieme, J., Luder, A., Wienhold, O.: Modeling of PLC behavior by means of timed net condition/event systems. In: 6th IEEE International Conference on Emerging Technologies and Factory Automation Proceedings (ETFA), Los Angeles (1997)
23. Heiner, M., Menzel, T.: A Petri Net Semantics for the PLC Language Instruction List. In: Proceeding of the Fourth Workshop on Discrete Event Systems (WODES), Cagliari (1998)
24. Michael Westergaard, H.M.W., (Eric) Verbeek.: Eindhoven University of Technology. CPN Tools. http://cpntools.org/
25. Horn, C., Hempel, L., Chemnitz, M., Stewin, P., Krüger, J.: STEUERUNG: advanced information security for critical infrastructures. In: Proceeding of the 9th Future Security Conference, Berlin (2014)

Cascading Failures: Dynamic Model for CIP Purposes - Case of Random Independent Failures Following Poisson Stochastic Process

Mohamed Eid[1]([⊠]), Terhi Kling[2], Tuula Hakkarainen[2], Yohan Barbarin[3],
Amelie Grangeat[3], and Dominique Serafin[3]

[1] CEA Centre de Saclay, DEN/DANS/DM2S/SERMA,
91191 Gif Sur Yvette Cedex, France
mohamed.eid@cea.fr
[2] VTT Technical Research Centre of Finland, Espoo, Finland
[3] CEA/DAMCentre de Gramat, CEG/DEA/STEX/LRME, 46500 Gramat, France

Abstract. Cascading failures are a challenging issue in Critical Infrastructure Protection (CIP) and related modelling, simulation and analysis (MS & A) activities. Critical Infrastructures (CIs) are complex systems of ever increasing complexity. A single failure may be propagated and amplified resulting in serious disruptions of some societal vital services. A dynamic model describing cascading random failures that occur following Poisson Stochastic Process (PSP) is proposed. The proposed model considers only independent failures. Additional R & D effort is necessary before extending the model to dependent failures.

Keywords: Cascade · Domino · Effect · Model · CI · CIP · MS & A · PREDICT

1 Introduction

Modern systems are more and more complex, distributed and interconnected. Be-cause of this ever increasing complexity, a localised single failure may be propagated and amplified through many interconnected systems leading to a serious crisis. One will then talk about "cascade effect". A full description of cascading failures may include both **structural and dynamical** aspects, [1]. Boccaletti [1], has reviewed models and modelling results of these kinds of systems. Formal **simulation models of critical infrastructure**, such as those developed by Conrad et al. [2], provide insight into cascading problems.

The graph theory provides a powerful mathematical basis for modelling distributed system as a set of nodes and links (edges). Some recent work even used graph theory-based modelling to assess n-order dependencies between critical infrastructures, such as the work described in [3].

Dynamic modelling aims at introducing the time into the description of the failures occurrence, propagation and mitigation. Robust crisis management strategies require-reliable capability of MS & A. A dynamics-based model is proposed in the paper assuming independent failures.

© Springer International Publishing Switzerland 2016
C.G. Panayiotou et al. (Eds.): CRITIS 2014, LNCS 8985, pp. 326–331, 2016.
DOI: 10.1007/978-3-319-31664-2_33

2   Overview of Cascading Models

Hernantes et al. [4], have identified four specific problems that appear to reoccur when CIs are challenged: (1) heterogeneity, (2) multiple and inconsistent boundaries, (3) resilience building and (4) knowledge transfer and sharing. They developed a **causal model** that captures the causes of crisis and the possibility of cascading failures.

In line with this causal modelling methodology, Li and Chen [5], developed a dynamic model for describing disaster evolution along **causality networks with cycle chains**.

Other researchers focus on **modelling the chain effects of the cascading events**. J.T. Rodriguez et al. [6], have proposed a **data-base approach** for assessing the potential damage that arise from various combinations of phenomena and locations. However, this method results in too many rules to model the complexity and the uncertainty of the problems (Qiu et al. [7]). Fang and Marle [8], have proposed a **simulation-based risk network model** for decision support in project risk management. This method accounts for the phenomena of chain reactions and loops, but neglects the detailed connections of information among the internal components of a cascading crisis event (Qiu et al. [7]). Wang and Rong [9], have studied the network **model of the chain reaction based on complex network theory**. They analyse the topological features of the network from only a macroscopic perspective (Qiu et al. [7]). All these methods cant combine the crisis chain reaction (**macro-view**) and the elements within the crisis event (**micro-view**) involved in the cascading event.

Ouyang and Duenas-Osorio, [10], propose **an approach to design or retrofit inter-face topologies** to minimize cascading failures across urban infrastructure systems. The paper introduces a global annual cascading failure effect (GACFE) metric as well as a GACFE-based cost improvement (GACI) metric.

Zhang and Peeta [11], propose a **generalized modelling framework** that combines a multilayer infrastructure network (MIN) concept and a market-based economic approach using the computable general equilibrium (CGE) theory and its spatial extension (SCGE) to formulate a static equilibrium infrastructure interdependencies problem. Zhang and Peeta [12], extend the framework to address the dynamic and disequilibrium aspects of the infrastructure interdependencies problem by using the variational inequality (VI) technique.

Ouyang [13], has made an extensive review on modelling and simulation of inter-dependent critical infrastructure systems (CISs) and broadly grouped the existing modelling and simulation approaches in six types: **(1) empirical approaches, (2) agent based approaches, (3) system dynamics based approaches, (4) economic theory based approaches, (5) network based approaches, and (6) others**. The model pro-posed in our paper could accordingly be considered as a **system dynamics based approach**. It considers only the independent failure events.

3   Overview on Dynamic Modelling

The independent cascading failures may be described under the form of an integral of a differential equation, Eq. (1). Fussell [14], uses the same integral equation as below, Eq. (1), and develops a solution based on Laplace transformation. Fussell considers the asymptotic solution only. Oppositely, Yunge [15], uses the same mathematical description (but in a differential form) to model the sequential occurrence of events in a given Priority AND Gate (PAG). Many other authors followed almost the same way of modelling and produced very interesting applications, [16–20].

Other researchers could solve the same problem using numerical techniques such as Petri Nets or Dynamic Bayesian Net (DBN). The use of a numerical technique does not allow to figure out the analytical solution.

In some other papers given in [21–28] interesting methods have been developed with solutions close to the proposed one. Two papers should particularly be underlined; these are [26,27].

4   The Description of the Algorithm

Let T be a cascade of failures described by the occurrence of the independent events e_i in a given order, $[e_1, e_2, e_3, ..., e_n]$. The corresponding occurring instants are defined by $[t_1, t_2, t_3, ..., t_n]$. The first event is e_1 and the last one is e_n. Each of these instances has its own probability density function ρ_n. The probability $p_n(t)$ that the cascade T happens within the interval $[0, t]$ is given by:

$$p_n(t) = \int_0^t \rho_1(\xi_1)d\xi_1 * \int_{\xi_1}^t \rho_2(\xi_2)d\xi_2 * ... * \int_{\xi_{n-1}}^t \rho_n(\xi_n)d\xi_n \qquad (1)$$

Where: $0 \leq \xi_1 \leq \xi_2 \leq \xi_3 \leq ... \leq \xi_n \leq t$ and ρ_i is the Poisson density function characterizing the event e_i $[\rho_i = \lambda_i * e^{-\lambda_i t}]$ and λ_i is the occurrence rate of the event e_i. The number n refers to the number of the elementary failures involved in the cascade T. Many authors have previously developed analytical solutions to Eq. (1) when the number of the events is relatively small, e.g. [14,15,26,27]. If the failures dependency is considered, the integral Eq. (1) will still be valid but not its analytical solution. If the dependencies are well-described, the integral Eq. (1) can, then, be numerically solved using Monte-Carlo Simulations or Petri-Net. The analytical solution of Eq. (1) and the corresponding quantities are given in details in [29].

$$p_n(t) = \sum_{j=1}^n C_j^n * (1 - e^{-(\sum_{l=n-j+1}^n \lambda_l)t}) \qquad (2)$$

The coefficients C_i^n are determined as following:

$$C_1^{i+1} = \sum_{j=1}^{i} C_j^i, \quad C_{j+1}^{i+1} = -\frac{\lambda_{i+1}}{\sum\limits_{l=i-j+1}^{i+1} \lambda_l} C_j^i, \quad and \quad C_1^1 = 1.0 \tag{3}$$

where, $j \in [1, 2, ..., i]$, and $i \in [1, 2, ..., n]$.

5 Conclusion

A cascade event T_n implies n well-defined successive random failures. Dynamic modelling is necessary if one should describe the temporal evolution of a cascading event. **Dynamic modelling** aims at introducing the time into the description of the failures occurrence, propagation and mitigation. Robust crisis management strategies require reliable capability of MS & A. A dynamics-based model is proposed in the paper assuming independent failures.

A cascading event is fully described by and integral equation that can be rewritten under a differential form, as well. If the elementary events involved in the cascading sequence are considered **independent**, the integral equation may have an analytical solution.

The cascading event may be characterized by: an occurrence probability, an occurrence probability density function and a mean occurrence time. These characterizing quantities can have analytical expressions if the n independent random failures follow a Stochastic Poisson process (SPP). Subsequently, the occurrence characteristics of the consequences and the related hazard can be determined as well.

If the failures dependency is considered, the integral Eq. (1) will still be valid but not the analytical solution. If the dependencies are well-described, the integral Eq. (1) can, then, be numerically solved using Monte-Carlo Simulation or Petri-Nets based algorithms.

Acknowledgments. The work presented in this paper has been partially realized and fully used in the frame of the EU collaborative project "PREDICT: PREparing for the Domino effect in Crisis siTuations", FP7-SEC-2013-1.

References

1. Boccaletti, S., Latora, V., Moreno, Y., Chavez, M., Hwang, D.-U.: Complex networks: structure and dynamics. Phys. Rep. **424**(2006), 175–308 (2006)
2. Conrad, S.H., LeClaire, R.J., O'Reilly, G.P., Uzunalioglu, H.: Criticalnational infrastructure reliability modeling and analysis. Bell Labs Tech. J. **11**, 57–71 (2006)
3. Kotzanikolaou, P., MarianthiTheoharidou, D.G.: Assessing n-order dependencies between critical Infrastructures. Int. J. Critical Infrastruct. **9**(1/2), 93–110 (2013). Copyright 2013 Inderscience Enterprises Ltd

4. Hernantes, J., Rich, E., Laug, A., Labaka, L., Sarriegi, J.M.: Learningbefore the storm: modeling multiple stakeholder activities in support of crisis management, a practical case. Technol. Forecast. Soc. Chang. **80**, 1742–1755 (2013)
5. Li, J., Chen, C.: Modeling the dynamics of disaster evolution along causality networks with cycle chains. Phys. A **401**, 251–264 (2014)
6. Rodriguez, J.T., Vitoriano, B., Mentero, J.: A general methodology for data-based rule building and its application to natural disaster management. Comput. Oper. Res. **39**, 863–873 (2012)
7. Qiu, J., Wang, Z., Ye, X., Liu, L., Dong, L.: Modeling method of cascading crisis events based on merging bayesian network. Decis. Support Syst. **62**, 94–105 (2014)
8. Fang, C., Marle, F.: A simulation-based risk network model for decision support in project risk management. Decis. Support Syst. **52**, 635–644 (2012)
9. Wang, J.W., Rong, L.L.: Research on chain-reacting network model of emergency events. Appl. Res. Comput. **25**, 3288–3291 (2008)
10. Ouyang, M., Dueas-Osorio, L.: An approach to design interface topologies across interdependent urban infrastructure systems. Reliab. Eng. Syst. Saf. **96**(2011), 1462–1473 (2011)
11. Zhang, P., Peeta, S.: A generalized modeling framework to analyze interdependencies among infrastructure systems. Trans. Res. Part B **45**(3), 553–579 (2011)
12. Zhang, P., Peeta, S.: Dynamic and disequilibrium analysis of interdependent infrastructure systems. Transportation Research Part B (2014). doi:10.1016/j.trb. 2014.04.008
13. Ouyang, M.: Review on modelling and simulation of interdependent critical infrastructure systems. Reliab. Eng. Syst. Saf. **121**(2014), 4360 (2014)
14. Fussell, J.B., Aber, E.F., Rahl, R.G.: On the quantitative analysis of Priority-AND failure Logic. IEEE Trans. Reliab. **R−25**(5), 324–326 (1976)
15. Yuge, T., Yanagi, S.: Quantitative analysis of a fault tree with priority AND gates. Reliab. Eng. Syst. Saf. **93**, 1577–1583 (2008)
16. Walker, M., Papadopoulos, Y.: Pandora 2: the time of priority-or gates. In: Proceedings of the IFAC Workshop on Dependable Control of Discrete Event Systems, DCDS07, Paris pp. 13–15, June 2007
17. Rai, S.: Evaluating FTRE's for dependability measures in fault tolerant systems. ieee trans. comput. **44**(2), 275–285 (1995)
18. Merle, G., Roussel, J.-M., Lesage, J.-J., Bobbio, A.: Probabilistic algebraic analysis of fault trees with priority dynamic gates and repeated events. IEEE Trans. Reliab. **59**(1), 250–261 (2010)
19. Merle, G., Roussel, J.-M., Lesage, J.-J., Bobbio, A.: Algebraic expression of the structure function of a subclass of dynamic fault trees. In: 2nd IFAC Workshop on Dependable Control of Discrete Systems (DCDS 2009), Bari, Italy (2009)
20. Merle, G., Roussel, J.-M., Lesage, J.-J., Vayatis, N.: Analytical calculation of failure probabilities in dynamic fault trees including spare gates. In: The European Safety and Reliability Conference (ESREL 2010), Rhodes, Greece (2010)
21. Yoshinobu, SATO: Safety assessment of automated production systems using microelectronics Quantification of the Priority-AND Failure Logic consisting repairable inputs events. paper given during the Yamanashi district Congress of the Japan Society of Mechanical Engineers, October 26, Paper N 85–0454 A (1985)
22. Walker, M., Papadopoulos, Y.: Qualitative Temporal Analysis: Towards a full implementation of the Fault Tree Handbook. Control Engineering Practice, Elsevier Science **17**(10) 1115–1125, ISSN 0967–0661
23. Yuge, T., Yanagi, S.: Quantitative analysis of a fault tree with priority AND gates. Reliab. Eng. Syst. Saf. **93**, 15771583 (2008)

24. Liu, D., Zhang, C., Xing, W., Li, R., Li, H.: Quantification of cut sequence set for fault tree analysis. In: Perrott, R., Chapman, B.M., Subhlok, J., de Mello, R.F., Yang, L.T. (eds.) HPCC 2007. LNCS, vol. 4782, pp. 755–765. Springer, Heidelberg (2007)

25. Manian, R., Bechta, J., Sullivan, K.J.: Combining various solution techniques for dynamic fault tree analysis of computer systems. In: Proceedings of the 3rd International High-Assurance Systems Engineering Symposium (HASE 1998) (1998). http://www.cs.virginia.edu/~dwc3q/soft_eng/papers/combining_solution_techniques.pdf

26. Long, W., Sato, Y., Horigome, M.: Quantification of sequential failure logic for fault tree analysis. Reliab. Eng. Syst. Saf. **67**, 269274 (2000)

27. Kohda, T., Inoue, K.: A simple method to evaluate system failure occurrence probability using minimal cut sets. In: Proceedings of ESRel 2003, Safety and Reliability Bedford & van Gelder (eds.), Swets & Zeitlinger, Lisse, pp. 923–926 (2003). ISBN 90 5809 551 7

28. U.S. NRC. Fault Tree Handbook, NUREG-094 (1981)

29. Eid, M.: A general analytical solution for the occurrence probability of a sequence of ordered events following poison stochastic processes. J. Reliab. Theor. Appl. **2**, RT&A # 03 (22), 21–32 (2011)

A Security Assessment Methodology
for Critical Infrastructures

Marco Caselli[1(✉)] and Frank Kargl[1,2]

[1] SCS Group, University of Twente, Enschede, The Netherlands
{m.caselli,f.kargl}@utwente.nl
[2] University of Ulm, Ulm, Germany
frank.kargl@uni-ulm.de

Abstract. Interest in security assessment and penetration testing techniques has steadily increased. Likewise, security of industrial control systems (ICS) has become more and more important. Very few methodologies directly target ICS and none of them generalizes the concept of "critical infrastructures pentesting". Existing methodologies and tools cannot be applied directly to critical infrastructures (CIs) due to safety and availability requirements. Moreover, there is no clear understanding on the specific output that CI operators need from such an assessment. We propose a new methodology tailored to support security testing in ICS/CI environments. By analyzing security assessments and penetration testing methodologies proposed for other domains and interviewing stakeholders to identify existing best practices adopted in industry, deriving related issues and collecting proposals for possible solutions we propose a new security assessment and penetration testing methodology for critical infrastructure.

Keywords: Critical infrastructure · Penetration testing methodology · Security assessment · Industrial control system

1   Introduction

"IT security assessment" is a process that encompasses the discovery of vulnerabilities of an IT infrastructure and the identification of related risks at business level. Vulnerability discovery is commonly also known as "security testing" and includes a large set of techniques that aim to verify if an information system achieves the intended level of security. Security testing techniques include different kinds of activities: analysis-centered activities (e.g. document-based design review), software analyses (e.g. code review) and practical tests on live systems with the purposes of penetrate infrastructures or disrupt their functioning commonly known under the name of "penetration testing".

In its most simplistic form, a security test involves running some automated security scanner, such as Nessus [1]. However, it is generally agreed that comprehensive security analyses typically involve additional activities such as manual

This work has been partially supported by the European Commission through project FP7-SEC-285477-CRISALIS funded by the 7th Framework Program.

© Springer International Publishing Switzerland 2016
C.G. Panayiotou et al. (Eds.): CRITIS 2014, LNCS 8985, pp. 332–343, 2016.
DOI: 10.1007/978-3-319-31664-2_34

test planing, preparation, conduction, and post-examination to be able to flexibly react to the system under test and identify more complex vulnerabilities that automated scanners will not find. In this case, the security tests but especially penetration tests should follow some structured methodology to ensure good coverage and valid, reproducible, and well documented results.

The development and use of structured security assessments and testing methodologies is motivated by several reasons. First of all, there are numerous vulnerabilities that may be difficult or impossible to detect when only using automated tools. Well guarded systems and infrastructures usually need human thinking more than brute force to be compromised. Security testing is also an indispensable input for any proper risk analysis. Conducting practical attacks allows to properly measure necessary effort from the attacker's perspective and can be directly used as an input for a correct risk estimation. Finally, companies use security testing and especially penetration tests to assess the ability of their network operators to successfully detect and respond to cyber-attacks.

The interest in penetration testing techniques has constantly increased in the last decade. Companies, organizations and governments provide numerous online services on the Internet and most of them face constant attacks of some sort. This creates the need to assess the security of systems which is served by a whole new security testing industry offering a broad range of security assessment services. Given the proliferation of self-designed and proprietary penetration testing methods, it is hard for customers to evaluate the quality of such offers. Some organizations and standardization bodies have thus decided to propose systematic and comprehensive methodologies that should serve as standards and enhance comparability of offerings.

Following standardized approaches has a number of additional benefits. A standardized methodology provides a certain confidence that no important steps or aspects of a test are forgotten by accident. As tests should be repeated after significant changes to the target system, following the same methodology also provides the possibility to compare multiple tests to identify whether a system got more secure after mitigation measures have been taken. A standardized approach and common reporting forms also allows to compare results with those measured on other similar installations. A generally accepted methodology may be required in cases where security tests are required from a legal or insurance perspective. Moreover, such a methodology simplifies negotiations between a security tester and clients about the scope of such tests.

Over the years, many standardized methodologies have been proposed. Despite that, none of the proposed methodologies specifically faces security challenges posed by critical infrastructures (CIs). To the best of our knowledge, the only guide focusing on industrial control system (ICSs) is the one developed within the US National Electric Sector Cybersecurity Organization Resource (NESCOR) [2]. The NESCOR methodology specifically focuses on testing electric utilities devices but lacks of a general approach to CI security assessments.

In this paper, *we propose a new security assessment methodology tailored to support security testing in CIs.* To define our methodology, we (1) *analyze security assessments and penetration testing methodologies from various domains* and (2) *interviewed stakeholders to investigate existing best practices adopted in industry, derive related issues and collect proposals for possible solutions.* Based on these two activities, *we propose a security assessment and penetration testing methodology for critical infrastructure that is founded in standard methodologies adapting their different phases and steps to requirements in CI.* This methodology aims to support ICS operators to assess security of CIs and assist pentesters in the activities of vulnerability searching and exploitation.

The rest of the paper is structured as follows. Sections 2 and 5 provide an overview on standard assessment methodologies and widely used pentesting tools. Section 3 analyses CI testing constraints and describes expected outputs from the operator's point of view. We detail our security assessment methodology in Sect. 4. Finally we discuss achievements and future works in Sect. 6.

2   Standard Methodologies

Over the years, many IT security assessment standard methodologies have been proposed. Among the most well-known standards are: OSSTMM [3], NIST SP800-115 [4] and ISSAF [5]. As the last years have witnessed an increasing concern for ICS security, some organizations have started working towards a standardization of security measures for industrial infrastructures. This is the case with the NESCOR methodology [2] that targets smart grids. In what follows we briefly outline the most important aspects of each of them.

2.1   OSSTMM

The Open Source Security Testing Methodology Manual (OSSTMM) is an open methodology for security testing that encompasses tests for every security aspect: from personnel qualification to physical security, from control of communication to electronic systems safety. The OSSTMM work flow is based on the identification of a type of security test (e.g. Blind, Gray Box, etc.) and the scope of the audit (Communication security, Physical security, and Spectrum security). The scope is further divided and defined by five "channels": Human, Physical, Wireless Communication, Data Network, and Telecommunications.

Once a type of test and a scope have been identified, the methodology leads the tester through seventeen operation "modules". Every module defines a specific target and several tasks that are needed to achieve it. Each module has an input and an output. The input represents the information needed to perform each task while the output is the result of the accomplished tasks.

Assessment results make use of security metrics, called Risk Assessment Values (RAVs), that quantify the security of the channels (e.g. measurement of the attack surface, the amount of uncontrolled interactions with a target, etc.).

2.2   NIST SP800-115

NISTSP800-115 provides organizations with guidelines on planning, conducting and evaluating information security testing. Even if the overall goal is to focus on some security assessment key elements, this publication provides also practical recommendations and technical information related to penetration tests.

The NISTSP800-115 work flow runs through three different phases: Planning (that concerns the collection of information regarding assets, threats, policies in use, etc.), Execution (that regards operational activities such as vulnerability identification and exploitation), and Post-Execution (that concerns the identification of vulnerability causes and mitigation strategies).

Within the Execution phase, the pentesting activity is further specified by three practical steps: "Review Techniques" (that analyzes assets and security policies in-place), "Target Identification and Analysis Techniques" (that describes how to identify potential targets), and "Target Vulnerability Validation Techniques" (that explains how to test discovered vulnerabilities).

Compared to OSSTMM, NISTSP800-114 provides a less comprehensive set of assessment activities but discusses the pentesting step with a more technical approach by giving specific recommendations and details.

2.3 ISSAF

The Information Systems Security Assessment Framework (ISSAF) is a peer reviewed structured framework designed by the Open Information Systems Security Group (OISSG). The methodology defined by ISSAF covers all the aspects related to security assessments: from an high-level perspective (e.g. business impact and organizational models) to practical techniques (e.g. security testing of passwords, systems, network, etc.).

ISSAF is divided into four main phases structured in different "activities". The four phases are: Planning (concerns all the operation needed to define a project plan for the whole assessment process), Assessment (defines the approach needed to evaluate the Information Security Risks within an enterprise), Treatment (implements a platform for taking decision about the identified security risks), and Accreditation (defines the steps needed to an organization to obtain the ISSAF certification).

The Penetration Testing methodology proposed by ISSAF consists of three phases and nine assessment steps. The three phases are: "Planning and Preparation", "Assessment", and "Reporting, Clean-up and Destroy Artifacts". The assessment steps go through the practical operations needed to identify and exploit infrastructure vulnerabilities. These steps are: "Information Gathering", "Network Mapping", "Vulnerability Identification", "Penetration", "Gaining Access & Privilege Escalation", "Enumerating Further", "Compromising Remote User/Sites", "Maintaining Access", "Covering Tracks".

ISSAF is as comprehensive as OSSTMM and more detailed than NISTSP800-115. However, the framework is less flexible than the other methodologies and cannot easily adapt to different kinds of IT environment.

2.4 NESCOR

The NESCOR Guide to Penetration Testing for Electric Utilities aims to support security assessments in smart grids. It is not a comprehensive methodology but focuses on the penetration testing phase providing a step-by-step procedure with high-level descriptions of penetration testing tasks and overall goals.

The NESCOR guide is divided into nine parts. Testing activities starts with the definition of a scope of the engagement. Then, pentesters have to analyze the architecture of the target system and, if possible, to replicate it in a safe environment. The testing process is divided into four main tasks: "Server OS Penetration" (identification of known or unknown vulnerabilities that can cause the attacker to be in control of the control servers), "Server Application Penetration" (exploitation of applications running within the control servers), "Network Communication Penetration" (communication eavesdropping and identification of protocol vulnerabilities), and "Embedded Device Penetration" (identification of physical attacks against ICS devices). The process ends with an overall analysis and a final process of result interpretation and reporting.

For each step of the methodology, the authors advice pentesters on the likelihood of a target system to be compromised (based on required skills by an attacker). This likelihood is expressed in colors: Green (easy target), Yellow (common target), Orange (unusual target), Red (complex target).

3   Critical Infrastructure Constraints

Developing a security assessment methodology for CI needs the input of different expertises (e.g. academia, ICS vendors, and ICS operators, etc.). We have collected viewpoints and industry requirements by interviewing experts to better understand present and future challenges that industries, governments and academia have to face to keep ICSs protected against common and targeted attacks. These interviews lead from the questionnaire presented in [6]. What follows is the result distilled from this analysis.

3.1   Security Deployment Limitations

There are several constraints in deploying security within CIs. Costs and available time are the most important. Costs play always an important role by limiting the available resources. Time constraints make it impossible to investigate all potential security issues and to properly deploy all effective security solutions within a CI.

Another limitation is the non-interoperability of off-the-shelf security technology and industrial control system devices. However, off-the-shelf tools and techniques are increasingly customized for CI components.

3.2   Security Tests

Most CI stakeholders already use security tests to check their infrastructures (e.g. stress, denial-of-service, and penetration tests, security code reviews, and formal code verification). While CI vendors apply many of these tests, CI operators almost exclusively perform stress and penetration test.

Only few experts consider "live" systems suitable for tests. Analyses are just performed during the setup process. However, situations in which the system is off-line for maintenance are also considered suitable to run specific tests. The reason are concerns that a test may affect the proper functioning of a CI and endanger physical processes, people, and company businesses. For example, SANDIA (a major United States Department of Energy research and development national laboratory) reported that a ping sweep performed during a test on ICSs caused a robotic arm to dangerously swing [7].

3.3 Pentesting Strategies

More than specific tests, our study investigates pentesting strategies already in place within specific critical infrastructures. This includes typologies of pentesting, remote access to infrastructures, and assessment outsourcing.

CI stakeholders use both white-Box and black-box penetration testing depending on the purpose of the test (e.g. vulnerability discovery vs. assessing defense reaction capabilities). Remote access is rarely used in CI testing. Not all CI operators agree to open their systems to the Internet. However, there are cases of specific tests performed through public networks to better simulate real attack scenarios. Finally, some CI operators agree on outsourcing part of the testing. In any case, outsourced tests do not substitute internal testing and a subset of the tests is always lead by CI owners. Moreover, outsourced tests are often performed on separate non-production devices or subsystems and they are rarely comprehensive for the whole infrastructure.

3.4 Penetration Testing Methodologies for Critical Infrastructures

The majority of stakeholders is not aware of any specific methodology focusing on CI (like NESCOR). However, some of them indicated that (non-public) customized proprietary methodologies for specific tests already exist. These methodologies are confined to a small set of companies and infrastructures.

All the interviewees agree on the value of a standard CI assessment methodology. However, not all agree on the level of detail and generality of such a methodology. On the one hand, there is the need of a comprehensive and detailed methodology that would make security testing on CI more organized/repeatable/comparable. On the other hand it is required to also provide specific best practices adaptable to concrete domains and systems. Still, there is agreement that the methodology should advice software and tools to be used, provide both specific tips and general guidelines about each testing aspect, and standardize the outcomes to the assessment process.

4 Critical Infrastructure Security Assessment Methodology

In this section we describe a security assessment methodology for CI based on the previous results. We do not aim to create a new approach from scratch.

Our methodology organizes CI stakeholders needs to specific phases of existing methodologies. The result is a lightweight security assessment methodology and a penetration testing tuned to constraints and requirements in CI.

4.1 Overview

Our methodology is conceptually split into two levels (Fig. 1):

- the **General Assessment** includes: the *Pre-Assessment* phase in which a company identifies the goals of the assessment and solves any bureaucratic and legal issues regarding the following operations, and the *Post-Assessment* phase in which the company evaluates the results and takes decision on vulnerability countermeasures and information disclosure.
- the **Practical Assessment** completes the General Assessment linking the aforementioned two phases. The Practical Assessment includes: the *Preparation* phase in which pentesters discuss technical details with system operators and prepare tools and strategies to be used during the test; the *Testing* phase where all the tests are performed; and the *Analysis* phase in which the results of the tests are documented and detailed.

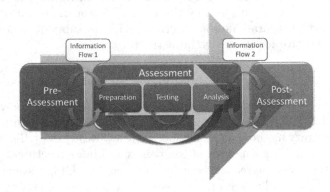

Fig. 1. Critical infrastructure methodology

The model illustrated in Fig. 1 shows also two *Information Flows* elements and two loops. The loops address the potential need to redo specific activities of a phase due to new information found in a following phase (e.g. requirements identified in the Pre-Assessment do not match with the results of the Practical Assessment and pentesters need further analyses and tests).

The reason to split the General Assessment from the Practical Assessment is twofold and answers to the needs raised by stakeholders during the interviews. First, this model increases the usability of the methodology. Stakeholders can substitute one of the two sections depending on their needs and connect the new activities by tuning just the connective information flows. Second, such a model improves the maintainability of the methodology in case part of it becomes outdated. In this case, stakeholders would have to update the related section of the methodology without altering the rest.

4.2 Security Testing Phases

Here, we discuss some phases of the methodology in more detail. The **Pre-Assessment** phase defines security assessment motivations and goals. This phase involves three different actors: the Chief Security Officer (CSO) or whoever is responsible for this function and may decide to approve the starting of assessment operations; the Chief Financial Officer (CFO) or whoever is representative for this function and may decide on the budget allocated for the assessment operations and about acceptable risks; and ICS operators that are responsible to contribute to the discussion from a technical point of view. The tasks of this phase include: description of security assessment goals, threat scenarios, identification of company assets, analysis of potential risks of a security test at business level, analysis of legal and contract obligations with stakeholders (e.g. warranties of suppliers). Moreover, involved actors have to agree on the assessment time plan (e.g. fitting infrastructure deployment or maintenance periods) and on the resources allocated to the further five phases of the methodology.

At the end of the Pre-Assessment phase, participants prepare a document summarizing all the outcome. The **Information Flow 1** defines the process of translation of such outcomes in practical directives for pentesters.

The **Preparation** phase involves two actors: ICS operators that report outcomes of the Pre-Assessment phase, and pentesters in charge of performing practical tests. The tasks of this phases include: definition of plausible attack scenarios, identification of a pentesting strategy, identification of the targets, organization of a test schedule. During the Preparation phase, involved actors constantly analyze the expected impact of the testing on the infrastructure. CI cannot be put in danger by a penetration testing even if the reason to perform the analysis is verifying that possibility. For this reason, ICS operators should implement specific safeguards and prepare an emergency plan in case a security test endanger people or infrastructure physical security. Alternatively, tests should only be conducted in safe lab environments. The final activity of the Preparation phase is the setup of the testing environment.

The **Testing** phase addresses the actual execution of the security tests performed by pentesters. This phase will be extensively discussed in Sect. 4.3. While performing the tests, pentesters log all the activities and related findings. In the meantime, ICS operators responsible for the emergency plan check and log the presence of testing side effects (e.g. cascading effects) on the CI that the pentesters may not be aware of. The two activity logs will be the input of the Analysis phase. It is worth noting that, in case a test shows severe vulnerabilities that can endanger the CI, the emergency plan should be triggered and prevent potential damages. The effect of such an event is the interruption of the methodology workflow and the immediate feedback to the Chief Security Officer.

The **Analysis** phase concludes the Practical Assessment. In this phase, pentesters report testing findings and rate the CI overall security, while ICS operators critically review the testing, contextualizing the problems and justifying any design or maintenance choices.

After the testing, ICS operators perform two further important tasks: they check if the status of the system has returned to normal (also removing any file or software used during the testing), and they apply fixes to minor and easy-to-fix problems and vulnerabilities (e.g., simple misconfiguration that does not need any further action to be discussed in the Post-Assessment).

At the end of the Analysis phase ICs operators and pentesters prepare a document thatsummarizes findings and security issues starting from the report of the Testing phase (**Information flow 2**).

The **Post-Assessment** phase involves two actors: ICS operators that present performed activities and findings of the Practical Assessment and possible countermeasures, and the Chief Security Officer or whoever represents this role in the company and may decide how to implement proposed countermeasures and whether to disclose found vulnerabilities. The output of the Post-Assessment phase is a document that details infrastructure vulnerabilities, established mitigations, and compliance to security legislation or policies.

4.3   Testing Phase

The Testing phase includes four testing processes with five operational steps: *Information Gathering, Architecture Analysis, Vulnerability Identification, Penetration,* and *Maintaining Control*; each process is targeting one task of the NESCOR methodology ("Server OS Penetration", "Server Application Penetration", "Network Communication Penetration", "Embedded Device Penetration"). The sequence of tasks defined by the NESCOR methodology may change to be compliant with the test schedule detailed in the Preparation phase.

In the **Information Gathering** step pentesters collect information on the CI (e.g. devices, software, personnel, or company policies). Depending on the type of testing (Black Box vs. White Box), pentesters can have some initial information at their disposal that helps them to better understand the environment.

In the **Architecture Analysis** step pentesters analyze collected information and focus on identifying possible targets within the CI. Several tools can be used during this phase (e.g., sniffers, device fingerprinters, disassemblers, etc.). The Architectural Analysis step will allow pentesters to confirm or discard attack hypotheses formulated during the Preparation phase.

Once one or more targets have been selected, pentesters perform a vulnerability scanning (e.g. using Nessus) in the **Vulnerability Identification** step.

In the **Penetration** step, pentesters try to gain access and obtain control of CI devices. This is a critical operation of the Testing phase as the attackers try to subvert CI's normal operations. In this step, frameworks such as Metasploit or customized tools are used.

Once access to a device is gained, pentesters move to the **Maintaining Control** step, retrieve any valuable information, and try to maintain control on the device by installing malicious code (e.g., root-kits). This step, can also lead to new targets (e.g. a device on a specific network may also link to different networks). If the target is still on scope (the target is in the list edited during the Preparation phase) the Testing phase loops back to the start.

Figure 2 shows the Testing steps performed within assessment methodology. The colors of the four testing loops refer to the colors used by the NESCOR methodology discussed in Sect. 2.4.

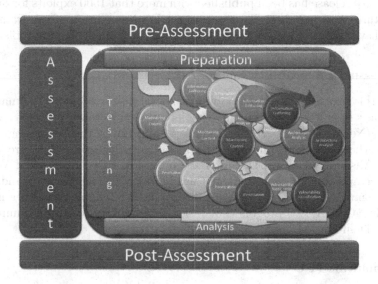

Fig. 2. Critical infrastructure methodology plus penetration testing steps (Color figure online)

5 Pentesting Tools

Availability of suitable security testing tools is of extreme importance for conducting effective and efficient tests and play also an important role in our methodology. Security experts developed different tools for many kinds of vulnerability checks and exploitations. However these tools are mainly focused on testing standard IT infrastructures (assuming Windows/Linux, TCP/IP, Web, Internet, etc.). Where industrial control systems (or more in general, critical infrastructures) deviate and provide specific or proprietary systems, software, and protocols, they are often not applicable. While a detailed discussion of penetration testing tools is beyond the scope of this paper, we want to conclude this paper by briefly listing the most important general tools and frameworks and the few ones that specialize on industrial control systems to provide a first starting point for practical application of our methodology.

5.1 Metasploit Framework

The Metasploit Framework [8] is one of the most known and widely-used penetration testing tools in the information security community.

Security experts and developers can use its open source platform to test a
wide range of systems and to write new exploits customized to specific targets
and tests. The extensible model provides to the user a comprehensive database of
exploits, payloads, encoders, no-op generators and several other auxiliary codes.
The last free release has been published with more that 1500 exploits for different
architectures and software. The commercial Express edition of the framework,
besides having more features, provides also ICS specific pentesting tools.

5.2 Nessus Vulnerability Scanner

Nessus [1] is probably the most popular vulnerability scanner on the market.

Nessus's operations rely on the description of vulnerability exploits written
in NASL (Nessus Attack Scripting Language) and run by the Nessus engine. The
tool does checks for four different categories of security issues: Software Vulnerabilities, Misconfigurations, Default Passwords, and PCI DSS Related Vulnerabilities (compliance for the Payment Card Industry Data Security Standard).

The commercial version of Nessus distributed by Tenable contains a number
of specific SCADA/ICS plugins that test a variety of devices from a number of
vendors (including ABB and Siemens) [9].

5.3 SamuraiSTFU

SamuraiSTFU [10] is a pentesting distribution used to perform security tests
specifically on ICS environments. Some key points of SamuraiSTFU are: a collection of free and open source tools for all aspects of SCADA and Smart Grid
pentesting, a comprehensive documentation on SCADA and Smart Grid architectures and protocols, a collection of PCAP samples captured over real environment networks, tools for Smart Grid environments simulations. Unlike other
general purpose pentesting distribution (e.g. Kali Linux [11]), SamuraiSTFU has
a clear focus on ICS where the main audiences are utilities and vendors in the
energy sector. Secondary audience are utilities from other CI sectors.

5.4 SCADA Strangelove Tools

SCADA Strangelove [12] is a group of Russian hackers specialized in SCADA
security. Besides running a blog dedicated to SCADA security, they also provide
a number of tools for general download. These include network scanners for
Profinet, password crackers for Siemens S7 PLCs, a metasploit module called
WinCC Harvester for Siemens SCADA software, and other similar tools.

The group also provides useful documentation, such as WinCC 7.x hardening
guide and a ICS/SCADA/PLC Google/Shodan Cheat Sheet (that can be used
to find target systems for specific protocols using Google or Shodan [13]).

6   Conclusions and Future Works

In this paper we propose a security testing methodology for critical infrastructures like ICS. We built on the structure of other and often more general testing methodologies and the input from industry experts. The resulting methodology provides a structure approach for security testing of CI systems where the individual phases discuss specific requirements and considerations for each step. To complement our proposal, we provide brief discussion of various tools especially suitable CI security testing. Due to space constraints we were not able to discuss the methodology in details. A more detailed discussion of our methodology can be found in deliverable 5.1 of the European CRISALIS research project [6] to be published soon via the website. We envision that availability of such a method will lead to security tests of CI to become more organized, repeatable and comparable. Future testing activities within the CRISALIS European project will try to apply the methodology and provide further feedbacks on its usability.

References

1. Deraison, R., Meer, H., Walt, C.V.D.: Nessus Network Auditing. Syngress Media Incorporated (2004)
2. Searle, J.: NESCOR Version 3 - Guide to Penetration Testing forElectric Utilities (2012). http://www.smartgrid.epri.com/nescor.aspx
3. Herzog, P.: OSSTMM 3–The open source security testing methodologymanual (2010). http://www.osstmm.org/
4. Scarfone, K., Souppaya, M., Cody, A., Orebaugh, A.: NIST Special Publication 800–115: Technical Guide to Information Security Testing and Assessment (2008)
5. Rathore, B., Brunner, M., Dilaj, M., Herrera, O., Brunati, P., Subramaniam, R.K., Raman, S., Chavan, U.: ISSAF 0.2.1 - Information Systems Security Assessment Framework (2006)
6. CRitical InfrastructureSecurity AnaLysIS (CRISALIS) (2012). http://www.crisalis-project.eu/
7. Duggan, D., Berg, M., Dillinger, J., Stamp, J.: Penetration testing of industrial control systems. Sandia National Laboratories (2005)
8. Metasploit, L.: The metasploit framework (2007). http://www.metasploit.com/
9. Tenable, SCADA Security. http://www.tenable.com/solutions/scada-security
10. UtiliSec, Samurai Project's Security Testing Framework for Utilities (SamuraiSTFU). http://www.samuraistfu.org/
11. Offensive Security Ltd., Kali Linux. http://www.kali.org/
12. Radvanovsky, R., Brodsky, J.: SCADA Strangelove or How Ilearned to StartWorrying and Love Nuclear Plant. http://www.scadasl.org/
13. Matherly, J.: Expose online devices, May 2013. http://www.shodanhq.com/

Automatic Fault Identification in Sensor Networks Based on Probabilistic Modeling

Stavros Ntalampiras[✉] and Georgios Giannopoulos

Joint Research Center, European Commission,
Via Enrico Fermi 2749, 21027 Ispra, Varese, Italy
stavros.ntalampiras@polimi.it, georgios.giannopoulos@jrc.ec.europa.eu
http://ipsc.jrc.ec.europa.eu

Abstract. This work proposes a mechanism able to automatically categorize different types of faults occurring in critical infrastructures and especially water distribution networks. The mechanism models the relationship exhibited among the sensor datastreams based on the assumption that its pattern alters depending on the fault type. The first phase includes linear time invariant modeling which outputs a parameters vector. At the second phase the evolution of the parameter vectors is captured via hidden Markov modeling. The methodology is applied on data coming from the water distribution network of the city of Barcelona. The corpus contains a vast amount of data representative of nine network states. The nominal is included for enabling fault detection. The achieved classification rates are quite encouraging and the system is practical.

Keywords: Linear time invariant modeling · Hidden Markov model · Fault diagnosis · Critical infrastructure protection

1 Introduction

Modern sensor networks include numerous elements for capturing various parameters of the environment under monitoring. In principle, these may produce homogeneous (e.g. only temperature) or heterogeneous (e.g. humidity and inclination) measurements. The trend suggests that the size of these networks is increasing in order to facilitate information gathering and subsequently derive a more accurate characterization of the process under monitoring. However, the increased size raises the complexity of the total framework and burdens real-time data processing. On top of that, not rarely, sensor networks suffer from various kinds of faults (sensor malfunctions, drifts, communication faults, power loss, etc.) which decrease the performance of the system. In such cases, prompt detection and isolation are of paramount importance towards avoiding information loss and/or misinterpretation of the ongoing situation.

The particular problematic falls within the scientific area of Fault Detection and Isolation (FDI), or simpler, fault diagnosis. It typically includes the detection

© European Union, 2016
C.G. Panayiotou et al. (Eds.): CRITIS 2014, LNCS 8985, pp. 344–354, 2016.
DOI: 10.1007/978-3-319-31664-2_35

of the fault (which refers to the time instant which the fault occurred) and its isolation (which refers to the location of the occurred fault). Fault identification corresponds to determining the nature of the detected and isolated fault, and is an element of significant importance since it may provide useful information for designing a proper accommodation strategy to minimize or even eliminate the consequences of the fault.

This article proposes a methodology for *fault identification* without the need of an analytical model of the underlying process generating the data while considering the cases of erroneous fault detections. We build on the findings of [1] and we model the relationships between the datastreams coming from the sensor network using a hidden Markov model (HMM) trained on the parameters of linear time invariant (LTI) models estimating the relationships. Subsequently the faulty data is automatically classified based on the HMM which most likely generated the particular data sequence (see Fig. 1). Concurrently the system is able to understand whether the data come from an already known class of faults as well as identify whether the data belong to the fault-free situation, thus achieving fault detection as well. Furthermore we present a method able to identify data which does not exist in the dataset. Dealing with unseen data is of significant importance since they are usually associated with one or more new fault types.

To the best of our knowledge, no approaches present in the literature consider a dynamic modeling approach with the model coefficients used to train an HMM for fault identification. The methodology is applied on data coming from the water distribution network of Barcelona, which comprises a Critical Infrastructure since its smooth undisrupted operation is of paramount importance for the quality of life of the citizens [2].

The rest of this article is organized as follows: Sect. 2 provides a representative picture of the related literature. Section 3 describes the joint usage of LTI and HMM for modeling the relationship between two datastreams. Subsequently Sect. 5 explains how unseen data is treated. Section 6 explains the experimental set-up and the dataset coming from the Barcelona water distribution network while the last section concludes this work.

2   Related Literature

Since in practical applications it is unrealistic to assume the existence of an accurate analytical model of the process under monitoring, the FDI community has steered its attention to *Computational Intelligence* (CI) methods, which have been recently employed for fault identification [3]. They may be based on quantitative (numerical) and/or qualitative (symbolic) information about the process of interest. Qualitative information is used in [4] where a fault-tree analysis was designed as an analytical troubleshooting tool by a team of knowledgeable managers, engineers, and technicians. Fault tree analysis is also used by Crosetti et al. [5] with a probability evaluation scheme. Fuzzy if-then relations have also been used in the fault diagnosis domain. Dexter [6] created fuzzy reference models to describe the symptoms of both faulty and fault-free plant operation and

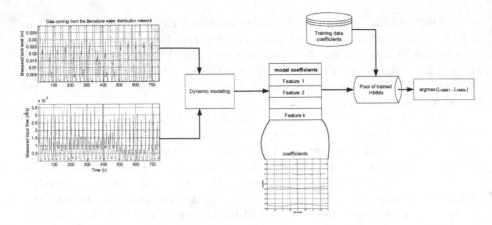

Fig. 1. Fault identification based on multiple HMMs. The class of the unknown data is determined by the HMM producing the highest log-likelihood.

subsequently used them to identify whether the system is operating correctly or a particular fault is present. Another work based on fuzzy models is reported in [7]. The authors obtain the fuzzy models using a modified regularity criterion algorithm while they optimized them by a genetic algorithm. Their methodology is applied on an industrial valve simulator to detect and isolate several abrupt and incipient faults in the system.

Even though qualitative CI approaches are effective, the derivation of accurate rules and/or fuzzy if-then relations is difficult, not to mention time-consuming and costly in case domain experts are involved. This makes them impractical for many engineering applications. Thus methods which can learn these rules "hidden" within large datasets are employed with neural networks constituting the primary tool due to their universal non-linear function approximation property [8]. Neural networks can model the behavior of a given system based on its produced input-output data. A work which employs NNs is reported in [9] where both artificial and real-world data were used to train NN agents for classifying between different motor bearing faults through the measurement and interpretation of motor bearing vibration signatures. Fault diagnosis in non-linear dynamic systems based on neural networks is described in [10]. This work uses a multi-layer perceptron network trained to predict the future system states based on the current system inputs and states. Afterwards, a neural network is trained to classify characteristics contained in the residuals and essentially performs fault identification.

Several works in the literature aim at exploiting the merits of both qualitative and quantitative approaches. Paper [11] exploits analytical redundancy via parity equation while neural networks are then used to maximize the signal-to-noise ratio of the residual and to isolate different faults. This methodology is applied for fault detection and isolation for a hydraulic test rig. Article [12] proposes the usage of multilevel flow models and ANN to develop a fault diagnosis system, with the intention of improving both identification and understandability of the diagnostic process and results. A feedforward ANN trained with the back-propagation algorithm is employed and when the faults are localized a diagnosis is performed by ANNs for either confirming the faults or offer an alternative solution and/or detailed information about the possible root cause. The application scenario is a Nuclear Power Plants simulator. A hybrid approach for fault diagnosis in 3-DOF (degree of freedom) flight simulator is proposed in [13]. They combine rough set theory with a genetic algorithm compute the reductions of the decision table. Then, the condition attributes of decision table comprise the input nodes of an ANN and the decision attributes are regarded as the output nodes of artificial neural network correspondingly.

To the best of our knowledge there are no approaches using multiple HMMs operating in the parameter space of LTI models for identifying faults in sensor networks. The HMMs may address nonlinearities existing within the data while they can be adaptive so as to deal with dynamic unstructured environments.

3   Modeling the Relationship Between Sensor Datastreams

This section explains the method used for modeling the relationships between datastreams coming from correlated sensors, meaning that the pattern of the relationship should remain consistent when the system operates in a certain state (faulty or not).

Let us consider a monitoring framework comprised of N sensors each of which generates a datastream. Denote by $X_i : \mathbb{N} \to \mathbb{R}$ the stream of data acquired by the i-th sensor.

Let $O_{i,T_0} = \{X_i(t), t = 1, \dots, T_0\}$ and $O_{j,T_0} = \{X_j(t), t = 1, \dots, T_0\}$ be the data sequence of the i-th and j-th sensors. In the following we assume that their relationship is characterized by a process $\mathcal{P}$ which is time-invariant or that every state of the system (e.g. nominal, freezing fault, etc.) can be approximated by a sequence of models even if it is time-variant (e.g. through a Markov process in the parameter space).

Therefore, the relationship between two generic correlated data streams X_i and X_j, X_j used to infer X_i, can be described through a linear input-output dynamic model of the form

$$X_i(k) = f_\theta\big(X_i(k-1), X_i(k-2), \dots, X_i(k-k_i),$$
$$X_j(k), X_j(k-1), \dots, X_j(k-k_j)\big)$$

where f is a function of linear time-invariant type in its parameters θ and k_i and k_j are the orders of the model. Following the logic of [14], we create an ensemble of dynamic models (e.g. ARX, ARMAX, OE, etc.) with various orders and select the one which best fits the datastreams (i.e. lowest reconstruction error) while low-order models are preferred. The model search algorithm minimizes a robustified quadratic prediction error criterion.

1. Build one HMM per faulty class,
$H_{f_1-f_N} = \{N_{f_1-f_N}, P_{f_1-f_N}, A_{f_1-f_N}, \pi_{f_1-f_N}\}$ from the vectors of parameters
$\theta_1...\theta_d$ each of which associated with a linear dynamic model applied to the
training data $O_{i,T_0,i=1,...,d}$ windowized using length M overlapping by $M - 1$;
2. Windowize the incoming novel data as above, which results in windows
$W = W_1...W_x$;
repeat
   | 3. j=1;
   | 4. Compute the parameter vectors of the $j - th$ dynamic model θ_j with
   | respect to W_j;
   | 5. Compute the vector of log-likelihoods $L_{W_{1...j}} = P(\theta_1...\theta_j|H_{f_1...f_N})$;
   | 6. Compute $argmax(L_{W_{1...j}})$ and assign the class with the highest
   | log-likelihood to window W_j;
   | 7. $j = j + 1$;
until (1);

Algorithm 1. The fault identification algorithm which models the relationship between two sensors by means of an HMM.

The second phase models the sequence of the model parameters by means of an HMM $H_{\theta_T} = \{N, P, A, \pi\}$, where N are the states, P the probability density functions with respect to each state, θ_T are the parameters of the training sequence, A the state transition probability matrix and π the initial state distribution. The model space is searched based on the log-likelihood criterion during the operational life. The model which produces the highest log-likelihood is selected out of the model library created off-line.

4   The Fault Identification Algorithm

The training phase of the proposed methodology creates one HMM per fault type while the testing one examines the probability that the novel data sequence was produced by the existing HMMs. The mechanism assigns the class associated with the HMM producing the highest log-likelihood to the unknown data. Based on the specific logic we essentially try to quantify the statistical similarity between the unknown data and the one available during training. The highest the similarity with an HMM, the most probable that this data sequence was generated by the specific HMM.

The fault identification algorithm is summarized in Algorithm 1. We assume a training set corresponding to $O_{i,T_0,1 \leq i \leq N}$ associated with each faulty class. We compute the d model coefficients over a predefined window of the sensor measurements of size M. They are used to train the HMM representing the specific class. In order to identify the HMMs with the best classification capabilities, we build a variety of HMMs with different parameters (number of states and Gaussian components) and we select the HMM based on the highest recognition rate criterion. The set of the constructed HMMs represents the set of classes

Table 1. The confusion matrix which includes the identification rates per frame with respect to the two frameworks in the following format: HMM/MLP (the respective overall averages are 82.5 %/79.2 %). The highest recognition accuracy for each class of faults is emboldened (abbreviations: N:Normal state, F1:Freezing abrupt additive fault, F2: Freezing incipient additive fault, F3: Negative offset abrupt additive fault, F4: Negative offset incipient additive fault, F5: Positive drift abrupt additive fault, F6: Positive drift incipient additive fault, F7: Noise abrupt additive fault, F8: Noise incipient additive fault).

	Predicted (%)								
	N	F1	F2	F3	F4	F5	F6	F7	F8
N	**87/78.4**	5.6/7.6	-/4.1	-/-	-/3.2	5.2/4	-/0.3	-/-	2.2/2.2
F1	-/-	**78.9/76.9**	-/6.5	6.7/3.3	2.4/-	-/-	-/-	-/1.3	12/12
F2	2.4/4.5	0.4/6.7	**83.2/80**	-/-	-/-	2/1.2	4.5/3.8	6.7/3	0.8/0.8
F3	-/2.8	-/-	1.1/-	**83.2/82.8**	3/2	-/-	9.5/9.2	-/-	3.2/3.2
F4	2.1/1.8	-/5.8	-/3.5	6.7/4	**84.4/79.8**	-/-	5/2	1.8/-	-/3.1
F5	5/2	3.2/3.5	-/5.1	-/-	1.4/1	**82.4/79**	-/1.4	3.8/3.8	4.2/4.2
F6	1.4/4.5	4.1/3.6	-/-	9.8/8.5	-/-	-/-	**82.4/81.1**	-/-	2.4/2.3
F7	5.3/-	2.5/3.1	5.6/2.9	-/-	6.7/9.8	0.3/3.7	3.2/7.6	**76.4/72.9**	-/-
F8	2.6/2.6	4.5/3.4	-/-	2/-	-/3.1	3.2/-	-/4.7	2.8/4.6	**84.9/81.6**

(left margin label: Presented)

in a 1-1 sense meaning that each HMM is associated with data coming from a unique system state.

When unknown data is processed, it is first windowized and the model coefficients with respect to each window are computed and inserted into the trained HMM. The log-likelihood vector is then calculated for window W_j and its maximum element is discovered revealing the HMM which best "explains" W_j. Finally the class represented by this HMM is assigned to W_j. The classification process is shown in Fig. 1.

The HMM models the evolution of the parameters derived while estimating the relationship pattern of the measured tank level and the measured input flow data streams. In other words X_i corresponds to $y_m(k)$ and X_j to $q_{in_m}(k)$. The measured demand follows a pattern imposed by the consumers and may be considered as a disturbance factor. During faulty conditions the specific relationship should exhibit alterations depending on the fault type, thus its monitoring is useful for fault identification purposes.

5   Dealing with Unseen Faults

It is of paramount importance that fault diagnosis systems operating on Critical Infrastructures posses the ability to deal with data coming from faulty classes which are not present in the available corpus. More often than not, the system under study may experience a faulty situation which has never been encountered before. The data associated with these conditions are not available during the development of the system making their correct classification impossible.

To overcome this type of problematic, in this work we pool the entire training corpus and create a *universal* model meaning that it estimates the probability

1. Train the universal HMM $H_u = \{N_u, P_u(x|\theta), A_u, \pi_u\}$ on the vectors of parameters $\theta_1 ... \theta_d$ each of which associated with a linear dynamic model applied to the training data $O_{i,T_0,i=1,...,d}$ windowized using length M overlapping by $M - 1$;

2. $T_u = min(Log - likelihoods)_{O_{i,T_0,i=1,...,d}}$;

3. Initialize the likelihood L;

repeat

    4. Acquire input data $x(t)$;

    5. Compute the log-likelihood $L(t)$;

    6. **if** $L(t) < T_u$ **then**

       | Unseen data is detected.

    end

    7. $t = t + 1$;

until *(1)*;

Algorithm 2. An HMM-based framework for novel data detection.

density function of the total dataset. Subsequently, as described in Algorithm 2, the statistical similarity between the HMM and the incoming novel data is used to process the datastream. Data characterized by high statistical similarity are considered as coming from the known during training classes. Differently, data with low statistical similarity are marked as *unseen*. Seen from unseen data are differentiated by means of a threshold T_u, which is set equal to the minimum log-likelihood of the training dataset. This process tags each data instance as either *seen* or *unseen* (meaning that it has been previously seen inside the corpus or not). Only data instances marked as *seen* are kept for further processing.

6 Experimental Set-Up and Results

This section provides details regarding the dataset coming form the Barcelona water distribution network, the parametrization of the proposed approach as well as a performance analysis by means of confusion matrices.

We employed the Torch framework (available at www.torch.ch) during both learning and validation phase. The maximum number of k-means iterations for cluster initialization was set to 50 while the Baum-Welch algorithm used to estimate the transition matrix was bounded to 100 iterations with a threshold of 0.001 between subsequent iterations. The number of explored states ranges from 3 to 7 while the number of Gaussian components used to build each GMM comes from the $\{2, 4, 8, 16, 32, 64, 128, 256$ and $512\}$ set. Finally the window length M was 100, a value which provided satisfactory reconstruction error during the preliminary experimental phase.

The HMMs have been configured in a fully connected topology (ergodic HMM), which means that the algorithm permits every possible transition across states while the distribution of each state is modelled by a Gaussian mixture model (GMM) with a diagonal covariance matrix.

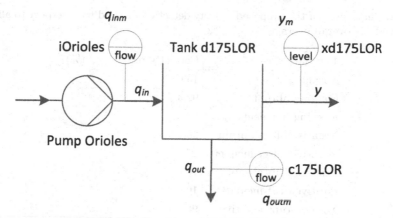

Fig. 2. The diagram of the Orioles subsystem belonging to the Barcelona water distribution network.

6.1   The Barcelona Water Distribution Network

The Barcelona water network considers 23 different districts covering an area of 424 Km^2 while serving about 3 million end users. It comprises a large scale infrastructure which includes 3 surface and 7 underground sources, 63 storage tanks, 18 nodes, 79 pumps, 50 valves and 88 demand sectors. The main sensors of the network include flow meters and pressure sensors [15]. Our experiments are focussed on the Orioles subsystem shown in Fig. 2. It has been chosen due to space limitations, still without loss of generalization since the specific method can be applied on any part of the network unaltered. The Orioles subsystem includes the following elements: (a) a tank (d175LOR), (b) an actuator with flow sensor ($iOrioles$), (c) demand with flow sensor (c175LOR) and (d) a level sensor (xd175LOR).

The dataset includes different fault types occurring on the elements of the network including both sensors and actuators: (a) Freezing: The faulty sensor provides identical measurements at the predefined fault time instant. (b) Offset: A constant magnitude is added to the sensor measurements at the predefined fault time instant. (c) Drift: A ramp function is added to the sensor measurements at the predefined fault time instant. (d) Noise: Random normally distributed measurement noise is added to the sensor measurements at the predefined fault time instant. Each fault may resemble one or more erroneous situations, such as power failure, communication error, sensor drift, etc. It should be mentioned that the faults are of both abrupt and incipient nature.

The sampling period T is one hour while the fault is appearing at sample $t_f = 100$ in $iOrioles$ pump sensor ($f_{q_{inm}}$). The dataset concerns a period of one year while the first 30 days were used to train each fault identification framework. The rest of the data is used solely for testing. Zero-mean Gaussian noise affected the datastreams with $\sigma = 0.1$.

Table 2. The results of the proposed novelty detection method with respect to all data classes and the overall average.

Test data class	Correctly recognized (%)
Normal	100
Freezing abrupt	92.3
Freezing incipient	96.5
Negative offset abrupt	96.1
Negative offset incipient	97.1
Positive drift abrupt	100
Positive drift incipient	100
Noise abrupt additive	98.1
Noise incipient additive	99.4
Average	**97.7**

6.2   Results

We present identification results derived from the application of two methodologies: (*a*) HMM, and (*b*) Multilayer Perceptron (MLP) applied on the ARX model coefficients. It should be mentioned that the system identification layer uses linear models of ARX(1,2) type for the extraction of the parameters used to train both the HMM and MLP mechanisms. The proposed approach is contrasted with the MLP which reflects well the current trend in the fault identification literature based on CI techniques (see Sect. 2). The MLP includes one hidden layer while it was trained using the back-propagation algorithm at a learning rate of 0.3. The number of nodes is half the total of the number of features plus the number of classes following a widely used empirical rule $((d + 9)/2)$. The Weka machine learning platform was used at this stage [16].

The confusion matrices of the two identification frameworks are tabulated in Table 1. The rates are given in the following format: HMM/MLP. It should be noted that experiments made with mode than one hidden layer did not provide improved performance. Overall we observe that the MLP framework produces lower rates than the HMM. The confusion matrix shows that the HMM method provides the highest rates for every system state including the nominal one. We infer that the rates achieved by the proposed approach are more than satisfactory.

Lastly the novelty detection component described in Sect. 5 was tested using a 9-fold cross validation scheme where each fold corresponds to one class of data (nominal or faulty). Thus we run the experiment nine times: each time one class remains unseen during training while the system is tested on it. The results are shown in Table 2. We observe that the method operates quite well across all data types providing an overall accuracy of 97.7 %.

7   Conclusions and Future Work

We introduced a fault identification framework for distributed sensor networks, the main novelty of which is the usage of an HMM operating in the LTI parameter space. The effectiveness of the proposed framework was carefully examined on data coming from the Barcelona water distribution network. The computational intensive part of the method lies on the training part which is to be ran only once and off-line. During operation it may run real-time since the involved algorithms (system identification and Viterbi) have low computational needs.

In addition, we wish to extent the proposed framework in five ways: (a) explore the usage of features derived from Echo State Networks [17] which may deal with the nonlinearities present in the data in a more effective way than LTI models, (b) develop a smart post-processing algorithm which corrects the decisions provided by the identification scheme, e.g. by eliminating unreasonable series or duration of decisions, (c) despite its rarity, it would be interesting to extent the present framework towards identifying simultaneously occurring faults by evaluating number of hypotheses equal to every possible combination of fault classes following the logic of [18], (d) conduct research towards developing a method for updating the fault dictionary automatically. We envisage a process that would group novel data based on their statistical similarity using e.g. the $K - L$ divergence. Thus, after detecting unknown data, new classes may be formed as soon as an adequate amount of data belonging to the same class is accumulated. (e) Design a cognitive level concatenating the faults decisions made on each subsystem for inferring the state of the entire network. The approach presented here can be extended in order to identify faults over large scale critical infrastructures in a straightforward way. The method could model the relationships existing among strongly correlated sensors and subsequently, by means of a cognitive level, aggregate the decisions made on a local level in order to assess the state of the entire network.

Acknowledgement. The authors would like to thank Prof. Joseba Quevedo and Dr. Miquel A. Cuguero of the Advanced Control System group (http://sac.upc.edu/) of the Polytechnic University of Catalonia for their useful and constructive insights regarding the dataset.

References

1. Quevedo, J., Alippi, C., Cuguero, M.A., Ntalampiras, S., Puig, V., Roveri, M., Garcia, D.: Temporal/spatial model-based fault diagnosis vs. hidden Markov models change detection method: application to the Barcelona water network. In: 2013 21st Mediterranean Conference on Control Automation, pp. 394–400 (2013)
2. Bashan, A., Berezin, Y., Buldyrev, S.V., Havlin, S.: The extreme vulnerability of interdependent spatially embedded networks. Nat Phys. **9**, 667–672 (2013)
3. Sobahni-Tehrani, E.: Fault Detection, Isolation, and Identification for Nonlinear Systems Using a Hybrid Approach. Concordia University, Canada (2008)

4. Zampino, E.J.: The extreme vulnerability of interdependent spatially embedded networks. In: Proceedings of Annual of Reliability and Maintainability Symposium, pp. 16–22 (2001)
5. Crosetti, P.A.: Fault tree analysis with probability evaluation. IEEE Trans. Nucl. Sci. **18**(1), 465–471 (1971)
6. Dexter, A.L.: Fuzzy model based fault diagnosis. IEE Proc. Control Theor. Appl. **142**(6), 545–550 (1995)
7. Mendonsa, L.F., Sousa, J.M.C., Sa da Costa, J.M.G.: Fault detection and isolation of industrial processes using optimized fuzzy models. In: The 14th IEEE International Conference on Fuzzy Systems, pp. 851–856 (2005)
8. Cybenko, G.: Approximation by superpositions of a sigmoidal function. Math. Control, Signals, Syst. **2**, 303–314 (1989)
9. Li, B., Chow, M.-Y., Tipsuwan, Y., Hung, J.C.: Neural-network-based motor rolling bearing fault diagnosis. IEEE Trans. Ind. Electron. **47**(5), 1060–1069 (2000)
10. Patton, R.J., Chen, J., Siew, T.M.: Fault diagnosis in nonlinear dynamic systems via neural networks. In: International Conference on Control, vol. 2, pp. 1346–1351 (1994)
11. Yu, D., Shields, D.N., Daley, S.: A hybrid fault diagnosis approach using neural networks. Neural Comput. Appl. **4**(1), 21–26 (1996)
12. Ming, Y., et al.: A Hybrid Approach for Fault Diagnosis based on Multilevel Flow Models and Artificial Neural Network, vol. 2. IEEE Computer Society (2006)
13. Duan, H., Xiufen, Y., Ma, G.: Novel hybrid approach for fault diagnosis in 3-dof flight simulator based on BP neural network and ant colony algorithm. In: IEEE Swarm Intelligence Symposium, pp. 371–374 (2007)
14. Bonissone, P.P., Xue, F., Subbu, R.: Fast meta-models for local fusion of multiple predictive models. Appl. Soft Comput. **11**(2), 1529–1539 (2011)
15. Quevedo, J., et al.: Validation and reconstruction of flow meter data in the Barcelona water distribution network. Control Eng. Pract. **18**(6), 640–651 (2010)
16. Hall, M., Frank, E., Holmes, G., Pfahringer, B., Reutemann, P., Witten, I.H.: The WEKA data mining software: an update. ACM SIGKDD Explor. Newsl. **11**(1), 10–18 (2009)
17. Funahashi, K., Nakamura, Y.: Approximation of dynamical systems by continuous time recurrent neural networks. Neural Networks **6**(6), 801–806 (1993)
18. Potamitis, I.: Single channel enumeration and recognition of an unknown and time-varying number of sound sources. In: 16th European Signal Processing Conference, Laussane, pp. 25–29, August 2008

Improving Situational Awareness
for First Responders

Francesca De Cillis[1], Francesca De Simio[1], Federica Inderst[2],
Luca Faramondi[2], Federica Pascucci[2(✉)], and Roberto Setola[1]

[1] Complex Systems and Security Lab, Università Campus Bio-Medico di Roma,
Via Álvaro del Portillo 21, 00128 Rome, Italy
{f.decillis,f.desimio,r.setola}@unicampus.it
[2] Department of Engineering, Università degli Studi Roma Tre,
Via della Vasca Navale 79, 00146 Rome, Italy
{federica.inderst,luca.faramondi,federica.pascucci}@uniroma3.it

Abstract. This paper aims at exploring a novel approach for indoor
localisation by exploiting data fusion. Specifically, personnel localisation
in rescue scenarios is addressed: the key idea is to increase the situation
awareness of rescuers. A pedestrian dead reckoning algorithm based on
waist mounted inertial sensors is designed to cope with different human
activities. The drifting estimate is re-calibrated by using information
gathered from the environment. The outcomes of experimental trials performed in a real scenario are reported.

Keywords: Situational awareness · Crisis management · Personnel
indoor localisation

1 Introduction

In the field of emergency management and response, there is a concept known
as situational awareness. In very basic terms, situational awareness is being
informed about what is happening so you can figure out what to do [3]. Situational awareness is information and analysis to facilitate efficient and effective
decision making, which is critical in emergencies. Improvements to situational
awareness could strengthen emergency response by offering to emergency managers the information to guarantee the health, safety, and welfare of the public
and of emergency responders. Currently, there is a gap between the information
that emergency managers get and the information they need to improve their situational awareness during emergency events. This gap becomes clear considering,
for example, the localisation of first responders: nowadays the only information
provided by the personnel to the commander are the description of the faced
scenario. Recently, a lot of efforts have been put to fill this gap by developing
indoor positioning systems (IPSs) to provide location information of people and
devices. Deep indoor scenarios, indeed, represent the most challenging area for
developing application due to the unavailability of Global Navigation Satellite

© Springer International Publishing Switzerland 2016
C.G. Panayiotou et al. (Eds.): CRITIS 2014, LNCS 8985, pp. 355–361, 2016.
DOI: 10.1007/978-3-319-31664-2_36

Systems (GNSS). A large part of the proposed solutions is based on proprioceptive sensors hybridised using networks of landmarks deployed by rescuers during
missions. These approaches mainly differ for the technologies of the landmarks.
In the EU Project LIAISON [11] RFID tags are considered. In the FIRE project,
the wireless sensor network SmokeNet [13] is adopted, similar to the lifeline proposed in LifeNet [6]. The Precise Personnel Location system (PPL) is composed
by wearable multi-carrier wide-band emitters and by receiving stations on the
emergency response vehicles. In the EUROPCOMM project [5], a network of
pseudolites is deployed outside the emergency area. On the contrary, the Personal Navigation System (PeNa) of the PeLoTe project [7] is designed to be a
stand-alone localisation system using laser based map-matching.

In this paper, the perspective proposed by the REFIRE project [2,8–10]
is adopted. Several low-cost highly standardized pre-installed landmarks are
embedded within existing safety devices (e.g., emergency lights): the landmarks
send their location information to the mobile devices carried by rescuers. The
mobile devices are also equipped with an Inertial Measurement Units (IMUs)
to continuously track rescuers and forward their positions to the commander
located outside the emergency area. The approach adopted allow the rescuer
to be localised without deploying any local network, as foreseen in [6,11,13].
Moreover, the additional equipment carried by the first responders is lightweight
instead of heavy laser, as proposed in [7]. Finally, the proposed algorithm does
not rely on external base station high penetrating electromagnetic wave as in [5].
The paper is organised as follows: Sect. 2 introduces the rescuer localisation
algorithm, Sect. 3 shows some experimental results in real scenario, and Sect. 4
proposes some concluding remarks.

2   Rescuer Localisation Algorithm

The Rescuer Localisation Algorithm (RLA) is a recursive procedure based on a
prediction-correction schema. To this end, rescuers are equipped with a mobile
device embedding a 9DoF IMU (triaxial accelerometer, triaxial gyroscope, and
triaxial magnetometer), considered as proprioceptive sensor forming a rough estimate of the position of the rescuer by using pedestrian dead reckoning (PDR)
in the prediction step. The IMU is placed at pelvis level and fixed to the
rescuer belt with body frame having x, y and z axes pointing to the left (Medio-
Lateral), forward (Antero-Posterior), and upward (Vertical), respectively. Landmarks are passive or semi-active RFID tags embedded within existing safety
signs. To reduce the dependence on wireless links to external data sources, the
RLA exploits the capability of RFID tags to store critical up-to-date building
information for local retrieval, according to the REFIRE standard [10]. Exploiting information from landmarks, the mobile device is able to provide a room-level
accuracy localisation during extended missions and to forward positioning information to the commander by means of 2G/3G/4G wireless networks (e.g., Public
Land Mobile Networks, PLMNs, or Professional Mobile Radio, PMR, such as
TETRA). In such a way, the commander can guide rescuers during missions,

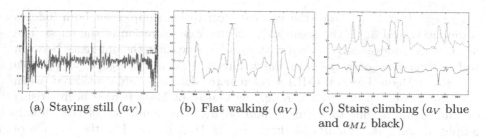

(a) Staying still (a_V)   (b) Flat walking (a_V)   (c) Stairs climbing (a_V blue
                                                                    and a_{ML} black)

Fig. 1. Accelerometer signals during different walking activities ($[g]$ vs time $[s]$) (Color figure online)

hence improving situational awareness and enhancing rescuers' safety and efficiency. It is worth noticing that the overhead of this approach is bounded to tag geo-referecing: this activity, however, is executed once, upon tag installation.

2.1 Prediction

Given an initial position, the user location is updated upon a motion event. To this end, the prediction step estimates the displacement and the heading of the user. The heading θ_k is computed from the attitude of the IMU by simple rotations to map the body reference frame into the absolute reference frame; the displacement l_k depends on the walking pattern. Thus, the prediction step is further decomposed into three phases: *Attitude Estimation* (AE), *Pattern Recognition* (PR), *Position Estimation* (PE). AE computes the attitude of the IMU using data coming from accelerometer, gyroscope, and magnetometer by means of quaternions, as proposed in [1,12]. Once the attitude of the sensor module is available, the Vertical (V) acceleration a_V along the gravity axes and the heading θ_k are computed.

PR identifies different walking activities. In rescue scenarios, only 3 patterns are considered: *staying still, flat walking, going up/down stairs*. The pattern recognition is approached as a sequential decision problem under uncertainty and it is implemented by a decision tree. To this end, a time window is applied to select and analyse b samples from the tri-axial accelerometer data. During *staying still* the noise covariance of the accelerometer measurements is considerably reduced as shown in Fig. 1(a), thus this pattern is identified by comparing the covariance of the vertical acceleration signal with an experimentally set threshold γ. When the rescuer is moving, the patterns *flat walking* and *going up/down stairs* are recognised by evaluating the dynamics of the V acceleration as in Fig. 1(b) and 1(c). Two different thresholds are set, e_1 and e_2. The first one, e_1, corresponds to the mean value of V acceleration normalised with respect to the n_u, which represents an anthropometric parameter calibrated on the user by experimental trials. It is used to divide the samples into two subsets, a_V^{MPI} and a_V^{MNI}, in order to compute the Mean Positive Index (M_{MPI}) and the Mean Negative Index (M_{MNI})

$$M_{MPI} = mean(a_V^{MPI} - \bar{a}_V)^2, \qquad M_{MNI} = mean(a_V^{MNI} - \bar{a}_V)^2 \qquad (1)$$

where a_V^{MPI} and a_V^{MNI} are the vertical acceleration samples for both indexes respectively and $\bar{a}_V$ is the mean value of the V acceleration in the burst. The norm of the indexes is compared with e_2, which captures the difference between *flat walking* and *going up/down stairs*. Finally, to detect the *going up or down stairs*, the Medio Latertal (ML) accelerometer data a_{ML} are considered: when the user moves up or down a rang, the Centre of Mass (CoM) begins rising or falling and a shift to a single limb occurs. The amplitude of this shift is amplified going down stairs as shown in Fig. 1(c). During PE, the position of the rescuer $x_k = [p_{x,k}, p_{y,k}, p_{z,k}]^T$ with respect to the absolute reference frame and its accuracy (i.e., the covariance matrix $P_{k|k-1}$) is updated according to the following equations:

$$\hat{x}_{k|k-1} = \hat{x}_{k-1|k-1} + l_k, \qquad \hat{P}_{k|k-1}^x = \hat{P}_{k-1|k-1}^x + Q_k^x \qquad (2)$$

where $l_k = [l_{x,k}, l_{y,k}, l_{z,k}]^T$ is the displacement of the rescuer during the sampling interval $[k-1, \ldots, k]$ and Q_k^x is the associated uncertainty. Both l_k and Q_k^x are computed according to the walking activities recognised.

2.2   Correction

The correction step refines the position estimate upon tag detection. According to REFIRE protocol, the tag provides its own position p_i, its orientation ϕ_i, and its accuracy w_i. Using these data, the position of the rescuer can be re-calibrated during long lasting missions. Since no ranging technique is adopted in this work, only the position of the rescuer is corrected, due to observability issues. When a rescuer is in the main radiation lobe of the tag, the reader receives information from the tag and the position is updated according to different strategies. If the PDR estimates the position of rescuer near the main radiation lobe and the tag reader perceives the tag i, the position is re-calibrated on the edge of the coverage area and the values on the leading diagonal of the covariance matrix is slightly decreased. If the PDR estimates the rescuer is inside the main radiation lobe of q tags and the tag reader perceives r tags, the position $\hat{x}_{k|k}$ is updated according to the following equations

$$\hat{x}_{k|k} = \hat{x}_{k|k-1} + L_k(p_k - [\hat{x}_{k|k-1}]_r), \qquad P_{k|k}^x = P_{k|k-1}^x + L_k S_k L_k^T \qquad (3)$$

where L_k encoded the accuracy of the tags, p_k is the block vector of the coordinates retrieved from the r sensors and $[\hat{x}_{k|k-1}]_r$ is a block vector containing r times the coordinates of the position of the rescuer, and S_k is computed as $S_k = \sum_{i=1}^r w_i(p_i - \hat{x}_{k|k-1})(p_i - \hat{x}_{k|k-1})^T$. If the PDR estimates rescuer far from the main radiation lobe of a tag i perceived by the reader, the position is reset on p_i and the covariance matrix is reset to the accuracy of the tag.

3   Experimental Results

Several experimental tests have been carried out to prove the effectiveness of the RLA. Specifically, we consider the basement of a hospital composed by a

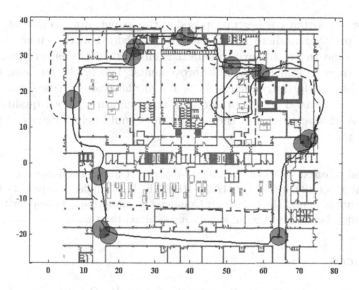

Fig. 2. Indoor results in the basement of the hospital: PDR path (dashed line), RLA estimate (solid line), tags (red square), main radiation lobe (grey circles) (Color figure online)

long corridor. During experiments, the rescuer is equipped with a waist-worn IMU MPU9150 MotionFit SDK device connected to a laptop PC via high speed USB. A CAEN RFID reader is connected to the same laptop via Bluetooth. The sampling frequency of the IMU is 50 Hz, the one of the RFID reader is 5 Hz, and a step is detected at 0.5 Hz. To this end, a synchronisation procedure is performed to align data on time.

Here, the results of a penetrating mission along the corridor are presented: data collected during the experiment have been post-processed using MatLab. The rescuer executes 500 steps overall, covering a distance of up to 300 m and traversing up and down stairs with several resting periods. The results of the experiment are depicted in Fig. 2. The PDR position estimate is compared with the RLA one. Specifically, in Fig. 2 the dashed line shows the path of the rescuer computed by PDR without RFID corrections. It can be noticed that PDR is not suitable by itself for deep indoor localisation: the positioning errors grow along the path and at the end of the experiment the accuracy is highly downgraded. The PDR estimate is improved remarkably when tags are used (solid line) and the target performance (i.e., room level localisation accuracy) is achieved using RLA.

4   Conclusion

Currently, there are some limitations on achieving situational awareness due to a gap between the information collected by emergency managers and the information that emergency managers need. To partially fill this gap, a rescuer localisation algorithm has been proposed in this paper: it takes advantages from smart environments, where RFID tags are embedded in the emergency signs. Although some successful experimental results prove the effectiveness of the approach, there is still room for improvements. The prediction step could be further enhanced by introducing more bio-mechanical activities and machine learning algorithms. The use of complex map, capturing both qualitative and quantitative characteristics of the environment could help for mission planning and map matching.

Acknowledgments. With the financial support of Directorate General Home Affairs (EC) Grant Home/2010/CIPS/AG/033 REFIRE This publication reflects the views only of the authors, and the European Commission cannot be held responsible for any use which may be made of the information contained therein.

References

1. Faramondi, L., Inderst, F., Pascucci, F., Setola, R., Delprato, U.: An enhanced indoor positioning system for first responders. In: Proceedings of 4th IEEE International Conference on Indoor Positioning and Indoor Navigation, Montbéliard-Belfor, France (2013)
2. Faramondi, L., Inderst, F., Panzieri, S., Pascucci, F.: Hybrid map building for personal indoor navigation systems. In: Proceedings of IEEE/ASME International Conference on Advanced Intelligent Mechatronics (2014)
3. Endsley, M.R.: Situation awareness global assessment technique (SAGAT). In: Proceedings of the National Aerospace and Electronics Conference, New York, pp. 789–795
4. De Cillis, F., De Simio, F., Faramondi, L., Inderst, F., Pascucci, F., Setola, R.: Indoor positioning system using walking pattern classification. In: Proceedings of 22nd IEEE Mediterranean Conference on Control and Automation, Palermo, Italy (2014)
5. Harmer, D., Russell, M., Frazer, E., Bauge, T., Ingram, S., Schmidt, N., Kull, B., Yarovoy, A., Nezirovic, A., Xia3, L., Dizdarevic, V., Witrisal, K.: In: EUROP-COM: Emergency Ultrawideband RadiO for Positioning and COMmunications. In: Proceedings of the IEEE International Conferenceon Ultra-Wideband (2008)
6. Klann, M.: Tactical navigation support for firefighters: the lifenet ad-hoc sensor-network and wearable system. In: Löffler, J., Klann, M. (eds.) Mobile Response. LNCS, vol. 5424, pp. 41–56. Springer, Heidelberg (2009)
7. Kulich, M., Kout, J., Preucil, L., Mazl, R., Chudoba, J., Saarinen, J., Suomela, J., Halme, A., Driewer, F., Baier, H.,Schilling, K., Ruangpayoongsak, N., Roth, H.: PeLoTe a heterogeneous telematic system for cooperative search and rescue missions. In: Proceedings of the 2004 IEEE/RSJ International Conference IROS (2004)
8. Pascucci, F., Setola, R.: An adaptive localization system for first responders. In: Proceedings of the 1st IEEE International Conference on Wireless Technologies forHumanitarians Relief (2011)
9. Pascucci, F., Setola, R.: An indoor localization framework for hybrid rescueteams. In: Proceedings of the 18th IFAC World Congress (2011)

10. Pascucci, F., Panzieri, S., Setola, R., Oliva, G., Marsella, S., Marzoli, M., Delprato, U., Borelli, G., Carpanelli, M.: In: A REference implementation of interoperable indoor location & communication systems for First REsponders: the REFIRE project. In: IEEE International Symposium on Safety, Security, and Rescue Robotics (2012)
11. Renaudin, V., Yalak, O., Tom, P., Merminod, B.: Indoor navigation of emergency agents. Eur. J. Navig. **5**(3), 36–45 (2007)
12. Sabatini, A.M.: Quaternion-based extended kalman filter for determining orientation by inertial and magnetic sensing. IEEE Tran. on Biomed. Eng. **53**(7), 1346–1356 (2006)
13. Wilson, J., Bhargava, V., Redfern, A., Wright, P.: A wireless sensor network and incident command interface for urban firefighting. In: Proceedings of the 4th Annual International Conference on Mobile, Ubiquitous Systems: Networking & Services (2007)

A Decision Support System for Emergency Management of Critical Infrastructures Subjected to Natural Hazards

Vittorio Rosato[1], Antonio Di Pietro[1(✉)], Luigi La Porta[1], Maurizio Pollino[1], Alberto Tofani[1], José R. Marti[2], and Claudio Romani[3]

[1] Italian National Agency for New Technologies,
Energy and Sustainable Economic Development (ENEA),
Casaccia Research Centre, Rome, Italy
antonio.dipietro@enea.it
[2] Department of Electrical and Computer Engineering,
University of British Columbia, Vancouver, BC, Canada
[3] University Campus Bio-Medico, Rome, Italy

Abstract. Natural hazards might damage elements of Critical Infrastructures and produce perturbations on the delivered services. In addition, (inter)dependency phenomena interconnecting infrastructures, may amplify impacts through cascading effects. In this paper, we present a Decision Support System (DSS) aiming at predicting the possible effects of natural hazards on the services provided by critical infrastructures. The system employs modeling and simulation techniques to forecast the effects of natural hazards on critical infrastructures services.

1 Introduction

Recent years have seen a growing number of Critical Infrastructures (CI hereafter) being severely hit by intense hazards manifestations. When a specific perturbation hits an infrastructure, cascading effects may occur due to systems's dependency, which propagates faults from one system to another. In this paper, we present a Decision Support System (DSS) which performs a complete risk analysis flow. The paper is organized as follows. Section 2 presents related works in the area. Section 3 describes Risk analysis concepts relating the occurrence of natural hazards with the functioning of physical components of CI. Section 4 presents the software architecture of the DSS and its main functionalities. Section 5 describes how the DSS reacts to seismic events, and presents a sample scenario to demonstrate how the system estimates the impact of the seismic event on a dependent system-of-systems.

2 Related Works

The European UrbanFlood project [3] was aimed at developing an Early Warning System (EWS) for the prediction of flooding in near real time. In the context

© Springer International Publishing Switzerland 2016
C.G. Panayiotou et al. (Eds.): CRITIS 2014, LNCS 8985, pp. 362–367, 2016.
DOI: 10.1007/978-3-319-31664-2_37

of the European Earth observation program Copernicus [4], a European Flood Awareness System (EFAS) was developed to produce European overviews on ongoing and forecasted floods to support to the EU Mechanism for Civil Protection. The Italian national project SIT_MEW [5] has focused on the implementation of an EWS to predict potential impact of seismic events on structures and buildings immediately following an earthquake. However, existing DSS do not simultaneously take into account environmental forecasts and (inter)dependency phenomena of critical infrastructures. This paper presents a novel class of DSS able to relate environmental forecasts to the dynamic of CI to estimate the possible degradation of the provided services.

3   Risk Analysis

In order to define the risk in terms of the loss of a service delivered by a Critical Infrastructure (CI), we provide the following formulation where R_{ij}^x is the risk of loss of the i-th physical component, located in a certain geographical area, belonging to the x-th CI and subjected to the natural hazard j:

$$R_{ij}^{(x)} \propto P(T_j)V(C_i^{(x)},T_j)I(C_i^{(x)}) \tag{1}$$

where $x \in \{1, .., N_{CI}\}$, $i \in \{1, .., N_{PC}^x\}$, $j \in \{1, .., T_{NH}\}$ with N_{CI} represent the total number of CI, $N_{PC}^{(x)}$ the physical components that constitute the x-th CI and T_{NH} the set of natural hazards. $P(T_j)$ is the probability that the natural threat T_j occurs in a certain area; $V(C_i^{(x)},T_j)$ is the physical vulnerability of the i-th component of the x-th CI w.r.t. the natural threat T_j; $I(C_i^{(x)})$ represents both the *impact* regarded as a Quality of Service (QoS) delivered by all CI and the relative *consequences* produced on the population, the environment and the industrial sector due to the loss of the i-th physical component.

4   Decision Support System Architecture

The proposed Decision Support System (DSS) can be logically represented in terms of five functional components or *functional bricks (Bn)*:

Monitoring of Natural Phenomena (B1): This functional block acquires geo-seismic, meteorological forecasts and nowcasting data which are then displayed in a GIS system in an appropriate format (i.e. territorial data, basic cartography, administrative boundaries, road network, hydrography and Census data).

Prediction of Natural Disasters and Events Detection (B2): This functional block, based on the information acquired periodically (meteorological forecasts, geo-seismic events and geographical information), is able to predict, within an estimated temporal horizon, the strength of a limited set of natural phenomena occurring in a specified area. For each threat manifestation T_j, the system employs specific forecast models to calculate the associated probability of occurrence $P(T_j)$ together with its strength s_j measured with the usual units of measure. Further, in order to consider an equal strength scale for all threat manifestations T_j with strength s_j, we defined a specific metric function F, called *strength transformation* s.t.

$$F : (s_j) \rightarrow [1,5] \tag{2}$$

which transforms the effective strength of the hazard into a phenomenological scale (Grade Scale) containing 5 levels (from 1 to 5).

Prediction of Physical Harm Scenarios (B3): This functional block evaluates the probability damage that each CI is likely to undergo due to the occurrence of natural events in terms of estimates of loss of functionality. In order to estimate the damage suffered from the physical component C_i of the x-th CI, by the Threat manifestation T_j, we first introduce two specific matrices, the Threat Intensity $S(C_i, T_j)$ and the Vulnerability $V(C_i, T_j)$ matrices. The first one, $S(C_i, T_j)$, is a function of the geographic location where the C_i element is located. It provides the strength s_j with which all threats are predicted to manifest at that specific location at a given time. The $V(C_i, T_j)$ matrix, in turn, is a function of the specific element C_i, accounting for the maximum perturbation strength. The physical Damage D to which an element C_i of the x-th CI is submitted by the threat(s) j will be given by overlying the two matrices:

$$D_{ij}^{(x)} = max\{S(C_i, T_j)V(C_i, T_j)\}, \tag{3}$$

The set of all $D_{ij}^{(x)}$ not vanishing will constitute the *Physical Harms Scenario* (PHS), which will be provided to the CI operators to alert them about the possible damages expected for the physical components of their CI.

Estimation of Impact and Consequences (B4): This functional block estimates the impact on the services delivered by the CI and the resulting consequences, due to the possible damage of the physical components estimated in B3. The system performs an optimization procedure aiming at maximizing the service level provided by the different CI by keeping into account the physical constraints associated to the CI, and the possible actions performed by the CI operator. As a test case of the described workflow, we report the case of a power distribution network subjected to possible physical failures due to natural hazards. For this case, we perform an optimization procedure that consists of the following steps: (i) execution of the load flow calculation to verify the feasibility of the network; (ii) application of a load shedding algorithm to emulate possible electrical operator actions; (iii) execution of an interdependency model (based on the I2Sim tool [1]), initialized with the electrical load values calculated in (ii), in order to evaluate the impact on the CI services. The aim of this procedure is to maximize both the power delivery to the loads and the level of services provided by the CI. This problem may be formally defined as follows:

$$\underset{L}{\text{maximize}} \quad Z(t) = Q^e(t, L, W^e) + Q^u(t, L, W^u)$$

$$\text{subject to} \quad 0 \le l_i \le P_i \ i = 1, \ldots, N, w_i^e \ge 0, \ i = 1, \ldots, N; w_i^u \ge 0, \ i = 1, \ldots, K$$

$$\sum_{i=1}^{N} w_i^e = 1, \sum_{i=1}^{K} w_i^u = 1, W^e = \{w_1^e, .., w_N^e\}, W^u = \{w_1^u, .., w_K^u\}$$

$$\tag{4}$$

$$Q^e(t, L, W^e) = 1 - \frac{\sum_{i=1}^{N}(1 - w_i^e)(P_i - l_i)}{\sum_{i=1}^{N} P_i} \in [0, 1] \tag{5}$$

$$Q^u(t, L, W^u) = \frac{\sum_{i=1}^{K} w_i^u Q_i^u(t, L, W^u)}{\sum_{i=1}^{K} S_i} \in [0, 1] \tag{6}$$

where l_i is the active (reactive) power demand value in MW (VA) of load i at time t; W^e and W^u are weight vectors needed to prioritize specific loads and services; $Q^e(t, L, W^e)$ represents a QoS index of the electrical network and reaches the maximum when all the loads l_i are consuming the expected power value P_i; $Q^u(t, L, W^u)$ represents a QoS index of the services provided by the CI that depends on the loads supplied and on the interdependencies phenomena and reaches the maximum when all CI are providing the nominal service level S_i.

Support of Efficient Strategies to Cope with Crisis Scenarios (B5):
This functional block provides crisis managers with a list, the *Decision List of Actions*, in cases where the DSS can provide further information needed to support a crisis solution.

5 The Earthquake Risk Assessment Workflow

In order to assess real-time the impact of earthquakes occurring in the considered scenario, the DSS constantly polls the Italian National seismic sensor network called ISIDe [2], to get epicentre and magnitude values of the latest seismic event occurring in the area of interest. If the magnitude of the seismic event is larger than 4 in the Richter scale, the DSS computes a theoretical shake-map to assess a preliminary PHS. Then, using the shake-map of the seismic event, the DSS will evaluate the set of PGA values associated to the shake-map and uses them to "refine" the PHS. Then, the DSS evaluates the impact on the CI using simulation models and GIS-based information.

5.1 Sample Scenario

In the following, we present a scenario where a synthetic seismic event, which has been simulated occurring in the Lazio region (Italy), where a set of dependent CI are located. The scenario consists of the following CI (Fig. 1): a MV power distribution grid feeding the water pumping stations, the hospitals and to the plants, whereas the water pumping stations supply water to the hospitals and

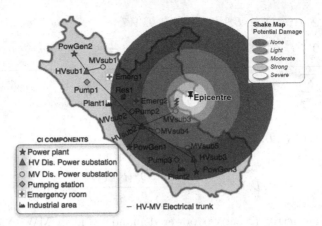

Fig. 1. Sample scenario: geographic representation the shake map relative to the seismic event. The lightning indicates the physical components that are estimated to be damaged due to the occurrence of the seismic event.

Table 1. Power balance (active power, MW) resulting from the load shedding actions.

Time	MVs2	MVs3	MVs4	Pump2	Res1	Emerg2	Plant1
12:00	15	6.5	11.5	1	15	2	10.5
12:10	7	0	10	1	7.5	2	7

Table 2. Critical infrastructure service layer.

Time	Water (Kl/h)	Patients healed per hour	Pieces produced per hours
12:00	375	4	4.5
12:10	375	4	3
14:00	375	4	1.5
18:00	375	4	4.5

the manufacturing plants. Our assumption is that the seismic event occurring at 12 a.m. affects a MV electrical substation (i.e. MVsub3) with the consequence that it is unable to satisfy the average electrical demand (Table 1).

The DSS attempts to solve the optimization problem defined in Eq. (4) considering the following parameters (Table 2):

$$w^e_{Emerg2} = w^u_{Emerg2} 0.5; w^e_{Pump2} = w^e_{Res1} = w^u_{Plant1} = 0.2; w^e_{Plant1} = 0.1; \tag{7}$$
$$w^u_{Pump2} = 0.3; P_{Emerg2} = 2; P_{Pump2} = 1; P_{Res1} = 15; P_{Plant1} = 15;$$

Table 1 reports the optimal solution where some of the electrical loads were disconnected as a consequence of the computed load shedding action. In general, the mere enumeration of all the possible solutions it is not possible. To tackle this issue, we defined a Genetic Algorithm (GA) to provide the best electrical network configuration that maximizes the objective function in (4). We consider each *chromosome* representing a load shedding configuration through a vector of real values *genes* of length N where N is the number of loads in the proposed electrical network. The real value of each gene represents the active power assigned by the load shedding configuration in the specific chromosome. For instance, the chromosome $(2.0, 1.0, 15.0, 1.0, 2.0, 15.0, 1.0, 12.0)$ represents a specific active power assignment to the *Emerg1, Pump1, Res1, Pump2, Emerg2, Plant1, Pump3, Plant2* loads respectively. A load shedding configuration represented by a particular chromosome is considered admissible if the constraints are satisfied and the resulting electrical network configuration is valid.

6 Conclusions

The Decision Support System described in this paper, attempts to solve the full risk analysis workflow, from events prediction to impact and consequences estimation of a scenario. Future work will focus on the DSS feature relative to the societal and economic consequences due to the loss of infrastructure services.

Acknowledgment. This work was developed from the FP7 Network of Excellence CIPRNet, which is being partly funded by the European Commission under grant number FP7-312450-CIPRNet. The European Commissions support is gratefully acknowledged. The authors wish to thank Dr. Gregorio D'Agostino who provided valuable comments and support to the writing of this work.

References

1. Ventura, C., Marti, J.R., Hollman, J.A., Juarez, H.: Mapping of interdependencies through integrated hazard analysis: Case study of a canadian university campus. In: 14th World Conference on Earthquake Engineering, pp. 12 17, October 2008
2. ISIDe, Italian Seismological Instrumental and Parametric Database. http://iside.rm.ingv.it/iside/standard/index.jsp/
3. UrbanFlood, FP7 UrbanFlood project (2012). http://www.urbanflood.eu
4. Regulation of the European Parliament and of the Council establishing the Copernicus Programme and repealing Regulation (EU) No. 911/2010
5. SIT_MEW, Italian National project co-funded by Italian Ministry of Education, Universities and Research (MIUR)
6. Rosato, V., Di Pietro, A., Aprea, G., Delfanti, R., La Porta, L., Marti, J.R., Lusina, P., Pollino, M.: Interaction between environmental and technological systems: toward an unifying approach for risk prediction. In: CRITIS (2012)

Progressive Recovery from Failure
in Multi-layered Interdependent Network
Using a New Model of Interdependency

Anisha Mazumder[✉], Chenyang Zhou, Arun Das, and Arunabha Sen

School of Computing, Informatics and Decision System Engineering,
Arizona State University, Tempe, AZ 85287, USA
{anisha.mazumder,czhou24,adas22,asen}@asu.edu

Abstract. A number of models have been proposed to analyze interdependent networks in recent years. However most of the models are unable
to capture the complex interdependencies between such networks. To
overcome the limitations, we have recently proposed a new model. Utilizing this model, we provide techniques for progressive recovery from
failure. The goal of the progressive recovery problem is to maximize
the system utility over the entire duration of the recovery process. We
show that the problem can be solved in polynomial time in some special
cases, whereas for some others, the problem is NP-complete. We provide two approximation algorithms with performance bounds of 2 and 4
respectively. We provide an optimal solution utilizing Integer Linear Programming and a heuristic. We evaluate the efficacy of our heuristic with
both synthetic and real data collected from Phoenix metropolitan area.
The experiments show that our heuristic almost always produces near
optimal solution.

Keywords: Critical infrastructure · Multi-layer networks ·
Inter-dependence · Progressive recovery · Modeling · Analysis

1   Introduction

In recent years the research community is becoming increasingly aware of the
fact that the critical infrastructures of a nation are heavily interdependent for
being fully functional. Let us consider the complex interdependencies that exist
between the electric power grid and the communication network. The power grid
entities, such as the SCADA systems control power stations and sub-stations.
Such SCADA systems receive the critical commands for proper functioning
through communication networks. On the other hand, electric power is imper-
ative for communication network entities, such as routers and base stations, to
operate.

This research is supported in part by a grant from the U.S. Defense Threat Reduction
Agency under grant number HDTRA1-09-1-0032 and by a grant from the U.S. Air
Force Office of Scientific Research under grant number FA9550-09-1-0120.

© Springer International Publishing Switzerland 2016
C.G. Panayiotou et al. (Eds.): CRITIS 2014, LNCS 8985, pp. 368–380, 2016.
DOI: 10.1007/978-3-319-31664-2_38

In order to understand the nuances of the interdependencies between multi-layered networks, the research community has made significant efforts over the past few years [1,2,4–6]. Although, quite a few models have been proposed to analyze such interdependent networks, most of the models are too simplistic. Thus, unfortunately these models fail to fully capture the complexities pertaining to the interdependence of power grid and communication networks. In [1], the authors assume that each entity in a network depends on exactly one entity of the other network. However, in a follow up paper [2], the same authors modify this assumption of theirs, simply because in the real world, an entity of a network can in fact depend on multiple entities of the other network.

The generalized model of [2] can account for *disjunctive dependency* of an entity in network A (say a_i) on multiple entities in the network B (say, b_j and b_k), which implies that a_i may be "alive" (functional) if either b_i or b_j is alive (functional). However, their model still cannot account for *conjunctive dependency* of the form that for a_i to be "alive", *both* b_j *and* b_k must be alive. Furthermore, it is quite likely, that in a real world network the dependency might be even more complex being a combination of both disjunctive and conjunctive components. For e.g., a_i may be alive if (i) b_j *and* b_k *and* b_l are alive, *or* (ii) b_m *and* b_n are alive, *or* (iii) b_p is alive. The graph based interdependency models proposed in [1,2,4–7], cannot capture such complex interdependency. In order to overcome these shortcomings of the models in the existing literature, we have recently proposed the *Implicative Interdependency Model* (IIM) [10] which uses Boolean logic to capture such complexities.

It may be noted that as entities of network A are dependent on entities of network B, which in turn depend on entities of network A, the failure of a small number of type A or B entities can trigger a cascade of failures in multi-layered networks resulting in a failure of a large number of entities. Suppose that $V(A) = \{a_1, \ldots, a_n\}$ is the set of entities of network A and $V(B) = \{b_1, \ldots, b_m\}$ is that of network B. Further, $A_f^O \subseteq V(A), B_f^O \subseteq V(B)$ represent the subset of A and B type entities respectively whose failure *originally*, results in the failure of $A_f^c \cup B_f^c$ through the cascading failure process. In this case, the set $A_f^O \cup B_f^O$, must be repaired to take the system back from its degraded state to its pre-failure state. Suppose that $A_f^O = \{a_1, \ldots, a_s\}$ and $B_f^O = \{b_1, \ldots, b_t\}$. Every time an element of A_f^O or B_f^O is repaired, the system moves towards its pre-failure state. However, improvement of *system utility* (formally defined in Sect. 3) after repair of an element $a_i \in A_f^O$ (say), may be quite different from that after repair of another element $a_j \in A_f^O$. Accordingly, the *sequence* in which the elements of A_f^O and B_f^O are repaired have significant impact on *system utility* during the recovery process. The goal of the Progressive Recovery Problem is to find the *repair sequence* of the elements of $A_f^O \cup B_f^O$, so that the *system utility* is *maximized* over the entire recovery process. The problem is described in detail in Sect. 3.

Utilizing the IIM model, we study the progressive recovery problem in an interdependent multi-layered networked system. We show that this problem can be solved in polynomial time for some special cases, whereas for some others, the problem is NP-complete. We provide two approximation algorithms for two special cases of the problem with a performance bound of 2 and 4 respectively. For the most general version of the problem, we provide an optimal solution utilizing Integer Linear Programming and as well a heuristic. Finally, we evaluate the efficacy of our heuristic using both synthetic data and real power grid and communication network data collected from Phoenix metropolitan area. The experiments show that our heuristics almost always produce near optimal solution.

2 Implicative Interdependency Model (IIM)

In Sect. 1, we indicated that the *Implicative Interdependency Model (IIM)* [10] was proposed to overcome the limitations of the earlier models [1,2]. If the network A entity a_i is operational ("alive") if (i) the network B entities b_j, b_k, b_l are operational, or (ii) b_m, b_n are operational, or (iii) b_p is operational, we express this in terms of *live implications* of the form $a_i \leftarrow b_j b_k b_l + b_m b_n + b_p$. Similarly, we can express the live implication for a B type entity b_r. We refer to the live implications of the form $a_i \leftarrow b_j b_k b_l + b_m b_n + b_p$ also as First Order Implicative Dependency Relations (IDRs), because these relations express direct dependency of the A type entities on B type entities and vice-versa. It may be noted however that as A type entities are dependent on B type entities, which in turn depends on A type entities, the failure of some A type entities can trigger the failure of other A type entities, though indirectly, through some B type entities. Such an interdependency creates a cascade of failures in multi-layered networks when only a few entities of either A type or B type (or a combination) fail. It may be observed that the IIM model is essentially a Boolean [3]. However, to the best of our knowledge, such modeling has not been previously used in analyzing progressive recovery techniques in interdependent infrastructure networks.

The IDRs can be formed either through a power-flow analysis of the multilayer network (similar to the ones carried out by the engineers at FERC [11], and also by the researchers at Columbia University [12] for the power grid), or by consultation with the engineers of the local utility and Internet service providers. It may be noted that it is possible that A type entities may depend on A type entities themselves, similarly, B type entities may depend on B type entities too. The IIM model can deal with such a scenario by not distinguishing between A and B type entities and treating them as a third type entity C. Moreover, the concept can easily be generalized to deal with networks with more than two layers.

3 Progressive Recovery Problem

Let $A_f^O \subseteq V(A), B_f^O \subseteq V(B)$ represent the subset of A and B type entities respectively whose failure initiates a cascade of failures and let $A_f^c \cup B_f^c$ represent the entities that failed due to the *cascading process*. So, the set $A_f^O \cup B_f^O$, must be

Table 1. IDRs for a power communication network

Power Net.	Comm Net.
$a_1 \leftarrow \phi$	$b_1 \leftarrow a_1 a_2$
$a_2 \leftarrow \phi$	$b_2 \leftarrow a_1 + a_2$
...	$b_3 \leftarrow a_1$

Table 2. $SUOT[T]$ for repair sequence (a_2, a_1)

Timestep (t)	0	1	2
$SUIT(t)$	0	40	110
$SUOT[T]$	0	40	150

Table 3. $SUOT[T]$ for repair sequence (a_1, a_2)

Timestep (t)	0	1	2
$SUIT(t)$	0	80	110
$SUOT[T]$	0	80	190

repaired to take the system from its degraded state back to its *normal functioning state* where all entities should be functional (alive). We call such a set $A_f^O \cup B_f^O$ as the set of *original failures* and for notational simplicity denote it by D_O. W.l.o.g, we assume that no IDR has an entity $d_i \in D_O$ on the LHS. Also, the entire set of *failed* entities i.e., $(A_f^O \cup B_f^O) \cup (A_f^c \cup B_f^c)$ is denoted by D_f. Suppose that $D_O = \{d_1, d_2, \ldots, d_p\}$, where $d_i \in A_f^O \cup B_f^O$. Obviously, the p entities of the set D_O must be repaired to take the system back to its *normal functioning state*. Suppose that only one failed entity $d_i \in D_O$ can be repaired in one unit of time. Since the real world utilities of the failed entities of D_f may be different, the sequence in which the entities in D_O are repaired becomes important. We illustrate this with the help of an example. Suppose that the IDRs of an interdependent power-communication network are as given in Table 1.

In this two layer network, when a_1, a_2 fail, we see that b_1, b_2, b_3 also fail. In order to return the system to its *normal operational state* both a_1 and a_2 must be repaired. However, whether a_1 is repaired first and then a_2, or the other way around, will have an impact on *system utility*. Suppose that the utility of an entity a_i is denoted by $u(a_i)$ and is defined as the benefit obtained when the entity a_i is operational. Similarly, we define utility $u(b_j)$ for entity b_j. Also, let $x_{a_i}(t)$ be the indicator variable for entity a_i such that $x_{a_i}(t) = 1$ if the entity a_i is operational at time t and 0 otherwise. Indicator variable $x_{b_j}(t)$ is defined similarly for entity b_j. We define *System Utility at Instance of Time t*, denoted by $SUIT(t)$ as: $SUIT(t) = \sum_{a_i \in V(A)} u(a_i) x_{a_i}(t) + \sum_{b_j \in V(B)} u(b_j) x_{b_j}(t)$, and *System Utility Over Time interval 0 to T* as $SUOT[T]$ as: $SUOT[T] = \sum_{t=0}^{T} SUIT(t)$.

In this example, $D_O = \{a_1, a_2\}$ and $D_f = \{a_1, a_2, b_1, b_2, b_3\}$. Let the utilities of the entities be as follows: $u(a_1) = 10, u(a_2) = 10, u(b_1) = 20, u(b_2) = 30, u(b_3) = 40$. In our analysis, we assume that if an entity $d_i \in D_O$ is fixed at timestep t, then all the entities fixed due to the cascade initiated by fixing of d_i are also fixed at timestep t, i.e., we ignore the cascade propagation time. If the repair sequence is a_2 followed by a_1, then a_2 and b_2 are operational at $t = 1$, and all of a_1, a_2, b_1, b_2, b_3 are operational at $t = 2$. If on the other hand, the repair sequence is a_1 followed by a_2, we have that a_1, b_2, b_3 are operational at $t = 1$ and all of a_1, a_2, b_1, b_2, b_3 are operational at $t = 2$. The $SUIT(t)$ and $SUOT[T]$ values at different time steps, corresponding to the two different repair sequences are shown in Tables 2 and 3. From this example, it is clear that the sequence in which the failed entities are repaired has an impact on the *system utility over time* $SUOT[T]$. The *system utility over time*, $SUOT[T]$, for the second sequence (a_1, a_2) is 190, whereas the $SUOT[T]$ for the first sequence (a_2, a_1) is 150. Clearly, the second sequence is preferable over the first. The goal of the progressive recovery problem is to identify the repair sequence in such that the *system utility over time* $SUOT[T]$ is maximized.

Algorithm 1. Polynomial Algorithm for Progressive Recovery Problem in Case 1

Input   : (i) A set S of IDR's of implications of the form of $x \leftarrow y$, where $x, y \in V(A) \cup V(B)$, (ii) A set of *original fault* entities $D_O \subseteq V(A) \cup V(B)$, (iii) A set of failed entities $D_f \subseteq V(A) \cup V(B)$, (iv) utility of each entity in D_f

Output: An ordering $\sigma(D_O)$ such that if the entities of D_O are activated in that order, the value of $SUOT[T]$ is maximized.

1: We construct a directed graph $G = (V, E)$, where $V = V(A) \cup V(B)$. For each IDR $x \leftarrow y$ in S, where $x, y \in V(A) \cup V(B)$, we introduce a directed edge $(y, x) \in E$.

2: For each node $d_i \in D_O$, we construct a transitive closure set C_{d_i} as follows: If there is a path from d_i to some node $x \in V$ in G, then we include x in C_{d_i}. We call each d_i to be the *seed entity* for the transitive closure set C_{d_i}. This physically means that if d_i fails, all elements in C_{d_i} fail.

3: Sort the *transitive closure sets* C_{d_i}'s, where the ranks of the closure sets are determined by the sum of the utilities of the failed entities belonging to each closure set. The sets with a larger sum of utilities of failed entities are ranked higher than the sets with a smaller sum. Return the seed entities of the sorted transitive closure sets as the required ordering of the entities of D_O.

---

4   Computational Complexity and Solutions

4.1   Case 1: Problem Instance with One Minterm of Size One

In this case, an IDR in general has the following form: $x_i \leftarrow y_j$ where x_i and y_j belong to networks A (B) and B (A) respectively. For e.g., in the IDR $a_k \leftarrow b_l$ belonging to Case 1, $x_i = a_k$, $y_j = b_l$. It may be noted that a conjunctive implication of the form $a_i \leftarrow b_j b_k$ can also be written as two separate implications $a_i \leftarrow b_j$ and $a_i \leftarrow b_k$. However, such cases are considered in Case 3 and is excluded from consideration in Case 1. The exclusion of such implications implies that the entities that appear on the LHS of a set of IDRs in Case 1 are unique. So, the in-degree is unity for each node $v \in V(G)$, G being the graph created by Algorithm 1. This property enables us to develop a polynomial time algorithm for the solution of the Progressive Recovery Problem for this case. We present the algorithm next. It may be noted that the description and analysis of this algorithm are similar to those of Algorithm 1 of [10].

   Time complexity of Algorithm 1: Step 1 takes $O(n + m + r)$ time, where $|V(A)| = n, |V(B)| = m, |S| = r$. Step 2 can be executed in at most $O((n+m)^3)$

time. A standard sorting algorithm in step 3 takes $O(|D_O|log|D_O|)$ time. Since, $|D_O| \leq n + m$, hence the overall time complexity is $O((n + m)^3)$.

Theorem 1. *For each pair of transitive closure sets C_{d_i} and C_{d_j} produced in step 2 of Algorithm 1, $C_{d_i} \cap C_{d_j} = \emptyset$ where $d_i \neq d_j, d_i, d_j \in D_O$.*

Proof: Consider, if possible, that there is a pair of transitive closure sets C_{d_i} and C_{d_j} where $C_{d_i} \cap C_{d_j} \neq \emptyset$. If $C_{d_i} \cap C_{d_j} = C_{d_i}$ or $C_{d_i} \cap C_{d_j} = C_{d_j}$, it means that $d_i \in D_O$ or $d_j \in D_O$ appears on the LHS of an IDR - this is a contradiction to our assumption that D_O is the set of *original* failures. So, let $C_{d_i} \cap C_{d_j} \neq C_{d_i}$ and $C_{d_i} \cap C_{d_j} \neq C_{d_j}$. Let $d_k \in C_{d_i} \cap C_{d_j}$. This implies that there is a path from d_i to d_k ($path_1$) as well as there is a path from d_j to d_k, ($path_2$). Since, $d_i \neq d_j$, there is some entity, say d_l, in the $path_1$ such that d_l also belongs to $path_2$. It may be noted that d_l may be d_k, yet d_l can not be d_i or d_j because in the latter cases either $C_{d_i} \cap C_{d_j} = C_{d_i}$ or $C_{d_i} \cap C_{d_j} = C_{d_j}$. W.l.o.g, let us consider that d_l be the first node in $path_1$ such that d_l also belongs to $path_2$. This implies that d_l has in-degree greater than 1. This in turn implies that there are two IDRs in the set of implications S such that d_l appears in the LHS of both. This is a contradiction because this violates the characteristic of the IDRs in Case 1.

Theorem 2. *Algorithm 1 gives an optimal solution for the Progressive Recovery Problem in a multi-layer network for Case 1 dependencies.*

Proof: We match the solution σ' of Algorithm 1 with the optimal ordering σ_{OPT}. We say that there is a mismatch at position r, when comparing σ' with σ_{OPT}, such that d_i is the rth entity in σ', while d_j is the rth entity in σ_{OPT} and $\sum_{x \in C_{d_i}} u(x) \neq \sum_{y \in C_{d_j}} u(y)$. So, when comparing σ' and σ_{OPT}, if there are no mismatch as defined, we say that the greedy Algorithm 1 does as good as the optimal solution. Otherwise, let r be the first position of mismatch from the left. By Theorem 1, we know that $C_{d_i} \cap C_{d_j} = \emptyset$ where $d_i \neq d_j, d_i, d_j \in D_O$. Since, the greedy algorithm did not choose d_j and chose d_i instead, it means that $\sum_{x \in C_{d_i}} u(x) > \sum_{y \in C_{d_j}} u(y)$. So, replacement of d_i with d_j reduces the total number of entities fixed at the rth selection of an entity in D_O to be fixed. This means that the $SUOT[T]$ value as achieved by greedy will be more than the optimal solution - this is a contradiction. So, the algorithm in fact returns an optimal solution.

4.2   Case 2: Problem Instance with Arbitrary Number of Minterms of Size One

In this case, the IDRs to be considered are in the general form of $x_j \leftarrow \sum_{i=1}^k y_i$, such that x_j belongs to network $A(B)$ and y_i belongs to network $B(A)$. For e.g., $a_p \leftarrow b_q + b_r + b_s$ is an IDR belonging to Case 2.

1. Proof of Hardness. We can show that the *min sum set cover (mssc)* [9] problem, which is shown to be $NP - hard$, can be reduced to a special case of the Progressive Recovery Problem if all the IDRs are in Case 2. This indicates our Progressive Recovery Problem is also NP-hard if all the IDRs are in Case 2. Following is a brief discussion of the reduction.

Min sum set cover (mssc). Viewing the input as a hypergraph $H(V, E)$, a linear ordering is a bijection f from V to $\{1, ..., |V|\}$. For a hyperedge e and linear ordering f, defining $f(e)$ as the minimum of $f(v)$ over all $v \in e$. The goal is to find a linear ordering that minimizes $\sum_e f(e)$.

For any instance I in *mssc*, say $H(V, E)$ is the input hypergraph. For each node $v \in V$, we create an entity b_v with $u(b_v) = 0$, and let $D_O = \{b_v | v \in V\}$. For each edge $e \in E$, we create an entity a_e with $u(a_e) = 1$. Also, we create an IDR of the form as $a_e = \sum_{v \in e} b_v$. Clearly, we construct a Progressive Recovery Problem instance in polynomial time with respect to the input size $|V|$ and $|E|$. We denote this instance by L. It is easy to check that if we can solve L optimally, we can also obtain optimal solution for I, since their objectives are equivalent. Hence, unless $P = NP$, it is impossible to solve Progressive Recovery Problem in polynomial time even if all IDRs belong to Case 2, which means it is $NP - hard$.

2. Optimal Solution Using Integer Linear Programming. Here we provide an ILP formulation for the Progressive Recovery Problem. Let $state^t_{a_i}$ (similarly $state^t_{b_j}$) be the indicator variable capturing the state of entity a_i of network A (similarly b_j belonging to network B) at timestep t. Let $state^t_{a_i} = 0$ if entity a_i is dead at timestep t, and $state^t_{a_i} = 1$ if entity a_i is indeed alive at timestep $t, 1 \leq t \leq |D_O|$. The state variables for entities b_j of network B are defined likewise. Let the indicator variable $u_t, 1 \leq t \leq |D_O|$ give the value of $SUIT(t)$ (defined in Sect. 3). The objective of the ILP can be written as **maximize** $\sum_{t=1}^{|D_O|} u_t$ where $\sum_{t=1}^{|D_O|} u_t$ gives the value of $SUOT[|D_O|]$ ($SUOT[T]$ is defined in Sect. 3). It may be recalled that the objective of the Progressive Recovery Problem is to find the optimal ordering in which the entities in D_O should be activated such that $SUOT[T]$ is maximized. The constraints of the ILP are as follow:

1. $u_t = \sum_{d_i \in D_f} u(d_i) \times state^t_{d_i}, 1 \leq t \leq |D_O|$: This constraint computes the value of $u_t, 1 \leq t \leq |D_O|$ as the sum of the utilities of all the entities which are alive in timestep t. Here, $u(d_i)$ gives the utility value for the entity $d_i, 1 \leq i \leq |D_f|$ and is provided as input to the problem.

Now, for each entity $d_i \in D_O$, let the indicator variable $act^t_{d_i} = 1$ if d_i is activated at timestep t and $act^t_{d_i} = 0$ otherwise, where $1 \leq t \leq |D_O|$. So, we have the following constraints:

2. $\sum_{t=1}^{|D_O|} act^t_{d_i} = 1, \forall d_i \in D_O$: This constraint ensures that each entity $d_i \in D_O$ is activated exactly once during the time interval $t = 1$ to $t = |D_O|$.

3. $\sum_{d_i \in D_O} act^t_{d_i} = 1, 1 \leq t \leq |D_O|$: This constraint ensures that in each timestep $1 \leq t \leq |D_O|$, exactly one entity $d_i \in D_O$ is activated.

4. $state^0_{d_i} = 0 \forall d_i \in D_f$: This constraint ensures that at timestep $t = 0$, all entities in D_f are in dead condition.

5. $state_{d_i}^t = state_{d_i}^{t-1} + act_{d_i}^t, \forall d_i \in D_O, 1 \leq t \leq |D_O|$: This constraint ensures that the state of an entity $d_i \in D_O$ at timestep t must be the same as that in timestep $t-1$ unless d_i is activated at timestep t. Also, if an entity $d_i \in D_O$ is alive at timestep t, it remains alive in timesteps $t+1, t+2, \ldots, |D_O|$.

Also, in general form, for each IDR of Case 2, say $x_j \leftarrow \sum_{i=1}^k y_i$, we have the following linear constraints. These two constraints ensure that entity x_j is alive only when at least one of $y_i, 1 \leq i \leq k$ is alive.

6.a $state_{x_j}^t \geq state_{y_i}^t, 1 \leq i \leq k, 1 \leq t \leq |D_O|$

6.b $state_{x_i}^t \leq \sum_{i=1}^k y_i, 1 \leq t \leq |D_O|$

For e.g., if we have an IDR of the form $a_1 \leftarrow b_1 + b_2$, for an instance of the Progressive Recovery Problem having $|D_O| = 2$, then this IDR, leads to the following constraints: $state_{a_1}^1 \geq state_{b_1}^1$, $state_{a_1}^1 \geq state_{b_2}^1$, $state_{a_1}^2 \geq state_{b_1}^2$, $state_{a_1}^2 \geq state_{b_2}^2$, $state_{a_1}^1 \leq state_{b_1}^1 + state_{b_2}^1$, $state_{a_1}^2 \leq state_{b_1}^2 + state_{b_2}^2$. Thus, given an instance of the Progressive Recovery Problem, we can compute the optimal sequence in which the entities of D_O should be activated by solving this ILP.

3. Approximation Algorithm for a Special Subcase.

In our Progressive Recovery Problem, we can transform the IDRs such that the RHS of each IDR consists of only entities of D_O. Considering the subcase of our problem such that utilities of all the entities are equal, the objective of this subcase of our problem is identical to that of the *mssc* problem [9] for which the authors provide a 4−approximation algorithm.

4.3   Case 3: Problem Instance with One Minterm of Arbitrary Size

In case 3, the general form of the IDRs to be considered is given by $x_j \leftarrow \prod_{i=1}^k y_i$, such that x_j and y_i are entities belonging to network $A(B)$ and $B(A)$ respectively. For e.g., $a_p \leftarrow b_q \times b_r \times b_s$ is an IDR belonging to Case 3.

1. Proof of Hardness.

It is possible to show that the *Minimum Latency Set Cover Problem (MLSC)* [8], proven as NP hard, can be reduced to a special case of the Progressive recovery problem if all the IDRs are belong to Case 3.

The Minimum Latency Set Cover Problem (*MLSC*). The problem is defined as follows: Let $J = \{J_1, J_2, \ldots, J_m\}$ be a set of jobs to be processed by a factory. Each job J_i has a non-negative weight w_i. Let $T = \{t_1, t_2, \ldots, t_n\}$ be a set of tools. Job j is associated with a nonempty subset $S_j \subseteq T$. In each time unit, a single tool can be installed by the factory. Once the entire tool subset S_j has been installed, job j can be processed instantly. The problem is to determine the order of tool installation in order to minimize the weighted sum of job completion times.

Similar construction scheme from Case 2 can be used. Let I be an instance of $MLSC$ and J, T be the corresponding input. For each $t \in T$, we create an entity b_t with $u(b_t) = 0$. For each $j \in J$, we create an entity a_j with $u(a_j) = w(j)$.

Also, for each S_j, we create an IDR of the form as $a_j = \prod_{t \in S_j} b_t$. By arguments similar to those given in Case 2, we know that even Case 3 alone is $NP - hard$.

2. Optimal Solution Using Integer Linear Programming. The Integer Linear Programming formulation for the Progressive Recovery Problem when the IDRs belong to Case 3 is almost identical to that when the IDRs are belong to Case 2. The objective function along with constraints one through five remain unchanged. Only constraint 6 changes to account for the change in the form of IDR from Case 2 to Case 3. An IDR in Case 3, in general form, say, $x_j \leftarrow \prod_{i=1}^{k} y_i$ can be represented by the linear constraints $k \times state_{x_j}^t \leq \sum_{i=1}^{k} state_{y_i}^t, 1 \leq t \leq |D_O|$. These constraints ensure that the entity x_j can be alive only when all the entities $y_i, 1 \leq i \leq k$ are alive. For e.g., let us again consider that we have an IDR $a_1 \leftarrow b_1 \times b_2$ and the instance of the problem has $|D_O| = 2$, then the linear constraints arising from this IDR are $2 \times state_{a_1}^1 \leq state_{b_1}^1 + state_{b_2}^1, 2 \times state_{a_1}^2 \leq state_{b_1}^2 + state_{b_2}^2$. Solving this ILP gives the optimal solution for this case.

3. Approximation Algorithm for a Special Subcase. If $\forall d_i \in D_O$, $u(d_i)$ are equal, we transform the IDRs such that the RHS of all the IDRs are subsets of D_O. Then the objective of our problem is identical to that of the $MLSC$ problem. A $2-$approximation algorithm for the $MLSC$ problem is given in [8].

4.4   Case 4: Problem Instance with Arbitrary Minterm of Arbitrary Size

In the most general setting, an IDR belongs to Case 4 and has the general form of $x_j \leftarrow \sum_{m=1}^{l} \prod_{i=1}^{k} y_{mi}$, where, as before, x_j and y_{mi} are entities belonging to network $A(B)$ and $B(A)$ respectively. For e.g., $a_p \leftarrow b_q \times b_r + b_s \times b_t$ is an IDR belonging to Case 4.

1. Proof of Hardness. Because the IDRs belonging to Case 2 and 3 are special cases of the general case i.e., Case 4 and the Progressive Recovery Problem has been proven to be NP-complete when IDRs belong to Case 2 and 3, so evidently the problem remains NP-Complete when the IDRs belong to Case 4 as well.

2. Optimal Solution Using Integer Linear Programming. When an IDR belongs to Case 4, it can be expressed in terms of linear constraints by applying a combination of techniques used to translate IDRs belonging to Cases 2 and 3 as discussed in the previous subsections. For e.g., if we have an IDR such as $a_1 \leftarrow b_1 \times b_2 + b_3 \times b_4$, we can re-write it as $a_1 \leftarrow c_1 + c_2$ (and translate it into constraints as discussed in Case 2), where $c_1 \leftarrow b_1 \times b_2$ and $c_2 \leftarrow b_3 \times b_4$ (these are IDRs belonging to Case 3).

Algorithm 2. Heuristic Algorithm for Progressive Recovery Problem in Case 4

1: set $ans = 0$
2: **for** $i = 1$ to n **do**
3:     **for** each node d_i that is not activated yet in D_O **do**
4:         Compute $influence_{d_i}$
5:         Compute $support_{d_i}$
6:     **end for**
7:     Choose an entity $d_i \in D_O$ with the highest influence value $influence_{d_i}$. If there is a tie, choose the one with the larger support value $support_{d_i}$. Choose one arbitrarily if tie still exists. Let $e \in D_O$ denote the entity chosen finally.
8:     Activate e and allow the cascade to occur. Remove any IDR from the set of IDRs if the entity on the LHS is fixed at this time step.
9:     $ans = 2 * ans + influence_e$
10:     $\sigma = \sigma + e$
11: **end for**
12: Output ans and σ.

---

3. Heuristic Solution. Our heuristic algorithm is a greedy one, i.e., we always want to obtain as much utility as possible in each time step. For an entity $d_i \in D_O$, we define $influence_{d_i}$ as the total gain (utility) obtained when entities get fixed following the cascade initiated by activating entity d_i alone. For instance, let us consider the following IDRs: $a_0 \leftarrow b_1, a_1 \leftarrow b_4 + b_2, a_2 \leftarrow b_1 + b_2 \times b_3, b_4 \leftarrow a_0, u(a_0) = u(a_1) = u(a_2) = u(b_4) = 1, b_1, b_2, b_3 \in D_O$. Then $influence_{b_1} = 4$ since by activating b_1, all of a_0, a_1, a_2 and b_4 are fixed after cascading. $influence_{b_2} = 1$, for only a_1 is fixed upon activation of b_2 and $influence_{b_3} = 0$. Entities with higher influence are preferred during each timestep, however, there could be a tie when multiple entities have the same influence value. In order to distinguish, we introduce another variable $support_{d_i}$. For each $d_i \in D_O$, we define $support_{d_i}$ to be the total number of appearances of d_i on the RHS among all IDRs. For instance, if we have $a_0 = b_1 \times b_2, a_1 = b_1 \times b_3, a_2 = b_1 \times b_4$, it is easy to see that all of b_i has influence 0. However, $support_{b_1} = 3$ since it appears thrice on the RHS and $support_{b_2} = support_{b_3} = support_{b_4} = 1$. In particular, if one IDR has the form of $a_1 = b_1 \times b_2 + b_1 \times b_3$, then $support_{b_1} = 1$ for such an IDR. So, whenever there is a tie, we will choose the entity with larger support value. If a tie further exists, we break the tie arbitrarily. Algorithm 2 gives the pseudocode for the heuristic algorithm. Input consists of a set of entities D_O which must be activated, a failed set of entities D_f with utility function $u()$, and IDRs. W.l.o.g, let $|D_O| = n$, $|D_f| = m$ and r is the total number of minterms in the IDR set. Let σ be the activation order obtained from Algorithm 2 and ans be the total system utility and we recall that we want to maximize the total system utility.

The running time of the algorithm is $O(n^2(m + r))$. We need to consider n time steps. During each time step, every entity in D_O is considered. Given an entity $d_i \in D_O$, it takes $O(m)$ time to compute its support value and $O(r)$ time to compute its influence value. Hence the total running time is $O(n^2(m + r))$.

5   Experimental Result

To study the performance of the heuristic solution for Case 4, we have conducted experiments both on real world data for Phoenix metropolitan area which is the most densely populated area of Arizona, U.S.A, as well as some synthetic data. An overview of the two types of data used in our experiments is as follows:

1. To consider a multi-layer network in a real world setting, we consider the dataset used in our work [10]. We have obtained the data for the power network of Phoenix metropolitan area from Platts (http://www.platts.com/) and that for the communication network from GeoTel (http://www.geo-tel.com/). The power network entities considered are powerplants and transmission lines while the communication network entities considered are fiber-lit buildings, cell towers and fiber links. The dataset consists of 70 power plants, 470 transmission lines, 2,690 cell towers, 7,100 fiber-lit buildings and 42,723 fiber links. Due to experimental resource limitation, we have considered five regions of interest in the Phoenix metropolitan area. For each of these five regions, we have constructed a set of IDRs from the power and communication network data using the set of rules described in [10]. For completeness, we describe the set of rules used: *(a)* For each generator to be alive, either the geographically nearest cell tower should be alive or the nearest fiber-lit building and the corresponding fiber link connecting the generator with the fiber-lit building must be alive, *(b)* To be alive, the fiber-lit buildings and the cell towers must have at least one of the two nearest generators and the corresponding connecting transmission lines alive, *(c)* The transmission lines and the fiber links are independent of any other entities.

2. We have also consider twenty datasets of synthetic data. Because of computational resource limitation, for each of these datasets we have considered

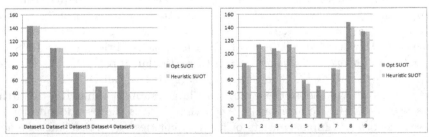

(a) Figure comparing optimal and heuristic solutions for the data for the Phoenix metropolitan area

(b) Figure comparing optimal and heuristic solutions for the randomly generated synthetic data

Fig. 1. Figure showing experimental comparison of the optimal and heuristic solutions

(1) a random number chosen among $\{2, 3, \ldots, 10\}$ for the size of D_O , (2) a random size for the set $D_f \setminus D_O$ which failed due to cascade, with the sizes varying from ten to twenty, (3) a random number of minterms of random sizes for each IDR. The number of minterms in each IDR is chosen randomly from $\{1, 2, 3\}$. The size of each minterm is randomly chosen from $\{1, 2, \ldots, 8\}$.

We have used IBM CPLEX optimizer 12.5 to implement the formulated ILP. We show the results of our experiments both on the real world data as well as the synthetic data in Fig. 1. We observe that in the real world data, the heuristic attains optimal solution in each of the five datasets. The reason for such a result is that the IDRs considered are quite simple because of the simple rules [10] as discussed previously- each IDR has at most two minterms and the size of each minterm does not exceed two. In case of the synthetic data, we have considered much more complex IDRs with much bigger sizes for minterms and much bigger failed set D_f. However, even in the case of the synthetic data, the heuristic attains near optimal solution in all the cases, with the ratio between the optimal and heuristic solution never exceeding 1.2 in any of the twenty datasets. In Fig. 1(b), we compare the optimal and the heuristic solutions for the cases where the latter deviates the most from the optimal solution. It can be thus seen that the heuristic performs quite well in our experimental setup.

6 Conclusion

In this paper, we study the Progressive Recovery Problem to maximize the *system utility* over the time when recovery of failed entities takes place in an inter-dependent network. We show that the problem can be solved in polynomial time in some cases, while in others it is NP-complete. We also provide two approximation algorithms and a heuristic to solve the problem in different cases. Experimental evaluations show that the heuristic attains near optimal solution in almost all cases.

References

1. Buldyrev, S., Parshani, R., Paul, G., Stanley, H., Havlin, S.: Catastrophic cascade of failures in interdependent networks. Nature **464**(7291), 1025–1028 (2010)
2. Gao, J., Buldyrev, S., Stanley, H., Havlin, S.: Networks formed from interdependent networks. Nat. Phys. **8**(1), 40–48 (2011)
3. Kauffman, S.A.: Metabolic stability and epigenesis in randomly constructed nets. J. Theor. Biol. **22**(3), 437–467 (1969)
4. Rosato, V., Issacharoff, L., Tiriticco, F., Meloni, S., Porcellinis, S., Setola, R.: Modelling interdependent infrastructures using interacting dynamical models. Int. J. Crit. Infrastruct. **4**(1), 63–79 (2008)
5. Parandehgheibi, M., Modiano, E.: Robustness of Interdependent Networks: The case of communication networks and the power grid. arXiv preprint (2013). arxiv:1304.0356
6. Nguyen, D., Shen, Y., Thai, M.: Detecting critical nodes in interdependent power networks for vulnerability assessment. IEEE Trans. Smart Grid **4**(1), 151–159 (2013)

7. Castet, J., Saleh, J.: Interdependent multi-layer networks: modeling and survivability analysis with applications to space-based networks. PloS one **8**(4), e60402 (2013)
8. Hassin, R., Levin, A.: An approximation algorithm for the minimum latency set cover problem. In: Brodal, G.S., Leonardi, S. (eds.) ESA 2005. LNCS, vol. 3669, pp. 726–733. Springer, Heidelberg (2005)
9. Feige, U., Lovsz, L., Tetali, P.: Approximating min sum set cover. Algorithmica **40**(4), 219–234 (2004)
10. Sen, A., Mazumder, A., Banerjee, J., Das, A., Compton, R.: Identification of k most vulnerable nodes in multi-layered network using a new model of interdependency. In: Presented at the International Workshop on Network Science for Communication Networks (INFOCOM workshop). arXiv preprint (2014). arxiv:1401.1783
11. Smith, R.: U.S. Risks National Blackout From Small-Scale Attack. Wall Street Journal (2012). http://online.wsj.com/news/articles/SB10001424052702304 020104579433670284061220
12. Bernstein, A., Bienstock, D., Hay, D., Uzunoglu, M., Zussman, G.: Power grid vulnerability to 3 geographically correlated failures-analysis and control implications. arXiv preprint (2012). arxiv:1206.1099

Model-Based Security Risk Analysis
for Networked Embedded Systems

Maria Vasilevskaya[✉] and Simin Nadjm-Tehrani[✉]

Department of Computer and Information Science,
Linköping University, Linköping, Sweden
{maria.vasilevskaya,simin.nadjm-tehrani}@liu.se

Abstract. Finding a balance between functional and non-functional
requirements and resources in embedded systems has always been a
challenge. What brings this challenge into a sharper focus is that
embedded devices are increasingly deployed in many networked applications, some of which will form the backbone of the critical information
infrastructures on which we all depend. The Security-Enhanced Embedded system Development (SEED) process has proposed a set of tools that
a bridge the two islands of expertise, the engineers specialised in embedded systems development and the security experts. This paper identifies
a gap in the tool chain that links the identification of assets to be protected to the associated security risks seen from different stakeholder
perspectives. The needed tool support for systematic prioritisation of
identified assets, and the selection of security building blocks at design
stage based on a risk picture of different stakeholders, are characterised.
The ideas are illustrated in a smart metering infrastructure scenario.

1 Introduction

Meeting the security needs of the society and the privacy needs of the individual
users of networked information systems is a subject for current active discussion.
While the generics of this challenging problem are being discussed by a spectrum
of scholars in an interdisciplinary manner, the technical development of new
types of systems and infrastructures is ongoing in parallel, with more applications
realised as networked embedded systems. The forthcoming vehicular networks
and smart grid infrastructures are examples of such a technological development
with economic sectors driving the development, waiting for the societal and
regulatory dimensions to catch up.

Embedded systems add new challenges to the existing map of security landscape since embedded systems were until very recently isolated from the rest of
information infrastructures, and their potential threat to societal and personal
security was both limited and local. With the advent of Internet of Things (IoT)
and higher rate of absorption of embedded devices in current applications, this
premise no longer holds. The earlier adopted approach of "adding on security"
which was already shown to be not an effective technique for enterprise systems
is definitely not an option in future IoT security. Hence, it is essential to address

© Springer International Publishing Switzerland 2016
C.G. Panayiotou et al. (Eds.): CRITIS 2014, LNCS 8985, pp. 381–386, 2016.
DOI: 10.1007/978-3-319-31664-2_39

systematic approaches to development of networked applications that include embedded devices.

A recent European project, SecFutur, combines reusable building blocks and a systematic process for constructing security-enhanced embedded systems [1]. In particular, we recognise that the security experts are largely outnumbered by the embedded systems engineers, and that the combination of the two expertise in every variant of networked embedded systems – a sector highly driven by economic returns, cost, size, or other form factors – is difficult to achieve in an efficient manner. We have therefore proposed a new process – called Security-Enhanced Embedded system Development (SEED) – that exploits security experts' knowledge in ontological repositories, to help a developer of an embedded networked system with no/little access to security expertise [2].

The proposed process starts with a (UML) functional model of a networked system on the one hand, and the knowledge captured about the security requirements in a *domain* on the other hand. To bridge the embedded systems and security worlds, we employ domain-specific modelling and ontology technologies. This process is supported by tools that (1) systematically search for involved assets in the functional models, and (2) systematically find countermeasures through the ontology-based repositories.

Our study of the gaps in SEED points towards the need for a link between existing risk analysis techniques and model-based system development process. The current paper asks new questions about their applicability in a critical infrastructure context, namely:

- How can the asset-driven assessment of required security properties be complemented by tools and methods that prioritise and select relevant assets?
- How can the stakeholder perspectives be utilised in deciding a higher or lower level of security within the design exploration space?
- Once the relevant assets are identified, how is the selection of security building blocks to protect them affected by the same stakeholder perspectives?

Section 2 describes the proposed method for prioritisation of assets and selection of countermeasures by linking to stakeholder profiles that addresses the questions stated above. We briefly illustrate the motivation for planned tool extensions by describing its application to a part of the smart grid infrastructure in Sect. 3. Exposure to the mathematical base of this method requires a lengthy account that is outside the scope of this paper. However, this paper shows that the step from that quantification to actual selection of countermeasures is highly dependent on a new component, namely the stakeholder perspective. Section 4 sums up the paper and provides directions for future work.

2   Linking Stakeholders and Risks

Critical information infrastructures have a lot of stakeholders whose preferences should be accounted for when deciding the appropriate level of security to demand during design stages. In the telecommunications sector for example, there is a growing number of end user devices all with their own characteristics (incorporating software and hardware from many different vendors), a number of network operators (wired and wireless), a number of communication system vendors (supporting various access technologies and incarnations of the same standards), as well as regulatory authorities that have their national interests. Similar characteristics are emerging in the vehicular telematics networks with both entertainment and automotive value-added functions emerging side-by-side with functions that enhance societal interests (e.g. the e-Call standard proposed in the European Union). Our earlier application of SEED has been in the smart grid domain, undergoing similar multi-perspective development.

This section refines the step that associates a measure for security. This measure rests on two components: assets automatically extracted within a system model and a set of stakeholders for the considered application. As an example of assets, our security ontology includes two types of assets: data that is in storage and data that is in transit between subsystems. Focusing on confidentiality and integrity as security goals, our current challenge is how to associate a "number" that characterises the absence of protection, e.g. integrity loss associated with an asset.

Here we envisage that the classic notion of risk [3] can be exploited. More specifically, we will consider confidentiality loss and integrity loss in the vein of a risk that needs to be averted. Hence, we will associate with the metric the two elements *likelihood* and *consequence*. While the simpler part is association of consequence with an asset, the association of likelihood of a breach of security in our model-based vision is computationally intensive.

The consequence assessment part of risk evaluation is typically carried out in consultation with stakeholders. For example, tools like CORAS [4] are formed around eliciting the costs of breaching security in connection with each asset. The notion of cost varies from one application domain to another and from one asset to another, but also from one stakeholder to another. There are also different costs depending on which security goal is violated. For example, for a utility provider as stakeholder the breach of integrity for end user electricity measurements are usually associated with high costs, while customer privacy (confidentiality) may have a lower relative priority. The right hand side of Fig. 1 visualises this idea. This stakeholder-parameterised version of consequence assessment can then be used in the decision process arriving at which asset(s) to prioritise for protection, or even in business decisions like who should bear the initial costs of an investment in a given security solution.

To compute the likelihood element of the risk is a more elaborate and demanding activity. First, a given system design and selected platform should be coupled with relevant attack models to obtain the likelihood to violate a certain security property. The left hand side of Fig. 1 depicts this process.

In order to support the computation of the likelihood in an efficient manner one has to choose a suitable formalism. Our current work [5] involves modelling attacks as directed acyclic graphs (i.e. attack trees) so that the combination of attacker behaviour and operations of a system leading to manipulation of assets

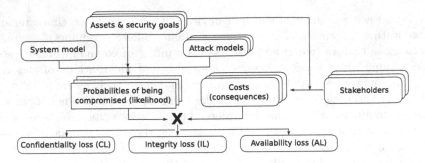

Fig. 1. Supporting the focus on relevant assets and security goals

can be probabilistically evaluated. An attack tree is an established representation of attack scenarios [6] formally defined [7] and extended with stochastic and time semantics [8,9]. Similarly, a system is formalised as a stochastic semi-Markov model that is an intuitive and powerful tool to represent dynamic aspects of a system behaviour. Finally, the combination of the likelihood and consequence are combined for each asset, and the outcome can be used as a means of ranking/filtering the important assets and the less relevant ones.

3 Smart Grid Illustration

We illustrate the novelty of the proposed asset selection and prioritisation on the smart metering infrastructure called Trusted Sensor Network (TSN) [1]. The TSN is built of a set of metering devices referred to as Trusted Sensor Module (TSM), database servers, client applications, and a communication infrastructure. The main goal of this system is to measure energy consumption at households and to associate measurements with the clients' data for billing purposes.

The overall specification of this case study consists of seven main scenarios that have a range of diverse security considerations. Consequently, there are many assets identified in these scenarios, e.g. measurements (meter readings), a set of user account data (customer, administrator, operator), a set of certificates (calibration, installation), communication configurations, functional settings, commands, control messages, etc. Additionally, as any large system the metering infrastructure has many stakeholders.

Let us assume that a realisation of tools and techniques mentioned in the previous section enables a per-asset characterisation of integrity/confidentiality loss seen from the perspective of different stakeholders. In this section, we focus on three assets, namely measurements (denoted by A_1), certificates (A_2), and commands (A_3). We also consider three distinct stakeholders, i.e. end users, the utility provider, and the national regulatory agency.

Violation of confidentiality and integrity of these assets has different consequences for different stakeholders. For example, for a utility provider, breach of the integrity of measurements is usually associated with high costs. A systematic misuse of the metering device can lead to manipulations at large scale and result in economic losses. However, the breach of confidentiality for the same measurement data is of a lower priority. Obviously, the picture is different for the user as a stakeholder. One can consider the national regulatory agency to be mainly interested in the availability dimension of the electricity supply and thereby, the breach of confidentiality of the measurement data has a lower consequence. On the other hand, a large scale manipulation of the commands issued to the sensor nodes, can be used in a scenario where national security is threatened.

Application of SEED allows systematically identifying the presence of above assets within a system model. Here, we propose that the calculated metrics introduced in Sect. 2 for all assets can be organised in a *stakeholder security profile* that shows losses for a stakeholder with respect to each asset. These profiles can be visualised as plots depicted in Fig. 2. Here, the selected assets are listed along the x-axis, and the y-axis shows the calculated confidentiality loss.

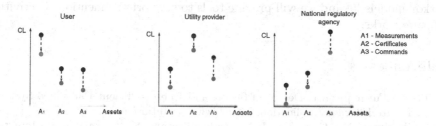

Fig. 2. Stakeholder security profile view

Next, guided by SEED, a system engineer selects a set of security building blocks (SBBs) to reduce the potential loss of security for stakeholders. Obviously, integration of any new functionality into a system will imply extra costs. In order to incorporate these costs and to distribute them among stakeholders, we need to evaluate how each stakeholder benefits when a certain SBB is integrated. We propose that the added benefit is expressed as a reduction effect that an SBB brings in terms of confidentiality (integrity, availability) loss for each asset.

As illustration, we consider three SBBs selected within the SecFutur project to be integrated into the TSM device: secure storage, anomaly detection, and secure communication. Secure storage and security communication reduce the likelihood of breaching integrity and confidentiality of stored data and transmitted data respectively. The anomaly detection, already shown to be viable in a prototype of the TSM [10], aims to reduce the likelihood of integrity loss for measurements stored in the device. Reduction effect of implemented SBBs is visualised in Fig. 2 as dashed arrows that shift the initial confidentiality loss (black dots) to lower values (grey dots). The placement of the dots and the scale of the reduction (the size of arrows) is a relative placement to visualise the intended use of the suggested techniques. This way, a system designer can analyse which stakeholders benefit most from integration of which SBBs and consider the cost-benefit trade-off for the implementation appropriately.

4   Summary and Future Work

Society depends on critical infrastructures for its vital functions, and these increasingly rely on embedded devices for their continued operation. The shift from the proprietary, isolated development of such networked applications towards large scale integration of off the shelf units necessitates a new mindset.

Our earlier work on SEED lays out a workflow for systematic identification of security needs of a system and selection of a suitable set of security mechanisms. In this paper we have characterised a missing part of the puzzle – the justification for prioritising assets as input to selection of security mechanisms. We suggested a bridge towards the traditional concepts from risk analysis, made specific in terms of integrity, confidentiality, or availability loss. This paper outlines the path to support the missing technology. Our ongoing work creates the mathematical underpinnings for the calculation of integrity/confidentiality loss using semi-Markov models [5] and we will provide tools to support the mentioned activities in future works.

References

1. The SecFutur project: Design of Secure and Energy-efficient Embedded Systems for Future Internet Application. http://www.secfutur.eu
2. Vasilevskaya, M., Gunawan, L.A., Nadjm-Tehrani, S., Herrmann, P.: Integrating security mechanisms into embedded systems by domain-specific modelling. J. Secur. Commun. Netw. 7, 2815–2832 (2013). Wiley
3. Alberts, C., Dorofee, A.: Managing Information Security Risks: The Octave Approach. SEI Series in Software Engineering. Addison-Wesley, Boston (2003)
4. den Braber, F., Hogganvik, I., Lund, S., Stølen, K., Vraalsen, F.: Model-based security analysis in seven steps – a guided tour to the CORAS method. BT Technol. J. 25, 101–117 (2007)
5. Vasilevskaya, M., Nadjm-Tehrani, S.: Quantifying risks to data assets using formal metrics in embedded system design. In: Koornneef, F., van Gulijk, C. (eds.) SAFECOMP 2015. LNCS, vol. 9337, pp. 347–361. Springer, Heidelberg (2015). doi:10.1007/978-3-319-24255-2_25
6. Kordy, B., Piètre-Cambacédès, L., Schweitzer, P.: DAG-based attack and defense modeling: don't miss the forest for the attack trees. Comput. Sci. Rev. 13–14, 1–38 (2014). Elsevier
7. Mauw, S., Oostdijk, M.: Foundations of attack trees. In: Won, D.H., Kim, S. (eds.) ICISC 2005. LNCS, vol. 3935, pp. 186–198. Springer, Heidelberg (2006)
8. Arnold, F., Hermanns, H., Pulungan, R., Stoelinga, M.: Time-dependent analysis of attacks. In: Abadi, M., Kremer, S. (eds.) POST 2014 (ETAPS 2014). LNCS, vol. 8414, pp. 285–305. Springer, Heidelberg (2014)
9. Almasizadeh, J., Abdollahi Azgomi, M.: A stochastic model of attack process for the evaluation of security metrics. J. Comput. Netw. 57, 2159–2180 (2013)
10. Raciti, M., Nadjm-Tehrani, S.: Embedded cyber-physical anomaly detection in smart meters. In: Hämmerli, B.M., Kalstad Svendsen, N., Lopez, J. (eds.) CRITIS 2012. LNCS, vol. 7722, pp. 34–45. Springer, Heidelberg (2013)

Author Index

Printed in the United States
By Bookmasters

Printed in the United States
By Bookmasters